T0386677

'A masterly London biography, surely the last word on a man, a myth—and a cat.'

Simon Jenkins, *The Guardian* columnist, and author of *A Short History of England*

'There are few more memorable stories of social mobility, enlightened entrepreneurship, civic leadership and inspiring philanthropy than Dick Whittington's. Michael McCarthy has provided perhaps the definitive account of his remarkable legacy along all these fronts, one which is as much a parable for the present as the past.'

Andy Haldane, former Chief Economist, Bank of England,
and Head of the Levelling Up Taskforce

'McCarthy's book explodes several comfortable myths. His Dick Whittington is a far cry from the familiar panto character: a successful (though often controversial) politician and immensely rich businessman. Less a biography of Whittington, and more a densely written portrait of an era, and especially the politics and economy of London at a crucial moment in its history.'

Nick Higham, former BBC News correspondent, and author of
The Mercenary River—Private Greed, Public Good: A History of London's Water

'A compelling read. McCarthy's deep research delivered with verve and pace forensically details the facts beneath the Whittington myth. And, as so often, truth beats fiction. This is a *vade mecum* to statesmanship, both mediaeval and modern, and a case study in the ethical bridging of the private sector and public service. Financier to three kings, including Henry V, protector of the people from abuse, city planner and developer, his philanthropic endowment continues 600 years after his death. Whittington's understanding of the power of liquidity, with his adaptability, trust and probity are all object lessons for public effectiveness today. And most important of all, McCarthy's assiduous curiosity does not, quite, kill the revered cat.'

John Campbell OBE, Chair of Campbell Lutyens, and author of
Haldane: The Forgotten Statesman Who Shaped Modern Britain

'It's time to turn again to the tale of Richard Whittington, the man and mayor, a life bound up so closely with the business, politics and society of London at a time of change—all vividly captured by McCarthy in this fascinating and entertaining account of a figure who continues to capture the imagination and whose charitable legacy survives to this day.'

Vincent Keaveny, Lord Mayor of the City of London

'I felt that I had been guided around all the nooks and crannies of medieval London and shown the daily lives, pastimes, rules and regulations, ambitions and differing fortunes of its citizens, embodied in the life of Richard Whittington. An erudite, enjoyable and illuminating read.'

Elizabeth Chadwick, historical novelist

'A remarkable story. Forget the cat: look at what Dick Whittington achieved in the City of London, for the crowning military triumph of Agincourt and his own legacy benefiting millions. I hope *Citizen of London*, through its vivid picture of the early 15th century, will resonate today and inspire new generations.'

Richard Graham, Conservative MP for Gloucester

'Michael McCarthy has rescued "Dick" Whittington from the pantomime! "Oh yes he has!" Crafting the history of Whittington's moral and social compass shown through his civic action, this book establishes his rightful place in the social and political history of British social welfare.'

Jonathan Parker, Professor of Society & Social Welfare, Bournemouth University

CITIZEN OF LONDON

VERA EFFIGIES PRECLAR DÑI DOMINI RICHARDI WHITINGTON EQVI. AVRAT.

Huius sparsa viri toti benesacta per orbem . . . ipsa monstrant indice qualis erit

The true portraicture of **RICHARD WHITINGTON** thrise Lord Maior
of London a vertuous and godly man full of good Works (and those famous) he builded
the Gate of London called Newgate which before was a miserable doungeon He builded
Whitington Colledge & made it an Almose house for poore people Also he builded a
greate parte of ye hospitall of S. Bartholmewes in westsmithfield in London. He also
builded the beautifull Library at ye Gray Friers in London, called Christes Hospitall:
Also he builded the Guilde Halle Chappell and increased a greate parte of the East
ende of the saied halle, beside many other good workes.

R. Elstrack sculpsit

MICHAEL MCCARTHY

Citizen of London

Richard Whittington

The Boy Who Would Be Mayor

HURST & COMPANY, LONDON

First published in the United Kingdom in 2022 by
C. Hurst & Co. (Publishers) Ltd.,
New Wing, Somerset House, Strand,
London, WC2R 1LA
© Michael McCarthy, 2022
All rights reserved.
Printed in Scotland by Bell and Bain Ltd, Glasgow

A Cataloguing-in-Publication data record for this book
is available from the British Library.

ISBN: 9781787387911

This book is printed using paper from registered sustainable
and managed sources.

www.hurstpublishers.com

And in worship now I think on the sun
Of merchandy, Richard Whittington,
That lode star and chief chosen flower.
What hath by him our England of honour,
And what profit hath been of his riches,
And yet lasteth daily in worthiness,
That pen and paper may not me suffice
Him to describe, so high he was of price

(Anon., 1436)

When one man out of a whole generation is selected by posterity as especially worthy to be remembered and had in honour, the choice seems to be influenced by that quality which we call force of character, the power, namely, which some men possess of impressing themselves strongly upon their contemporaries.

Walter Besant and James Rice, *Sir Richard Whittington:*
Lord Mayor of London (1881)

It has been Whittington's singular fate to become the hero of a popular tale which has found an ultimate lodgement in the nursery. The Whittington of the old ballads, chap-books, and puppet play started life as a poor ill-treated orphan in the west of England and made his way to London on hearing that its streets were paved with gold. Arriving in a state of destitution, he attracted the commiseration of a rich merchant, one Mr. Hugh FitzWarren, who placed him as a scullion in his kitchen, where he suffered greatly from the tyranny of the cook, tempered only by the kindness of his master's daughter, Mrs. Alice. From this state of misery, he was presently released by a strange piece of good fortune. It was the worthy merchant's custom when sending out a ship to let each of his servants venture something in it, in order that God might give him a greater blessing. To the freight of the good ship *Unicorn* Whittington could only contribute his cat, which he had bought for a penny to keep down the vermin in his garret; but the vessel happening to touch at an unknown part of the Barbary coast, the king of the country, whose palace was overrun with rats and mice, bought the cat for ten times more than all the freight besides. Meanwhile her owner, unconscious of his good luck and driven desperate by the cook's ill-usage, stole away from Leadenhall Street early in the morning of All Hallows day, and left the city behind him, but as he rested at Holloway, he heard Bow bells ring out a merry peal, which seemed to say: Turn again, Whittington, Lord Mayor of London.

James Tait, 'Richard Whittington', *DNB* (1885–1900)

Other successful merchants lived in London at the same time as Whittington; others filled the high and responsible office of Mayor as often, and with as much honour and credit; others received kings with as much dignity; others maintained the liberties of the city with as much determination; others were as charitable, as generous, as patriotic, and as prudent. Yet Whittington outshone all the citizens of his time. He alone was regarded, even in his lifetime, as *flos mercatorum*, the flower of London merchants.

Walter Besant and James Rice, *Sir Richard Whittington:*
Lord Mayor of London (1881)

CONTENTS

CONTENTS

Dedication at front of book
To Rosalind, Lewis and Liberty

ACKNOWLEDGEMENTS

The eve of the 600th anniversary of Richard Whittington's death in 1423, seems a fitting moment and an opportunity to bring the life and achievements of the real 'Dick' Whittington to the fore. Any work on Whittington, born towards the end of the 1350s, in the decade after the cathartic, ruinous and dislocating Black Death, is inevitably bound to be a combination of what we know and is recorded, what we can broadly piece together by events and fragments of history elsewhere and what we must surmise and speculate. This work is a combination of all three.

Like countless others who have experienced the pantomime in childhood, I grew up with a lingering fascination with the story of 'Dick Whittington' and passed this to my own children. This parabolic story has travelled with me throughout the years since. A childhood fascination developed into a later life curiosity about the real Whittington. Who was he, where did he originate, why and when did he come to London, who encouraged and facilitated his career and what could we learn about his impact as mercer, civic leader, lender, and social reformer, while still retaining the heart of a story that has touched millions of people and for whom it continues to resonate as history, parable and entertainment. What is rooted in fact, what can we reasonably surmise. Where are we confined to guesswork, and to proposition and supposition. How reliable can his story truly be, some 660 years after his birth, with fact often lost or incomplete, frequently clouded or simply no longer available.

I was attracted most by the social and political framework of the Whittington story and have found myself often attending meetings in streets and places where Whittington made his way, built his career and continues to be recorded or celebrated. There are few places even in the modern global 'City' of London that don't have some resonance with the man, his exploits and his time. I have been fortunate that many of my enquiries have been met with surprising interest and enthusiasm, underscoring perhaps that for those of us who have encountered Dick

ACKNOWLEDGEMENTS

Whittington in childhood the story does indeed travel with us in adulthood and parenthood. I began my initial research some years ago, drawing on the assistance and expertise of Gloucestershire Archives and Gloucestershire Library Services in tracking down often rare, dusty and arcane material that convinced me that there was a significant real-life story to tell of which the pantomime version was a popular, if entertainingly caricatured, reflection. My interest was sparked further, significantly so, by later discovering Caroline M Barron's excellent seminal 1969 paper on 'The Man and the Myth' and encountering the work of Jean Imray and Sylvia Thrupp. The Mercers Company were also very helpful in my early enquiries. The rest, as they say, is history.

The timely publication of this book owes much to the efforts of two people. I am most grateful to John Campbell OBE for giving me his time to discuss the initial synopsis of the book; for his continuing advocacy of the subject and for introducing me to Michael Dwyer, Publisher and Managing Director at C. Hurst & Co, who saw immediately its principal contention, that Richard Whittington, not just his pantomime alter ego, should have a far more prominent place in the public space. I am grateful for his confi-dence in the book from the outset. From our initial conversation on its merits and appeal, to his unfailing support and oversight towards its release. His critical eye has made the book more meaningful and appealing. I would also like to record my thanks to Peter Sonneborn who was most supportive of the book and who was instrumental in facilitating the foreword written by Sir David Wootton. I also wish to record a belated vote of thanks to Professor Jonathan Parker, Director of the Centre for Social Policy at The University of Bournemouth who encouraged me in my interest a few years ago by allowing me as a Visiting Professor to engage his students on the part played by Whittington and his contemporaries in the development of medi-eval social policy and interest group politics. There was and remains a remarkable story to tell.

As the 600th anniversary of his death approaches and after a pandemic that draws some parallels with Whittington's own time in London, this seems an appropriate moment to bring him back into the spotlight. There is still much we do not know and probably never will about London's 'four times mayor'. There is a longstanding and continuing debate about the date and circumstances of his birth in Gloucestershire and about the timing of his arrival and early years in the capital. This book neither seeks to, nor can it, tie up the several loose ends of his achievements or the more intimate lacunae of Whittington's early and married life but it is intended to help rekindle popular interest in a figure who played an increasingly significant role in the City, in the Commons and at Court for nearly 30 years, during the eventful reigns of 3 successive English kings.

Questions still abound. Not least, was Richard Whittington already a successful mercer who had made his mark elsewhere before he was 'announced' in London in 1379 or had he arrived as a young boy to take up an apprenticeship that would later launch his career. There is much debate over his precise birthdate and the markers range from as early as 1350, through to the mid-1350s and later to 1359 and these variants influence the timing of his arrival in London and his age and standing at the moment he first comes to public notice. Was he already a 'made man', a known figure in London's landscape by this date, having proved himself here or in Gloucestershire before then. And what was his precise connection to the man who would 35 years later award him the sobriquet Citizen of London.

Returning to those I wish to thank. The time and expertise invested by Russell Martin in proofing and shaping the book is evident in the finished article. He has my appreciation and my great estimation of his skills. My appreciation is also due to the production and marketing teams at Hurst who have helped turn a voluminous manuscript into an eye-catching book intended to attract and resonate with a wide general readership. Specific thanks are due to Daisy Leitch, Head of Production; to Mei Jayne Yew, Lara Weisweiller-Wu, Emily Cary-Elwes, Raminta Uselytė and to Alex Bell for his work on the index.

I also owe a huge thanks to Simon Jenkins, Nick Higham, Professor Jonathan Parker, Elizabeth Chadwick, Richard Graham MP, Andy Haldane, John Campbell OBE and to London's current Lord Mayor, Vincent Keaveny for their early and enthusiastic endorsements of Citizen of London.

I would also like to express my great appreciation to Sir David Wootton, for graciously agreeing and taking the time to write the foreword. A highly pleasing and symmetrical contribution from someone who as a Common Councillor in 2002 and as the 684th Lord Mayor of London 2011–2012 followed in the footsteps of Richard Whittington who first took office in those positions in 1384 and 1397.

Finally, I would like to record my appreciation to my family. My son Lewis will recall many early conversations on what direction this work

ACKNOWLEDGEMENTS

might take. I have valued his continuing interest and know he is excited that the endeavour has reached fruition. To my daughter Liberty a more recent thank you for your skill and imagination in creating a new website to accompany the book.

Above all, there is one person to whom I owe an appreciation that can neither be measured nor scripted here. To my wife Rosalind, for her unwavering support, her boundless generosity and her continuing encouragement when I was consumed by researching and writing this book ... thank you for everything, I could not have envisaged or achieved this **without** you. *Semper Amare.*

FOREWORD

Alderman Sir David Wootton

The office of the Lord Mayor of London is probably the best known civic office in the world (it was 'Mayor' in Richard Whittington's day; 'Lord' came later). I had the honour of holding that office in 2011–2012. I was conscious at the time, and am even more conscious now, that the office is a unique combination of history and tradition; and modern adaptation and relevance.

The Mayoralty may not be the oldest civic office in England and Wales: that title may go to the Shrievalty—High Sheriffs in the English counties and Sheriffs in the City of London—which goes back to Saxon times. The concept of 'Mayor' came to England with the Normans and has remained since then as the head of almost all our municipalities: ceremonies which give recognition, status and validation to important aspects of community life; civic leadership, exhibiting, supporting and endorsing those qualities of behaviour and conduct which are in the best interests of public life.

Today the Lord Mayor of London—the official title but frequently referred to as 'Lord Mayor of the City of London' to distinguish the office from that of the (relatively) recently created Mayor of London, the party-political, executive, four-year-term mayor of the whole of London—retains the civic functions of all mayors but in other respects is unique: as Head of the City Corporation, the Lord Mayor has much involvement in events relating to the Monarchy and the Royal Family—the Lord Mayor is the Lord Lieutenant for the City of London—and events of national significance, and, the City of London being the leading international financial centre of the world, spends probably the majority of the time in office promoting financial and professional services both in the City and throughout the United Kingdom, and 'UK plc' generally.

Both of these themes—'national' and 'business'—have their origins in history: Mayor Whittington did much in both. Both lie in the basic 'deal' which originated with William the Conqueror, that the Crown—long on political power but short on cash—would allow the City, the business centre since at least Roman times, to (continue to) go about its business so long as the City—short on power but long on cash—recognised the Crown as the political power and responded positively to the monarch's requests for funds. We see much of all these elements in this book.

The principal features I describe have remained in place down the centuries. The City remains independent of government and, because it is party-politically neutral, the City Corporation regularly provides politically neutral platforms for Ministers to make important statements on matters of policy across a wide range of subjects.

There are, however, differences from Whittington's day: a transformation in the international aspect, given the travel which is now possible, from trading alliances with a small number of continental European cities to promoting trade and investment links with a large number of business centres on every continent; continued adaptation to take in sustainability and climate change, and innovation, new kinds of business and new technologies—fintech, regtech, AI—so that the City remains relevant today.

The Lord Mayor now has the benefit of a private residence in Mansion House, although it is more of a working space: Richard Whittington had to make do with living at home. Mayors in Whittington's time tended to be owners of City businesses—proprietorial, those with a significant ownership interest in their businesses—while today Lord Mayors are more likely to be professional people, those whose foremost contribution to the businesses in which they work is their own skill, qualification, time and effort. The financial arrangements have been changed so that the holding of office does not require significant personal expenditure on the part of the holder.

Lord Mayors today like to work closely with others, and in a way co-ordinated with others, in the City Corporation: the phrase 'One Team' is frequently heard to describe the contemporary approach; a phrase unlikely to be heard in former centuries. Similarly, Lord Mayors today like to develop continuity, of theme and action, with those who went before and those who will follow.

The processes of election of both Lord Mayors and Sheriffs are now well established and free of interference from outside the City: the imposition of a Lord Mayor on the City by the monarch, as with Richard

Whittington's first term, is unlikely to be seen again. Nor is it likely that we will see again a monarch avoiding a debt by declaring it extinguished and exiling the lender from the country.

Among the adaptations to suit contemporary economic, political, cultural and technological circumstances, the City continues to demand from its Lord Mayors and other civic leaders the highest standards of behaviour and conduct, in their personal, working and public lives—personal gain is not permitted, and compliance in full with the Nolan Principles of Public Life is required. Aldermen will not these days be found making personal loans to the monarch.

In my reading of Dr Michael McCarthy's excellent, scholarly and highly readable book I found many elements which I have encountered in my time in the City: the importance of sheep and wool connects with my membership of the Woolmen's Company; references to the battles of Crécy and Agincourt with my membership of the Fletchers and the Bowyers; Leadenhall, which features early in Richard Whittington's time in the City, is in the Ward of Langbourn, of which I am the Alderman; my near namesake Nicholas Wootton was Mayor at the time of Agincourt; and Mayor William Sevenoke came from a town of that name with different spelling in which I live.

Richard Whittington died in 1423, after a lifetime of aspiration, hard work and application, commercial success, business and political acumen and navigational skills, community awareness, consciousness of and sensitivity to the circumstances in which others lived and a genuine wish to improve the conditions and the lives of others. He showed that progress in the City is not restricted to those already in it and that there are always opportunities to be taken. The Mercers have much to celebrate as they mark in 2023 the 600th anniversary of his death. My only regret is… no cat.

Alderman Sir David Wootton
July 2022

(Alderman Sir David Wootton is Alderman for the Ward of Langbourn in the City of London. He served as Sheriff in 2009–10 and as the 684th Lord Mayor of London in 2011–12. He is a member, and has been Master, of a number of City Livery Companies. He was a solicitor, a partner in a City law firm.)

INTRODUCTION

On 17 January 2017, the Birmingham Hippodrome announced that more than 100,000 people had flocked to see 'the world's biggest panto'. They had come from as far afield as Australia, Hong Kong, Japan and the United States to watch *Dick Whittington*. The cast had spent 180 hours on stage serving up 72 performances of a much-embellished and historically meandering folk tale. For the record, this remarkable 'run' produced 375 loads of washing for the theatre's wardrobe department. It is quite arresting to visualise this number of people booking seats, handing over their money and making often complex travel arrangements to spend little more than a couple of hours in a packed theatre during such an exceptionally busy period of the year and at a time when countless other forms of entertainment and diversion were on offer and available nearer to home. All in the name of one of Britain's most renowned folk characters, who, unlike many of the other great pantomime figures, has a deep and influential basis in fact. Though the embellishments, diversions and 'facts' have been something of a hostage to folk memory, and later to the draw of the box office, the essential conceit (or perhaps allegory) of a young rural lad making his way to fame and fortune in late-14th- and early-15th-century London has held broadly, very broadly, true for 600 years. This is a remarkable testimony to Whittington's fame, to the charm and appeal of his character, to his continuing aspirational resonance across six centuries and, of course, to the story's sustained entertainment value. By the time the Hippodrome opened for its panto season in December 2016, quite literally millions of people had watched a performance of the Dick Whittington story since it was first enacted before a London audience at the Stationers' Hall in 1605. When Whittington died at his home at St Michael Paternoster in April 1423, the population of London was barely 50,000 and mostly illiterate, and the 'social media' of the age was essentially word of mouth. Yet even then his name and his achievements were arguably better known and more accurately celebrated than in the modern pantomime version of his life.

1

Indeed, it might be argued that, as with many stories and legends handed down the centuries and to ever larger audiences, the embellishment and the thirst for entertainment get in the way of an even better story—*the truth*. This is by no means a criticism; quite the contrary: we should celebrate the enormous enthusiasm and dedication invested in keeping the rudiments of his story alive and enthralling for so long and to such popular acclaim. So, the intention here, in this book, is to get behind the scenes, scrape off the greasepaint and discover who the real Richard Whittington was and, in a nod to those millions who have happily paid to encounter and be charmed by his alter ego, endeavour to recreate what we know of a figure who is real and a story which, for want of being there, can be reasonably surmised.

* * *

600 years after his death and despite this prodigious exposure, we know surprisingly little about 'the real Dick Whittington', his extraordinary life or the circumstances in which he forged it. Yet he was a real and historical figure who, it is claimed, was celebrated in Parliament by Henry IV as 'the pulse of the nation'. Many of us know the popular mythology associated with his pantomime character—an impoverished country lad earning a crust as a scullion in a household in London, a city where the streets were said to be paved with gold, enduring difficult and discouraging times, which caused him to leave and then famously 'turn again', returning to the capital to make his fortune, marrying the daughter of a wealthy merchant, and rising to become mayor not once but three times. And, lest we forget, all was achieved with the help of a legendary lucky cat.

But how much is true, why has this tale endured for so long, and why have so many flocked to see it enacted? Why does it excite us as children and still engage us in adulthood? Why does it resonate with and charm us, and what basis of fact is there in this life-affirming tale that celebrates the 'poor boy who made good'? Is the story of Dick Whittington simply a diverting folk tale, a religious parable or a theatrical take on real events? Perhaps it is an amalgam of all of these. This account of Richard Whittington, the first detailed book for 140 years, aims to go some way in finding out. And if you are wondering why attention was drawn to the efforts of the wardrobe department in the Birmingham production, it is because the real Dick Whittington had rather a lot to do with finery, adornment and ostentation, not least in his endeavours with the Great Wardrobe of three English kings. In fact, he owed his fortune to it.

INTRODUCTION

The Sonne of Marchaundy

The first literary reference to Whittington was published in 1436. *The Libelle of Englyshe Polycye*, a polemic in favour of mercantilism, would surely have won Whittington's approval. The identity of the author is unknown and much disputed, but he was impressed enough by the mercer's achievements to offer a glowing epitaph, referring to Whittington as the 'sonne of marchaundy'.

> And in worship nowe think I on the sonne
> Of marchaundy Richarde of Whitingdone,
> That loodes starre and chefe chosen floure.
> Whate hathe by hym oure England of honoure,
> And whate profite hathe bene of his richesse,
> And yet lasteth dayly in worthinesse,
> That penne and papere may not me suffice
> Him to describe, so high he was of prise,
> Above marchaundis to sett him one the beste!
> I can no more, but God have hym in reste.[1]

This salute to Whittington's influence as a merchant adventurer was a central theme of Samuel Lysons's history of 1860, which asserts that Whittington's importance lies in 'the liberal views which he introduced into trade, raising it from mere pedlary into legitimate commerce'.[2]

Whittington first appears in popular folklore in the late 16th century though there is no substantive evidence of the story being systematically handed down generation by generation following his death in 1423. However, writing in 1569, the chronicler Richard Grafton had little doubt about the qualities that had set Whittington apart; a figure whose achievements and fame were, and deserved to be, passed on in popular eulogy. He captures the essence of Whittington's moral and social intent in his summation that 'This worshipful man so bestowed his goods and substance to the honour of God, to the relief of the poor and to the benefit of the common weal that he hath right well deserved to be registered in the book of fame'.[3]

Writing in his seminal *Survey of London* (1598), John Stow describes the mid-century interventions made to Whittington's tomb at St Michael Paternoster. Presented as a necessity of repair, these amounted to a wilful and avaricious excavation of his burial place by the very authority charged with its safety and sanctity. The rector of St Michael's, Thomas Mountain, evidently believed that Whittington's celebrated will had pointed to the interment and concealing of a great bounty, which in his view the Church could put to far better use.

This Richard Whittington was in this church three times buried: first by his executors under a fair monument. Then in the reign of Edward VI, the parson of that church, thinking some great riches, as he said, to be buried with him, caused his monument to be broken, his body to be spoiled in his leaden sheet, and again the second time to be buried; and in the reign of Queen Mary the parishioners were forced to take him up, to lap him in lead as before, to bury him a third time, and to place his monument, or the like, over him again, which remaineth and so he resteth.[4]

By this time, more than a century after his death, Whittington would have been known to Londoners not for any dramatisation of his life but for commonplace matters of fact, evident in the practical good works he had funded in their city, not least the construction of almshouses, work to the splendid Guildhall, and the financing from his will of the rebuilt Newgate Prison. They would not have known him, but many would have known *of* him, his memory elevated and prolonged by tangible and enduring acts of charity and civic munificence rather than his successes as a mercer or his tenure as their mayor.

It was not until the early years of the 17th century that a production of Whittington's 'life' was first enacted before a theatre audience. On 8 February 1605, *The History of Richard Whittington, of his lowe birth, his great fortune, as yt was played by the Prynces Servants* was performed at London's Stationers' Hall.[5] Whether its subtitle, implying the progress of a boy of low birth to great riches and the company of princes, is the original source of the pantomime legend is uncertain. More likely, this was the first structured staging of a popular piece of local folklore that had been doing the rounds for many years, perhaps for generations. Since Whittington's endowments were in plain sight, his name may have been introduced as a personal metaphor for the general successes of young boys arriving in London from the shires in the 15th and 16th centuries. Presumably, this proved a success, because on 16 July of that year a licence was granted for the publication of a ballad called 'The vertuous Lyfe and memorable Death of Sir Richard Whittington, mercer, sometyme Lord Maiour'. However, we cannot be certain since neither the play nor the ballad nor any account of their reception is known to have survived.

The translation of Whittington's story to the stage may have reflected the general aspirations of Londoners of all classes in the period. This is hinted at in the political satire and anti-Scottish comedy *Eastward Hoe* written by Ben Jonson, George Chapman and John Marston and performed at Blackfriars on 13 January 1606 by the Children of the Queen's Revels.

Though not centred on Whittington, the line 'when the famous fable of Whittington and his pusse shall not be forgotten' makes clear that the story and the reference to his cat had been around for some time.[6] London's playwrights were catching up and testing its wider appeal. Although he is mentioned only very briefly, there is a nod here to popular touchstones at an uncertain moment in England's political and social stability. Had he been around to see it, Whittington might well have enjoyed the 'parable' of a London goldsmith and his household of two daughters and two contrasting apprentices, one given to morality and industry, the other to ambition and villainy. In the brief imprisonment of its authors for offending the king with their anti-Scottish references, he might also have recognised echoes of life under Richard II. Another reference to the Whittington 'legend' is also found about this time in the work of Thomas Heywood, a writer who had popularised sometime between 1592 and 1600 the aspirations of the city's apprentices in *Four Prentices of London*. Heywood referred to Whittington in the second of his 'history plays', *If You Know Not Me, You Know Nobody*, published in 1605. We find him referred to as well in a satire by Francis Beaumont, *Knight of the Burning Pestle*, first performed in 1607.[7]

Whittington held an enduring fascination for Londoners throughout the course of the 17th century, so much so that we find that exceptional eyewitness to London life, Samuel Pepys, recording in his diary on 21 September 1668 having attended a meeting that morning at St James where 'the Duke of York did of his own accord come to me' and then gone 'To Southwark fair, very dirty, and there saw the puppet show of Whittington which was pretty to see; and how that idle thing do work upon people that see it, and even myself too'.[8]

* * *

That Cat

So, what of the enigmatic cat, 'the famous fable of Whittington and his pusse', which Jonson, Chapman and Marston referred to in 1606? This feline association with Whittington must have been in circulation for some time before then, but is there any evidence that Whittington kept a cat, let alone benefitted from the prodigious 'good luck' it is said to have brought him? Much of the modern support for the existence of his lucky charm centres on two excavations, in 1949 in the grounds of Whittington's former home at St Michael Paternoster and at a house in Gloucester said to have been built around 1460 by his nephew. Four hundred years later, during the excavations to lay the city's new drainage system, the foundations of the house were exposed to reveal a bas-relief of a young boy cradling a cat.[9] The rest, as they say, is history. Or maybe not. St Michael's is first recorded in 1219 as St Michael of Paternosterchierch, its name almost certainly associated with the manufacture of 'paternosters' (rosaries) in nearby Paternoster Lane. In 1361, the church had incorporated 'Riole' into its name. Later corrupted to 'Royal' and assumed to have had some association with the monarchy, in fact the term is said to derive from the area of La Riole near Bordeaux from where many of London's vintners, Geoffrey Chaucer's father among them, imported their wines into the cellars of Thames Street. The church was destroyed by the Great Fire of 1666 but was later rebuilt in 1694 by Christopher Wren. It is reported that during the fire itself or in the building's subsequent reconstruction, Whittington's tomb was finally lost.[10] Perhaps, but the legend gained a new twist during a further programme of rebuilding more than 250 years later in 1949, following bomb damage inflicted during the war. Renewed attempts to locate Whittington's grave amid the rubble-strewn site failed to find his body but did produce, of all things, a mummified cat. A tongue-in-cheek reference to the legend is incorporated in the modern south-west window, which depicts him with a cat and probably originates from a 17th-century engraving of Whittington by Renold Elstracke, which shows him with one hand placed on a skull, later replaced by his allegedly popular mascot and talisman.[11]

There is a left-field claim that Whittington's association with a lucky cat derives from his lifelong campaign to rebuild Newgate Gaol. Here the story goes that after its almost complete destruction during the Great Fire of London in 1666, the prison was rebuilt in 1672 and its association with Whittington sustained by common reference to it as 'The Whit'. In a study of London, a century later, the archivist Henry Chamberlain describes the original medieval gate (of the Whittington prison) as featuring four niches each supporting a life-size figure. Three represented the virtues of Peace, Security and Plenty while the fourth was a figure wearing a cap bearing the name Libertas and at her feet lay a carving of a cat, apparently an allusion to Whittington and presumably commissioned by his executors, who must have had a valid reason for displaying this association.[12] A contemporary of Chamberlain, the naturalist and antiquarian Thomas Pennant, claimed that a niche incorporated into the new gaol in 1672, also bearing the form of a cat, was a replacement for that which had originally been sculpted nearly 250 years earlier.[13] Whittington's story, with the cat ever more prominent, became an increasingly popular theme of 'chapbooks' for children in the 18th and 19th centuries. Its chief breakthrough, however, came with its popularity as a pantomime theme, appearing first in this form in a performance at Covent Garden in 1814 of *Harlequin Whittington, or the Lord Mayor of London*.[14]

There have been many explanations for the appearance of a cat in the Whittington legend and these include the assumption (consistent with the pantomime version) that cats were used to rid merchant ships of rats. This gained currency given the outbreak of the Black Death in 1348 and subsequent visitations of plague and pestilence. The story that Whittington had served as a houseboy in a large London house during his apprenticeship offered another explanation, as cats were employed to keep the cellars and larders free of vermin. Then there are the more eccentric elucidations. The flat-bottomed vessels used for bringing coal to London from the northeast of England during Whittington's lifetime were known colloquially as 'cats', but this ranks as a frivolous explanation as there is no evidence of Whittington's association with the coal trade. Frankly, it is nonsense. So, too, is another explanation, which suggests that the word 'cat' is a corruption of the prevailing French term 'achat' used by London merchants and shipowners to describe their purchases. Further afield, cats were commonly identified in medieval Europe as the 'familiars' of witches and heretics but also as the bringers of safety and good luck to the upstanding and religious—a means of keeping such witchcraft and heresy at bay. Then there is the rather more evidence-based role of cats in safeguarding the storage of cloth. In the Flemish city of Ypres, at this time one of Europe's leading wool and cloth centres, cats were deployed in large numbers to destroy the colonies of mice that nested in, gnawed away at, and bred and multiplied in the piles of finished cloth produced from English wool. The story goes that this worked for a time, until the cats themselves replicated the very nesting behaviour they had been employed to terminate. Soon a feral and aggressive cat population had supplanted its former prey and came to mimic their habits, burrowing ruinously into expensive cloths and procreating. The solution was plain if somewhat fantastical: simply exterminate the colonies by hurling them from the vertiginous roof of the Cloth Hall. Another version of 'cat throwing' or *kattenstoet* links this practice with the onset of spring, when the cloth had been sold; a practice also associated with the killing of heretics and ungodly philosophers and thinkers. There is some truth in this at least. Evidence for *kattenstoet* is found in the city chronicles for the years 1410–20, by which time this macabre tradition is thought to have been at least 300 years old, having originated in the city's Ascension Fair during the late 1120s. In the 15th century, albeit fifty years after Whittington's death, the event was moved to the second week of Lent and cats were dispensed with on what came to be known as 'Cat Wednesday'.[15] Happily, in modern times, woollen effigies have been substituted for the real thing.

We may never uncover the truth of Whittington's association with the cat, if indeed there is one, but a firm and popular link had been made by the middle of the 17th century. A 'black-letter ballad' of 1641 held in the British Museum, titled 'London's glory and Whittington's renown; or a looking glass for the citizens of London; being a remarkable story how Sir Richard Whittington … came to be three times Lord Mayor of London, and how his rise was by a cat', has been cited as the earliest story of Whittington and the first reference to his cat. The introduction to a reprinted version published by the Villon Society in 1885 sets out to distinguish fact from fiction.

> The popular story of Whittington and his Cat is one in which a version of a wide-spread folk-tale has been grafted upon the history of the life of an historical character, and in the later versions the historical incidents have been more and more eliminated. The three chief points in the chap-book story are, 1, the poor parentage of the hero; 2, his change of mind at Highgate Hill by reason of hearing Bow Bells; and 3, his good fortune arising from the sale of his cat. Now these are all equally untrue as referring to the historical Whittington, and the second is apparently an invention of the eighteenth century.[16]

Invention it may have been, but the story of London's famous mayor and his feline mojo continued to draw interest well into the 19th century, arguably reaching its peak with the publication of the then two main academic works detailing his life, Samuel Lysons's *The Model Merchant of the Middle Ages* (1860) and *Sir Richard Whittington: Lord Mayor of London* by Walter Besant and James Rice (1881).[17] A more populist though partial treatment had been given earlier in Thomas Keightley's compendium *Tales and Popular Fictions* (1834) and then in chapbooks such as E Carr's *Story of Sir Richard Whittington* (1871) and WA Clouston's *Popular Tales and Fictions* (1887). The century closed with James Tait's portrayal of Whittington in the *Dictionary of National Biography*.[18]

A succession of brief studies followed in the 20th century. Some, like Osbert Sitwell's 'true story' of Dick Whittington, were characteristically whimsical and edged the shores of credibility.[19] Meanwhile, the memorial pamphlet published jointly by the Gloucestershire councils and the Mercers' Company in 1959, to mark the 600th anniversary of his presumed birthdate, took the celebratory route and helped to firm up the contention of the present book that Whittington enters the world sometime around 1358–9 and not eight to ten years earlier.[20] Elsewhere, Michael Whittington's short study of 1988 is distinctive in placing his kinsman within the much broader and affinitive context of his family and offers a valuable localised insight into Richard Whittington's early circumstances.[21]

Notwithstanding the popular, the serious, the eccentric and, in some instances, the overly romantic pictures that the literature provides of Richard Whittington's life and circumstances, we have only truly come to understand his extraordinary influence on medieval London, and the extent of a legacy that continues to flourish in the present day, through the seminal work of Jean Imray in *The Charity of Richard Whittington: A History of the Trust Administered by the Mercer's Company 1424–1966*,[22] Caroline M Barron's sweeping study of *London in the Later Middle Ages*,[23] and Anne Sutton's expansive history of *The Mercery of London: Trade, Goods and People*.[24]

The work which provided the chief inspiration for this book was Barron's 1969 paper, 'Richard Whittington: The Man Behind the Myth'. It is over fifty years since she produced what remains the definitive study of Richard Whittington, a detailed essay directed at a more learned audience. Arguably, there has not been a single book dedicated to Whittington and aimed at a wider lay readership since the over-admiring Victorian account of London's famous mayor produced by Walter Besant and James Rice in 1881. It is 650 years since an insignificant young boy of 10 or 11 was lifted above the limited horizons of rural Gloucestershire and dispatched to the heaving sprawl of late-medieval, post-plague London, where he would make such an impression that we still celebrate his achievements today. If Whittington had a window on our present age, he might well recognise some of the exigencies and issues he encountered in his own time. History has a habit of repeating itself. Perhaps this is an appropriate moment to revisit them, and to explain in more detail what that pantomime fuss is all about.

1

HOME

The tiny settlement of Pauntley lies ten miles north-west of Gloucester, and seven miles south-east of Ledbury. The Domesday Book records the village as Pantelie, held under the ownership and administration of Ansfrid de Cormeilles. In 1086, there were just three households paying tax.

In 1066, the manor of Newent was held by Edward the Confessor, forming part of the royal estate centred on Westbury on Severn. Following the Norman Conquest, the lands were bestowed by William I on his relative and counsellor, the influential William Fitzosbern, Earl of Hereford, and from him they passed in grant to the Benedictine Abbey of Cormeilles, in what is now modern-day Eure in France. In many ways, this is where the Whittington story begins. On the death of Fitzosbern in 1071 Walter de Lacy, one of William the Conqueror's leading commanders, was honoured for his endeavours by the seizure and grant of some 120 manors, about two dozen of which were in what is now modern-day Gloucestershire. They included Pauntley and the adjoining area then known as Ledene, deriving its name from the modest river Leadon. Walter's niece married the upwardly mobile landowner and tenant-in-chief Ansfrid of Cormeilles, who later came to own Pauntley, Ketford and other places near Newent, which formed part of his wife's dowry. By 1086, Ansfrid was lord of Pauntley and fourteen other estates.[1] Today, his burgeoning demesne reads like a glossy heritage tour of some of Gloucestershire's most historic villages, many invested with 'the honour of Cormeilles', before fragmenting and passing to several landowners in the early 13th century.[2] Fitzosbern had founded the Benedictine monastery of Cormeilles in Normandy in 1060, and the fruits of conquest provided him with both the opportunity and the resources to enrich his favoured religious house by investing it with endowments granted to him during his early years in England. These included the manor of Newent, its church and all tithes and offerings, together with the abundant, game-rich woods and all assarts that belonged to Newent, Stanling, and Boulsdon with the chapel. Of most interest, he also granted to the Abbey of Cormeilles the church of Taynton, together with the modest chapel of Pauntley, part of the estate which later fell to the Whittington family.

Of these settlements, only Dymock and Newent could be reasonably described as 'villages'. Pauntley itself was little more than a loose necklace of scattered tiny farms and isolated smallholdings, essentially part of Newent's expanding hinterland. Bordering the ancient Forest of Dean, eight miles north-west of Gloucester, Newent had been settled since Roman times and in 1086 it remained the area's only notable market centre. It was granted market rights later, by Henry III in 1253. Dymock fell under a different stewardship, that of the Cistercian monastery at Flaxley established in the early 1150s by Roger, son of Milo Fitzwalter, Earl of Hereford. Valued for its iron workings and agriculture, it would later help drive the local wool trade with London.

By the end of the 12th century, it was to Newent that this sparse collection of hamlets and holdings looked for food, supplies, trade and entertainment, and the bustling religious and administrative centre of Gloucester where the principal trade and pilgrim routes to Oxford and London, and to the Midlands and Bristol, converged. Newent was a long-established focus also for trade with Wales, a gateway to the small foundries of the Forest of Dean, which would supply the archers at Agincourt three centuries later, a moment which figures in Richard Whittington's own story. Its chief asset was its mill, a vital facility for small estates like Pauntley. By the 1170s, Newent's parish church was well established and in 1181 this church, together with those at Taynton and Dymock and the chapel at Pauntley, was reconfirmed to Cormeilles as part of a grant to the abbey by the Earl of Leicester. At the same time, Henry II granted Cormeilles the right to operate a forge and burn charcoal on the manor, striking a modern note in the production of cinders for the ever-multiplying potholes on its main roads.

Newent had to work hard to sustain its trade, zealously guarding its relationship with the scattered settlements along the Welsh border and those tucked away in the denser reaches of the Forest of Dean. The rivalry between what its inhabitants proclaimed was now a small 'town' and the much larger regional 'capital' of Gloucester is evidenced in an inquiry held in 1253 to establish the veracity of claims that Newent had become so successful that it was undermining trade at Gloucester and at the small port of Newnham on Severn. Its sheer, and perhaps aggressive, vitality was demonstrated in the ruling that, rather than undermining its competitors, it contributed to the region's wealth by enabling Welsh cattlemen to trail their beasts to the markets at Ross on Thursdays, Gloucester on Saturdays, Newnham on Sundays, and Newent on Fridays—though Newent did upset Gloucester's dominance of the corn trade. Whatever the charges, the inquiry appears to have supported the grant of its market charter. In the late 13th and early 14th centuries, the town's establishment of a fulling mill was instrumental in its development as a centre for weavers, dyers and fullers. In 1313, Edward II granted buoyant, enterprising Newent a new Friday market. By the time of Richard Whittington's birth in 1358–9, records at Gloucester Abbey refer to the family's demesne at 'the market town of Newent'.

Newent prospered well from its relationship with the Welsh drovers who brought their cattle to market there, enjoying something of a regional reputation for fine meat and produce. By the 14th century it numbered cooks, butchers, a cordwainer, a glover, a skinner, a tailor smiths, hoopers, mercers and a wheelwright among its tradesmen. It had become a popular and reliable place to purchase bread, meat, mustard, vegetables, corn, dyes and cloth, not to mention strong local ale and prized eels from the Severn, much of which also found its way to market at Gloucester. By the middle of the 14th century more than twenty of Newent's citizens kept alehouses or traded ale. In turn, Gloucester supplied its upstart neighbour with wine, salt, fish, leather goods and finished ironware. Yet by the time of Whittington's birth a decade later, it stood devastated, its industrious and resourceful population decimated, the once reliable supply of tenants and labourers savagely depleted. Many of the survivors chose to abandon it. It had barely recovered when the young third son of the Whittington family left in 1369, bound for London.

So, what of Gloucester: why did this much larger place, among the wealthiest towns of England, having strong trading ties with London in the south and Bristol in the west, not provide an outlet for Richard Whittington's future? Regardless of the ambitions and vitality of nearby Newent, Gloucester was the area's principal town by far, an important trading hub and one of England's leading ecclesiastical centres, boasting in its remarkable abbey church one of England's most celebrated visitor attractions and a notable centre of education and learning. Though its population was less than 5,000 at the time of the Black Death and twenty years later had been reduced by at least a third, it had shown a resilient determination to rebuild and move forward. Gloucester has been described as experiencing the economic problems that affected many English towns in the period following the Black Death but 'the inherent strength of its position as a centre of trade, administration, and communications brought it through them without any dramatic change in its fortunes'.[3] Among English towns, it ranked sixteenth in terms of wealth in 1334 and fifteenth in 1377. Though its importance nationally had shown signs of decline, it continued to sustain some measure of economic stability and produced modest spurts of prosperity for its small but enterprising merchant class in the half-century after 1375.[4]

As 'Glevum', the town claimed a notable Roman history and later developed a significant Saxon heritage. Its location as a gateway to Wales and to the South-West and the Midlands, and its access to the road from Oxford to London, gave it a strategic commercial and military importance. As its abbey church acquired a wider renown, the town's status as a religious destination soared. A monastery dedicated to the honour of St Peter and St Paul had been founded in 681 by Osric, under-king of the Hwiccas.[5] Nearly 350 years later, in 1022, Wulfstan, Bishop of Worcester and York, reordered the abbey's secular priests as a Benedictine community and rededicated its mission to St Peter. In 1058 his successor at Worcester, Bishop Aldred, commenced the rebuilding of the church and in 1072 a transformative plan for Gloucester began to develop with the appointment by William the Conqueror of a new abbot. It was Serlo who rebuilt the church of St Peter after its partial destruction by fire in 1088, and it was under his direction that an ambitious vision for Gloucester began to unfold. A monastic community believed to have comprised just two monks and eight novices on his arrival in 1072 numbered 100 by the time of his death in 1104.[6] By the Middle Ages, the abbey was firmly established as one of England's leading religious destinations, a place of coronation and burial for kings. Walter de Lacy, from whose line the Whittington estate at Sollers Hope would descend, had been lain to rest at the abbey in 1085. Robert Curthose, the Conqueror's own son, was buried there in 1134. The nine-year-old Henry III was crowned at Gloucester in 1216 and Edward II, who had died at Berkeley Castle, was buried there in 1327.[7] Yet, Gloucester's greatest asset lay not within the confines of its abbey yard but in its outlying fields. In the 14th century, the wool trade at Gloucester was so vigorous and profitable that the town was able to invest even more significantly in church improvements, sufficient in the years before the Black Death to remodel the choir and, hugely ambitiously in the 1350s, to commission the Great East Window, then the largest in the world. This, just a few years after the town and the abbey's Benedictine community had been decimated by the plague. The city was also home to Kingsholm, a royal residence near the abbey, the 'palace at Gloucester' to which William I repaired during the Christmas Witan of 1085 when he commissioned the Domesday survey.[8]

Here were the places and horizons familiar to Richard Whittington as a young boy of ten or eleven. He would have seen at first hand that twenty years after the Black Death, Gloucester had recovered sufficiently to rebuild its economy in grain and malt, supplied by small farms and villages located in the Severn and Avon hinterland; that it once again acted as the provider of a wide range of foodstuffs and manufactures, much of it transported down the Severn to the expanding port of Bristol; and that it still managed to sustain a small but wealthy merchant community with strong trading connections with London. He may have heard the labourers employed at Pauntley or the fishwives in the market whisper that Gloucester also thrived through its vigorous 'black economy' centred on the regular smuggling of grain and other foodstuffs to the south coast for illegal export to France. He might have observed from the produce served at his family's table that even after the ravages of plague the town had revived and had the benefit of a burgeoning supply chain of foodstuffs, including exotic imports such as pepper, dates, raisins, almonds, plant extracts and oils. If he travelled into town, he would have seen at first hand that its busy cloth and dyeing industry had also recovered because it was well placed to import by road and by river commodities such as woad, alum, madder and soap from Southampton and large quantities of wine from Bordeaux.

Yet, if he had listened to his mother's likely explanation for sending him to London, he may also have learned that despite its apparent vibrancy, Gloucester was struggling to compete with Cirencester, Tewkesbury, Worcester and Bristol, and other towns whose names would become familiar to him later in his London career—Coventry, Nottingham and Newark. Listening to the din that rose from the make-shift timber-and-reed shacks on the riverside and the clamorous hammering as he passed the workshops of Gloucester's acclaimed stonemasons, he would have understood that much of the town's working population was engaged in the production of manufactured goods. The abrasion and crashing of metal would also remind him that much of its craftsmanship was centred on metalworking—the production of armour, arrowheads, pots and pans, locks and keys, swords, and other weaponry. He would learn, soon enough, that war was good for business. He would know too that weaving was hugely important to the local economy and that it was also well known for profiteering. In the 1350s, forty-three men of the craft had been prosecuted for price rigging—an activity, though in a different trade, that would present one of the most significant and enduring challenges of his later life as London's acclaimed mayor. And, in common with every child born just a decade after the Black Death, he would have heard the horror stories, assimilated the crude, handed-down statistics and seen for himself, on the family estate at Pauntley, its impact upon labour, servitude and agriculture. Yet, if there was one overriding example of the changes that had been wrought and that were still reshaping the countryside and economy about him, it would have been the ubiquitous presence of sheep, the wealth it had begun to generate, and the increasing shift to wool over agriculture.

* * *

The acquisition of the manor house by the Whittington family in the early 14th century brought substantial tracts of woodland and access to a 'great park', three-quarters of a mile to the south-east, a notable landmark on the route to Gloucester. A trackway connected the estate, which was less than half a mile away, with the well-travelled route from Newent to Ledbury, and it was barely a mile distant from the Gloucester Road. By the middle of the 14th century the parish had consolidated into two distinct parts: the more expansive of the two was located north-east of Newent, while the smaller, barely one-fifth the size of the main settlement of Pauntley, lay between Oxenhall and Newent. At the time of Whittington's birth, taken in this study as 1358–9, local roads were once more rattling with trade to the Forest, to South Wales, and to the religious centres of Tewkesbury, Worcester and Hereford. The main commercial routes to the ports of Gloucester and Bristol were also showing signs of recovery.

Whittington's manorial home, Pauntley Court, was well appointed, commanding a site above the narrow, twisting Leadon but screened by a thin arc of woodland, its singular near neighbour the 12th-century chapel. The isolated steadings which both served and relied on the estate were concentrated on meadowland near the narrow waterway.

Poor Dick Whittington

The *Victoria County History* describes the Whittingtons of Pauntley as the most prominent and wealthiest of the smaller lay lords at the end of the medieval period, owing their advancement to the changes wrought after Domesday in the acquisition and consolidation of farmsteads within the enlarged manors.[9] Some valuations of Pauntley, at the time of Richard's departure, were deemed to be modest and have encouraged the view that the family estate was under financial pressure, perhaps giving credence to the myth of the poor country boy who makes his way to London where the streets are 'paved with gold'. It is an attractive prospect, but the Whittingtons were by no means impoverished. At the time of Sir William Whittington's death, Pauntley was assessed at the equivalent of a knight's fee, about £20 per annum. When his youngest son left for London, the family held estates in both Gloucestershire and Herefordshire. They also had wealthy and influential connections that would serve them well throughout the next half-century. The Whittingtons were not, however, the leading family in the area; that status fell to the Berkeleys, with whom they were interlinked; but they were certainly far more advantaged than the pantomime story would have us believe. Indeed, the hero's departure for London is proof of that, and it is evident that his coat of arms was not that of 'a newly risen man', but one to which he was entitled by birth. According to an earlier authority, Whittington's lineage can be traced to the family which held the estate at Sollers Hope in Herefordshire in the 13th century and that from which he originated at Pauntley in Gloucestershire in the mid-14th. Drawing on Samuel Lysons's work of 1860, *The Model Merchant of the Middle Ages*, Besant and Rice remark that following the death of Whittington's father, 'The estate of Pauntley became the jointure of Dame Whittington, who thus possessed for life two estates, and could not have been badly off'.[10] Writing in the 1880s, they assure us romantically that the Whittingtons 'were of a good old race, and lived on their own lands, which were farmed for them by three *villains*', adding in what amounts to pure conjecture that 'The estate would yield enough and to spare of corn and grain, cider and mead, hay and grass, cattle, sheep and bacon for their own use; while the woodland, which then formed so large a part of every country estate, was hunted over by the sons of the house for venison and game'.[11] This overlooks the fact that at the time of his departure around 1369–70, Richard was a boy of ten or eleven, his middle brother Robert was just two years older, and their much older brother William is reported as having a sickly and fragile constitution. It is hard to imagine any of them hunting and foraging.

2

WHITTINGTON

Whittington's origins and circumstances at the time of his departure for London have exercised imagination and invited scrutiny since the work of Richard Grafton in 1569. The popular mythology that has built up around the pantomime version of his life has embellished him as a folk hero but has distorted what firm evidence we have about his background in Gloucestershire, his time in London, his achievements there, and the purpose and fabric of his legacy. It may disappoint some readers, but it is best to state at the outset that I can find no substance for a rise to such influence derived from the endeavours or the presence of a cat. This seems to be no more than enticing embroidery, evolved in the later populist celebration of his life to provide a theatrical and entertaining device for his transformation from country urchin to mayor of London and the confidant of kings. It is an essential part of the 'magic' of the Whittington rags-to-riches story. Deploying his rat-catching cat as the means of his exceptional good (and real) fortune suggested that anyone could make their way to the top with a slice of good luck. More deeply, perhaps, it is a metaphor for human progress amid the threat and consternation visited by plague. In common with other folk tales, the content is to some extent a mixture of fiction and truth. The introduction of a cat helps both to explain and to symbolise his good fortune to a fascinated audience who first encountered him nearly 200 years after his death, a lengthy vacuum into which are introduced a variety of ingredients intended to promote and celebrate that most singular of human characteristics—self-improvement. And, of course, theatre demands precisely that: *theatre*. There are features of the Dick Whittington story that do contain a truth, and these are not to be underestimated or dismissed. He is a country lad and does make his way to London at a young age. He does enter the household of a wealthy gentleman, and he almost certainly is tasked in his early years of service with a range of dispiriting and thankless chores as a means of earning his keep and fulfilling the pre-terms of his apprenticeship. It is true that he does make his mark with the master of the house and later with his daughter, who eventually becomes his wife, and in some accounts their names are also known. We know too that he does make his fortune and becomes mayor of London, though whether he at some point determines to leave the city but is summoned to return by the peal of church bells is another matter. And it is conceivable that the household may have acquired a cat to keep rats and mice at bay and that it fell to the young Whittington to ensure that it did. There is a basis of truth in most fantasy.

So, what of the truth itself, as we claim to know it? Writing in the *Dictionary of National Biography*, James Tait drew on Samuel Lysons's earlier study of Whittington's origins, noting that Lysons 'gave strong reasons for identifying his father with Sir William Whittington of Pauntley, who married (after 1355) Joan, daughter of William Maunsell, sheriff of Gloucestershire in 1313, and widow of Thomas Berkeley of Cubberley, who held the same office at least three times'.[1] And that Whittington bore the arms of the Pauntley family, with a mark of cadency and a difference of tincture and crest.

Arguably, it was Ansfrid de Cormeilles who set the Whittingtons on their way, through his marriage to a niece of the powerful Walter de Lacy. Through this union, Ansfrid acquired as many as twenty manors in Herefordshire and Gloucestershire, among them Sollers Hope. In the 12th century Pauntley passed from William de Solers to his son Richard and then later still to his grandson Walter, whose son Richard rendered services and a regular income to the Benedictines of Cormeilles Abbey who secured their rights to Pauntley's church in the early 13th century, against the claims of the Whittingtons' distant kin, the Solers who held the manors at Hope and Aston in Herefordshire. The two families were related through marriage with descendants of Ansfrid. Over time, various estates and holdings held by the Solers passed to Margaret, the wife of Walter de Stokes, creating connections with another local estate, Stoke Orchard. Richard Whittington's eldest brother William (the sixth William Whittington, who died in 1379) would marry Joan Archer, daughter and heiress of Geoffrey Archer of Stoke Orchard, sometime between the death of her first husband in 1365 and her own demise, childless, in 1369. Margaret's properties were divided between her two daughters. It was one of these, Isobel, the wife of Simon de Solers, who inherited the manors of Hope and Pauntley. These remained in the Solers family until 1310, when ownership of title was referred to an Inquisition on the death of a descendant, Sir John de Solers. It is here that we see the rise of the Whittingtons in Gloucestershire. To illuminate this further, we need to trace their line from the first William Whittington.

The Whittingtons in Gloucestershire

According to a family source, the home of William Whittington has never been identified. He was not from Herefordshire but, according to Michael Whittington, apparently 'emerges from the shadows in South Warwickshire not far from Haselor'.[2] Whether he was a well-heeled merchant or a prosperous farmer is unclear but he was wealthy and far-sighted enough for his son William Whittington II to marry Hawise, sister and heiress of Hugh Aguillon, lord of Upton near Alcester. Like the Herefordshire marriages, this proved to be an advantageous and upwardly mobile union. Hugh was the last of an ancient family line, and on his death in 1284 William III succeeded to the manor of Upton. The Whittingtons continued to live at Upton-Haselor until the inquiry of 1310 established their rights in Gloucestershire, through the Solers branch of the family, intimated in a reference to 'a certain John', son of Aguillon's sister Maud. The *Victoria County History* remarks of Upton that

> nothing is known of the ownership of the manor until 1284, when Hugh Aguillon died holding the manor of Upton. His widow Ellen claimed dower in the manor. He left no children, and his heirs were his sister Joan, then aged 80, and his nephews Hugh Trenchevent and William de Whitenton or Whittington, and a certain John, son of his sister Maud. The greater part of the manor passed to William Whittington, who settled it upon himself and Joan his wife in 1314 and was still in possession two years later. A similar settlement was made in 1347 upon another William and Joan Whittington.[3]

The multiplicity of Williams and Joans, and the two distinct directions from which the family developed, invite confusion and need unpicking,[4] but what seems clear is that it is from the Herefordshire line rather than Warwickshire that the connection with Gloucestershire was upheld. The marriage of William Whittington III to Solers's daughter Maud was the means by which the manor of Pauntley became vested in the Whittington family. 'William III's marriage and his son's succession to the estates of the

Solers family set the Whittingtons on an upward course in the social scale and as substantial landlords [they] must have been saved the necessity of pursuing whatever means of livelihood their forebears had previously adopted.'[5] However, this William was dead before 1310. After the inquiry of that year, when Edward II declared him to be the son of William Whittington III and Maud de Solers, daughter and heir to Sir John de Solers, lord of Hope and Pauntley, it was *his son* William IV, Richard Whittington's grandfather, who acquired Pauntley and Sollers Hope. Married to Joan Lyvet, daughter of Roger Lyvet of Haselor, in 1314 he settled the manor of Upton on himself and his wife. He is presumed to have relocated to Pauntley sometime after 1314 because he represented Gloucestershire at the Lincoln Parliament of 1327. Knighted by 1325, he died in 1331 aged 47 and was succeeded by Richard's father, Sir William Whittington V.

Accordingly, in 1331, Richard Whittington's father found himself the master of three estates, Upton in Warwickshire, Sollers Hope in Herefordshire, and Pauntley in Gloucestershire. We can see why each of these counties, even today, lays claim to the family's most famous son. Like his father before him and his sons William, Robert and Richard after him, Sir William would represent Gloucestershire in Parliament, in his case in the year of the Black Death, 1348. He is a significant figure in the family history for several reasons: the identity of his wife; the long gap between their first and last sons, which indicates that his eldest, also William, was the product of a much earlier marriage; the charge of outlawry made against him and his subsequent isolation; the question whether, before his death in 1358–9, it was he who had predetermined his youngest child's dispatch to London ten years later; and the nature of his relationship with the household to which Richard would be bound.

Marriage, Births, Deaths

The key to unlocking who married whom and when their children came along lies in determining the date of Richard's birth and the identity of his mother. The exact date is unknown though widely contested. The joint Mercers' Company and Gloucester City and County pamphlet settled on 1959 to celebrate the 600th anniversary of his birth but acknowledged that it 'may be called a date of convenience, as absolute documentary proof is lacking of the date of Richard's birth'.[6] Whittington's birth has been dated by some writers as early as 1350, which seems unlikely as he would have been approaching thirty when we first hear of him in London in 1379. Nor does it appear to fit with what we do know about his mother and father and the timing of their marriage. Others place his birth at 1354–5, which would put him in his mid-twenties in 1379. This, too, jars with other dates and episodes. On the other hand, there is good reason for settling on 1359 as rather more than a mere 'date of convenience' for his 600th 'birthday'. Writing in 1968, Jean Imray, the highly respected archivist to the Mercers' Company, centred her study on Whittington's later years and specifically on the work of his charity, rather than on his origins. She too leaves open the possibility of 1359 in a simple footnote.[7] The principal authority on Richard Whittington, Caroline M Barron, tells us that 'Richard Whittington was born at Pauntley in Gloucestershire, the third son of Sir William Whittington and his wife Joan' and that 'his father died on 8th September 1358 when his eldest son William was 23 years old'.[8] Barron doesn't identify the maiden name of Richard's mother, or the exact year of his birth, but it is conceivable that he arrived in the year of his father's death, 1358–9. A parliamentary résumé describes Richard as the '3rd s. of Sir William Whittington (*d*. 1358) of Pauntley, Glos. by his w. Joan Maunsell, bro. of Robert'. There is no mention of his eldest brother, as he was deceased by the time Richard entered Parliament in 1416.[9] On the face of it, modern scholars appear to have accepted that there is no definitive record of mother or birthdate and have opted for flexibility. If we cannot find certainty in the modern sources, then we must return to the three principal accounts of Whittington's life written in the 19th century to see if they can shed any light. The first of these is Samuel Lysons's work of 1860, developed further by Walter Besant and James Rice in 1881, and a subsequent account published by the Villon Society in 1885.[10]

Lysons's history is a curious medley of fact, fiction and supposition. In an otherwise detailed and sturdy history, he meanders into the dubious and distracting territory of Whittington's cat. Geography and 'stock' are recurring themes. From the outset, he remarks that Whittington's origins in Gloucestershire are disputed by claims of his birth in Herefordshire, Somerset, Shropshire, Staffordshire and even Lancashire. He asserts that his researches, in the British Museum, allow him 'to prove most satisfactorily the pedigree' of his subject. Through a definitive examination of armorial bearings, he concludes that those of the Lord Mayor of London 'are identical with those of Gloucestershire and Herefordshire'. All other claims are summarily dismissed. 'The arms of our hero which appear on the Ordinances of the college and on the hospital which he founded, are identical to those of the Gloucestershire family.' He goes on to add:

When you know all that I have to tell you of Richard Whittington, I think you will agree with me that we ought not to readily concede the privilege of having him as a Gloucestershire worthy, descended from Gloucestershire stock, if not actually born in the county, the probabilities, however, being in favour of the latter supposition, though inasmuch as there were no parish registers at the time when Whittington was born, nor until more than 100 years after his death it would be difficult to fix it with any certainty.[11]

So, there we have it, the geography apparently sorted.

The third history cited above, written by an author known only as 'TH', edited by Henry B Wheatley and published by the Villon Society in 1885, concludes that 'Nothing is known of Richard's early life, either as to when or how he came to London'. It contests the view that Whittington might have been born in 1360, because he would have been too young to have made his mark in London in 1379. Yet 'TH' leaves the door open to this very possibility, remarking that Richard's contribution to the City's gift to the king was the lowest figure among the contributions. This, as the present work suggests, may indicate that he was very young, of limited means, quite possibly supported by a third party, and encouraged to 'announce himself'.

Richard Whittington was the third son of Sir William Whittington, knight, of Pauntley, Gloucestershire, and it is assumed, by some writers, that he was born in or about the year 1360. We must, however, place his birth at an earlier date, for his name appears in the city *Letter Book*, H, fol. 110a (as Richard Whyttingdone), in the second year of Richard II (A.D. 1379), as a contributor of five marks towards a loan to the city authorities; about four-fifths of the subscribers contributing the same, which is the lowest figure among the contributions. This is the first appearance of Whittington's name in the city books.[12]

Surely the answer lies in the sequence of marriage and births. There is a window of four years at most between the marriage of Richard Whittington's parents in 1355 and his father's death in 1358–9, and it is further narrowed by the fact that his brother Robert precedes him by just two years. Almost certainly, this places Richard's birth at 1358 or even 1359. Much of the confusion about the marital and birth dates may lie instead with the third and oldest brother, William, named after his father and known to be significantly older than his two brothers. This suggests that William was the product of an earlier marriage by his father; that his marriage to Joan was a second union for both partners; that Joan was much younger than her husband, who was 49 or 50 by this time; and that

William was not the full brother of Richard and Robert. During the swearing-in to his first term as mayor of London in June 1397 Richard Whittington attested that he was the third son of Sir William Whittington of Pauntley and Joan Maunsell, daughter of William Maunsell and widow of Thomas Berkeley. He reaffirms this when he enters Parliament in October 1416, when he again describes himself as the third son of Sir William and Joan. On his death in 1423 he makes provision in his will for these same parents. Yet the maths, as they say, does not compute. So, who is brother William's mother and his father's first wife?

It is easy to understand the confusion surrounding the timing of Whittington's birth and his parenthood. The family's circumstances were complicated from the outset by Sir William's failure to gain royal sanction for the marriage of a young widow, so soon after the demise of her first husband. Given that his eldest son William is said to have been as much as twenty or so years older than his two younger 'brothers', it is reasonable to conclude that the three were not full siblings: Robert and Richard being the children of a second marriage, with their father marrying their younger mother late in life.[13] The question is why. This short and, for Sir William, twilight marriage must have been under considerable financial pressure from the start. It was joined barely seven years after the Black Death when the Gloucestershire economy was only just beginning to recover and when the value of land and agriculture was compromised by the lack of labour and, where it was available, by a surge in costs. The failure to secure royal approval to marry the widowed Joan meant from the outset that Sir William was deemed an 'outlaw', and he would have been deprived by the king of the very income from his land and property that he would have expected to rely upon as his part of the marriage settlement and as the basis of the family's prospects.[14] He was certainly no farmer and had few accomplishments as an estate manager. He had sat briefly in Parliament in 1348, but any ambitions there had been foreclosed by his military duties. The sketchy picture we have of him is one of an ageing career soldier, no longer in service, and perhaps temporarily without benefit of a pension, with a much younger new wife and possessed of an estate producing relatively little return to meet their needs and match his ambitions. His prospects must have looked bleak. For her part, pending the termination of outlawry, Joan may have been unable to secure the full settlement due to her from her earlier marriage to Sir Thomas Berkeley of Cobberley. Given the social circumstances of her rush to remarry and the cloud produced by royal disapproval, she is likely to have found herself shunned by members of her own family for shedding her widowhood so quickly.

Here was a not unfamiliar situation of illiquid wealth tied up in land and property, but exacerbated by a royal sanction imposed on the drawing of any income because of the circumstances of that marriage, and with few other means available to support a family of five and the wider household. At the time of Richard's birth, the family certainly had status if somewhat dented and some notable assets if somewhat illiquid, but little in the way of ready money. Worse was to come. The father Richard never knew would once again find himself on the wrong side of the law. Either around the time that his mother was pregnant, or when Richard was in his first year, his father fell ill, took to his bed and died soon after. Was his death hastened by the promulgation of outlawry brought against him at the hustings court in London on 3rd September 1359 by William de Southam for the non-payment of debt?[15] Southam is referred to elsewhere as the vicar of St Lawrence Jewry in 1356.[16] Whatever the reason or the circumstances, Richard Whittington's father died an outlaw with debts outstanding. At the time of his death in 1358–9 the family held estates at Pauntley valued at 8 marks per annum and at Sollers Hope and Hopton in Herefordshire but were encumbered with the offence of outlawry because of Southam's plea of debt.[17]

Richard's arrival would have mattered little to his elder brother, a generation older and now burdened with re-establishing the estate, or to a middle brother just a couple of years ahead of him, to whom he would have been a source of competition. There would be no future for Richard Whittington at Pauntley once he had reached an age when the cost of feeding and clothing him and an opportunity to make something of himself could be found or laid elsewhere. A local option would have been service in the large and wealthy household of a 'superior' family. He might, for example, have been presented by his mother to the Berkeleys, with a view to becoming a page, but if she did this then he must not have been suitable. Based on the scant evidence of an engraving of Whittington made some time in his fifties, Lysons suggests, somewhat wildly, that he may not have been fair enough of face or of figure to join what then resembled a minor regional court. 'Now poor Richard Whittington (to judge by Elstrack's portrait of him in mature age) did not possess in his youth the face or figure likely to make an elegant or interesting page, but he evidently was of that more practically useful class of whom the adage justly says— "Handsome is that handsome does".'[18]

So now, he was to go to London. How and where to he probably had little idea, except that his host or sponsor would almost certainly have been someone acquainted with his father and approved by his mother. His future education and purpose in life would have been given considerable thought before his family entered into any agreement or undertaking ahead of his departure.

* * *

For a boy of ten or eleven raised in the rural backwaters of a minor estate, Gloucester must have seemed the very centre of England. The town had begun to recover after the plagues of 1348 and 1361–2, even though many of its merchants and craftsmen had perished. At Llanthony Secunda Priory and the Abbey of St Peter, one or the other of which may have been responsible for Richard Whittington's earlier schooling, less than half of the monks had survived. The qualities of the abbey are well documented, but the vitality and wealth of Llanthony Secunda at the time of the Black Death, when it owned 97 churches and 51 well-appointed manors, ranked it as the sixth largest Augustinian house in England. It was only as Whittington departed that the flow of pilgrims associated with the abbey returned to earlier levels with a regular stream of worshippers once more arriving in Gloucester. The town itself had regained some semblance of its earlier energy. Yet even now the fields beyond the town were still shorn of workers and Whittington's mother, widowed for a second time, would very likely have struggled to meet the rates demanded by the new itinerant class of labourers. Pauntley had at least been spared the abandonment that ravaged the neighbouring settlements of Bromsberrow, Kempley and Oxenhall. Elsewhere, the old ways had been turned upside down and new opportunities beckoned. At Dymock and throughout the rich grassy Ryelands, there was hardly a man at work in the fields, and the land had been left to sheep. Here the landowners were now among the wealthiest in the area. The transformation and its impact locally would shape Whittington's career in London. 'Sheep's gold', they might have called it.

3

DEPARTURE

How would Whittington have been informed of his imminent departure? It would have fallen to his mother, perhaps supported by a male relative, acting both as a legal witness and for the boy's comfort—someone from Joan Whittington's own family, a Maunsell from Lypiatt perhaps. There is good evidence that Whittington maintained contact with the Maunsells long after his departure to London. In February 1394, for example, by then a prosperous mercer and a notable lender at court, Whittington lent his uncle Philip Maunsell the sum of £500. Maunsell would later default on the loan but conveyed the manor of Over Lypiatt in Gloucestershire by way of settlement. And how might the reason for the boy's departure have been explained to him? Was it that the family really could no longer afford another mouth to feed, or that as the third son of a knight and former landowner he was simply now of an age when he was expected to move on and commence the long climb to a self-sustaining career? Were there other factors at work?

Given the general remoteness he displayed to his brothers in later life, it may be that they were not close and that his mother had responded to the dissonance. It would be perfectly understandable for a young boy, displaced from the family home, to harbour a long-term sense of detachment from and perhaps resentment towards those he believed had rejected him and forced him out. William, a sickly character, was in his late twenties or early thirties and is unlikely to have had much in common with a child of eleven. It was to him that the management of the estate now fell, and his priorities would have turned to raising his own family. We know little of William's marriage to Joan Archer, which is thought to have taken place sometime after 1365, other than that his wife died in 1369. As a widower, perhaps with young children, often unwell and with

29

an estate to manage and a household to feed, it would have fallen to William as the head of the Whittington family, rather than to his step-mother Joan Whittington, to send Richard on his way. Robert, the middle brother, was a far more robust and purposeful character, aware that he was likely to inherit Pauntley sooner rather than later. In the short term, he was marked for military service and may have viewed his younger brother as a cuckoo in the nest.[1] There appears to have been little love lost between the two; they barely engaged with each other and built quite separate distinguished careers, one in the capital, the other in their home county of Gloucestershire.[2]

The one notable exception to the 'distance' they kept did not occur until 45 or more years later. In October 1416, accompanied by his son Guy, Robert arrived unexpectedly in London to urge his influential younger brother to support their presentation to Parliament against the violent intentions of a local rogue, Richard Oldcastle. Whittington's acquiescence turned apparently on the alleged affront posed to the family name and reputation, rather than any kindly disposition towards his older brother. A combination of factors shaped Whittington's general detachment in later life: the death of his father either just before his birth or during the early months of his infancy; his mother having to raise him as a single parent; her having to overcome the social and financial circumstances associated with successive widowhoods; and the outlawry of her second husband for debt and the stain on both his and her own family name. If these circumstances resulted in Richard Whittington's aloofness and detachment in later years, they may also have been instrumental in making him the strikingly enterprising and self-reliant figure who served as London's mayor four times and achieved much more besides.

What would he have taken with him to London? A leather bag perhaps, containing the meagre personal effects of a boy of eleven. A modest chest of clothes, a fine pair of boots, his best tunic, a comb fashioned from horn, a hymnal. Perhaps a farewell gift from a tutor at the abbey or the priory, a popular work on the lives of the saints by the influential Bartholomew of Trent. Into his satchel his mother would have inserted family papers and warrants for identification, including an introductory letter to his sponsor secured with the Whittington seal. Might there have been a fashionable French purse containing a small sum of silver coin and a signet ring in memory of his father? He would have owned little else.

The term 'conject' became obsolete in the late 14th century, around the time that Whittington left his family, but was still in sufficient currency to allow us to conject how his departure might have unfolded. Arrangements would almost certainly have been made for him to depart from Gloucester, where he would have been placed in the care of someone able to transport him quickly and safely to the capital. His family would not have wished him to be exposed any longer than necessary to the rigour and dangers of a week-long journey to London. Arriving in Gloucester from Pauntley, the departure party would probably have entered the town across the meadow at Alney Island, easing their way past the fishermen and mongers on the banks of the Severn; idling the horses on to Ebridge Street before passing St Mary de Grace and Holy Trinity and the remains of the old Mint; making their way up Westgate Street, perhaps cutting across the marketplace to the Fountain Inn near the Boothall, where reputation had it that Henry III had stayed when he was crowned at the abbey church.

His mother would have sought advice and recommendation as to which type of fellowship and means of transportation it was best to entrust her youngest child. Perhaps this offers a clue to the identity of Whittington's sponsor and to his destination in London. At this time, the Gloucester to London Road, and notoriously that between Oxford and High Wycombe, had a reputation for outlawry and sporadic attacks on travellers. Assuming that Whittington was making his journey in 1369 or 1370, there would have been the further uncertainty occasioned by the latest outbreak of plague, which we now know to have been severe, consuming between 10 and 15 per cent of the population.[3]

This alone would have been reason enough to move quickly, purposefully and under the protection of someone who was very familiar with the road and knew both its physical and its metaphorical 'twists and turns'. Someone who knew when to gather pace and when not to; someone who knew how to distinguish between casual curiosity and unwelcome attention; who knew where to rest the horses and to find a secure bed for the night; who was well versed in spotting the signs of trouble and how to avoid or even deal with them if he had to; whose apparent reason to be on the road was perfectly evident and whose purpose there enjoyed the oversight of a master who would have resources and the law at his disposal if his man was waylaid or his goods were abused or stolen; who understood that on this particular journey that was exactly what he would be conveying—his master's goods—but by far the most precious he had transported to date. That someone was almost certainly an experienced London carter, well known on the road, exceptionally familiar with its geography, welcome at its staging posts. Quite possibly, he was one of the new echelon of carters who had fought in and returned from France, was resilient and aware of the world around him, knew how to look after himself and had taken up the opportunities that burgeoned with London's expansion after the plagues of 1348 and 1361–2. A young soldier or pikeman who had served at Crécy in 1346 or during the Siege of Calais in 1347 would be in his early forties in 1369–70, and his history and his civilian work should have kept him fit and alert. Such a man was of a type recruited by a master also familiar with soldiery, organisation and discipline, a merchant who himself or whose family came from a military background.

All forms of travel had their drawbacks. While there was much to be said for safety in numbers during a six- or seven-day journey, it was also the case that group travelling, for example with groups of pilgrims from Gloucester to Southwark and Canterbury, had the severe drawback of slow progress and of having to obtain food and secure safe and hospitable accommodation for large numbers. A pilgrim 'caravan' would progress at the pace of its slowest member, and was prone to many diversions and unplanned stoppages along the route. A young and relatively genteel boy was bound to be a subject of unwarranted curiosity. Large and scattered gatherings, moving slowly and tending their sick and feeble along the way, were an easy target for thieves, hucksters and kidnappers. As for the most obvious choice of simply saddling a couple of fast horses and riding hard for London, this too had evident disadvantages. Foremost, this was an expensive option, and the riders would need to change horses along the route, adding further to the initial outlay. Second, a boy of Whittington's age would be neither experienced or robust enough to make such an arduous journey at the pace required. It would place a further watchful burden on his companion. Third, it was precisely this type of express travel that was most likely to attract, not deflect, unwelcome attention. Why just a man and a boy, why the hurry, what were they carrying or concealing? In almost every way, the carter option was the most sensible for mother, son and sponsor. It also had the merit of 'normalcy'. The carter could arrive in Gloucester laden with goods, making the outward journey financially worthwhile for his master, and could return with the boy sitting amid a reduced load, helping perhaps to offset the mother's costs. Perhaps it is here that the popular image of 'Dick Whittington' gained currency. If they were to avoid attracting undue attention, the boy would hardly have travelled in his best attire; he would more likely have dressed himself in his oldest and most worn clothing which, as the days moved on and the dust kicked up, would have given him the appearance increasingly of an unkempt ragamuffin. Most observers would have taken him for the carter's own son. Arriving in London, he may well have looked ragged, depleted and unwashed, like any other of the numerous country lads that daily made their way through the city's gates.

As for recommendation and approval of his 'minder', Joan Whittington would have sought confirmation close to home that the man selected to convey her youngest child was of suitable calibre and character. How might she have done this? One answer would have been to consult the opinions of leading merchants in Gloucester whom she would know socially or by reputation and who would have had knowledge of the sponsor and his man. At this time, there were five or six she might have chosen to consult: wealthy, well-connected men all of whom were highly regarded within the confines of the town but who had built their fortune and reputation through their commerce with London and Bristol. Gloucester's most notable merchant at this time was William Heyberare, whose civic involvement in the town had begun in 1359 and would last for over thirty years. First appointed bailiff in 1361, he went on to serve until 1384. Heyberare was well known in London's merchant and political circles; he regularly undertook commissions for the Crown, and represented Gloucester in Parliament on as many as nine occasions. He moved freely in Gloucestershire's 'landed' circles and was elected a knight of the shire five times. A prominent figure in the town's religious affairs, known for his religious endowments, his kinsman of the same name had served as chaplain of St Mary de Crypt in 1353 and was rector by 1357. Another potential consultee was Thomas Pope, a member of a wealthy Gloucester goldsmithing family and later a bailiff and the founder of a chantry in Holy Trinity church. John Head (or Anlep) was well known as a successful draper and cloth exporter, who in his will left the sum of 20 marks for the upkeep of Gloucester's quay. John Monmouth, merchant, landowner and by 1373 lessee of the nearby manor of Elmstone Hardwicke, might have been suitable; as might John Banbury, a thriving corn exporter running much of his business down the Severn to the port of Bristol.

Pope, Heyberare and Head were the most likely to be known to the Whittingtons, each the leading figure in families that had been prominent in the town since the early 14th century. Yet if Joan Whittington had sought their opinion, she would have done so primarily because they were most likely to be acquainted with her son's London sponsor and to have used the services of his carter. If they were consulted, it was because they would confirm her instincts and reassure her decision. As for the carter, a fellow entrusted with this special task is likely to have been someone who not only transported goods for these men but who also acted as a secure 'postal service' conveying and safeguarding covenants, affidavits, bills of sale, and even payments to their associates in London and those of his master in Gloucester—quite literally a safe pair of hands. There was little opportunity for the boy in Gloucester, for its merchant class was being increasingly displaced by and becoming dependent on its trade with Bristol. London, they may have assured her, was the place for her son to make his fortune.[4]

* * *

At this time, moving precious goods and small loads between towns fell increasingly to 'horse hauling' (the *carreta*). Transport by horses was expensive but it had the advantage of being fast and the higher cost could be offset by the capacity to make more journeys than could be achieved using mules or donkeys. Horse hauling and the use of oxen were favoured to draw the heaviest loads. Their carts now dominated agricultural transport. Following the Black Death, the use of packhorses on many estates had either ceased or dwindled. Carts were capacious, generally reliable and the medieval equivalent of the modern-day articulated lorry, able to carry anything. For mercers conveying expensive fabrics, which needed to be rolled or folded, stacked to fill every inch of space, hidden from view and protected from the elements, they were a well-proven option. Had the boy expressed surprise or reservations that he was to be transported in this way, rather than by unburdened horse or by packhorse, the carter would have explained that the packhorses they would overtake along the route were now the favoured choice of pilgrims and for slow-moving trade in which the modern merchant was disinclined to invest. They would soon die out, he might have added confidently.

Oxen were stronger and could carry more, perhaps double the horse load, but horses pulling the same weight as oxen could cover up to twenty miles an hour while the oxen might achieve two or three at most. It would never do for an impatient time- and money-conscious mercer. Everything had to be done 'by yesterday'. There were schedules to keep, terms to fulfil. A greater profit lay in goods being unloaded quickly from the cogs on the Thames or the Severn at Bristol and dispatched expeditiously to the large fairs and markets. The real gains lay not just in shifting the goods about more quickly but in moving the money needed to invest in them and the money received for selling them much faster than ever before; in shortening the gap between transactions and recognising that it was money itself that was the true commodity because it had so many uses and purposes and could unlock not just one but a whole sequence of transactions and opportunities, some of which would have nothing to do with mercery at all. Richard Whittington would later raise this to an art form. By employing horses to draw his goods, the merchant might recover his outlay and secure a profit two or three times more than if he had transported them by oxen. Using this more expeditious means, he would not have to borrow so much or risk having payments outstanding for extended periods. One might call it 'certainty'.[5]

4

TO LONDON

We can imagine that in a few moments Gloucester was gone—already a memory trailing in the dust of a horse-hauled cart that moved faster than any the young Whittington had ridden before, his safety and passage entrusted to a man he had probably met only a few hours earlier. If the horses were as fast and spirited as their master might have claimed, they would make light of the twenty miles to Northleach, a village already well known for its Cotswold wool and a regular stop for a carter transporting that commodity to London. As they approached from the old Roman road, they would have observed a group of regular-sized burgage plots facing east–west and, beyond, a triangular marketplace, a few stone houses, and the tower and ancient chancel that still form the oldest part of the church today. Northleach was already steeped in the wool trade, but the great wealth that would fund the expansion of its famous 'wool church' would come after Whittington's death, over fifty years later. Even so, he should have seen enough to grasp the importance of sheep and their wealth-producing effect on the medieval economy. The success of sheep raising in the parishes surrounding Northleach was already the stimulant for an era of prosperity for the town, which had a central role in the Cotswold wool trade between the late 14th and the early 16th centuries.[1] The woolmen based there gathered the crop from surrounding villages and supplied it to London merchants and the agents of foreign merchants for export to the Continent. 'The greatest woolmen of the fifteenth century ... were those of the Cotswolds for this district seems to have gained greatly in importance as the wool centre at this time. The chief meeting place of the woolmen and export merchants was the village of Northleach, right up on the wolds.'[2]

On that first night perhaps, they might have bedded at one of the smallholdings where the age-old lines of agriculture had been severed by the plague and which now combined a measure of sheep rearing with providing hospitality to the numerous and diverse travellers who regularly came this way—some bound for Gloucester, some heading towards the steep Roman Fosse Way that served the old capital of Corinium, by now Cirencester. Northleach would be a convenient stopover, close to the ancient Saltway. Then up early to embark on the next stage of their journey to Burford, mid-way to Oxford, the one place other than Bristol and London that Whittington would have known something about if he had studied with the monks at St Peter's or Llanthony Priory. The aim would be to press on with speed, keeping close to the shallow Windrush below, making later for the old Saxon town of Witney twelve miles west of Oxford. But first there was Burford, even then a fine-looking straggling market town famed for its 11th-century royal charter and an Augustinian priory that offered rest to travellers on those frequent occasions when its bustling inns were full to the rafters.

A few miles beyond they would have passed the hamlet of Minster Lovell and perhaps catch a glimpse of the original church dedicated to St Kenelm. Would Whittington have recalled the story of Cynehelm, the boy king of Mercia and martyr? Maintaining a good pace, they would have completed the segment from Northleach to Witney a little before midday, in time to feed and water the horses and enter the imposing medieval church of St Mary the Virgin to view its remarkable wall paintings and join the Angelus. Here was another handsome town enriched by 'sheep's gold', replanned in the previous century by the bishops of Winchester, who had their wool collected and weighed in its fine new Wool Hall. It was smaller than Oxford and Banbury but bustling with trade and enterprise and, like most of the places Whittington would encounter, showing firm evidence of its recovery from the decimation wrought only twenty years earlier—so significant that as many as 400 properties were now paying poll tax, many of them homes to weavers, tanners, wool merchants and flour millers. There was wealth and improvement here. He would have taken in, just as he had at Northleach and Burford, that wool was the means to both.

Then it was on to Oxford, the axis for important routes from Northampton to Salisbury, Winchester and Southampton, and from London to Wales via Gloucester, the Forest of Dean, Hereford, and Brecon.[3] This was a revered place, celebrated for its learning and for the favour it drew from successive kings and through which the royal court frequently travelled on its way to Woodstock. In the year of Whittington's death, 1423, the route to Gloucester would change, and Oxford would be bypassed. Had he been alive, he would have travelled instead via the new Gloucester to London road winding through the village of Faringdon and crossing the Thames by the recently built stone bridge at Abingdon, which would have unlocked the navigable inland port of Henley just forty or so miles west of London. It is unlikely he had ever been this far from home and he had probably only heard of the wonders of Oxford, its streets populated with confident, well-built stone houses, fine courtyards, resplendent churches and, even then, a student body of 1,000.

Had he rested here, his first encounter with Oxford would have taken place almost 200 years after Henry II had facilitated its expansion by banning English students from attending the University of Paris in 1167. Now, two centuries later, it flourished as England's primary centre of learning, its first chancellor appointed de facto in 1201. Oxford's foundation colleges had developed from medieval halls of residence. University College had been established in 1249, Balliol in 1263, and Merton in 1264. Exeter followed in 1314, Oriel in 1326 and the Queen's College in 1341. Though not yet constituted as colleges, St Edmund Hall (1226) and Hertford (1282) were also well established as centres for teaching. In 1355 Edward III had paid tribute to the university for the services rendered to the state by its distinguished alumni. Whittington would not have known that in the year of his visit one of Oxford's most notable students, John Wycliffe, a graduate of Merton and briefly Master of Balliol, had gained a bachelor's degree in theology and was already on his way to becoming one of the university's most distinguished figures though not one of those 'collaborative' contributors the king had in mind. Instead, he would make his mark as an existential threat to the English state, the most articulate political and religious reformer of his time, who would attract the acquiescent support of the Black Prince and John of Gaunt. Wycliffe's call for the royal divestment of all Church property and his increasingly popular views on predestination and attacks on the papacy would give rise to the anti-establishment Lollard movement and to civil unrest. In January 1414, thirty years after his death, Wycliffe's flame still burned brightly, and a reluctant, much older and wiser, Richard Whittington would find himself instructed by Henry V to lead an inquiry charged with identifying and seizing the property of those Lollards who continued to follow his teachings and were 'still at large'.

Passing through in 1369–70, had he been able and equipped to investigate, Whittington would have discovered that, despite the charm of its celebrated buildings and an outward appearance of vitality and purpose,

Oxford was not quite what it seemed. In the years immediately after 1348 many of its halls had fallen vacant and its commercial strength had waned. Oxford's student population had declined to as little as one-third of its pre-Black Death number.[4] Within fifteen years the university had salvaged a modest recovery driven by the acquisition of cheap land and the reassignment of lost titles 'freed' by the plagues of 1348 and 1361–2. Student numbers were replenishing quickly and on the face of it trade was once more on the up. Yet for all its finery and intellectual energy, Oxford was once more on the brink of an imminent decline that would not be reversed until the final years of the century, by which time Richard Whittington was mayor of London and beginning to envision how he could create a college of his own. Had he been afforded time to explore Oxford at greater length, he would have come across an altogether different tract of land that the colleges had wisely avoided, an unenclosed site to the north-east of the town extending to thirteen acres, which a few years later a local jury would record as 'a dump for filth and corpses, a resort of criminals and prostitutes',[5] and which presented a much sharper picture of the decline and poverty that Whittington would encounter time and again during his near-forty-year civic career.

* * *

After Oxford the topography changed sharply from the soft and welcoming landscape encountered in the early stages of the journey, that of the gentle verdant slopes of the Cotswolds grazed by large herds of sheep and overlooked by tall stands of oak and beech, dotted with honey-coloured hamlets.

Stokenhurst would normally have been the short next stage had the cart been laden with goods, but Whittington's carter may have judged it safer to avoid the forests of Aston Rowant, then rife with local brigands. Instead, they may have chosen to depart from Tetsworth a little after dawn, having decided to run hard and aim for High Wycombe. It was fifteen miles distant and, if they could make it there by midday and be on the road again within a couple of hours, they would be within five miles of Uxbridge by nightfall. Uxbridge spilled into the parish of Hillingdon and neighbouring Cowley, and it was difficult to know where their respective boundaries began and ended. Charing Cross was now a tantalising sixteen miles away.

Continuing by this route, a traveller would have passed the manor and moat at Northolt, constructed only fifteen years earlier but destined to be flattened and rebuilt on a smaller scale just a year later.[6] They would venture next over the Green Ford to a well-used watering hole in the place called the Worm Woods, before pushing on to the expanse of the great manor of Tyburn, in the parish of St Mary le Bone. We shall presume they were bound for Bishopsgate. In the closing miles of their route, it would have been evident that beyond the city walls life remained harsh, gruelling, cruelly displaced even twenty years after the Black Death. Countless families had lost their breadwinner and many their employers too. Among the remaining landowners, few could or would offer paid work on the terms demanded by a greatly depleted supply of labourers increasingly aware of their scarcity and enhanced worth. Many landowners denounced the proposition of higher labour costs as a mischief, as an affront to the social order or, worse, as equivalent to sedition. Men who had survived the horrors of France, common and titled alike, had made it home only to be struck down by an unseen enemy in the summer and autumn of 1348, or later by the predator that followed in the spring of 1361. Some of the smaller manors that marked the final few miles into London were little more than skeletons, with little flesh to their bones and no head to do their thinking. They must have stood in marked contrast to the scene that would open as Whittington approached the city walls at Bishopsgate.

* * *

Here he would have encountered the Bethlem Hospital founded by the Priory of St Mary of Bethlehem. It was a notable point of entry situated on land gifted in 1247 by the crusader and former sheriff of London, Simon Fitzmary, to the Bishop of Bethlehem to serve the needs of paupers. A century later, failing for lack of funds and repair, the hospital had been taken under the wing of the City of London and had begun to concentrate on mental health, offering its services to people afflicted with 'madness' and the 'falling sickness' (epilepsy). By the 1360s it had become a fearful place where 'inmates' were often manacled, restrained by chains, subdued and suppressed by corporal punishment and where there was a great and terrible noise and unhappiness. Its name was corrupted initially to Bethlem and subsequently to one which we now associate with uproar, turmoil, mania and distress—Bedlam. As one writer puts it: 'Those troubled in mind had to compete for beds with lepers, the blind, the crippled, the toothless hags and the abandoned children, scrabbling for scraps of bread and cheese, a jug of ale and a bed of straw,' but later 'Bethlem developed an appalling reputation and only the most desperate made their way to its battered wooden door. Bethlem became a byword for thieving, degeneracy and institutionalised corruption.'[7]

In the distance, a first glimpse would have been offered of London's numerous churches and, flourishing at their side, some fine early examples of the tall brick-and-timbered houses that had begun to spring up across the city from St Clement to All Hallows—bold proclamations by the senior clergy and the city's merchant princes of London's increasing finery, confidence and wealth. In the eyes of an awestruck young lad who had witnessed nothing larger than Gloucester, barely a tenth of the size, they may have seemed like streets of gold. In the town he had left behind few people of any means made their homes on the riverside unless they were fishermen, families working the flatboats that brought in goods from Bristol, or poor farm tenants. The land beside the Severn was generally deemed too low-lying for significant development and was vulnerable to flooding. Here in London, the situation was the opposite, with increasing numbers of people judging they were safer and more likely to find employment within the city, with the result that it was once more threatening to burst at the seams. The thirst for suitable land within its present confines could not be slaked. Twenty years later the frequent and wilful demolition of tenements and the ever-pressing need for quay space and storage, not to mention the appropriation of large and fine tracts of riverside land by merchants, nobles and the Church, would send prices through the roof. Even as Whittington arrived, men who had once devoted the entirety of their energy and investment to a single trade were now merely dabbling in it, having recognised that they could make more money from the buying and selling of land, for the accommodation of both goods and people and at either end of the wealth spectrum. These far-sighted investors and developers could estimate where the port needed to expand, where importers would pay a premium to store their goods securely, where the wealthy would covet land for their mansions, and where the common folk of England's largest city, accelerating in numbers by the day, needed a simple roof over their head. Whittington would arrive in a London where a new class of entrepreneurs sought not only to identify and acquire new opportunities but also to gain possession, by fair means or foul, of existing property that could be 'turned' or recycled at great profit—liabilities that could and would become lucrative assets. Decrepit tenements were being deliberately run down, and after their tenants were ejected they were held empty, while demand for the land spiralled, before being sold for a king's ransom. By 1369–70 many parts of London were simply beyond the reach or prospect of ordinary people, many forced out by the very wealth they had helped to create. If he had cocked an ear, Whittington might have been able to detect the distant periodic boom of ordnance being tested at the new community at Portsoken, east of Aldgate, where a colony of foundries and workshops had been established on cheap open land to provide cannon for the king's navy and equipment for his troops. In contrast, he would soon hear of the lavish developments beyond Holborn Bars where wealthy merchants were buying up land and constructing large and opulent houses whose like most Londoners had neither seen nor imagined.[8] On the opposite side of the river even tawdry, down-at-heel Southwark was being transformed, with castles for bishops and inns for travellers. Everything in London was about commodity, supply and price.

* * *

Had he entered the city via the holy entrance marked by the stone lintel carved with a mitre, Whittington would have encountered more churches in Bishopsgate ward and along the route to Leadenhall than in the entirety of Gloucester and Bristol combined—St Botolph, St Augustine, St Andrew Undershaft, St Ethelburga, St Martin Outwich (endowed by the wealthy Oteswich family for their personal salvation), St Mary Axe, the Priory of St Helen and, in the distance, St Peter upon Cornhill, atop the highest point of the City of London. On the opposite corner stood his destination, Leadenhall, situated in Lime Street ward, where carts were forbidden to loiter for any length of time. The household of the man who would take him in, oversee his apprenticeship, sponsor his early career and embed him in his family is said to have occupied much of the building, one of the finest and most well known in London, roofed in lead and noted for its fine tall windows. Yet its location and distinction also reflected those eccentric and characteristic aspects of London that have marked the capital's urban development for a thousand years: the juxtaposition of great wealth and ruinous poverty, of calm quietude and reverberating clamour, of pleasant fragrance and arresting stench. To the rear of its magnificent elevations stood London's principal and often stomach-churning poultry market. The court at 'Leaden Hall' which formed the market had been paved fifty years earlier and was intended to signal a much wider transformation of London's streets. It was also reputed to have encouraged greater attention to the cleansing of the city. Looking about him and taking in the pervasive stink and noisome activity of Leadenhall's environs, Whittington may have felt somewhat differently.

5

LEADENHALL

There is no record of whether the household into which the young Richard Whittington arrived was based in the street of Leadenhall or in the landmark building from which it took its name. The street itself was among the most prominent in London, linking Bishopsgate and Cornhill, one of the city's three ancient hills, in the west to St Botolph Street and to Aldgate, variously interpreted as 'old gate' or 'all gate' or 'ale gate', in the east. We can speculate that Whittington was admitted to the house of that name since we find him leading a significant corporate endeavour in 1408–9 to save the iconic building from further decline by making possible its eventual purchase by the City of London in 1411. It is also likely that the family into which he was received leased rather than owned Leadenhall. Notable for its size, ornamentation and, famously, its lead roof, Leadenhall is largely undocumented throughout its early history. There is a view that the draper Sir Simon Eyre was the 'founder' of Leadenhall, when in fact he was its redeveloper, replacing the original manor hall with a public granary, grammar school and chapel in 1440 as a gift to the citizens of London, whom he would come to represent as mayor in 1445.[1]

There is a possible connection between the building and its central characters. It is conceivable that the Nevilles were acquainted with the Fitzwarins and that the two families had been comrades in arms during the early years of the war with France and in the border engagements with the Scots. In turn, there may have been a similar connection between the Fitzwarins and the Whittingtons. There are also hints of a closer relationship, even perhaps of kinship, and these would deepen and consolidate around 1402 more than thirty years after Richard's arrival. The more we examine the apparent interconnections between these two names, the locations associated with them, and the social and commercial networks that revolve around them over a period of 200 years, extending from the early 13th to the early 15th century, the more we might conclude that Richard Whittington did not arrive in London or at Leadenhall by chance. Indeed, his arrival here and at this time underscores the reality that Whittington was very far from his pantomime portrayal as a homeless and ragged country waif who tramped the streets of London seeking food, shelter and employment. Not only were the two families almost certainly known to each other, but this process also followed a well-established tradition for young country boys, whose families wished to ensure a future for them and either already had established connections and opportunities to place them as apprentices to enterprising sponsors in London or else were more than willing to purchase the creation of such opportunities. In Richard's case the former applied, as the Fitzwarins and Whittingtons were already known to each other, formally and circumstantially, though the full extent of the relationship may not have been known to him.

* * *

The Fitzwarins had arrived in England with the Norman Conquest, their ancestor being Warin de Meer, about whom details are scarce. The family do not come to notice until a century later, by which time they are established in the Marches, on the border with Wales, where they happen to then hold the castle of Whittington in Shropshire. It is the three sons known as Fulk who relate in various ways to the Whittington story. We encounter Fulk I when Henry Plantagenet rewards him with the royal manor of Alveston in south Gloucestershire for his support of his mother, the empress Mathilde, in her struggle against King Stephen for the English throne. The family also acquired the manor of Whadborough in Leicestershire and were known latterly as the 'lords' of Whittington and Alberbury (Salop) and Alveston (Gloucs).[2]

On Fulk's death in 1171 the manor fell to his young son Fulk II, who also held the manor at Wantage in Berkshire; this later fell to Whittington's sponsor, Sir Ivo Fitzwarin, whose burial place in the parish church of St Mary is marked by a unique brass figure of him resplendent in knight's armour. As a child, Fulk Fitzwarin II was raised for a time as a ward of Henry II in the royal household at Windsor. In 1195, however, he is recorded in the Royal Council—the *curia regis*—as being in debt to the king in the sum of 40 marks for the tenure of Whittington Castle. He died in 1197 with the debt outstanding and it passed, bearing a fine, to his eldest son, Fulk III.

The subsequent and violent struggle over the ownership of Whittington Castle lies at the heart of the folklore that developed around the 'legend' of Fulk Fitzwarin III in the closing years of the 12th century. The demesne of Whittington had been granted originally in 1114 to the energetic 'castle builder' William Peverel during Henry I's sorties along the Welsh Marches. In 1165, his grandson Henry Plantagenet granted the lordship to the king-dom of Powys and the castle passed to Roger de Powys and then to his heir Maurice. However, Maurice's right to title was challenged by Fulk II, who had contested the ownership for some years, insisting that it lay instead with his family as part of an earlier and wider land settlement involving the Crown and the Peverels. In 1195 Fulk II believed he had finally secured the right to Whittington, but as he had never acquired a written contract of freehold to substantiate his case, the claim had no standing in court. Whittington remained beyond reach, still in Welsh hands at the time of his death in 1197. In April 1200, it was Fulk III who took up the challenge, offering £100 for the title, more than twice the sum conceded by the Crown's favoured contender, Maurice of Powys. The offer was dismissed by King John, ostensibly to preserve stability on his troublesome border. John's fractious relationship with Fulk's father may also have played a part. Whatever the reason, the king affirmed that Whittington should remain in the hands of the Powys family and restated their right of title on Maurice's death in August 1200. Within six months an aggrieved Fulk III was in open rebellion and had marshalled a robust group of followers to challenge the king's ruling. Run to ground by a force of over 100 knights led by Hubert de Burgh, in April 1202 Fulk's group sought sanctuary at Stanley Abbey near Chippenham. Following a series of violent skirmishes, an accom-modation was finally reached on 11 November 1203 when Fitzwarin and 30 of his followers were pardoned. In October 1204 the payment of a much-inflated fine of 200 marks was deemed by the Crown as sufficient for the Fitzwarins to finally receive their 'right and inheritance' at Whittington. The lordship descended thereafter in the Fitzwarin family, but not without further turbulence which yet again placed their tenure at grave risk.[3]

In 1223, Whittington Castle was besieged by Llywelyn ap Iorwerth of Gwynedd as he sought to drive out the English and expand his territory into Powys and the Welsh Marches. During the summer of 1265 the castle was again taken from the Fitzwarins by Henry III and this time, along with several other border strongholds, was ceded to Llywelyn ap Gruffudd, as part of a settlement that would eventually recognise Llywelyn as Prince of

Wales. Following his defeat and death in December 1282, it was finally restored to the Fitzwarins. In 1295, over ninety years after Fulk had 'finally' secured right of title, it fell to Edward I, following his defeat of Madog ap Llywelyn at Maes Moydog in Powys, to confer on his grandson Fulk V a hereditary peerage and the title of Baron Fitzwarin.

The Fitzwarin connection with the Whittingtons becomes evident fifteen years later with the birth of William Fitzwarin in 1310 at Whittington in Shropshire. Grandson of Fulk V, 1st Baron Fitzwarin, son of Fulk the 2nd Baron and Alianore de Beauchamp, and known as William le Frere, he would contract plague in 1361. He died at Wantage on 28 October that year and was buried in the family church of St Mary. Sometime in 1336 he married the wealthy Amicia de Haddon, daughter and heiress to Sir Henry de Haddon of Stourton Caundle in Dorset. This branch of the family is referred to as Fitzwarin of Caundle Haddon.

William Fitzwarin has been described as

> a member of an important family whose estates centred on Whittington (Shropshire) and Wantage (Berkshire). The head of the family had been summoned to Parliament as a baron since 1295, and Sir William Fitzwaryn was himself called to the great council of 1342. He and his son remained close to the main line, and their arms were those of Fitzwaryn of Whittington with a difference.[4]

William must have enjoyed some early success as a knight as we find him appointed governor of Montgomery Castle in North Wales in the early 1330s and rewarded by Edward III for his services with the town of Wilton in Wiltshire and the manor of Powerstock near Bridport in Dorset. In 1339 he was active in Flanders as a member of Edward's guard and later deployed to Scotland during the Second War of Independence. He returned to Flanders in 1340 and must have managed to combine valour in the field with sufficient resources to afford his own retinue of men because in 1342, with the Hundred Years War under way, we find him serving again in northern France, having attained the rank of knight banneret, a title that could only be conferred by the sovereign on the field of battle. He is described as having in his retinue one knight, eight esquires and ten mounted archers.

On 11 July 1346 Fitzwarin was a commander in the vanguard of the English and Welsh forces that sailed for France to sustain a campaign that would result in the seizure of Caen, the inflicting of Edward's infamous *chevauchée*—the laying waste of the French countryside—and the iconic triumph of Crécy. In 1348 Fitzwarin was installed as a Knight of the Garter and in 1349 he was appointed knight to Queen Philippa. Seven years later in September 1356, by this point 46 years of age, he is reported as serving as a commander under the Black Prince in the victory at Poitiers, although others suggest that he is confused here with his elder brother Fulk. There is some dispute about the year of birth of his son Ivo (Hugh), some sources reporting this as 1343, seven years into his marriage to Amicia, which would make him about 26 when Richard Whittington arrived in London around 1369–70, while parliamentary records report his birthdate more specifically as 30 November 1347, a date more consistent with his status as a minor at his father's death in 1361.[5]

During his minority, Ivo was for a short time one of Queen Philippa's wards, but in 1362 she granted custody of his estates to third parties, which he recovered on proving the age of 22 in February 1369, enabling him to take possession of significant landholdings and rental incomes at Wantage in Berkshire, Wilton in Wiltshire and the manors of Pitney, Wearne and 'Ilebrewers' in Somerset, together with numerous properties in Dorset. His early childhood seems to have been spent in Wiltshire and latterly at Wantage, but, like his father, he would spend many of his later years abroad on military service. By the time that Whittington arrived in London in 1369–70, Fitzwarin was in his early twenties, already wealthy, embarking on the first stages of a notable military career and well connected with the city's merchant community. Having proved his age and his right to his father's lands, he is thought to have been knighted at this time. To all intents and purposes, he was a young man 'on his way', and determined to make something of himself, a quality he may have recognised in the young boy who presented himself at his door. His trajectory was further assured by a well-chosen marriage in 1372 to Maud, one of four daughters and co-heiresses to the immensely wealthy Sir John d'Argentine. The union would add significantly to his inherited wealth and give him a share of Argentine property in Essex, Surrey and Cambridgeshire. By the early 1380s he is described as 'a prominent landowner' and one whose subsequent military and public achievements mark him out as 'a man of importance in both local and national affairs'.[6]

Whittington was therefore joining the dynamic household of an ambitious young soldier and entrepreneur who would go on to sustain a military career in France and Scotland, serve as a castellan in the Marches, and represent three different counties in Parliament, and who was, from what little there is to glimpse of him, an outward-looking and well-connected merchant and investor with the run of one of London's best-known houses. Here Whittington could be apprenticed to his future trade, in a household in which he would have an opportunity to observe and absorb everything. An apprenticeship at this stage could span anything between seven and twelve years and, for mercers, typically lasted eight years. This usually involved being accommodated under the roof of the sponsor or master, becoming an integral part of his household. In turn, this would require undertaking chores and duties in addition to learning the intricacies of his trade. Given that the master would train, house, feed and sustain him, the apprentice's family was expected in most cases to contribute a premium for the privilege, regardless of the master's own financial circumstances.

Fitzwarin hardly needed the money; it was the principle and acknowledgement of his mentoring and hospitality that mattered. At the time of his death in 1414, Fitzwarin held estates in Somerset and Dorset, almost certainly in right of his wife, but was also independently wealthy, holding the hundred of Wantage, two parts of the manor of Wantage together with land at Lymington and Fordingbridge, and property in Sussex, Oxfordshire, Cornwall, Dorset, London and Devon. It is also possible that he derived rents from land and fisheries in Surrey. By this time, Whittington would also be immensely wealthy in his own right, and the bond between the two families would be far stronger than either could have imagined 45 years earlier. Yet on his arrival he would learn that there was already much that connected them. We might suppose that in taking Whittington into his household and effectively acting as the boy's guardian and mentor, Fitzwarin's instincts were both protective and commercial. Unlike Whittington, he had been raised by and been close to his father, but in the years since his father's death and those of his minority he must have experienced something of the vacuum that his young charge had grown up with and of which no doubt the boy's mother had made him aware. On the other hand, he was cultivating his business interests in London and it is reasonable to assume he needed someone he could trust to run errands, gradually take on duties while he was away on military service, develop as a mercer's apprentice, learn all he could, and provide either a one-off or, more likely, a continuing financial and social return on his 'investment'. These were common considerations in any such sponsoring relationship. In some instances, such arrangements were also based on a different form of mutuality, the future marital interests of the two families. These would emerge much later. However, Fitzwarin was aware of a more substantive link between them that may explain how Whittington came to land at his door rather than that of a more conventional sponsor.

6

CONNECTIONS

In the absence of a father and assuming a male relation had not taken up the matter, it would have fallen to Whittington's mother to contact Fitzwarin, explain her aspirations for her youngest son, and prepare the way for his new life in London. Almost certainly she would have offered some financial provision for him to take Richard under his wing. We might imagine that his first meeting with the boy took place in the solar (the private quarters) at Leadenhall and that Fitzwarin opened by explaining that his chief interest lay in campaigning and that he would be away frequently from London but would give Whittington as much time as he could and put in place the means and the people to guide him towards a career in mercery. Beyond that it would be up to him to make his way and possibly even to provide further recompense for Fitzwarin's generosity. The boy's mother would have told him that his new master was not yet married and that he was at the call of his commander, Edward of Woodstock, the Black Prince. He had no heir, nor perhaps had he yet acquired an assistant to help him with his affairs or run his errands while he was abroad. Fitzwarin may have pledged to take her son into a household where he would probably serve for a time as a houseboy learning all there was to know about the workings of a large London house and its expenditure. This would provide invaluable practical experience. He would see important people and diverse interests come and go, which would stand him in good stead as he made his way in the city. He was to observe and learn from whoever came here and to absorb not only the craft of mercery but also its ways and means. His chores would embrace the kitchen (a determining feature of the pantomime story) where he would also learn the source and the price of commodities and grasp the importance of buying well and efficiently.

51

The work might be gruelling and without apparent purpose, but he would probably learn more about the practicalities of London life from the housekeeper and servants than he would from their master. They would be his mentors among the shops and stalls of Eastcheap and Poultry and the markets at Billingsgate and Smithfield and in the over-sized chicken coop that served as Leadenhall market. To reassure him that this was designed to serve his long-term prospects, Fitzwarin may have assured the boy, and his mother, that on the successful completion of this 'practical education' in the ways of the household he would, within a year of his arrival, take him into service as his apprentice.

With the basics out of the way, Fitzwarin would surely have addressed the question which Whittington must have wrestled with throughout his journey to the capital: why here and with this man? Why would Richard Whittington of Pauntley Court, a boy of eleven unknown to him, stand this day in the house of Sir Ivo Fitzwarin in the very heart of the City of London? Was he aware that his mother had not written speculatively, nor without some prior association between their families? Would Fitzwarin have related there and then the more detailed context of their relationship? His father Sir William, the Baron Fitzwarin of Wantage, had been dead eight years and his mother was the Lady Amicia, daughter of Sir Henry de Haddon of Stourton Caundle in Dorset. His father had been known as William Fitzwarin le Frere—brother of the legendary Fulk Fitzwarin, 3rd Baron Fitzwarin of Whittington. The boy's eyes might have widened at the mention of his own family name. His host would have related that during the wars in the Marches, Sir William Fitzwarin was master of Montgomery Castle, appointed by the king himself. That he had fought alongside Edward in Flanders in 1339 and in the same year was sent north to harry the Scots, and by 1342 he was back in France but now with the rank of banneret. If the boy had appeared surprised when he first heard mention of Whittington Castle, he must have been even more so when Fitzwarin revealed that the knight who had served under his father's banneret for the first time in northern France in 1342 was none other than Richard's own father, Sir William Whittington. They were comrades in arms. The elder Fitzwarin had been personal bodyguard to Queen Philippa, fought alongside the Black Prince at Poitiers and survived the brutalities of France, the guerrilla campaigns of Scotland and the skirmishes in the Marches, only to be taken in his bed by the pestilence in 1361 shortly before Hallowmas.[1]

Fitzwarin might then have turned to the part played by Richard's own father, reminding the boy that at the beginning of the century there was much dispute about the ownership of Pauntley. Various families had claimed title, a term he would do well to mark as it would feature commonly as he made his way in the city. He would have explained that when such matters were in dispute a special court heard and resolved the claims of the competing parties. He would have referred to the note written by Richard's father which stated that during the travelling inquisition of 1311 a magistrate had declared him to be the son of William Whittington and Maud de Solers, and therefore the next heir to John, son of Thomas de Solers. And he would have reminded the boy that this family, the Solers, had held Pauntley since it was extracted from the grasp of the Abbey of Cormeilles. On affirmation of his father's inheritance the manor and estate of Pauntley were reunited. The rest Richard would have known. Sir William had married Richard's mother Joan Maunsell, daughter of William Maunsell, the scion of a leading family, and the recent widow of Sir Thomas Berkeley.

The immediate family detail he knew but what followed may have been unfamiliar. The house of Fitzwarin reached back to the Conqueror and its ancestral home at Whittington Castle was won in the 'lists' by the first of its name. Fitzwarin may have remarked that both families had been wronged by the law, explaining that his ancestor Fulk Fitzwarin had been outlawed in his dispute with King John over the family's right to Whittington. Here was the news he would have wished most to impart: Richard's father had not only served as a young knight under the banneret of Sir William Fitzwarin but he had also become his close and trusted friend. More than that, Richard's father may have been a kinsman—as he now believed Richard was to him. As for his arrival at Leadenhall, Richard's father had known that he, Sir Ivo, held from his father land in the county of Hampshire and estates and holdings in Sussex, Oxfordshire, Cornwall, Devon and Dorset. In London, he had been aware that the Fitzwarins held extensive property, including the freeholds of shops and tenements; that the family also dabbled in mercery. And if it was true, he would have known, because he would almost certainly have visited this very house, that Fitzwarin's occupation of Leadenhall derived from another of their joint acquaintance, Sir Ralph Neville, 2nd Baron Neville de Raby, a fellow soldier and companion.

Leadenhall

There are no official records of the Fitzwarins holding Leadenhall, only circumstantial evidence including Richard Whittington's personal determination in 1409 to save the then semi-derelict building from further decline and render it to the ownership of the City of London. This suggests he had at least some association with it. The earliest mention of Leadenhall market dates from 1296 and refers to a mansion built by Sir Hugh Neville, who constructed the mansion around a courtyard that opened onto Leadenhall Street. Although the origin is uncertain, the name is likely derived from the mansion's lead-based roof.[2] Stow's research told him that 'in the yeare 1309, Leadenhall belonged to Sir Hugh *Neuill* knight, and that the Ladie *Alice* his widow made a feofment thereof, by the name of Leaden hall … to *Richard* Earle of Arundell and Surrey, 1362'.[3] A detailed account of Leadenhall's history is provided by AH Thomas, who offers an insight into the intricate shifts of ownership and part ownership of the building and of its parts during the period of interest here.[4] In the 1350s the building was owned by John de Neville and his wife Alesia, who were childless. Thomas relates that during the 14th century a series of deeds were drawn up 'evidently designed to raise money on the remainder of the property, while securing to them and the survivor of them a life interest'.[5] Although it is a tenuous link, we know that Sir William Fitzwarin was well known to the Nevilles, who on 22 October 1357 acquired the greater part of Leadenhall for the duration of their 'joint lives' while another with whom Fitzwarin had served, Sir William de Bohun, Earl of Northampton, acquired the remainder of the building. What does become clear is that parts of the entitlement are acquired by other parties and are sublet over the next twenty or thirty years. Thus, in August 1362 the messuages (properties) and 'reversions' were conveyed to Sir Richard Fitzalan, Earl of Arundel, who married de Bohun's daughter. Most striking perhaps is Thomas's discovery that between June 1377 and February 1380 the outright ownership of Leadenhall lay with Sir John Hawkwood, leader of the so-called White Company of mercenaries. Here was another who had learned his trade under Edward III and served under the Black Prince at Poitiers, but he spent most of his subsequent life domiciled in Florence.[6] The courtyard to the rear of Leadenhall was initially a meeting place for poulterers, and it is believed that all poultry brought to London had first to be taken to Leadenhall for sale.[7] As for the building into which Richard Whittington was introduced, it is thought to have remained, at least in main part, in the Neville family, and we are left to speculate that either before or after Sir William Fitzwarin's death in 1361 his son Ivo occupied a part of Leadenhall, using it as his London base and commuting from time to time to the family estate at Wantage.

In 1394 the owner of Leadenhall, Alice Neville, died and in 1397, the year Whittington first served as mayor, the focus of the market shifted from poultry in favour of cheese mongering. By the early 1400s, part of Leadenhall was used to store and sell a wider range of provisions for Londoners, and this function is seen as the starting point for the City's interest in the site. By 1409 the Fitzwarins had vacated the building and removed themselves permanently to Wantage. Their departure and Leadenhall's uncertain future must have influenced, with Whittington's recommendation, the City of London's decision to acquire the building. A consortium of Whittington and his close associates John Hende, Thomas Knolles, John Shadworth, William Staunton and William Askham acquired it on behalf of the City of London in 1409 for the sum of £566 13s 4d.[8] In 1411 the site was formally established as a food market and granary for the city.[9]

* * *

Like many nobles who divided their time between soldiery and enterprise, Fitzwarin saw an intricate, even indivisible, relationship between property and the income it produced: not simply as the means to build a wider enterprise and to grow his own and England's wealth but also to sustain the country if war continued to drain her coffers. It seems clear that Whittington's mother knew of the family connections and that she instigated his arrival here. It is conceivable that both fathers had pledged support for each other's families in times of need and she was 'calling this in'. For his part, the ambitious and diversely deployed Fitzwarin needed someone young, eager to absorb what he hoped to impart and invest, in every sense, to ensure the continuing prosperity of the house of Fitzwarin, and perhaps one day to establish and secure his own. He was also in a hurry. With England almost permanently at war, soldiery offered scant prospect of a long or secure life.

Here perhaps was the deal. As Whittington grew older and learned his craft, he would come to represent Fitzwarin's interests and would be well regarded and respected for doing so. In the early stages of his career Fitzwarin's name and reputation would give him access and passage. Sir Ivo's wealth, connections and influence would give him leverage. Eventually Whittington would be the means to their mutual growth. Fitzwarin would be his mentor and patron and later his investor. And though he might consider them to be related in some way, he would continue to remind the boy that he was foremost his employer and his landlord.

7

FIRST DAY

Waking London

How might Whittington's first day, perhaps in the company of his new master, have unfolded? At the hour of six a peal of bells would sound the Angelus, heralding the formal start of the city's life. Within the hour the markets would be thriving. This was the best time to see London. Even before the churches called their parishioners to prayer, the rumble of carts, the cracking of loose stones under the weight of produce, the snorting and scraping of horses, the exhortations of their masters, and the thrum of slowly building activity were already framing the hours ahead. There was the sound of people tearing up the street, bursting with early morning energy, youthful shouts, ribald yells and hurried greetings. Garbled messages would be thrown into the air as London's runners and errand boys raced past each other. From the ovens and the 'cook shoppes' on Bread Street would arise the aroma of *pain de mayne* and the tang of rye. From Leadenhall early risers could distinguish the competitive efforts of at least three churches by a tuneful carillon, a repetitive clang, and a sonorous boom: St Peter's Cornhill, St Edmund Lombard and All Hallows. The ringing was a belated prompt to worship and endeavour, conferring purpose and accelerating the pace of activity already coming to life within the city's ancient confining walls. London went about the preparations for its business very early indeed, unremitting but good-natured. A blur of people, pack-horses, oxen, carts, goods and manufactures, materials and produce, and all manner of domestic animals, was already in full flow with purpose known, destinations set, routes mapped. The meeting of Cornhill with Bishopsgate, a favoured and well-established place of assembly, marked an important signpost to direct people and trade to all parts of the city. At this confluence sat Leadenhall, imposing, known to all and strategically placed; a landmark to guide you to your destination, wherever you were bound. Here, early in the morning, you could see small herds of cattle being led to market down-hill from Bishopsgate, the drovers manoeuvring their keep through the knots of people that had begun to thicken around the crossroads, and loiter at the 'cooke shoppes' that had begun to spring up all over the centre of the city—medieval 'fast-food outlets' and 'pop-ups'.

In the opposite direction, above All Hallows, the streets were by this time in the grip of remorseless redevelopment directed by foremen in their leather jerkins with wide belts stuffed with mallets and chisels as they barked at migrant labourers and issued instructions to pairs of nerveless carpenters hired to secure timber scaffolding to the elevations of half-formed buildings. Anyone casting their eyes two storeys above would espy the sure-footed acrobats who took their life in their hands as they skipped across the spans and lowered their hoists to receive the next consignment of staging. It was an entertaining and instructive eye-opener for any new-comer to the city. What might have struck them more was the height of these fine houses, commonly reaching three storeys, a rare few even higher, placing them visually and culturally at odds with the unsophisti-cated squat tenements to which they posed a threat or which they already displaced. In the narrow streets below, Whittington might have found himself encountering small groups of women weighed down with consign-ments of ripe fruit and recently dug vegetables, chunks of damp soil cling-ing to their roots, stuffed into a capacious rush basket strapped to their backs with two more slung over their shoulders. They would have trudged stoically, eyes to the ground, bodies bent and flexing under the shifting weight of their produce—little more than beasts of burden. Turning around, he might have observed small handfuls of men encrusted head to toe in yellow dust, who looked as if they might have avoided the curfew and slept rough in the street. Then there were the road-weary pedlars cajoling mules overladen with bolts of cloth, amid a cacophony of rattling pots, trinkets and metalware: everything was tied to everything else. Even at this hour they would have proclaimed their presence, extolling the mer-its of their merchandise, boasting its special worth and its quite remark-able origins, 'unique in the whole of Christendom'. It would have been a familiar sight and cry, for they were the type of pedlars Whittington was accustomed to seeing at Newent and Gloucester on market day. Now, he was in the heart of expansive, exotic London, a wide-eyed young boy excited to experience everything that one of Europe's greatest ports had to exhibit or proclaim, ready to absorb and savour it all. A city with walls built to keep the invader out, these were now far more of a confinement to its straining population, recovered from the most recent pestilence. As many as 50,000, and far more on market and feast days, squeezed into this open-topped cooking pot. These were London's robust, purposeful citizens: inmates, more like, said many observers.

It was during the 1370s and later in the 1380s that the chronicler Jean Froissart established himself as a keen and wry observer of London, its people and the ups and downs of the war with France, and as a regular visitor to the European cities and trading centres that London engaged with. He offered a broad context from which he could observe the attributes and deficiencies of England's thriving capital. Londoners were, for him, the most dangerous and turbulent element within a very proud and dangerous people: stern, hardy, brave, able to withstand and recover from slaughter, acquiring courage from their reverses, and given to brawling and disorder.[1]

To an observer of the London 'ant-hill' of 1370, Fitzwarin's first piece of advice might well have been: 'If you are going to make your way here, then be sure to look beyond the confinement of the city's walls'. That's where London's future and that of his young charge surely beckoned, a nod to the imperative of trade, far and wide. In the meantime, there was no better education in the economic geography or the social mapping of London than simply walking its streets and taking it all in. It was no more than fifteen minutes' walk along the primary route from Leadenhall to Cornhill, then on to the Stocks at the junction with Poultry, which teemed with people early in the morning. As a mercer of sorts, much of Fitzwarin's business would have been conducted in the dense web of back streets bounded by Cornhill, Lombard Street and Gracechurch Street, an area that also included the churches of St Michael and St Edmund Lombard. Here the crumbling tenements were interspersed with many drapers' houses and workshops,[2] and the 'mysteries' that were anchored to their parishes.[3]

Keen to get Whittington off on the right foot, Fitzwarin may have pointed out those he dealt with regularly and instructed him, even then, to make a mental note, reminding him that he would be running errands and taking orders to them before the week's end. On the eve of the new decade London was a place frantic with the conveyance of goods and trade, overstuffed and unable to house its current population, and a magnet for thousands more who would happily breach its gates and overrun its quays in the belief that it would offer them shelter, employment, trade, prosperity and safety.[4] A ceaseless heave of people crammed into streets often no more than nine feet wide and fifteen high. Here they were wedged tight between cramped, decrepit tenements and the mushrooming of lime-washed shops and workshops that formed the frontage to larger and better-built dwellings, recently fireproofed with roofs of tile or stone, that served as both home and workplace to many of the city's tradesmen and merchants. Each was determined to give no quarter to its neighbour. Each was an open invitation to insanitation and pestilence. Typically, a barrel of green slimed water stood to the side of those still crowned with thatch; from their gables hung long rakes for clawing away burning straw.[5] As Whittington plotted his way, it must have seemed that every piece of available land was forced with buildings or development. He would not have encountered such density or constriction in his short life. Yet in a London where it seemed there was a church at every street corner, he would soon be able to navigate the dense and often dark inner passages of the city by the edifices it had erected to God.[6] By the time he reached All Hallows, he would have encountered at least five churches, established signposts to the city's less accessible thoroughfares.

Crossing Lombard Street, they would arrive in the vicinity of St Benet Gracechurch where a small corn market flourished on an adjoining plot. At Cornhill the business of drapery had long since displaced the enterprise from which it derived its name and the sale of grain had been relegated to the streets below. From there they might have continued into Candlewick ward, one of the then 24 divisions of the City of London.[7] Whittington would need to explore them all, recognise their landmarks, understand their commercial protocols and their political loyalties, and build an awareness of who controlled them both officially and unofficially.

Discovering London this way, trailing behind his new master, he would also observe how Fitzwarin's bearing and dress announced him as someone of great measure. Two hours after Angelus, the streets were even more packed with people shortcutting between Poultry and 'Cheap', some going about their business in and out of the dismal workshops, while into the churches trundled those with the time and inclination for prayer. Wading through the rank atmosphere that clung beneath the overhanging eaves, the progress of a figure like Fitzwarin would be marked by the tugging of hats fashioned of straw and burlap, the doffing of woollen and fur caps, and the gentle clasp of linen and hemp coifs. It would seem that everyone in London wore something on their head. Riders would offer an evidently wealthy man of bearing their salutations; carters and barrow boys would draw to one side lest they kick up dust. Even the feral children and beggars that seemed to infest every other doorway and churchyard would show such a figure appropriate courtesy.

Where might Fitzwarin have taken his young charge then? After all they would have been pushing their way through the crowds for some time and there was still much to see. Perhaps to one of the highly popular 'cook shoppes' that had sprouted opposite St Mildred Poultry, determined not to have their appetite dulled by London's abominable stink. Might Fitzwarin have been among those leading citizens who had taken up this affront to the senses with the city's mayor, John Chichester, a wealthy goldsmith, just a few months earlier? After all, what else were mayors for if not clearing the city of ordure and emanation, an expectation that Whittington would remember when his own time arrived? Then he would apply his considerable energies to the abominable infestation of Walbrook and the Fleet.[8] The former was a dumping stream for every imaginable form of waste while the latter was corrupted by the gross spoilage of London's butchers, tanners and leather workers.

The stench was one thing, but far more diverting would have been the exceptional quality of the fine houses and mansions which burgeoned despite it. Whittington knew only of Gloucester, though he may have visited Bristol once or twice to meet distant relatives who lived in a decaying pile on the Berkeley lands at Bedminster. Neither would remotely offer comparison with London's perpetually transforming townscape. In Leadenhall and Gracechurch Street alone there were probably three times more imposing residences than in the whole of Gloucester and Bristol combined. Here drapers and mercers had set a fashion for tall imposing houses faced with brick baked in the Flemish clay pits close to the river-bank, which compensated for London's lack of good local stone. Their height was one surprise, but many of the buildings were also far wider than he would have encountered elsewhere, frequently incorporating shops and workshops within their frontage, though few at this time were glazed to any extent. Instead, most featured timber shutters that folded down to form long shelves suspended over the street by chains or supported from below by sturdy pedestals. Upon them drapers laid tightly wound bolts of cloth of considerable variety and quality, and in baskets below they deposited unruly heaps of 'remains' through which the impecunious would sort, sift and search for a bargain. Had he peered through the tiny windows he would have glimpsed a prodigious, if fragmented, backroom industry barely illuminated by the weak flicker of cheap tallow candles set in blackened spikes, rank with cow suet. The entrances to the best houses were to the rear, approached through expansive courtyards often planted with lush gardens and boasting their own stabling. In the most sought-after plots adjoining and facing the fine church of St Clement Eastcheap and in a handful of pleasant streets above St Mary Abchurch, wealth and ambition jostled for position. Ever larger houses presided over the choicest ground, not least on those parts of the riverbank which afforded the installation of a small private jetty, a notable status symbol for wealthy merchants and bishop 'princes'. Indeed, in the very year Whittington arrived in London the City objected to one such structure for its overly ambitious proportions, nineteen feet by five feet and towering seven feet above the Thames.[9]

Some of the grander houses, many of which were home to mercers and drapers, had frontages of nearly forty feet embracing their shops and rented premises, sometimes with tenements attached or situated nearby. The hall was usually entered from the courtyard, a green space adorned with flowers, shrubs and low trees of fruit and berry, and patches of darker earth cultivated with vegetables and tidy rows of culinary and medicinal herbs. It was common to encounter servants cutting flowers for the hall and the chambers and uprooting all manner of roots and legumes for the pot. Entering such a space, you were almost remote from the city, in a different world brightened by scent and birdsong, a far cry from the grime and clamour in the street on which the house had staked its frontage. Further along, smaller but no less impressive, homes had begun to elbow out the old tenements that housed the commonalty, fuelling a growing problem of homelessness exacerbated further by London's demand for labour—ironically much of it to serve its latest development cycle—and the arrival of large numbers of rural migrants looking to the city for work.

With each pace a visitor could see how the new and the grand were displacing the old and the humble, forcing overcrowding elsewhere. Empty messuages had begun to spring up throughout the city and Whittington would have been among the few able to read the painted signs that proclaimed their acquisition by this individual or that mystery, for the purpose of improvement or wholesale replacement. On every street, high or low, and at each turbulent junction, there stood an edifice to God. Was there any place with more churches and chapels, monasteries and convents, almshouses, hospitals, colleges and charnel houses than late-14th-century London? Most were intended as highly visible, and often deeply personal, examples of 'good works': monuments to high salvation frequently funded by the proceeds of low trade, testaments in this life to a fear of the next.

If this imagined journey had continued in the direction of Lombard Street, Fitzwarin and Whittington might have contemplated the two over-bearing mansions which flanked St Mary Woolchurch. The ancient church had been dwarfed by their recent arrival; they were taller by far than any others the boy would have encountered previously. They were said to have exceeded three storeys. Could that be possible? Had he scrutinised the arrangements of their windows, he might have concluded that there was indeed another floor, though of lower proportions than the three which supported it—a mark of London's unbridled growth and vain prosperity. Noting his interest, Fitzwarin might have remarked to him that the upkeep and adornment of many of London's fine churches were in the gift of one trade or another, the *territoire* of the wealthier guilds.[10] It was hardly surprising that their leading lights should seek recognition in this life and solace in the next by constructing their conspicuously fashionable new homes on the adjoining plots. Many years later, as guilds became 'companies' and acquired their royal charters, the erection of their sta-tus-driven, purpose-built halls would follow a similar pattern. For now, they were still few and far between and offered only a slender glimpse of what was to come. Only the tailors in 1331 at Threadneedle Street and the goldsmiths in 1357 at Foster Lane are known to have had halls erected and dedicated specifically to the business and social congregation of their fraternity at this time.[11]

For the first half of Whittington's life in London, most companies con-tinued to meet in premises that either formed part of or were adjacent to the parish churches with which their trade was associated historically. The pace quickened significantly after the granting of royal charters in the 1390s and continued during the first half of the 15th century so that by 1450 at least 28 halls had been erected to serve the needs of London's companies. Here, in these grand domestic and corporate gestures, was the evidence of successful commerce, embellished further by the halls' asso-ciation with the saving of souls. They were pointers to a new London in which economic opportunities were plentiful and for which enterprising men would give thanks to God through endowment and edification at home, at work and at prayer. What better course could there be than to erect and flaunt your fine mansion on the plot that adjoined your parish church? Was this not the crux of all good business? A forward-looking investment in salvation, an insurance for life, and reassurance at death. If you had prospered in this life and sought to do so in the next, then the course was a simple one: build your house next to that of God. Then take care to thank him for it with endowments, ornamentation and provision for sustenance, repair and prayer.

* * *

If the development of halls towards the end of the century was something of a self-proclaiming, if yet still relatively sparse, indication of the emerging 'corporate' London into which Whittington was introduced, there was another far more important prize by which the city's ancient trades sought to measure themselves and be measured by their peers. Many of the guilds were already looking sharply to the future. They were shedding their old ways, dusting themselves down and rapidly reconstituting themselves so they might secure the vital royal charter that would affirm them as a company. Yet it was a slow and arbitrary process in the gift of the king and subject to whimsy, favour and preferment. While many guilds had assumed the trappings, both real and literal, of a company by the turn of the century, the conferment of a royal charter would elude most of London's great mysteries for many years still. The mercers were notable among their number.

During the reign of Henry V (1413–22), 111 crafts are recorded as operating in London 'all of which seem to have had some fraternity or "mistery" organisation, though not all had received from the city authorities formal powers of self-government'.[12] Yet at the time of Whittington's death in 1423, nearly thirty years after the mercers had belatedly acquired their own charter, the incorporation of most of London's leading guilds was still some way off. To a large extent this slow progress may reflect the peculiar characteristics of the trade: how well was it organised; was it uniform in its objectives or captive to uncertainty or factionalism; what merit did it perceive in incorporation; was it well regarded in the eyes of the king; was it influential at court? Yet the simplest explanation for the relatively few charters granted by Henry's reign was surely cost. Incorporation was an expensive business, a costly privilege priced in some instances by the value of its political expediency to the king. Typically, it was the preserve of the wealthiest fraternities, driven in turn by determined and astute leaders. The mercers fell within this group. But what are we to make of the hugely wealthy fishmongers, who built more halls than any other fraternity? They did not incorporate until 1433, forty years after the mercers. Or the cordwainers, frequent allies of the mercers, who achieved company status a further six years later? Both were rich enough in corporate terms. Perhaps they lacked the 'leadership' to pursue their ambitions or did not have the status to 'deserve' conferment. Or were their ambitions thwarted by those who had already acquired their charter and were not keen to see their privileges diluted? Whatever the explanations, it was not until after 1500 that the so-called Twelve Great Companies of London were finally embedded in London's constitutional arrangements and their perceived order of status was acknowledged formally: led by the mercers and followed in order by the grocers, drapers, fishmongers, haberdashers, ironmongers, vintners, goldsmiths, skinners, salters, merchant taylors and clothworkers.[13]

Fast-forward 300 years and we find the arrangements have held almost to the letter. London now has 110 ancient and modern trade associations and guilds, virtually all styled as the Worshipful Company of their craft, trade or profession, each contributing as they did then to the city's (and today to the nation's) life through charitable giving, the funding and facilitation of educational and economic opportunity, the development of cultural and social programmes, and a dynamic process of networking. These are activities and inclinations that London's most celebrated mayor would recognise and might claim no small part in helping to establish. The ancient traditions developed before and immediately after Whittington's lifetime also continue to endure, most notably in the voting rights of the modern-day liveryman—the '*enclothed* freeman'—for London's lord mayor, sheriffs and City of London Corporation, which, Whittington would be reassured to discover, still retains extensive local government powers.[14] The one notable change is that the skinners now fall sixth and the merchant taylors seventh, but they acknowledge their previous ranking by alternating each Easter. Some say this is the source of the phrase 'at sixes and sevens', though Chaucer refers to the phrase much earlier in 1374 ('Lat nat this wrechched wo thyn herte gnawe, But manly set the world on sexe and seuene').[15] It's a good story either way.

* * *

In the case of the mercers, nearly a quarter of a century would pass following Richard Whittington's arrival in London before they finally achieved the recognition that had eluded them for so long, and he would play an influential role in securing its conferment. Long before then, he would conclude that while having a royal charter was an invaluable corporate asset, the status and influence of having your own man as mayor was arguably the greater prize. London's attraction as a place to do business was also driving significant change, evident not least—as it is today—in the array of nationalities, languages, dialects, ethnicity and origins of its street and market traders. This too would have widened Whittington's eyes; he had no experience of the melting pot that London had already become by the opening of the 14th century, let alone how it would have transformed by the start of the next. However, London's diversity came at a different form of price, with frequent outbreaks of resentment and violence towards foreigners, reminiscent of that inflicted upon the few Italians robust or assured enough to remain following the bankruptcies of the great banking houses in the 1340s. More recently, the spiteful attentions of English traders and merchants had turned to the lowlanders from Flanders and Brabant who had staked a claim in the city's rising prosperity and who were denounced and attacked for challenging an Englishman's domestic privileges—his control over markets and his right to fix prices. Generally, most Londoners were grateful for the choice and cheapness of the foreigners' goods and content with the familiarity with which these alien traders went about capturing their attention and their business. Here, within the narrow sun-starved streets, in the heaving press of London's markets, and in the persuasions of their goods and merchandise, the callow Richard Whittington would first comprehend the vitality of trade, the fiercely outward-facing commerce of London, and the essentials of commodity, choice and price. His seasoning in London's trade would be steepened by his initial duties as a houseboy in the Fitzwarin household and as an errand boy and 'runner' in the Fitzwarin business.

At the close of his first day he would have heard for the first time, and would hear each night thereafter until his death in 1423, the announcement of curfew at eight during winter and at nine in the summer, proclaimed by the bells of four of the city's most familiar churches, St Giles without Cripplegate, St Mary-le-Bow in Cheapside, St Bride's in Fleet Street and All Hallows Barking.[16] It was a resonant start to a resounding life in England's greatest city.

8

PLAGUE

The Black Death

The twenty years prior to Richard Whittington's arrival in London were marked by a series of events and opportunities that transformed the city and its commerce and that would bear directly on his own life and career. The aftershocks of the Black Death continued far beyond the immediate trauma of 1348–50, producing far-reaching impacts—social, economic, physical and psychological—not only in London but upon the nation at large. Despite the unimaginable nature and scale of loss and the overhanging fear that plague might return at any time, the effects of the Black Death shaped a remarkable period of resilience and enterprise, both individual and collective, often in the least expected quarters. The changes it forced, encouraged or simply accelerated were little short of remarkable: a far-reaching 'disruptive' impact on ownership of land and title; a reordering of assets and entitlement that led to speculation and accelerated urban development, no more so than in London; a transformation in the faltering practices and structures of England's agrarian economy; a deep and far-reaching aggravation of the rural labour supply, already showing signs of depletion after decades of falling birth rate, high mortality and the draining effect of men conscripted for war; and the impetus it gave to wage bargaining and in turn to the enactment of the Statute of Labourers in 1351, which reacted to the spiralling price of scarcity by reversing labour costs to pre-Black Death levels. The Black Death also accelerated conditions in which the issuing of the Ordinance of the Staple in October 1353 became irresistible, regularising designated 'staple ports' where the trade in specific goods could be presided over by the 'mayor of the staple', the office to which Richard Whittington would be appointed half a century later, both for Westminster and for Calais. The weakening effect of the

Black Death on the continent of Europe contributed in 1354 to Edward III's resumption of the Hundred Years War, which helped drive economic recovery; while the resumption of hostilities also fuelled the unrelenting demands of three English kings for tax revenue and for loans, for which the 'cash-rich' Whittington was frequently the first port of call. The events of 1348–50 also had a particularly transforming impact on the reorganisation of England's wool trade and on exports, regulation, diversification, and distribution. A combination of early-14th-century population decline, the concentrated decimation of the population brought about directly by the Black Death from 1348, the resulting scarcity of labour, and an improvement in income and living standards for many among the remaining population was instrumental in producing a shift in both the economic and the social psyche that drove consumption and the demand for luxury goods and fashion; in turn, this contributed to the resurgence of the port of London and the undiminishing vitality of its great artery, the Thames.

In London, the loss of many landowners and titles and records resulted in a freeing of land and spurred a fresh tide of opportunism and investment by new and enterprising landowners in grand housing, in the development of tenements and workshops, and in improvements to port infrastructure—quays, warehousing, workspace. This almost cathartic upheaval also extended to a quickening in the erosion, already under way, of the old guild system and the assertion of the pre-eminence of 'the company' over the artisan. The decades following 1350 saw in London the consolidation of a powerful, wealthy merchant class and accelerated the spirit of adventurism. The ancient interrelationship between politics and commerce would also deepen and was no better evidenced that in the intensification of competition for the ultimate prize—the mayoralty of London. For many of the wider population who had survived the onslaught of the Black Death, their faith in God and the clergy was severely tested and in some instances sundered. Teaching and learning were also badly affected, as many of England's monastic houses were laid low, removing a vital educational resource. The Black Death decimated the poorer rural clergy, reducing and weakening the literate capacity of England's clergy generally for some decades. Religious and arts projects were abandoned for lack of finance or skilled management and labour. On the other hand, the impact of the Black Death on French-speaking educators, clergy and nobility accelerated the displacement of French by English at court, in law and in commerce. And all the while there remained the spectre of unpredictable, ineradicable plague, both calamitous and galvanising, lying in wait, biding its time, until the next opportune moment. In 1361–2 it would cut a swathe through London's youngest and most vulnerable, its children.

* * *

In 1370 Whittington encountered a London still undergoing a huge transition—in its foreign ambitions, in its commerce and labour relations, in lending and investment, and in social mobility, fashion, consumption and aspiration. Politics, the economy, foreign relations, religion, and the city's ancient craft traditions and representational structures were either transforming or in flux. Lives, businesses and careers had been destroyed, but in their place the city, its people and its economy were already well on the road to recovery, and Whittington arrived at a moment of mushrooming enterprise and striking opportunity, perhaps the beginning of a renaissance. Yet for all its vitality and prosperity and the ceaseless day-to-day churn of its diverse constituencies, it was the deeply embedded fear of plague and the harrowing prospect of its return that continued to haunt England at large and the populace of its vigorous and increasingly mercantilist capital in particular. That the Black Death should have ravaged a nation and a city so buoyant and self-propelling, just two years after the glory of Crécy, was stupefying. How could it be so?

We know far more about the Black Death today than we did even just twenty years ago, let alone seventy when much of the intense curiosity about its origins, characteristics, demography, pathology, and impacts was first generated.[1] Indeed, as this book was being written, new scientific evidence was brought to light on the 'causes' of the Black Death, which at the very least may raise questions about the carrier role of the eternal pantomime villain—the rat.[2] There is not space here to either debate or reference the sheer volume of work on each of these complex and much contested aspects of the plague. Estimates of mortality and their methods of calculation vary considerably, at their most extreme ranging between 20 and 60 per cent. There are also marked variances in localised mortality rates (in manors, monasteries, towns) and between social groups (peasants, landowners, nobility, higher and lower clergy, children and adults). However, some general context is required to assess the legacy of the Black Death with regard to population and economy, and how this may have shaped the circumstances in which Richard Whittington made his way in London after 1370.

One of the more recent studies of the Black Death offers a precise time and circumstance for its arrival in England, placing this in early June 1348, when it was brought into the tiny entrepôt of Melcombe Regis (others widely report Weymouth as first point of entry), located between Southampton and Dartmouth, by Gascon sailors aboard one of two boats that had departed from the English port of Bordeaux three weeks earlier to supply the south coast wine trade. Benedict Gummer reports that its progress was rapid; within a fortnight it consumed its first English victims before sweeping at speed through the rural south-west. In a matter of weeks, it had invested the region's capital, Bristol. Spreading swiftly by road and river, it next overtook the settlement of Thornbury, destroying its 'regular, peaceful estuarine existence',[3] before advancing towards Whittington's own home ground of Gloucester. It consumed in its path the necklace of riverside hamlets that beaded the Avon and Severn before infiltrating the radial networks of rural tracks, bridleways and watercourses of Somerset, Gloucestershire, Herefordshire and Worcestershire and breaching the Severn into Wales. Philip Ziegler estimated its arrival in London around the end of September, and it certainly had the capital in its grip by November.[4] The sheer weight, cramped conditions and appalling sanitary habits of London's population were effectively an open invitation to plague and ill health of any kind, and the Black Death took few prisoners. Michael Harrison notes that, unlike the Romans, later governments and inhabitants of London failed to construct an extensive system of sewers to contain the spread of disease and that 'the use to which London's rivers were put was a use envisaged by those who abstained from building cess-pits and sewers'.[5]

Edward I had made some effort to stem the literal tide of filth, issuing a series of ordinances against the fouling of the noxious Walbrook, but the very fact that these were measured in the plural illustrates the basic natural tendency of his subjects to reoffend. London's civic leaders were no more effective. It didn't help that at the beginning of the 14th century large parts of the city fell outside the mayor's jurisdiction. In 1300, almost half of the city's entire enclosed area was under the control of parties other than the mayor and Corporation.[6] Even after the passing of the Black Death, matters would improve only marginally and intermittently. One wonders what the young Whittington would have made of the Walbrook in 1370, before turning in revulsion from the stench of its effluence. 'Filth running in open ditches in the streets, fly-blown meat and stinking fish, contaminated and adulterated ale, polluted well water, unspeakable privies, epidemic disease, were experienced indiscriminately by all social classes.'[7] He would hardly have imagined that it would fall to him one day to oversee the clearance of London's unutterably filthy watercourses, but for now, like everyone else, he would have had to simply accept the assault on his senses as an everyday normality. Twenty years on from the horrors of 1348–50, London, like most English towns, remained cramped, pervasively unhygienic, and in many of its wards nothing less than shockingly squalid. It was still hopelessly inattentive to the lessons of the Black Death and the vicious return of plague in 1361–2 and 1369. Among the legacies Whittington would leave to his adopted city fifty years later would be a material improvement in its sanitation and in the quality and supply of water. His was a belated recognition that what had killed people in huge numbers in 1348, and again through other forms of pestilence during these later episodes, was not simply the toxins borne by plague itself but the sheer lack of resistance to them on the part of a population whose health was frequently fragile, whose mortality was placed in the balance by even the slightest of downturns in diet or living conditions, and who were exceptionally vulnerable to the insanitary conditions in which they worked, ate and slept.

Europe is thought to have lost up to 25 million people between 1347 and 1351 to the Black Death. Rather than ascribing it to millions of plague-infected rats swarming off ships, infiltrating watercourses and occupying every nook and cranny of medieval settlements, urban and rural, at least one modern study asserts that the fundamental truth of the Black Death lies elsewhere, in the form of human 'ectoparasites', typically lice and fleas, associated with filthy, bug-ridden clothing, insanitary conditions, and unclean and untutored medical care. Research at the universities of Oslo and Ferrara, centred on simulating outbreaks of plague in nine European cities, has concluded that the lice and fleas on humans (not rats) were more likely to have been responsible for spreading the disease. In seven out of the nine cities studied, the 'human parasite model' was a much better match for the pattern of the outbreak. 'The conclusion was very clear. The lice model fits best. It would be unlikely to spread as fast as it did if it was transmitted by rats. It would have to go through this extra loop of the rats, rather than being spread from person to person.'[8]

The Black Death was not the first time London had experienced a great and numbing catharsis. In the years 1130, 1132 and notably 1135–6 large areas of the town had been consumed by a series of terrifying blazes that had rampaged through its flimsy timber buildings, gorging on the air trapped between their interlocking eaves and incinerating the welcome invitations offered by their thatched roofs. These fires left in their wake a huge loss of life and the decimation of large numbers of houses and workshops and much of London's embryonic 'City'. This was the immensely destructive outcome of reckless development and flawed construction, fuelled by the growth in trade and by the residential needs of a burgeoning population, precisely the issues Whittington would encounter as mayor. By 1200, London's population had expanded to between 20,000 and 25,000, more than double that of 1066, and was already more than three times the size of England's next most populous town, York, and more than four times that of Bristol.[9] In 1300, the city's population may have been as large as 80,000, by far the greatest urban concentration in England and at 'the peak of its medieval size'.[10] Yet well before the arrival of the Black Death, the population of both England and London was already in decline, attributed to high rates of mortality, disease, deprivation and accidents, and the toll taken by long, continuous periods of war both at home and abroad. The Black Death has been extensively blamed for England's economic and population decline in the two decades or so after its passing, yet the population of Europe's leading military power was already waning before the first of its citizens manifested the symptoms of the great plague.

> By 1348 the reputation of English arms can rarely have stood higher and the King's prestige was at its zenith. But the glory was meretricious and the cost in money and manpower mounted steadily. Edward's crown was pawned to the Archbishop of Trier, his debts to the Bardi and Peruzzi were enormous, the rich merchants and the city of London had been repeatedly mulcted, taxes had been raised as high, perhaps even higher than was prudent. England was a still rich country but it was under severe financial strain and the strain was beginning to tell.[11]

Estimates of the population of England at large at the beginning of the 14th century vary widely. Amyat puts the national figure at around 4.5 million.[12] In 1948 Josiah Russell provided a widely held estimate of 3.7 million at the outbreak of plague, but he also noted subsequently that other writers held the famines of 1315–7 as the high mark of England's population and that it was already in decline before the Black Death.[13] His estimates were rejected by Postan, who considered them far too low, venturing that the population in 1348 could have been as high as 6 million. Wrigley and Schofield provided a further updating and revision of the estimates in 1981.[14]

Numbers on the eve of the Black Death are widely contested. Population estimates inevitably shape the accuracy of mortality levels and vice versa. The contemporary chronicler Ralph Higden of Chester certainly went too far in claiming that 'scarcely a tenth of mankind was left alive', while an unknown recorder at Malmesbury was almost certainly too cautious in reckoning that 'over England as a whole, a fifth of men, women and children were carried to the grave'. Most of the records we have from the period are highly localised and not ideal for wider extrapolation. Record keeping had fallen generally to the local clergy, to the clerks of small towns, to the owners of manors and landed estates, to scriveners and lawyers dealing with wills and property, and to officers of the state, and it centred frequently on assets, transactions, production, employment, payment of rent and, of course, tax collection. These records largely form the basis on which population estimates have been drawn. It didn't help that the suddenness and savagery of the Black Death not only dealt a huge blow to the population at large but also cut a swathe through those responsible for making and maintaining records. The persistence and geographical dispersal of plague also meant that much of the population was taken during the early months of 1349 when the onslaught was even more virulent. There was little time or inclination to save records over lives.[15]

9

A NUMBERS GAME

Before examining some of the headline estimates for population and mortality, it is essential to recognise that major changes in the economy and in patterns in England's demography were already under way and evident before 1348. The Black Death may have compounded or accelerated these changes, but it was not the sole driver or explanation for them. It is wise to tread with caution. Drawing on the earlier work of MM Postan,[1] Bruce Campbell has written that the economic expansion of the earlier Middle Ages owed little to any qualitative change in its make-up or to technological advancements and that in the absence of this technical progress 'expansion was made possible by a rise in the population'. As standards of living fell in the late 13th and early 14th centuries, so rates of mortality increased and 'these were high enough to determine the overall trend in population'.[2] Rather than the decline being due either solely or overwhelmingly to the Black Death, it may have been that other great trauma, the Great Famine of 1315–7, more than forty years earlier, which marked 'the turning point between the early medieval rise in population and the late medieval decline. The equilibrium which had once existed between population and economy was shattered well before the Black Death, and the explanation for it is to be found within the economic system.'[3] Or, if we refer to Postan, the causes lie in the 'essential processes of a society held in by physical ... Malthusian checks'.[4]

So why is this important and what does it have to do with Richard Whittington? The oversimplified answer is that England was 'overpopulated' at the start of the 14th century, but the failure of agriculture and the decline in production led to an irreversible change which became wrapped up in the further consequences of the Black Death, although they predate its arrival by some decades. From 1300 England's population was in decline and by 1348 the need to find alternatives to falling agricultural yields had already begun to shift the agrarian economy away from agriculture in favour of sheep. The Black Death *accelerated* rather than originated these developments. Thus, an improvement in people's living standards after 1350 generally associated with the Black Death may well have been well under way before it arrived on English shores. England's economy was faltering long before the trauma of 1348. From 1300, and perhaps as early as the 1280s, urban rents had begun to fall away; in the countryside land under cultivation had contracted sharply; demand for manufactures had dipped; unemployment was rising. As the economy shrank, so too did the size of England's population.

Just as they had been at the start of the 14th century, production and population were by 1348 once again out of balance, but now the problem was that there were *too few* people. Scarcity of labour meant that incomes would rise, and people would have money to spend for the first time in decades. By 1400, real wages would be 20 to 30 per cent higher than in the decade prior to the Black Death. There were other supporting factors: the emergence of new industries, the 'corporatising' of commerce, London's swift recovery through investment in housing, infrastructure and trade, and a renewed and sustained ripple in the vitality of the Thames and its corridor. Most of this improvement in incomes occurred after 1370, and Richard Whittington found himself well placed to exploit it. 'Population change, however, was now the constant and all-important factor, and other factors had their full effect only because this one was present on such a scale.'[5]

A fierce debate has raged for more than seventy years on whether the events of 1348–50 were the cause of population decline in the second half of the 14th century or whether numbers were already shrinking for other reasons—poverty, famine, ill health, war, child mortality; a multi-layered inability to restock the population. The contention here is that the Black Death accelerated and exponentially increased a fall in the population already under way. Yet by 1370, in some of England's larger towns at least, the curve had begun to recover. JMW Bean, for example, asserts that by 1400 the long arc of national population decline was over.[6] This recovery offers useful context to Whittington's own progress as it spanned the first thirty years of his career when he made his first fortune, first took office as London's mayor, shifted his business into luxury goods and foreign trade, became a leading supplier of goods to the court, struck most of his loans, and enjoyed his first taste of political influence. The entrepreneurial energy, shifting patterns of investment across traditional craft boundaries and ensuing financial rewards achieved by agile groups of outward-looking London merchants during the late 14th and early 15th centuries, of whom Whittington was an integral member as a civic and social standard-bearer, must surely be associated with some stabilisation in the population at large or more likely with largely London-centred growth and in-migration, since 'The fearsome spectre of recurrent plague, swingeing mortality rates, and a preoccupation with death, are not readily compatible with an age of vitality'.[7]

In London, the availability and more efficient use of capital, together with an overwhelming spirit of what might loosely be termed merchant adventurer capitalism and an influx of labour that was also accompanied by an atypical high-level demand for goods and services, drove England's economic engine to a much earlier recovery which saw London's merchant community pushing the boundaries of enterprise, home and abroad, strengthening their economic powers and increasing their wealth and political influence. Towns with strong local economies and a continuing demand for their goods or services—such as the traditional cloth centres of Coventry and Norwich, the wine ports of Bristol and Southampton, the small ports of Chichester, Boston and Lynn, and coal-producing Newcastle—also managed to ride out the commercial shock of the Black Death and were likewise partly aided by in-migration. Conversely, England's rural population experienced a sharp decline following the Black Death, overwhelmingly the result of high levels of mortality but latterly because there weren't enough families left to repopulate the countryside at the required rate or else people simply feared or chose not to do so.[8] There was also a rebalancing within and between rural areas themselves, instances where trade and prosperity had shifted to emerging centres of enterprise like the West Riding, to settlements in the hinterland of the Essex ports and, in Whittington's home patch, to the wool towns of the Cotswolds and the weaving settlements around Stroud.[9]

The decline in fertility in the second half of the 14th century remains one of the most striking outcomes of the Black Death. Many of those who survived found a world turned upside down; the oversupply of labour of earlier decades had been eradicated, and their skills or services were now in demand and for much higher reward. Whether peasant, artisan or merchant, they were able to benefit from their labour, their craft or their investment, providing a sounder basis for sustainability, self-improvement and consumption. This produced opportunities and economic conditions that favoured entrepreneurs, merchants and financiers like Richard Whittington. Yet the aftershock of plague, the sheer uncertainty of life, and a widespread desire to live for the moment also produced restraint, in reproduction. Perhaps this was a contributing factor in the lateness of Whittington's own marriage and in its absence of children.

* * *

So, to what extent did the Black Death impact on numbers nationally and within London itself?[10] A catastrophic reduction in England's population during the second half of the 14th century, which, at its outer limits, some have placed as high as 65 per cent, appears to jar with evidence in London and in England's larger towns of enterprise, commercial expansion and prosperity, and with the Exchequer's ability to raise taxes and loans to finance a long-running war. Writing in the mid-1960s, the demographer Goran Ohlin famously captured the dangers of stretching calculations and assertions based on limited or disputed evidence too far: 'they are not only afflicted with the uncertainties that beset statistics but actually contain such curious elements of speculation and guesswork that they must regretfully be dismissed altogether'.[11] In his wide-ranging work on the Black Death in 1969 Philip Ziegler estimated the death toll at one-third of the population.[12] Surveying the 'evidence' in the early 1980s for the wide range of estimates, John Hatcher drew from 'the present state of knowledge' a national death rate in 1348–9 of between 30 and 45 per cent, and this continues to find a broad consensus of agreement.[13] Hatcher noted that 'the seductive charms of quantification have frequently proved too tempting for historians accustomed to courting cold favours from indirect evidence'.[14] Such 'indirect evidence' includes much-disputed extrapolations of tenant holdings on agricultural estates; calculations of male generation replacement rates; the use of multipliers of taxpayers to calculate the national population; assumptions based on graphs of long-term population change; projections based on flawed mortality rates and widely varying local burial estimates for plague victims; and national population assumptions derived from manorial and monasterial transcripts. Even where records are available, the sheer variance in the reportage of mortality rates renders wider extrapolation difficult, as figures from estates near Whittington's home at Pauntley show.[15] In 1991 Barbara Harvey suggested that the population of England on the eve of the Black Death may have been as high as 6 million.[16] In 1996 Jeremy Goldberg judged that 45 per cent was a likely estimate, a loss of 2.16 million lives if we accept a national population of 4.8 million in early 1348; while in 2004 Ole

Jørgen Benedictow arrived at a much higher level of 62.5 per cent, which would stretch losses to 3 million. If we accept that the much higher pre-Black Death population suggested by Harvey's earlier population estimate of 6 million is accurate, this would correspond to 3.75 million deaths.[17] Whatever the precise figure, it was certainly immense; the impact on human life was monstrous, the effect on London transformative.

What is clear is that at the outbreak of the Black Death, England was effectively overpopulated in relation to its productivity and the ability of the economy to support its people. The ensuing increase in output, income and general prosperity in the final quarter of the century can be explained as a combined rebalancing of population, production, output, prosperity and consumption. In short, fewer people with more money to spend, or, in other words, a more efficient harmonising of capital, land and labour, accompanied by what we might term a shift in psychology. The Black Death is the means of 'balance'.

The Psychology of Plague

One of the most intriguing outcomes of the Black Death was its impact not simply on weight of numbers but on attitudes to death and uncertainty, on the capacity of individuals and communities and of tightly knit and often overlapping 'economic communities' to recover and prosper. What factors and considerations drove their responses to plague and what impact did it have on the individual and group psyche? In London, we see evidence, particularly after 1370, that the city at large, its merchants, its commonalty, its rural incomers and its foreign trading partners, came through the trauma relatively quickly, determined to get on with life and make a living. Opportunities arose, were created and were exploited. Arguably, the physical assault of the Black Death and the endemic fear that it would return in some form at any moment were almost certainly drivers for and not a brake on recovery. We can trace this in the conditions the Black Death helped to bring about or expedite: in the fostering of resilience and a new buoyancy in agricultural prices; in the recalibration of the wool and cloth industries; in London's rise to dominance over the staple and cloth trades; in a third-quarter restoration of seigneurial prosperity; in the development of a wider merchant adventurism; in the erosion of serfdom and the assertion of labour rights and just reward; in the growth of consumption; in the attempts by the state to put the brakes on self-improvement and ability to consume through the Sumptuary Laws; in the shift from ancient trade practices and the prevalence of the solitary crafts-man towards combination, collaboration and the chartered company; in the construction and improvement of churches by the wealthy in gratitude for survival in this life and as a down payment on salvation in the next; in the inclination of ordinary people with increased earnings and ability to pay for goods previously out of reach to spend now and fret later; in the increasingly influential role of women in enterprise, establishing charities and funding good works; in the enlarging and sharpening of the competi-tion for London's mayoralty; and in the determination of City and Parliament to assert their independence from the Crown. As if the Black Death had simply been a figment of the imagination, it did not deter, either in economic or human terms, successive English kings from raising men, arms and taxes to pursue their martial ambitions. The Black Death and the plague that followed in 1361–2 may have galvanised England, providing a systemic rush of national adrenalin.[18]

10

RECOVERY

Londoners had fared better than most during the half-century before the Black Death because of their access to food, employment, and the variable attentions and skills of England's greatest concentration of physicians, barbers and apothecaries. After 1350 the city was also able to rebuild more quickly, aided significantly by the rural in-migration of those desperate to seek greater opportunities for work. This inward flow of labour and skills and a revitalised demand for goods and services ensured that London's recovery was far better sustained than elsewhere. Despite the human and economic trauma and the loss of as much as 30 to 40 per cent of its population, London not only retained but strengthened further its hegemony as England's economic engine. The flourishing of its port, the expansion and improvement of its infrastructure, and ready access to the Continent's principal manufacturing centres placed it not only as England's most dynamic centre but by 1370 arguably Europe's also. Richard Whittington had arrived at the right place at the right time.

The trauma of plague was twofold: the sheer physical decimation it wrought on a hapless population ill prepared to deal with it, and the impact on the mind and sense of purpose. For some it shook the foundations of their social and religious certainties, while for others it had a surprising, almost cleansing effect. The Black Death had a powerful liberating impact on London's reduced but energetic merchant class, who were presented with unexpected opportunities to transform their enterprises, accumulate wealth and assets, and in the process energise the city's economy. A new breed of entrepreneurs emerged, fearful no doubt of the ravages they saw about them but driven, in some cases relentlessly, by the conceit that salvation lay in honourable trade, hard work, the accumulation of wealth, and investing a portion of this windfall in religious endowments and in acts of social improvement. This was evident in the work ethic which characterised England's wool trade, a barometer of national recovery and personal advancement. 'Not only did Englishmen begin to see what a fortune there was to be made in wool, in trade and in the creation of monopolies, but the trade itself began breeding the type of adventurer who was in time to expand it in a score of different directions.'[1]

A similar attitude could be found among ordinary Londoners and in many of the rural migrants who flocked into the city, great numbers of whom had lost their families, their masters and their livelihoods. In many cases they, too, were presented with a hitherto unlikely opportunity for advancement, if they could seize it, arising from the unexpected shortage of labour. Even for the poorest of Londoners, the Black Death 'brought about a revolution, a revolution, most importantly, that fed upon itself, for a man who a generation before had hoped only to feed his family began to be aware of luxury on every side. And so he began demanding a share of it.'[2] Fear of plague was well justified; it would return to London next in 1361–2, when around 20 per cent of the population is estimated to have been lost nationally, with children and young people most severely affected. It visited again in 1369–70, the year Whittington arrived, but this time was largely confined to York and the North. London was ravaged by further visits of plague or viral outbreak throughout Whittington's time in the capital. These occurred four times more in 1375, 1400, 1407 and 1413. It was, according to one writer, only in the mid-1370s that 'plague really began to bite hard into the traditional manorial economy. From 1375, for the first time in the 14th century, money wages did not conform to the movement of prices, for low prices did not force down wages as they had in the 1340s. Costs rose, rents fell, vacancies increased, and the lords were clearly troubled.'[3]

In the wake of successive physical degradations of health and well-being, what finally set off the Peasants' Revolt of 1381 was the unavoidable reality that the 'burden of old and new taxation was too much to bear'.[4] After the revolt there followed other significant epidemics, not regarded as plague, which attacked London indiscriminately, most notably a long bout of debilitation between 1389 and 1393 occasioned by famine, sickness, poor sanitation and dysentery. The mortality rates suggest that some sections of the population were neither recovering their bodily defences and general health nor sustaining their volume during this time.[5] Drawing on Hatcher's work and Russell's earlier projections, Bolton highlights the divergences in population estimates, and refers to 'possible maximum and minimum population estimates' that appear to plot a sharp collapse after 1350. These continue downward until their lowest point around 1400, before levelling out for half a century.[6] Yet England's capital continued to thrive and succeed in winning trade not only aboard but from other English towns and regions, and its wealthiest citizens were numerous enough, well enough and rich enough to invest, consume and dispense largesse like never before. Perhaps like modern capitals, late 14th- and early 15th-century London had become something of an economic bubble better insulated than its rivals and more able to shed and replace its population. Of interest here is the impact of plague outside London and specifically in respect of Richard Whittington's dispatch to the capital city in 1369–70. Bolton tells us that in areas close to Pauntley plague had swept through relentlessly. Thus, on the Cotswold manors of Winchcombe Abbey 'the plague brought the disintegration and regrouping of holdings'. Yet

> the only direct evidence of the impact of the Black Death on Gloucester concerns the canons of Llanthony Priory who (in a record of a century later) were said to have lost two thirds of their number, 19 out of 30, at the first outbreak of the plague in 1349. Gloucester Abbey appears to have lost about a quarter of its complement of monks.[7]

Whatever else we may remark or conclude of the second half of the 14th century, England suffered from, and yet was still able to rise above, both the recurring fear and the revisitation of plague. By 1370, because of London's location, its concentration of court, governance, law and state apparatus, its physical and human assets, its unrivalled access to resources, its fostering of an exceptional and spirited entrepreneurial outlook, its ability to replenish its population and labour supply from outlying areas and to attract expertise and investment from abroad, and its growing share and dominance of an otherwise declining wool trade, the capital was able to recover and prosper like no other English town or city. It was in any case as much as ten times larger than its nearest competitor. The likes of Bristol, York, Norwich, Coventry, Hull, Newcastle or Southampton can hardly be described as London's 'rivals'. They had their respective pieces of cake and in most instances also recovered well, but essentially these were regional centres, while London's chief imperatives were to dominate the English economy and foreign trade. Wool and cloth provide good examples.

Wool

London's economic recovery was driven in large part by fundamental shifts in both the wool and the cloth trades, by the increasing displacement of foreign merchants, and by a shrinking of geography, notably a consolidation around scale and the ascendancy of the Thames. The transformation that would most closely shape Whittington's career path was the pronounced shift from agriculture to the raising of sheep. This was already in full swing by the time of his birth in 1358–9 and had become the mainstay of the English economy long before his arrival in London a decade or so later. With Gloucestershire's Ryelands on his doorstep, having made his way to London through a Cotswolds in thrall to sheep and taken in the wealth and vitality of the wool towns, he could hardly have had a better starting point for his commercial education.

England was on the cusp of a century or more of transformation which would see landowners compensate for the loss of labour and produce that supported their traditional markets and income by clearing their lands of agriculture and populating them with sheep. England's chief export, and the source of its wealth at the time of the plague, was primarily raw wool for the most part sent for 'finishing' to cloth makers in Flanders. Gradually though, the technology for cloth making used on the Continent was appropriated by English manufacturers, and around mid-century started an export of cloths that would boom over the following decades.[8]

Export of wool had been in decline since the early 1300s, demand from Flanders and Florence had reduced sharply, and the east coast ports of Hull and Boston had been severely hit. In the decade before 1300 the small Lincolnshire town of Boston had exported far more wool than London. Yet, by the third quarter of the 14th century England's better-resourced, more efficient and far more politically and commercially sophisticated capital city was by far the dominant force in what was then, perversely, an ebbing trade. The loss endured by England's traditional wool-exporting centres was London's gain as wealth, investment, acumen and trade concentrated in the south-east.[9] In a savagely depopulated countryside, agriculture gave way to pasture, providing a huge accelerator to the cloth and woollen industry—to London's enormous profit.

'Rents dwindled, land fell waste for want of tenants who used to cultivate it' (Higden) and 'many villages and hamlets were deserted … and never inhabited again'. Consequently, landed incomes fell. The bulging piles of manorial accounts which survive for the period of the Black Death testify to the active land-market and the additional administration caused by the onset of plague. But all too often the administration consists of noting defaults of rent because of plague.[10]

It helped enormously that London was the nation's centre of political and economic power and that England's commercial and military adventures were driven from there. It was this convergence of political, economic and military purpose that accelerated the rerouting and consolidation of the wool trade in London. In part, this decline was a consequence of the hugely successful story of English wool in the previous century, a 'golden goose' for English kings seeking to raise revenue through excessive taxation, draconian export duties, and the restriction of trading routes and by allowing the Staple to erect protectionist barriers that severely narrowed the choice, competition and risk presented by foreign trade.

In 1310–1 England exported 35,509 sacks of wool and barely any cloth; by 1392 this had fallen to 19,000 and by 1448, 25 years after Richard Whittington's death, wool exports had crashed to just 60 per cent of that total, barely 21,000 sacks, of which two-thirds were now cloth. What mattered more to London was share. In 1370, the capital commanded a third of the national wool export. When Henry IV appointed Whittington as collector of the wool custom in 1401, it was more than half and was then exported almost exclusively by wealthy London-based merchant adventurers, among whom he was a leading figure. London not only dominated the Company of the Staple, but its merchants were also pre-eminent in the wider lucrative trading relationships that England enjoyed with the Netherlands, the Italian manufacturing centres of Florence and Milan, and the great ports of Venice and Genoa. This offered new horizons for men like Whittington and his circle: 'The period of decline and stabilisation was the age of the middleman dealer, who grew in importance as peasant farmers took the place of the great demesnes. It was also the age of monopoly, of high taxes and of the English Company of Merchants of the Staple.'[11] The oversight awarded to Whittington, first as collector of the wool custom and then (from 1405) as mayor of the Westminster staple and (from 1406) of the Calais staple, was more than sufficient for him to turn a handsome profit. For Whittington, the far more important 'return' was political, the opportunity to be close to the levers of power. This is consonant with the template established by Edward III, who clearly understood the seduction of influence and the possession of direct access to king and court. Even though, as Eileen Power notes, Parliament was able to assert itself through the wool trade, 'Parliament was rising side by side with the wool trade, and the first appearance of the commons, that is the knights of the shire and the burgesses, was almost contemporaneous with the first specific wool tax.'[12] Whittington was notable in choosing not to immerse himself there, probably concluding that Parliament's power was intermittent, diffused, slow to congeal and remarkably fast to dissipate; there he would have been just one voice among many. It was also a place frequently at odds with England's kings and their advisers. Throughout the course of his career, with the single exception of the parliamentary session of October 1416, Whittington chose instead to assert his influence at 'close quarters' through the mayoralty, through access to the court and through royal lending.

Cloth

During the same period, imports of foreign cloth into England had pared down from 3,302 sacks in 1310–1 to a figure described as 'negligible' in 1447–8.[13] Trade with the principal centres of cloth manufacture in the Low Countries and Italy had virtually come to a standstill as English domestic production displaced them. Yet the circumstances and outcomes of decline would produce in the late 14th and early 15th centuries, the period when Whittington was most active, a transfigurative shift in the structure of the industry and the market. In 1300, it was foreign merchants who dominated the market, shifting English cloth through ports as different and far apart as St Ives, Lynn, Southampton, Newcastle and an already declining Boston. Fifty years later, as the effects of the Black Death lifted, these dispersed and small-scale arrangements were already being superseded. Production, volumes and markets were under threat or in flux, but what London particularly and England generally benefitted from was the rationalising and reorganisation of production at home and seizing market share and control. It was not so much an issue of small or large scale but of increased share achieved through exclusion, rationalisation, capitalisation and highly effective management. This is how London and just a few key centres in England thrived in what would become a declining market. Exports were now largely in the hands of English merchants and had consolidated around the two ports closest to the centres of cloth production, Bristol for the Cotswold trade and Yarmouth for East Anglian worsteds. In London, the foreign merchant prevailed for a time but was on his way out by 1370 and soon displaced by London's own merchant community. Collaboration continued, but control gradually passed to English traders, even in their dealings with the Hanseatic League. Average annual export of English cloths soared in the forty years after the Black Death from 2,000 cloths in the early 1350s to over 40,000 by the early 1390s. The growth in domestic demand also surged, probably doubling during this period. These two sets of circumstances, the capture by London of the lion's share of the declining wool trade and its seizing of a still vibrant and rising cloth trade, are essential in understanding the conditions in which Richard Whittington developed his expertise and his wealth.[14]

The raising and lending of finance and the organisation of trade had also undergone a sea change since the late 1340s. A new wave of ambitious and far-sighted English entrepreneurs and lenders had sailed into the void created by the devastating dispatch and subsequent bankruptcy in 1345 of the Crown's Italian bankers,[15] and were already looking beyond the economic and political limitations of the small guilds and traditional crafts towards merchant adventurism, finance and banking. In the early years of his reign, Edward III had taken a positive view of the Italians, regarding them as accomplished traders and sophisticated investors, likely to strengthen English commerce and shorten the learning curve of London's merchant class. Even more usefully, they had the means and the experience to provide him directly with what he wanted most, loan finance, the facility that would figure so prominently in Whittington's own dealings from the early 1380s with three English kings. The pattern followed the same template of risk and reward that Edward had established fifty years earlier, first with the Italians and, from the mid-1340s until his death in 1377, with a small caucus of English lenders. He had offered the Italians commercial opportunities, freedom to acquire property, and, in the case of the Genoese and Florentines, unpopular rights of domicile. Leading Florentine merchants and bankers were able to secure rights of residence in breach of English statute, impose a lucrative diversion of customs that were due to local offices, and acquire enviable privileges from the king to buy and export wools for an entire year without having to comply with the Ordinance of the Staple. Not surprisingly, such preferential treatment went down badly with London merchants, who denounced the Italians as alien profiteers bent on excluding the English from their own markets and trampling on their domestic rights.

Increasingly fearful that they would lose what they had lent already, the Bardi, their rivals the Peruzzi, and the Acciaiuoli found themselves locked into a spiral of reckless lending, convinced that by pandering to Edward's ever-escalating demands they would somehow stand a better chance of eventual repayment. It was a catastrophic misjudgement. In 1343 Edward III extinguished his enormous debt by simply refusing to honour it and peremptorily expelling the Italians. It was the signal for English merchants and 'bankers' to step into the vacancy at the heart of government. There was no shortage of takers.[16]

11

LONDON'S MERCHANT CLASS

On the eve of the Black Death, the leading figures in Whittington's own fraternity were already embracing a more expansive, diverse capitalism which centred on using the profits of mercery to fuel lending and investment in property and development and in the commissioning and distribution of fine wares from the Continent. Lending to the Crown for both personal and state purposes was now the preserve of English merchants and a handful of extravagantly wealthy bishops. Mercery had ceased to be defined by a singular trade, location or activity and was fast evolving as a 'process' reflecting, better than any other, the integration rather than the separation of investment, risk, manufacture and distribution. Moreover, mercers could offer their services 'at scale'. If in 1348 this 'expansive' outlook was still in its early stages, by 1370 it was being given full rein. It is in the transformations brought about by each of these events—a pronounced shift in the economic and financial order already under way before 1348 and the prodigious 'accelerator' provided by the Black Death itself—that we see the motivation for and the ingredients of Richard Whittington's rise to wealth and influence. 'London was important to the Crown because of its wealth: this is why the relations with the city of London took up a considerable amount of the time both of English kings and of their counsellors. It was not simply convenient for the king to get on with the city of London: it was crucial.'[1]

By 1370 London was once more overcrowded, a combined dynamic of personal and national recovery and of in-migration and economic concentration, but also an outcome of the purgative effect of widescale demolition and redevelopment.[2] Alongside its indigenous shortage of labour, the city found itself short of housing for those who now flocked in seeking employment and shelter. Land and title had been freed up, and there was money and a mindset for development and growth, though they were largely appropriated by a watchful and opportunistic merchant class which recognised quickly that the thirst for good land would push prices through the roof. At the beginning of the 13th century London's merchant class had been relatively small, segmented by guild, and concentrated in the densely packed streets from which each conducted its trade, clustered around the parish churches from which each fraternity or mystery had either evolved or to which each was bound. At this time, the city's merchants, wealthy and impoverished, lived, worked, married, raised their families, prayed, died and were buried within intensely localised confines defined by their craft and their pastoral affinities. Within these parameters and very occasionally outside them, their members were known to or aware of each other. They met at the same taverns and churches, they often combined for work, they sometimes shared the cost of materials, they raised and paid back investment with each other, they collaborated to lay off risk, and they traded property and opportunities. They married their sons and daughters off to their friends and associates within the guild, and supported the ambitions of members who sought political or civic office. Now, a new order was in the making in which wealth and commerce would challenge and then gradually supersede the old dependencies of the landed knights and aristocracy, often by assimilating them through marriage and preferment. London's merchant class was socially aspirational and politically ambitious, flaunting its wealth through what we might term conspicuous consumption. Fashion was the most obvious marker of a desire for greater status and a determination to 'get on'. In turn, this acted as something of a driver for self-fulfilling high-end commerce and manufacture. It also had a political context. In the wider picture of England's trade, economy and taxation, the Sumptuary Laws of 1337 and 1363, either side of the Black Death, were means by which the Crown and its supporters in the City and in the guilds sought to diminish further the role of 'alien' merchants in London's trade and curtail their influence over lending, investment and acquisition of property.[3] These laws can be seen to have issued not only a caution to domestic social climbers that they should 'know their place', but also a warning to foreign merchants to 'leave this place'.

If the 1351 Statute of Labourers[4] had been the blunt end of the English state's effort to beat down economic improvement and reinforce the old order, the Sumptuary Law of 1363 was intended as a scythe to mow down an even more insolent breach of social place, the threatening imitation of their 'betters' by an increasingly wealthy and numerous merchant and artisan class, through fashion, acquisition and consumption. This was regarded as a preposterous infringement of the hallowed ground occupied by the nobility, senior clergy and state officials: a social affront that bore the hallmarks of something far worse, a political incursion on their coveted status, preferments and privileges.

The commercially astute, socially ambitious and politically engaged merchant class had moved quickly in the decade after the Black Death to first stabilise and then expand its economic power, aided by formalising its distinction from the old craft traditions and structures. This had consequences for fashion, for social advancement, and for spending on what the Exchequer might have deemed frivolous ornamentation and self-aggrandisement—and, worse still, at the very moment when its coffers were depleted. The first Sumptuary Law of 1337 had sought to limit the social aspirations of the merchant class by restricting choice and expenditure on goods deemed to be above their station. These were defined as certain luxury cloths, foods, beverages and furnishings. The law was designed to prevent breaches of rank, reinforce existing social hierarchies, sustain class distinctions and strengthen morals. It was also intended to boost the economy by promoting English cloths and manufactures and by restricting the wearing of imported furs. The containment of excessive expenditure on 'fashion' by those deemed unworthy to sport it was essential in imposing the social order. Even knights were instructed not to exceed the accoutrements and furnishings of their rank. However, the sheer momentum of social and economic change had already overtaken the capacity of the 1337 statute to slow it, let alone arrest it. The radicalisations produced by the Black Death simply swept it aside. The Sumptuary Law of 1363 promised a more robust effort to rein in such ambitions and restore the social equilibrium.

This too aimed to control social advancement, restricting the wearing of cloths and fashions of superior design or material. Once again, it claimed that misplaced aspirations would injure the domestic cloth industry. The importation of silk and lace by Lombards and other foreign merchants based in England was forbidden. Mercers were at the heart of the trade and the aspiration. Garments of silk, damask and velvet were deemed beyond the place and the privilege of the commonalty, though often not beyond their means. Nor could they wear manufactures of gold or adorn themselves with rings, chains, buckles and clasps or fine brooches. Wives and children were also deterred from even aspiring to own or display such luxury and ostentation while female servants could wear items only to a limited value. Women were instructed to dress according to the position of their fathers or husbands. The sporting of fur was to be confined to the ladies of knights with a rental estimated above 200 marks a year; the wives of certain craftsmen and yeomen were prohibited from wearing cloth of gold or sable, the statute asserting this as the exclusive preserve of the royal court; cloths of gold and silk of purple were restricted to female members of the royal family; the daughter of an esquire could not wear velvet, satin or ermine; and, at the bottom of the social heap, the wife or daughter of a mere labourer was forbidden to wear clothes beyond a certain price or a girdle garnished with silver. By this means, the city's craftsmen and artisans, many of them drivers of London's prosperity, were alienated from the very goods they produced, prisoners of their own unique skills. This occurred at a moment when London's richest citizens were fuelling demand and driving consumption to match their wealth and social ambition, creating a thriving market for the most desirable goods their money could buy, including the commissioning of enviable homes. Already in the year Richard Whittington arrived in London, the stretch of riverside from Baynard's Castle to the Tower of London had largely been prospected and gobbled up by entrepreneurs and 'developers' who for the most part had made their wealth in London's traditional economy. Merchants were mapping, shaping and buying a stake in London's future, along its principal artery: creating space for warehouses and sites for workshops and industry, bidding for secondary land to house the many people who flocked to London to work its golden river, and, most conspicuously, colonising the very banks of the Thames to erect the grandest houses and episcopal 'inns' that London had yet seen.[5]

Acquisitiveness and extravagance were leavened in part by charitable works, endowments and projects to support the Church and clergy, a guilty acknowledgement perhaps that many among London's merchant community had benefitted from the swingeing impact of plague on the Church. Here too the outcome was transformative. A significant proportion of England's clergy were consumed in 1348 and again in 1361–2. The physical and psychological trauma was all the sharper because it brought with it a spiritual void, perhaps in the certainties its survivors had formerly held, but more so because it simply decimated the middle ranks of the Church, particularly in the countryside, removing much of its quality and dismantling its local command and administrative structure. Plague had far-reaching effects on the confidence of the senior clergy and on the confidence of lay communities in the Church as an institution.[6] In its wake, it left empty churches, abandoned chapels, and a marked deterioration in the quality and performance of those recruited to fill the shoes of the thousands it had lost. Metaphorically and literally, the Church needed to be rebuilt after 1348, and the commercial endeavours and social aspirations of London's wealthiest citizens would play a significant part in its practical reconstruction and its social recovery.

While plague had the effect of cutting down as much as 40 per cent of the capital's population, for many who survived it provided a unique opportunity to reprice the value of their labour. For some who would never have imagined it, this too would bring prosperity and social aspiration. As for those heading into London in the immediate aftermath of the great pestilence, the hastily issued Ordinance of Labourers of 1349 was only partly successful in imposing a return to pre-plague wage levels. The shortage of skilled labour to rebuild and redevelop London, including its many churches, meant that for this purpose wages would and did continue to rise. The ensuing Statute of Labourers of 1351 sought to reimpose the servile order and re-embed social and economic privilege by preventing labourers from 'profiting from plague', but change and disenchantment had already set in and would reach a watershed in the eventful summer of 1381.

The circumstances of and savage response to the Peasants' Revolt stand out in the national conscience as a violent and deeply divisive dismissal of the needs, rights and aspirations of the commons. Yet while much of rural England was still trying to recover its economic stability and direction thirty years after the Black Death, by the early 1380s London had begun to restore its commercial strength, increased its wealth, and further imposed itself as England's economic engine, home and abroad. For the surprising numbers of those who could now afford it, consumption had become a highly visible barometer of prosperity. Ironically, the restraints imposed by Edward III were effectively cast aside by the ostentation favoured by his grandson. While most ordinary Londoners craved bread simply to survive, the privileged and the commercially successful grew more so and acquired ever greater means to remain so. Perhaps most comically this was seen in the appetite for preposterous, eye-catching footwear—the late-14th-century 'winkle-picker'. London's wholly unsuitable streets revelled in the curious spectacle of gilded young men and their elders, whose weight was often too great to take more than ten paces unaided, sporting the continental craze for 'crackows'—sharply pointed footwear stiffened with animal bone that was attached to a string at the knee to raise the elongated toe from the mud and slime below and packed tight with sheep wool to prevent it from curling. Imported from their city of origin in Poland, they were soon copied and turned out by the cord-wainers of Bow Lane, Pancras Lane and Watling Street and in the work-shops of neighbouring All Hallows.

Yet even this fixation was soon surpassed by that for imported skins and furs transmuted into a medieval 'must-have' by the sharp wit and industry of London's skinners. Formerly the preserve of the court and nobility during Richard II's reign, fur became a propeller of wealth-defining fash-ion sought and driven by London's merchant community, by a burgeoning Westminster 'secretariat', and even by members of the high-ranking clergy. The fashion for fur collars and the trimming of fine gowns, muffs and gloves, and softening of caps and hats disregarded all bounds and pre-mium. In the final quarter of the 14th century London boasted a signifi-cant constituency of men and women wealthy and confident enough to dismiss sumptuary restraint and conspicuously willing to stand out from their friends and peers. Workshops and tenements on Budge Row and Cornhill seethed with enterprising trades tirelessly cutting, sewing, stitch-ing, gluing, trimming and polishing some manner of good that required fur. The currency of the skinners was never higher, and they had England's new youthful king to thank for it. Under Richard II the importation of furs, primarily from the Baltic, simply soared. From 1 July to Michaelmas 1384—a matter of just three months—a total of 382,982 skins of Baltic origin were shipped to London mainly by the Hansa, of which 377,200 were squirrel, the rest mostly ermine and beaver. Later, between 1 March and 30 November 1390, the volumes were still high and the origins and proportions similar: of 310,035 skins of Baltic origin, 306,900 were squir-rel, the rest beaver, ermine and snow weasel; just 13,589 skins were imported from elsewhere.[7]

Competitors, 1393

London's economic performance cannot be assessed in isolation from that of its European neighbours, whose own pace and strength in working through the trauma of the Black Death presented both gains and deficits to the city's trading ambitions. National and local recovery depended on how individual nations and their leading manufacturing and trading centres responded to the Black Death's impact on their industry, suppliers, com-petitors and, in some instances, adversaries. London's performance is instructive. Despite its early-century growth and its partial recoveries after the plagues of 1348 and 1361–2, by 1370 the city's population still fell well short of the leading cities on the European mainland. Florence, for example, was already one of the five largest cities in Europe by 1300 with an economy and population inflated by the manufacture of woollen cloth and by an extraordinarily wealthy and far-reaching banking sector that had also embedded itself firmly in London. By the third quarter of the 14th century, it was arguably the leading centre of European culture, the intellectual and artistic hub of the Continent at large. The city's promotion of humanism and an indefatigable belief that man himself was the measure of all achievement had, like its commerce and banking, infiltrated the mercantile economy and lifestyle of England's largest city. Just across the Channel, England's great adversary, France, also promoted the confidence and glory of its principal city, assured that, despite the ravages of almost continuous war, the territorial incursions of successive English kings, and the rapacious commercial energy of London, it was the inhabitants of Paris still 'who could, with some justification, look upon their city as the greatest in Christendom'.[8]

A quarter-century later, Venice was reaching the zenith of her power. Londoners were well aware of the Italian city's own claim to be the greatest trading nation on earth, her commercial prowess evidenced by her enormous galleys berthed at Galley Quay that traded refined luxury wool brought in from Spain alongside more customary items such as canvas, silk, fustian, felts and fine pelts. During the 13th century, Galley Quay's length and its proximity to the Tower of London had established it as the favoured anchorage for Venetian shipping and for foreign merchants trading exotic spices, fine silks and sweet sugar for England's own precious commodity—raw wool—to which the Venetians had become proficient in 'adding value' by selling it on to the cloth-manufacturing centres of Milan and Florence. In turn, this extraordinary demand for wool and its flip trade in fine goods created an added value for London itself in the development of port infrastructure. In his enthralling account of the history of the Thames Peter Ackroyd notes that

> There was so much trade that in the fourteenth and fifteenth centuries major centres for ship-building and ship-repairing were established at Shadwell, Rotherhithe and Deptford—in which quarters they remained for four hundred years … The presence of these docks meant in turn that the riverside became populated by tradesmen such as coopers and sail-makers who joined the porters and labourers in acquiring their income directly from the Thames.[9]

Trade with Venice was central to London's growth in the late 13th century, to its recovery in the second half of the 14th century, and to its durability in the first quarter of the 15th. Here, after all, was another city ravaged by the Black Death which had rebuilt not only its population but also its buildings and infrastructure and which had fired up its mercantile economy. An exuberant and outward-looking city, Venice had accumulated vast corporate and individual wealth that it put to highly efficient use— both political and economic—at home and abroad, and London was a favoured destination for both. While London's prosperity was closely bound to its great river, the horizons of Venice were far wider. As John Julius Norwich puts it, she 'belonged to the sea'—the 'Mistress of the Mediterranean'. Norwich tells us that by 1400 Venice was the greatest seafaring force in Europe with an estimated 3,300 vessels and 36,000 sailors, assuring her exceptional authority and safeguarding her trade in both domestic and foreign waters.[10] Yet this was just one part of her merits. To her wealth, infrastructure and commercial nous she brought something that no other leading European city could offer, a unique access to the luxury goods of the eastern Mediterranean, craved by North European consumers, and for which they would pay a premium. By then, London had become a primary centre for demand and its merchants, among them a far-sighted Richard Whittington, saw extravagant opportunities for trade and collaboration with their Venetian counterparts. Meanwhile, in the colder waters and less travelled outreaches of the far North, a spirited and often precarious expansionism would also bear positively on London, further diversifying its economy and sharpening its appetite for investment and risk. London's association with what became the Hanseatic League had extended well over a century by the time Whittington had first sight of the city. In 1266 Henry III had granted the German 'Hansa' of Lübeck and Hamburg a charter to establish their business in England, and in 1282 their counterparts from Cologne arrived to form the most powerful, and arguably the most far-reaching, overseas trading colony in London. Developing and trading as a loose coalition of commercial centres, at its height the Hanseatic League eventually encompassed as many as 170 towns and cities across a huge arc of northern Europe. It fell to Henry's son Edward I to take the relationship to the next level. In the so-called Carta Mercatoria of 1303, Edward offered a raft of tax and customs concessions to the Germans to help galvanise England's trading position in return for their establishing a formal presence on the Thames.[11] London was acknowledged as a 'kontor city' but was not awarded status as a full member.

Trading from a fort-like community on Ironbridge Wharf, with its own warehousing, church, weighing house and tenements and 'known as the Steelyard after the beam used for weighing merchandise', the Hansa shipped grain, timber, furs and flax from Russia and Poland to the lowland ports of Flanders and the Scheldt into London and exported English wool, cloth and other manufactured goods eastward.[12] Half a century later, the establishment in 1356 of semi-regular meetings of the League centred on Lübeck gave further impetus to its expansion into Poland, Gotland, Russia and Norway, extending and connecting Europe's markets ever further afield and, like the Venetians, evolving strong defences against piracy. London's merchant community was exceptionally placed to benefit, both as traders and investors, from this commercial colonisation of the North.[13]

London's domestic control of English manufacture and commerce meant that everything else was taken care of. Domestic marketing and distribution fell increasingly to London's own merchants working hand in hand. So much so, as John Clapham explains, that the Hansa 'did not then travel about the country. Instead, they sat close in their walled "factory" by the Thames, the Steelyard ... and if they retailed Rhenish wine it was a grievance. The London vintners would see to distribution and sale.'[14] In this, London's 'adventurers' were far more powerful and self-determining than their much smaller counterparts in the north of England where the Hansa remained strongly embedded and where it was able to keep local entrepreneurs more in check and more subordinated to the League's own interests. 'The Hansards, with their control of the northern continental markets, and privileges won from the English Crown, had kept down "adventuring" in cloth from the northern ports of England in the fourteenth and fifteenth centuries.'[15] This contrasted sharply with the League's experience in England's capital in the later 14th and 15th centuries when 'the Londoners fought them; concentrated their business on the Netherlands, when Antwerp, rising into its short-lived commercial splendour, became an excellent market' and later under Edward IV (1442–83) 'not only shipped more broadcloth from London than all foreigners, including the Hansards, put together, but approximately as much as all the other ports of England'.[16] In his work on 'London's triumph', Stephen Alford speaks of a prior contentment for centuries among the city's merchants to confine the limits of their trade to the Low Countries, France and the Baltic and notes that it was not until 1620 that 'their ambitions were without limit', demonstrated by a trading nexus that by then would embrace Russia, Persia, the far-eastern Mediterranean, Africa, the colonies in North America and even Japan.[17]

However, this diminishes evidence that the template for this great flourishing of global trade had begun to be forged two centuries earlier and overlooks London's significant Italian trade. Despite the limitations of their vessels, the constraints imposed by the Hundred Years War, the constant threat of piracy, and the vagaries of both marine and terrestrial cartography, by the beginning of the 15th century London's merchant adventurers had long-established and far-reaching geographical and supply chain partnerships with Iberian and Italian traders through the great seafaring entrepôts of Genoa and Venice, which in turn fostered intermediary trade with the ports of southern and eastern Spain, the Levant and China. In northern Europe, London's extensive relationships through the Steelyard and the wider Hanseatic League had by 1420 already opened routes (which Whittington himself may well have invested in) that enabled London to capture trade as far afield as Russia, Poland and northern Scandinavia. Indeed, 30 years earlier, and 235 years before the accession of Charles I, it was Richard II in 1390 who had seen the opportunities for encouraging and extending England's foreign trade in the first of the Navigation Laws, designed to ensure that all imported and exported goods were carried in English ships. It was an attempt to widen London's trading horizons and to strengthen the domestic shipbuilding industry centred on the Thames. While it may be true that in the mid-14th century London was 'a modest satellite of a European system of international trade whose weight was settled firmly in the middle of the continent',[18] by its close and the completion of the first quarter of the next its trading outlook and position were far more adventurous and internationalist. There is a powerful echo of Whittington's London in Alford's observation that the city's alternating accommodation of and raw hostility to immigrants would prove to be a continuing characteristic of its growing economy during its next period of expansion, noting that, while 'London had in the sixteenth century an impressive ability to absorb new arrivals into its social fabric' and that 'ordinary Londoners had to come to terms with outsiders who threatened their livelihoods', at times Elizabethan London 'crackled with hostility and threatened violence'.[19] Two centuries earlier, London could be similarly threatening, both to impoverished immigrants and to its wealthy and cultured alien merchant community. Indeed, it was the seafaring Venetians and Genoese who were most frequently on the receiving end of a general distrust and dislike of foreigners that at times spilled over into outright racism, casual violence and, in a few instances, premeditated murder.

12

MERCERS

This Company, in former times, consisted chiefly of such as sold rich Silks brought from Italy, and who lived, for the most part in Cheapside, St Laurence-Jewry, and the Old-Jewry; afterwards the Mercers were generally Merchants. (Robert Seymour, 1735)[1]

By 1327 the power and prosperity of the city's guilds had grown to such a level that the City was able to press Edward III, a boy of fifteen in his first year as king, to concede a charter, as much anti-foreigner in its purpose and spirit as it was protectionist. This required alien merchants to sell their goods within 40 days and to lodge with English hosts so that their activities could be observed and their efforts to acquire property made known and frequently thwarted. Apparently, the young king never forgot the overbearing attitude of the City, and by 1335 he was confident enough to make clear his need of foreigners and his determination to 'import' them. He welcomed their trade, valued their enterprise, and actively sought their willingness to lend to the Crown in return for commercial and social concessions. Their freedoms were restored and underlined again in the renewal of the statute in 1351, yet anti-foreigner sentiment would persist throughout the entire course of Edward's reign, driven by accusations that aliens were leaching English trade, subverting London's prosperity, and appropriating valuable land and buildings. For some they were little more than spies. In 1369 the mistrust of Flemish merchants was so pronounced that Edward was obliged to issue a royal proclamation intended to protect them from a rising tide of verbal and physical assault. Their grip on London's trade was also threatening the ways and means of the city's ancient and highly protective guilds. In 1376, the year before his death, the contempt and revolt broke through into the proceedings of the Good Parliament.[2]

The guild system was already thirty years down the path of an irreversible reconstruction by the time Whittington arrived in London around 1369–70. The polarisation of the traditional guilds and the new companies was consolidated further during the last quarter of the 14th century and the first quarter of the 15th.[3] London provided an intensely competitive stage for the emergence of a powerful and wealthy 'merchant-craftsman' who looked beyond the financial, production and geographical limitations of those who had traditionally made and sold a narrow range of products on their own doorstep. While these developments were the natural and predictable outcomes of a need for both scale and specialisation in the economy, they were given formal impetus by the overbearing and often frantic needs of successive English kings for loans and revenue raising. The award of a royal charter became both an incentive and a reward for trades who saw early the commercial and political value of their 'corporatisation' as companies. By the third quarter of the century many of the old guilds had either been pushed aside or subsided in favour of intricate livery companies layered with restrictive rites of membership and exclusions based on levels of wealth and influence far beyond the means of a traditional craftsman. Affirmatory 'gatekeeping' devices such as expensive ornate livery were intended to ensure that the new companies would confine and prosper as professional oligarchies.[4] The Fishmongers had been among the first of London's guilds to receive a royal charter in 1272. The Armourers' Company and Founders' Company followed in 1324. However, it was Edward III, ever mindful of the limitations of his Exchequer, who gave active and open encouragement to a wave of new livery companies in London.[5] At the start of his reign in 1327 royal charters were conferred upon the goldsmiths and the grandly named Guild and Fraternity of St John the Baptist in the City of London (later the Merchant Taylors). The vintners would secure their charter in 1363 and the drapers in 1364. Though arguably pre-eminent among London's companies by the close of Edward's reign in 1377, the mercers would have to await their royal charter until 1394. Richard Whittington would have an active part in securing its conferment.[6]

The Mayoralty

The pursuit by the guilds and companies of the great civic prize, London's mayoralty, was also transforming as Whittington arrived in the city, becoming far more focused, contrived and competitive as the opportunities and influence associated with the office multiplied and strengthened. This was hardly surprising as London's mayor enjoyed in his own right authority over a wide range of regulatory powers as well as serving as the principal instrument of the Crown in its efforts to govern, intervene in or interfere in the affairs of the City. He could issue precepts on the part of the king without reference to the 24 aldermen or the Common Council. Formally at least, the mayor had the last word in disputes between London's rival companies and presided over the revision of their regulations and ordinances. Consequently, by the mid-1370s the candidates for the mayoralty were more numerous and more ambitious and their constituencies better resourced and organised than ever before. The guilds were also more politicised and more aggressive in their efforts to place their man and their trade at London's helm.[7] The mayoralty had long been an expression of London's wealth and commercial importance, but now, with Edward's health failing and the prospect of a young and inexperienced successor in the wings and with England increasingly listless, there was a growing confidence in both the mayor's and the City's potential to influence not only the course of London's governance but wider matters of state. Driving this prosperity and exerting a demand for greater political and fiscal influence was a powerful, affluent and progressively self-confident merchant class which was successfully transitioning into banking, investment and merchant adventurer capitalism. Wool remained hugely important but not simply for its own sake. It had become a vehicle for drawing the profits necessary to invest elsewhere, in other commodities, in land and development, or to furnish the loans that would enable London's merchants to buy their way into the king's favour, secure attractive sinecures, and trade cash for opportunities that would bring them social status and further commercial gain.

London's merchant class not only exercised an influence that was economic, social and political but now expected to do so, and this would bring it into regular conflicts and stand-offs with England's next three kings. For much of the next fifty years this at times volatile relationship alternated between courtship and enmity. Yet one thing was clear: the prosperity of this class and of London itself was essential to the Crown's military and territorial ambitions. Mercers were at the heart of this relationship, for good or for ill.

Mercers

Mercery had originated as a generally itinerant business associated chiefly with those who produced relatively low-grade goods in their workshops and sold what they could locally, but also toured and traded at the great regional fairs, carrying and hawking their wares from their beasts or off their backs. Later generations of mercers would invest great effort, expense and elaborate forms of cultural and financial exclusion in rejecting and renouncing any hint of association with what they regarded as the inferior and unseemly business of 'pedlary'. Their name and trade are held to derive from the French *mercier* and before that from the Latin *mercator*. Historically, trade had been separated into two main divisions, the 'staple' and the 'miscellaneous', the latter developing as mercery. In the 19th century the archivist and publisher John Gough Nichols claimed the name derived from *merces*, the plural of *merx*, a Latin word signifying *any* kind of ware or merchandise which was brought to market. However, it is evident that by the middle of the 12th century, whether he traded from his own doorstep or hiked and hawked his way to the country fair, the mercer's business was already established as that which promoted the trade of linen, raw silks and other cloths.[8]

Nor were mercers disparate individuals with few bonds, lacking wider purpose and embarking on a precarious, fragmented trade. By the early 1100s they were already organising themselves to become more concerted and more efficient. Like other London guilds, they spoke of themselves as a 'fraternity' bound by common interest and their attachment to their favourite saint. Consolidation was ensured by their geographical concentration. In the reign of Henry II, we find the workshops and stalls of London's mercers congregated in an area close to 'the Chepe' market, between Friday Street and Bow Church, a place defined and known as 'the mercery'. 'The Mercers had existed from the reign of Henry II, receiving their charter from Richard II. At first they were general dealers in linen, haberdashery, and imported goods; later they specialised in fine textiles. Their first London site was on the north of Cheapside, where their hall was later built.'[9]

London Mercers

Around 1190 Thomas, the son of Theobald de Helles, and his wife Agnes, sister to Archbishop Thomas à Becket (1120–70), granted to the master and brethren of the Hospital of St Thomas the Martyr of Acon a piece of land formerly owned by Becket's father Gilbert, himself a mercer by trade.[10] It was here thirty years later that a monastic order founded in the Holy Land and dedicated to Becket established the Hospital of St Thomas of Acon. Stow also reports that during his own lifetime it was well established along with St Paul's as a notable free school.[11] Writing in 1892, Sir John Watney tells us that a copy of this grant is recorded in the Mercers' Company's 'register of writings' and makes clear that 'the fraternity of Mercers were constituted patrons of the hospital'. He presents it as the first record in existence of the association which afterwards became the Mercers' Company.[12]

The association between the hospital and the mercers continued until the Reformation and, in Watney's words, formed 'a good example of the connection of secular guilds and ecclesiastical foundations in the middle ages', secular guilds being established for the promotion of trade and alms deeds, and ecclesiastical foundations for devotion and alms deeds.[13] Until their incorporation in 1394, and for some time after, the mercers continued to attend the parish church of the Hospital of St Thomas of Acon, adjourning for business in an adjoining hall. The wardens' accounts refer to a meeting in 1390—which Richard Whittington would have attended—when an assembly was held 'en la sale de Seynt Thomas a Acres' at which the wardens were chosen, and the previous year's accounts were scrutinised and signed off. Watney reports that meetings of the company were also convened at the aptly named 'Prince's Wardrobe', a tavern in Old Jewry. After the granting of their charter and still lacking a hall of their own, the newly 'incorporated' Mercers' Company continued to meet in a room at the hospital or at the church. In 1413 the company purchased from the hospital a modest room and chapel which became known as the 'Sale del Mercerie' or Mercers' Hall. Watney writes that the Church of St Thomas of Acon was held in great esteem by other fraternities and by ordinary Londoners at large. For many, it was outranked in importance only by St Paul's itself. Whittington would have witnessed and later participated in some of the frequent torch-lit processions held by the city's fraternities, their members and the civic dignitaries who led them, clothed head to toe in the elaborate liveries that identified their company or marked their office.

In his *Survey of London* written 400 years after Henry II's death, Stow offers an imaginative reconstruction of the south side of Cheap ward, describing 'a great conduit westward' in which there 'were many fair and large houses, for the most part possessed by Mercers up to the corner of Bow Lane'. These houses, he adds, 'in former times were but sheds or shops with solars [upper chambers] over them.'[14] A more contemporary reference to the trade is found in a property deed of 1235, which records a gift made to the priory of Haliwell by Serlo le Mercer, who served as London's mayor in 1214 and then for four further terms between 1217 and 1221. This forms the basis for Stow's later certainty about the location of mercery trading in London since it alludes by name to an area known as 'the mercery' in the parish of St Mary-le-Bow, a space which then hosted shops, stalls, workshops and tenements associated with those engaged in the trade, though it also accommodated an assortment of drapers, goldsmiths, grocers and other merchandisers.

Less than a century later the term meant something altogether different; the 'mercer' now presented himself as an outward-looking entrepreneur searching for and commanding new markets both for supply and sale and on a much greater scale. He had evolved as

> very clearly, the true merchant type—the man who may go overseas, like Aelfric's merchant, taking miscellaneous cargoes out and bringing others in; who, whether he goes overseas or not, is ready to trade wherever he sees chance of gain and in any commodity that will give him a profit; whose main chance of profit—always a mystery and a sinful mystery to the medieval mind—lies in the different values that men living far apart may attach to articles of commerce.[15]

This reference to trading overseas is of great significance as the mercer was also seen as a bulwark against commercial incursion by alien merchants. A lawsuit of 1304 documents the successful defence of the mercer's trade against foreign interests and effectively identifies and entwines his business with the freedoms of the City of London itself. Here, at the beginning of the 14th century, mercers are described as a 'commonalty', a like-minded group bound by shared interest and some degree of organisation. The association that would be incorporated ninety years later under royal charter as the Mercers' Company was originally a trade guild, and much of its ethos, structure and regulatory framework can be traced to the early medieval period when men and women working in the same crafts or trades combined in informal associations or fraternities for mutual benefit and protection. In return for an oath or pledge and a modest fee, the guild looked after its members and their families if they fell on hard times. It paid for their funerals and might have represented members in legal actions and in the settlement of trade disputes. Initially, these fraternities or 'misteries' conducted their business in the churches, monasteries or hospitals—St Thomas of Acon offering a fine example—to which they had formed their original attachments, contributing, in turn, with the good works and endowments, initially 'privately' driven and family-based, that would burgeon from the early 14th century and give rise to the more public-spirited, 'civic' endeavours that Richard Whittington is associated with. Dinners and feasts were originally held in private homes or in favoured taverns until, in the 15th and 16th centuries, they invested their wealth in the fine purpose-built halls which proclaimed their status as the city's great livery companies. Whereas the term 'mercer' had formerly described an itinerant conveyor of cheap cloths or a shopkeeper dealing in small wares, from the early 1300s we find his role and his status elevated. He is now more widely regarded as a 'trader' or distributor, operating on a much greater scale and with goods of higher worth. His horizons have also widened, and he is as likely to import from Italy as he is to export from Yorkshire or East Anglia.

On the eve of the Black Death, London's mercers were associated chiefly with the export of English woollen cloths and their principal imports were the finest Flemish silks and linens and the even more rarefied luxury products of the great Italian cloth centres. Even so, the trading interests and the goods offered by the mercer were relatively fluid. There was certainly no obligation to confine himself to 'mercery'—though most chiefly handled textile goods, often as exporters. Nor was there a rigid division between wholesale and retail trading even though, as Stow puts it, 'the great men of the Companies were usually wholesalers'.[16]

The ordinances of the Mercers' Company provided for the election of four members each year to govern it and stipulated that its members should dine together once a year. If any member should be ruined by wrongdoing, by loss at sea, through loss from debtors or from bodily weakness and could not earn a living, the company would provide alms to alleviate hardship. The ordinances of 1348 laid out the fees to be paid to the company for the privilege of apprenticeship, specifying that 'no one should take on an apprentice who has carried packs around the country and been one of those called peddlars, nor one who is the son of a villein'.[17]

* * *

Anne Sutton has written that 'If the Mercers of London had a golden age, it was the fifteenth century: they had a continuous run of prosperity, more aldermen and mayors than ever before ... and a higher proportion of well-off men'.[18] Yet, what is striking is that the first half of the century was a period when the English and London economies were in retreat. Despite this, mercers—among them the most prominent of all, Richard Whittington himself—continued to prosper, to create exceptional wealth, to excel in business, dominate civic affairs, promote social reform and endow good works, to extend their influence at Westminster and in the Guildhall, and to consolidate the Mercers' Company as London's pre-eminent trade body. Perhaps there was simply something intrinsically enterprising about mercery and about the practitioners it attracted that enabled it to prosper corporately and individually in a way that eluded the other great companies and trades of the day. Was this an outcome of the type and background of the candidates that mercers selected for apprenticeship, did it lie in the quality and rigour of their training, or was it derived from the compass and commercial foresight of their financial interests or their agility in spotting and exploiting opportunities before their competitors? Or was it something entirely different, something more philosophical rooted in their *raison d'être*, something which infused commerce with a high social morality and an unshakeable self-confidence that in promoting enterprise they were also doing God's work? Was the reward for endeavour on earth the assurance of a secure and peaceful afterlife? Certainly, most other trades believed this, and the mercers had their fair share of the corrupt and the criminal, but if the mercers were held to be the pinnacle of London's companies, then what set them apart? The answer may lie in 'vision'. Mercers understood that business was changing; that as wealth increased the demand for luxury goods would percolate downwards and then enlarge; that far from being a brake on ostentation and conspicuous consumption, the Sumptuary Laws had simply advertised and amplified how demand was changing and would continue to evolve and grow. Collectively, individually and in their 'partnering' with foreign merchants and other trades, mercers recognised that the horse had already bolted. There were now two lucrative markets for luxury goods, the rarefied demand produced by king and court and the much larger demand exerted by the wider nobility and a spendthrift merchant class consumed by consumption.

Merchant Adventurers

Towards the end of the 13th century, sometime around 1280, there emerged another trading force that shared many commonalities with mercery and included within its ranks leading mercers. English merchant adventurers had their origins in the trade with the Low Countries and with Brabant in particular. Their chief métier was overseas trade and shipping. Many within their ranks chose to settle in the centres they traded from. It was natural that they should develop a close association with London's mercer community, and their spiritual common ground is evident in their initial assembly as the Fraternity of St Thomas à Becket of Canterbury. Their arrival was formalised by a royal charter from Edward I sometime between 1296 and 1300. Anne Sutton points to an overlap in the membership of the two fraternities and to the ascent from the early 1400s of London mercers to an increasingly dominant position within the merchant adventurer community trading with the Low Countries. In doing so, she refutes the view that the Company of the Merchant Adventurers of England was created much later, at the end of the 15th century.[19]

Stephen Alford has described the Company of Merchant Adventurers as looking out for the interests of English merchants and says that 'by the fifteenth century this powerful organisation was dominated by London's mercers'.[20] The mutual self-interest of Antwerp and London traders turned on the former's need for English cloth while English merchants relied on Antwerp for its market, for its networks, and for the investment and distribution services that in turn assured their wealth. The English presence was a far cry from the type of permanent and formidable trading outpost that Cologne merchants had established in the Steelyard in London, but they were by 1400 a notable feature of Antwerp's commercial districts, some taking permanent residence there, some passing through on a regular basis, and many more increasingly drawn by the city's sheer energy and the benefits of its financial infrastructure. Indeed, by the early 1400s the English had reversed the traditional position in which foreign merchants had established themselves in London by installing a remunerated 'governor' in Antwerp to promote and oversee their continental interests.[21]

A free-standing body, they neither originated from nor developed as a specialised interest group within the Mercers' Company but emerged instead as an independent and functional response to the demands of England's burgeoning foreign trade. Nor were mercers the only influence, for the membership was drawn from a wide catchment of traders, investors and shippers, reflecting the increasing complexities, specialisation and opportunities associated with England's trade overseas. The merchant adventurers developed particularly close ties with the Merchants of the Staple during the latter part of the 14th and throughout the 15th century, and this may explain why for a time Richard Whittington was or was perceived to be one of their number. As mayor of the staple at both Calais and Westminster, he would almost certainly have been an influential figure within both companies. One of Whittington's own apprentices, William Cavendish of Suffolk, admitted to the Mercers' Company in 1403, provides an example of someone who straddled both groups and who leaned increasingly to overseas trade as a merchant adventurer. During the latter part of the 14th century and throughout the century that followed, the Mercers' Company gradually yielded the conduct of foreign trade to, first, the Company of the Merchants of the Staple and then to the merchant adventurers while at home the domestic trade in woollen cloth was substantially in the hands of the drapers by the early 1400s.

13

POLLUTION

Shifts in the organisation, scale and rewards of trade in favour of the few were accompanied inevitably by less happy outcomes for the many. An increase in the volume and velocity of manufacturing and industry in London during the 14th century produced a challenge for its leaders and citizens more typically associated with our own age—pollution.[1] Attempts by the City to staunch London's literal tide of filth were largely futile, ignored, mocked and abused by man and beast alike. Whittington may have been forgiven for thinking that some of its practices were more typical of the rural areas he had left behind.

> For all its pride, its magnificence, and its bustling activity, Chaucer's London still retained some of the characteristics of a country town ... It seems likely that only the proximity of the open countryside can have saved from deadly disease the closely packed inhabitants of a town where open channels for liquid refuse ran through the streets into the streams and ditches, where pigs rooted in the garbage, where butchers slaughtered their beasts in Fleet Street and lepers were often found wandering at large.[2]

No sooner had one stretch of Walbrook been cleared and its foul contents deposited in carts than Londoners resumed their disregard of good health and their disdain for good order and simply refilled the void. A visitor or newcomer unaware of the hygiene practices in the streets around the once free-flowing Walbrook and Fleet might have found themselves having to dodge the feculence and slosh hurled from upstairs windows into the streets and ditches below. Into this putrid slick and slime pigs dipped their snouts, dogs scooped their paws, and geese and fowl pecked at the residue of slop and scurf that overlapped the side of the ditches on market days. When the rain fell, it swelled the contents, returning the bloated mess almost back to the very doors and openings from which it originated. Amid this fetid mire, people somehow went about their business, some having done it in the ditches in the first place. They would press on, navigating carefully or disregarding their steps entirely, as if the wall of noise they generated somehow insulated them from the ordure at their feet, the catch in their throat, and the pall in the air. A young apprentice, unfamiliar with the territory, carrying goods and messages, fetching orders and inventories, had to gather his senses, step gingerly through, and keep his eyes peeled while his ears thrummed with London's din. The city's markets must surely have been the most difficult to negotiate, as you had to keep your wits and feet in alignment amid the cacophony of sale and purchase, commerce and manufacture, begging and giving, wailing and shouting, bargaining and settling, befouling and cleansing, and the inexhaustible handling, lifting and setting down of goods, produce and people. These frantic days were also marked by common courtesy and by acts of uncommon generosity, by boundless interventions and unfathomable argument, and occasionally by dark threats and spontaneous retribution. For the most part, the ordinary citizens of London—heads down, purpose set—would hardly have seemed to notice the corruption hurled from above or lying at their feet.

* * *

Coal

The tumult of commerce and industry, the stink and press of the population, and the diverting scale of London's household debris would have been an immense contrast to what Whittington had known at Newent or Gloucester. Yet this was not the only pollution affecting the city. While its citizens may have resigned themselves to necessity and to the pitfalls of household debris, London was both mesmerised and afflicted by a more toxic and invidious pollutant—coal. The manufacturing and financial attractions of a 'miracle fuel' that could energise industry for days on end and at lower cost were at first exhilarating. By 1300, imports of coal from Tyneside had become an established requirement of London's metal-casting industry.[3] Driven by a combination of military, domestic and commercial demand, the city's foundries and workshops had become increasingly reliant on its intense sustaining heat. Its 'benefits' were soon in question, however. Coal's toxic effects, smoke, ash and poisonous residues, were so concerning they had become a cause of significant social unrest. So much so that in 1306 Edward I was obliged to issue a royal proclamation prohibiting the use of sea coal in the city's furnaces, and for a time London's foundries and smithies reverted to wood and charcoal.

> Henry III had granted a charter to the town of Newcastle, by which the inhabitants were impowered to dig coal; which is the first occasion on which coals are mentioned in England. Those professions which required large fires, as dyers, brewers, &c. began now to use coal in London; of which the nobility and gentry complained to the king, as being a public nuisance: this produced a severe proclamation against the use of sea coals, under certain penalties.[4]

By mid-century the tide had turned, and the very citizens who had railed against its use were now coal's most vociferous market, demanding it for cooking and heating. It was cheap, plentiful, and burned stronger and for longer. It helped too that Edward III now championed the merits of London's trade with the north-east, apparently favouring use of the magical fuel in his own quarters. With a war to fight and an army to supply, Tyneside coal was soon on its way to support his military endeavours at Calais. By 1370 its merits were established, and its trade regulated. It had earned the approval of City, commonalty and court.[5]

> Edward III licensed the men of Newcastle to dig for coal outside the walls and, in ordering the miners of Gateshead his special protection in 1368, expressed the view that it would be valuable to have coal taken to all parts of the kingdom. Coal was still mainly used for smith's work; but with the increase of chimneys towards the end of the century it was beginning to be burned in private houses also.[6]

Demand for coal had a marked impact on the Thames, creating and driving a market for strips of ugly, nondescript, cheaply bought riverbank, perfect for mucky coal and for the even grimier industries that would follow. This would accelerate sharply during Whittington's time in London, and many of his guild and among his own associates invested in the opportunities it generated. As industry boomed on the back of cheap fuel, the demand for coal was thought to be insatiable. The 'cats' that brought it in required more quay space and this drove the acquisition of adjoining land for wider development. The need for new wharves and jetties to unload the cargo was obvious to anyone, but the real prize lay in serving the needs of the enterprises that would clamour to be nearby. Where there's muck there's brass, one might say. Workshops, timber yards, land for maintenance and repair, sites for foundries, riverside plots for warehousing and storage, fields for stabling: the uses and opportunities seemed endless.

So relentless was this trade and its infiltration of London's life that the Corporation finally appointed four officials to 'meter' the coal. Rather than measuring its deleterious impact on people and buildings, its threats to existing livelihoods and the enterprises and communities it displaced, the Exchequer saw in it an unimaginable bonanza—a windfall opportunity for extracting new revenue; one which also brought economic benefits to the north of the kingdom. Meanwhile the streets below Lothbury, notorious for the screeching of metal and their interminable clangour, were made even more objectionable by the viscosity of inferior coal burning in numerous tiny foundries. By the time Whittington had completed his apprenticeship, the Corporation saw these streets as the heart of London's industry and the workshop of England. London needed to *manufacture*, not simply to trade.

However, just as there had been consequences in the early years of the century, so there were repercussions on the eve of Whittington's arrival in London, angrily wrapped in an edict from Edward III in 1369 to put an end to the slaughtering of large animals within the city walls, partly for the carnage left to rot in the streets by London's butchers but chiefly for the selling of meat polluted by acrid soot from London's innumerable hearths and fires. Until then a multitude of beasts had been led through the city each week to be butchered and skinned in the lanes adjoining the markets.[7] It was not just the drovers and the butchers whose noses were put out of joint. As London industrialised, its citizens and its Corporation found there was a price to pay for progress. The arrival of coal, and the recognition that it had become an unhealthy and unwelcome pollutant, also proved to be a serious inconvenience for skinners and pelterers whose own trade depended on the butchering of livestock. They, too, had to remove their activities to the outskirts of the city. London's households, who formed a large part of the problem, would now have to journey to the slaughter grounds at Bow and Knightsbridge to procure the freshest and cleanest meat. Later, in 1391, during Richard II's reign, it was the turn of the nobility, the higher clergy and the wealthy merchants who had accumulated in the grand properties that had sprung up in the north-west of the city to rebel against the mind-numbing butchering of beasts on Holborn Bridge. Finally, in 1393 a deeply insanitary but evidently plausible solution was achieved: the butchers would cut up their offal and deposit it midstream into the Thames from boats.[8]

On this much-abused river the arrival and clustering of the shallow 'cats' that transported the coal was having a quite different effect. They were taking up space and impeding the fast work of the wherries and the lightermen that made short journeys darting between the cogs anchored midstream, moving their cargo bit by bit to the nearest quay or jetty. Boatmen complained that the congestion was forcing them to take chances in plying their own ancient trade. When approaching London Bridge, the prudent had usually taken the wider, slower channel under the drawbridge to avoid the rapids that rinsed and boiled around the huge stone piles and timber 'starlings' that supported the structure. Now they were forced beyond the safety of the 'pool' and found themselves pushed mid-river, ever closer to the swirling current and rocks. At their traditional berths the coal was scooped up relentlessly by a forest of treadwheels and cranes powered by windlasses. London's industry and its landscape had moved on.

While coal became indispensable to many forms of manufacturing and production, an angry revolt was building in the city's grander quarters along Cornhill, among the stallholders on East Cheap and Poultry and within emporia that sold finer goods in the Stocks. Shops and stallholders complained that customers were deterred by the residue of soot that descended on their goods. Trade was falling away, revenue had shrunk, and taxation would be leaner, harder and therefore harsher to raise. Affluent households resumed long-standing traditions, the use for example of sweet-smelling applewood that gave off a light aromatic smoke with little spitting. Although useful for scenting the air, it was wholly impractical as it burned down quickly, as did the birch used to rekindle its ash. Even thorn and yew, pleasant as they were, could not compete with the enduring heat of coal. Eventually, even these households simply chose to 'lump' it, and with good reason; after all, it was they who profited most from the economic and investment opportunities coal brought in its unpleasant but lucrative wake.

Nowhere was coal in greater demand or used on such scale or with more purposeful results than in the street celebrated for its metalware. Lothbury was an endless source of fascination for most Londoners.[9] It was a place of mild terror which belched smoke, radiated intense heat, volleyed frightful showers of sparks, and launched spumes of hot ash that alarmed the mindful and bewitched the adventurous. Here the ear-splitting din of metal crashing and clanging on metal never relented. This was how it got its name, 'Lothbury', a corruption of 'loathsome', a verbal reaction to the prolonged abrasion, scouring and filing of the ironmongery and utensils manufactured in its neighbourhood. It was matched in clamour and turbulence only by the naval foundries at Portsoken.

Yet it was one of the most essential destinations in London, a thunderous warren of forges, smithies, armourers, artificers and metal-related workshops that supplied most of the city's households with their pots, pans, knives, skewers, plates and hooks, and probably anything else they required. The finer and more fashionable workshops had migrated to the less noisome streets adjoining St Margaret's, and the servants and stewards of the wealthiest households had followed. But ordinary Londoners, visitors enthralled by its spectacle, and Flemish merchants who exported the city's metal goods to Brabant held fast to Lothbury and to the stalls and counters that fronted its cramped fire-belching workshops. Like any houseboy or apprentice of his time, Whittington would have plied his master's trade to the craftsmen who had remained at its core, to those who had moved 'upmarket' to St Margaret's and, wider still, within an industrious and densely commercial quarter of the city bound by Lothbury to the north and by the great markets at Cheap and Poultry to the south. From Leadenhall, it would have been easy to race along Cornhill to its junction with Broad Street, formed by another of the city's favoured spots, the Stocks. And if Sir Ivo Fitzwarin had business at the river, Whittington could have followed his nose—day or night—southward along Walbrook to Dowgate, through the Vintry to the quays at Queenhithe. There was very little out of reach or likely to catch an ambitious, enthusiastic young apprentice out of breath in this densely and conveniently compressed city. London and Fitzwarin's business were at his feet.

14

OSMOSIS

In the second half of the 14th century, though buffeted by market, political and military fluctuations, wool remained England's primary export and its chief source of commercial revenue, the lodestar for London's mercantile ambitions. England's economy had shown signs of recovery throughout the 1360s, and the year before Whittington's arrival from Pauntley marked a twenty-year high in cloth exports. After a short period of uncertainty at the turn of the decade, London's business would strengthen further in the late 1370s, going on to displace its chief competitor, Flanders, as a ruinous six years' war (1379–85) unhinged Flemish stability, markets, investment, and ability to trade effectively. Elsewhere, the outbreak of the Ciompi Revolt in Florence in 1378 and a fall in the quality of its goods, combined with a shift in the production of cloths to rural areas in other parts of Europe, created a vacuum that England and its voracious capital were perfectly, almost solitarily, placed to exploit. As he began to make his first sales at court in the mid-1380s, Whittington might have looked back and acknowledged that events abroad had contributed favourably to his progress at home. Such events were not confined to an upheaval in the markets but were also the result of currency stability.

Crisis of Coin, 1370

In 1370, still a young boy, he would not have been aware of one such development that would shape his future career—a continental shortage of precious metals and therefore the means to create money. Arguably, 1370 marks the beginning of a depression in Europe.[1] As a result, one might argue that this was *not* the best timed of arrivals. The average output of coin from England's mints had begun to fall from 1350 and continued to do so until 1417, at times sharply. The lowest period of coin production lasted from 1375 to 1407, spanning many of Whittington's formative and most successful years, and producing a powerful dampening effect on prices.[2] Yet this may help to explain Whittington's lifelong elevation of cash over all other assets. If coin was in short supply, and Whittington later excelled in accumulating and hoarding it, then we can see why his acuity was celebrated and why borrowers, three kings among them, would beat a path to his door. In the words of one who studied the fluctuations of coinage, circulation and value in the 1370s, the French scholar, mathematician and bishop Nicholas Oresme, 'it is clear without further proof that coin is very useful to the civil community, and convenient, or rather necessary, to the business of the state'.[3]

Arriving from a small Gloucestershire estate, still riding out the legacy of plague and the death of a father he had not known, and exposed to the vagaries of crop yields, declining farm rents and lost agricultural dues, here was a boy familiar with the insecurities of being 'asset rich, cash poor'. Hardly the down-and-out pantomime character on which his popular fame is based, he had nevertheless experienced life in a household squeezed by failing resources and financial necessity. His family had sailed precariously close to the wind: an ageing outlawed father unsuited to estate management; a mother unschooled in its uncertainties, who had lost two husbands, whose entitlements were uncertain and who had been left to fend for her children; and an elder brother too frail and ill-equipped to assist her. Wasn't the fragility of Pauntley and his own family's lack of cash at least part of the context for his dispatch to London? He was hardly likely to hanker after a rural life or its dubious blandishments.

The young Richard Whittington was probably fortunate in embarking on his career as London underwent a difficult and stormy period, part of which he would witness as an apprentice. The social, economic and political events that overtook the city in the 1370s prepared him for the opportunities that would follow as he made his way as a freeman and mercer in the decade after. We can only speculate that under the tutelage of Fitzwarin, and others within his circle, Whittington learned at first hand that London's trade and its brittle political relationship with the Crown were shaped by 'a city governed by officers of its own appointment, holding its own courts, brooking no interference from the King's justices, passing its own laws for the regulation and preservation of its trade, and, practically, more independent than it was to be later on, under the Tudors and Stuarts'.[4]

It was against a background of change, tumult and opportunity that Whittington would have commenced his first year at Leadenhall probably as a houseboy, instructed to assist anyone who required his services, and, if the panto version of his life has any ring of truth, the demands placed upon him might have been made at any time and for whatever menial purpose. This was the practical side of his education, often low-level household tasks, deemed to provide a functional means of testing his mettle and his willingness for hard work. They were early practical lessons in upkeep, presentation, pricing and budgeting; and an opportunity for Fitzwarin to observe the character and resilience of the boy. It may not have been what Whittington had expected in his first year, but the lessons would stay with him throughout his life. He was to learn the ways and means of a grand and busy London house, familiarise himself with its suppliers, and respond to the needs of its master and his associates and visitors; absorb everything and observe everyone. It was likely to have been only one part of his obligations to Fitzwarin and to his own family. We can imagine that his mother would have set aside some savings to enable him to continue his formal education, schooled perhaps one or two days a week by a Greyfriar or one of the freelance scholars then establishing schools for grammar and mathematics in London.[5] There was one nearby, housed in a tavern on Lombard Street. If this was the case, his spare evenings, such as they were, would have been devoted to assignments and preparation. His programme of education would have combined schooling in the subjects deemed essential to advanced scholarship with a firm requirement to understand the economy and management of a large household. Fitzwarin himself may have set aside time to instruct the boy in the arts of commerce and law and perhaps in civics and governance. A Greyfriar could offer a choice of tuition in Latin, French, mathematics, sciences, theology, grammar and the principles of *ars dictaminis*, so that one might learn how to compose formal letters and become skilled in rhetoric.[6] As both a merchant and a soldier, Fitzwarin might have had him understudy his scrivener so that he would grasp the basic principles of law, already under strain as demands grew for English to supersede French in government and in the common court.

Life's Essentials

Above all, a mercer had to understand the impact of demand and supply on the value and pricing of commodities, and here the lessons provided by

117

London's markets were invaluable.[7] In the reign of Edward II, London's fishmongers traded from stalls in Bridge Street, a market which preceded Billingsgate and Old Fish Street.[8] A houseboy would learn that April was the start of the flat fish season, that cod was plentiful from November to Easter, and that in the summer months eels were a favoured London staple. Those from the upstream traps and those brought into the old fish wharves from Kent were held to be the best and therefore the most expensive. Stockfish was available all year round, and the best salted herring could be found at Stockfishmonger Row at London Bridge.[9] Anything caught near the wharf at Dowgate, where the effluviant Walbrook emptied into the river, or close to Baynard's Castle, where the deeply mudded Fleet was riddled with all manner of vermin, was to be avoided if you valued your health and had the wherewithal to purchase elsewhere, though few Londoners enjoyed that privilege.[10]

In the late 14th century, the Thames was plentiful with fish, and wider varieties were brought in from the east coast ports and some from northern Europe. A wealthy household like Fitzwarin's might eat fish four or five times a week, mostly caught locally and often driven into controversial 'trammels' upriver. Many years later, as London's mayor, Whittington found himself having to regulate the persistent abuse of stocks that he must have consumed as a young apprentice. Herring was brought in from Yarmouth, barbels from the small ports of Devon and Cornwall, and cod from Grimsby and 'King's town upon Hull'. There was some early trading of fish in the area around 'water gate', which three centuries later developed as Billingsgate,[11] but it was from the minor wharves around Queenhithe, where small inshore boats sold mussels, whelks and oysters direct from their nets in the Thames and from the 'mongers' at Trig Lane and Friday Street, that most Londoners bought their fish.[12] Fresh oysters were highly prized, and during the summer months salmon was brought in from as far as Scotland to sate the appetite of those who could afford it.

Understanding the market in fish was bound to be instructive for a young man with one eye on fulfilling his household duties and the other on assimilating whatever he could about the operation of London's guilds and the mechanics of its economy. This was not simply a matter of learning about the quality and pricing of an essential staple or the differences between 'stock fishmongers' and 'salt fishmongers'[13] and their respective territoriality and influence, though a passing knowledge of a trade that had secured its first royal charter in 1272, more than 120 years before the mercers, would serve Whittington well when he embarked on his mayoral career. An attentiveness to the practices and ambitions of a trade that stood at the very heart of London's most basic needs was clearly worthwhile in economic terms, but it was also something of a 'political education'. Expeditions to London's fishmongers served to emphasise both the pace at which and the way in which London was changing at this time.[14] What happened in the fecund waters of the Thames determined activity and opportunity on its banks and its neighbouring streets. It impacted directly on the budget and wellbeing of every London household, and it shaped the politics of many of the city's 24 wards. The catching, distribution, sale and availability of fish were barometers of London's political and economic 'weather'. The shifting needs and interests of the fishmongers also affected trades wholly unrelated to fish but dependent on the river for quite different reasons. This interconnectedness of London's economy was a lesson to take note of. For example, many of the small waterfront tenements and shops that formed the old fishmonger communities were surrendered to the demand for space on the wharves exerted by the dyers and the tailors. Landlords sold premises where, in some cases, they had traded for over 200 years, literally beneath the fishmongers' feet. They continued to attend their favoured churches and taverns but the old 'shoppes' and corners disappeared, swept up by those with wealth and political connections. Some moved out to Barking and East Smithfield where there was more room and greater certainty. It was all an instructive example of London's spatial needs and enforced elasticity.

In the role of houseboy, for a short period before embarking on his formal apprenticeship in mercery, Whittington would have been required to accompany the cook or kitchen servants to shop not only for fish but for meat, vegetables and bread, learning how to extract the freshest produce and best prices from the fishmongers on the wharves and the butchers at Smithfield; to barter with sharp-faced shopkeepers and tricksome pedlars at the Stocks, and to compete with the ruddy wives of Eastcheap for a rare bargain. Eventually, he might be trusted to go on his own, no doubt relieved to get out of the house. Here was an opportunity to learn about the difference between the best cuts of neck and shoulder, loin and haunch, or where and from whom to buy the freshest lamprey and the juiciest eels, or how to distinguish between trout and bream, perch and pike, sole and flounder and plaice. He could observe how the fishmongers broke out the grey fleshy meat from the large brown crabs and snapped the armoured orange fingers of crayfish scooped from the centre of the river. He would estimate the variable quality and texture of mussels and scallops or observe the tell-tale shape and colour of oysters brought in on squat fishing boats from the wharves of Kent. In this way, Whittington might have begun to acquire the singular knowledge that was the purpose and the product of his endeavours: the price of everything and the value of buying low and selling high.

* * *

In the matter of household chores, we might imagine that Whittington, not yet twelve years old, was put to fetching the kindling and lighting the fires in the kitchen and bedrooms, stocking the great hearth in the hall with logs and faggots, and ensuring an endless supply of fine candles and cheap tallow for light throughout Fitzwarin's cavernous house. He would also have been involved in waxing and polishing furniture, turning beds, cleaning floors, and preparing the hall for a regular merry-go-round of suppers and formal dinners. He might have been dispatched by the butler or cellarer to one of the vintners trading on Upper Thames Street or in the lanes around St Martin in the Vintry, to help him transport and store regular orders of Rhenish and Gascon for Fitzwarin's cellar. Allowing the panto to intrude here for a moment, he might well have been responsible for setting the cats to catch the rats and string them by their tails. Other tasks would have included firing the lanterns at the front of the house and the braziers in the courtyard to light the way, placing pots of lavender and lily in the porch to scent the entrance, and keeping the fire barrels topped with water. He would have welcomed guests, taking their cloaks and helping to stable their horses; then returning inside to serve at the table and replenish their wine, toing and froing from the kitchen for hours on end; and always in readiness, long woollen jerkin at hand, to show them out and retrieve their rides—rain, wind or snow. And if they were too drunk to mount safely, the boy might have been instructed to fetch a lantern into the street and summon a cart to collect them and take them home.

When the servants were washing the pots, scouring the trenchers, and storing the bowls and plates, it would be the young houseboy who found himself carrying out the slops and the remains to the pigs and fowl. Leftovers of uneaten meat might be taken to the old soldiers and cripples who begged outside St Dionis Backchurch on Fenchurch Street, named ironically after the patron saint of France and well known for its fine garden and dry shelter. A wealthy household might also require a houseboy to help maintain the vegetable patch, edged with rows of bay and chervil, clary and fennel, rosemary and sorrel. He might be directed to collect honey from the skeps and spoon it into pots covered with muslin squares tied tightly with flax to preserve it through the winter. And as nothing was wasted, he might learn how to employ a thin blade of smooth wood to scrape out thicker layers of wax which were then scooped into shallow oaken boxes to solidify in the cold air of the stables or outbuildings. Here was the means to impose the deep shine required for the household's fine panels and furniture. To the houseboy also fell the task of pouring the thick fat left over daily from cooking into an assortment of half-size former wine barrels, where it was left to set and thicken. If it was mutton fat it would be used to fabricate the crude tallow candles relegated for use in the minor and ancillary rooms. He could find himself charged with scouring the soot and spalling from the heavy pots or, on feast days and for large suppers, sent to collect suckling pigs, capons, hares, and sides of beef and venison in a small handcart that might be painted in the house's colours to ward off any interference by thieves and urchins. Finally, there was the worst of scutwork, assigned by rote, that all servants dreaded: the opening of the latrine and access to its contents for collection by the well-paid fellows who collected the night soil or 'gong', the wonderfully named 'gong farmers' ('gongfermours').[15]

During the early years of his apprenticeship Whittington would have run errands across the city and to the quays, where he would have seen at first-hand how vacant land at the riverside was being scooped up for the storage of goods. Entry to and from the river, and space for docking and warehousing, were already under intense pressure from London's own merchant community but this was compounded further by the needs and displacement caused by Venetian and Genoese merchants, who were commissioning ever larger vessels to carry more cargo, both into London and out again. It was well understood that London could lose out to the Lowland ports and, at home, to Southampton and Bristol, which had already cornered much of the Bordeaux trade, if it failed to create more quay space and superior warehousing. Genoese carracks at this time could exceed 100 feet. For their part, the Venetians were concerned that their ships would soon not be able to venture beyond Queenhithe, and urgently needed to concentrate their goods and warehousing in the deeper water away from the silt and effluence, close to a riverside that could expand to support them. This thirst for space and for purpose-built depots and stockrooms that were fire- and theft-proof, and that would allow goods to be held securely until the market was ready to accommodate them, became an increasingly important driver not only in the development of the port but also in the pronounced investment in riverside land, in localised infrastructure, and in the grand housing that stretched down to the banks of the Thames as the city's merchants cultivated new ways to divert profits from their traditional activity as mercers, drapers, grocers, fishmongers, goldsmiths and vintners. Each of these trades had long-standing and often lucrative stakes in import–export and in ship-owning, so it was natural they should turn their attention to opportunities presented at the riverside by the irrepressible demand for land, infrastructure and port services.

As his familiarity with Fitzwarin's business increased and his knowledge of London expanded, Whittington would be removed from his household chores and indentured as an apprentice mercer. Initially, he would serve as a runner and errand boy for his master's business, the world a mere sail away from the river that lay at his doorstep, trading with places he had never heard of and for which there were not yet detailed maps. If his training was thorough and imaginative, he would learn not only the substance and service of mercery but also some of the detail of its supply chain, including wool production, drapery, tailoring and the like. It was all about osmosis, a thorough immersion in the building blocks of his trade. He would be on hand to check the arrival and dispatch of his master's goods, hurrying back and forth to provide reports on shipping, their cargo and their arrivals and departures, dipping in and out of the workshops and warehouses to ensure goods were ready for loading, storage or distribution. He would spend his day attending suppliers early each morning with orders, returning samples of cloth back to Leadenhall, rushing back with his master's comments and approvals, ferrying orders and commissions to and from patrons and clients, delivering invoices and settlements, conveying messages to Fitzwarin's importers and captains, and concluding arrangements with carters to collect and deliver raw materials and finished goods, near and far. In the evening he would return home to pore over orders and accounts before readying himself to start all over again the following morning.

* * *

The streets that neighboured Walbrook were the worst. Here, the shallow trenches intended to improve London's hygiene were frequently overrun with a sluggish dark stew of household waste, rotting food, human ordure, animal remains, and the daily accumulation of horse, pig and chicken droppings propelled into them by the very householders who railed at their aldermen about the cleanliness of the city and the quality of its water.[16] 'It was never very navigable being only 12ft to 14ft wide and very shallow'; in 1288 it had to be 'made free from dung and other nuisances'. But by 1383 it was 'stopped up by divers filth and dung thrown therein by persons who have houses along the said course'.[17] The town planner Michael Harrison tells us that the Walbrook had a long history of pollution and that London's Corporation had long failed in their duty to follow the lead provided by the Romans in creating cesspits and sewers. The Walbrook was left to do the job. Quite literally. In Edward I's reign ordinances were passed to prevent or limit it from choking up, but these were largely ignored, and, in any case, the more practical solutions of engineering and disposal were eschewed as too interruptive or too expensive. Neither king nor Corporation rushed to offer investment. Yet a Roman dwelling at the end of Walbrook at the corner of the modern Queen Victoria Street, excavated in 1868, was found to sport a balcony overhanging the water-way. Hardly surprising, then, that it has been remarked that 'the river's condition in later times would not have encouraged the use of this balcony'.[18]

The streets that radiated from Lothbury were well known to the city's mercers and apprentices. Coleman Street, Threadneedle Street, Throgmorton Street and Swan Alley thrived with the workshops of silk makers and needleworkers—trades and skills essential to London's luxury goods market.[19] In the narrower lanes you might find yourself cast in darkness by the closely interlocking roofs and eaves that shut out the sunlight. One moment you might be threading your way through decrepit rows of poorly lit and densely packed tenements, barely able to see ten yards ahead; the next you would suddenly emerge into a brightly lit open space, the sun bursting through, illuminating edifices erected to God in his magnificence: the splendour of St Mary Colechurch, St Mildred Poultry and St Christopher's, and the exceptional house built by Sir Robert Fitzwalter. Cutting along to Basinghall Street or to Moorgate, Whittington would come to Old Jewry, a favoured residential choice for London's mercers. Once it had been the bustling centre of a diverse and exotic enterprise, but by now there was no longer a single family or merchant of the Jewish faith resident anywhere on this street or in the whole of London. For any mercer's apprentice there were frequent trips to purchase or collect fine bolts of cloth from the cloth market near St Nicholas Shambles. As London's mayor in 1397, Whittington would oversee the establishment of

its first permanent cloth market, proposed the previous year by his predecessor, Adam Bamme. As he acquainted himself with the geography and
economy of London, he might have cut along Coleman Street where he
would first enter civic life in 1384 as a common councillor and where in
1431 John Sokelyng would bequeath his brewery, the famous 'Cock on the
Hoop', to the vicar and parishioners of St Stephen's Coleman Street, then
a chapel of ease to the parish church of St Olave Jewry. The bells of St
Olave's would summon London's cloth merchants to trading at Blackwell
Hall a quarter of a century later.[20] Whittington might then have passed by
another St Olave's, that on Hart Street, where he is said to have kept a
house before his marriage to Alice Fitzwarin, a popular misconception as
the building in question was not constructed in his lifetime.[21] It was in St
Olave's graveyard that the tomb lay of the charcoal burner who gave his
name to Coleman Street and to its ward and who provided an inscription
that aptly captures the path that Whittington himself would later follow:
'Here lies before his maker Robert Coleman who has striven in this life to
earn his place in the next. God be willing.'[22]

15

APPRENTICE

As he was away much of the time in the service of the king, it is possible that Sir Ivo Fitzwarin would have arranged for Whittington to attend the workshops of his associates, enabling him to watch and learn; note how the merchant treated each customer as if they were his only one, grasping the importance of retaining their patronage, why they returned and how the merchant sustained this relationship; and to observe the quality of goods and the attentiveness of service that he had to must provide if he was to become a mercer in his own right. Whittington was enormously fortunate in having Fitzwarin as his mentor and somewhat young father figure. Few trades actively tended to the welfare of their young apprentices. Exposure to danger, accidents and disability, and the prospect of loss of employment and lifelong hardship, were part of the risk deemed worthwhile in securing the prize of becoming a freeman. Some masters hardly gave it a thought. Welfare was not their responsibility, so why concern themselves?

After all, the guild was the ladder to advancement, apprenticeship its first rung. You had to take the rough with the smooth. The game was to climb from there. Few would make it to the very top, but the prospect of doing so compensated for the tribulations of the ascent. Apprenticeship was promoted and regarded, both in London and among aspirant families in the shires, as an immense privilege, bringing opportunities for wealth, status, respect. It also enhanced the likelihood of a good marriage, often to a relative of the master in whose household the apprentice took service. For the great majority of entrants, the completion of an apprenticeship and their elevation to freeman and to membership of the guild or company were probably the height of their ambitions and their capabilities, and for the most part offered them a good and reasonably affluent life. For others it was a route into politics, by intent or preferment, a gateway to the wards, election as an alderman or common councillor, even sheriff, and in rare instances to the mayoralty itself. With the right skillset and the support of influential patrons, it would be a lucrative door to the Palace of Westminster. It might widen horizons and enrich lives through travel and trade in the great manufacturing and commercial centres of Europe. In spiritual terms, it provided the means to celebrate the glory of God, to erect monuments to his greatness, and to carve a path to salvation through enterprise, endeavour and charitable works.

An aspiring mercer might be instructed to keep this in mind as he trudged around the city's innumerable workshops and quays, or found himself on arduous cart journeys to fetch and carry wool from north to south, or lamented having been dispatched for days on end to tiny ports and flea-ridden taverns on the Essex and Sussex coasts. He might lean back and think on it when he was ploughing through heavy ledgers and cargo inventories and bearing the brunt of whatever had gone amiss or had failed to meet his master's expectations. A demanding master would require someone with a good head for quayside arithmetic, a working knowledge of Norman French and even the commercial patois needed to make himself understood by the Venetians and Genoese at Queenhithe and Gallions Reach. He would be expected to know the tides and the queuing and anchoring protocols of the Thames, be able to get his head around the intricacies of import and export duties, and understand the difference between scavage and tronage.[1] If he was a mercer's apprentice, he would know why the Italians and Flemish favoured Cotswold and Hereford wool, who were the most reliable suppliers, which alien merchants would pay the best price, and how his master could make the best of it. An astute lad serving his time in London in the 1370s would know too that a new echelon of consumers was emerging who placed great value on luxury goods, on being seen to be different, to be ahead of the pack. For them, the richness of the products in which Whittington would later specialise lay not simply in the quality of the cloth but in its refinements and finishes and in where and how these enhancements were made. Italian products were highly valued and sought after. This was a rarefied market, and the affluent stood apart and drew value from their primacy. Most importantly, they would pay handsomely for the privilege, happily conceding a premium price because the product and service that attended it were not commonly attainable.

126

APPRENTICE

The Assumption of Risk

Long before that he would absorb the basic mantra 'buy low, sell high' but also recognise that the role of the mercer was evolving and segmenting. This was happening commercially, culturally and at great pace. The old ways were being thrust aside or confined to those who could not afford or lacked the social profile to make the step up. The pursuit of charters, the introduction of religious ritualisation and expensive liveries within the guilds, the codifying of self-worth, and the gatekeeping of those who were welcome and those who were not were the window dressing to the most transforming change affecting London's mercers, an irrevocable shift in self-perception and economic purpose. Their métier lay in procuring the materials that the craftsman needed and in selling on the finished article. The essence was specialisation, with functions performed by different players, one a producer, the other a distributor. Where the mercer differentiated his service, and what enabled him to demand a premium for the goods he selected, priced, distributed and increasingly guaranteed, was his covering of 'risk'.

Here was the basis for a new relationship with his suppliers, funding their work, enabling them to focus on production, making better use of their skills and reducing their costs; offering them a guaranteed price for high quality and availability on demand and the prospect of repeat business; doing away with the small trader's traditional need to haul his goods around the country; transforming logistics by providing his own carters; and, where appropriate, providing his suppliers with the finance or joint investment to expand. Here was the template for the modern mercer, a more efficient, productive, specialised enterprise in which he bore the financial risk, cut his costs through efficiencies, and increased his profits through improvements at every stage—investment, manufacture, supply and distribution. Finally he would deliver to the market at large or to the customer direct for an additional premium. Better still, this market, these customers, and the mercer's time and enterprise were concentrated in or supplied from a single commanding place, London.

If Whittington had been asked in his early teens what he had observed so far of his chosen trade, he might have responded that the mercer grew wealthy by investing in the production of others and by his ability to identify opportunities and supply the goods to sate them. Mercers didn't become wealthy simply by carting materials from Gloucestershire to London or finding an accomplished craftsman to turn them into desirable goods for which affluent people would pay a premium; the most successful were those who knew what the market wanted or how to create a market that did not previously exist, and those who enabled the craftsman to concentrate on what he excelled at: craftsmanship. The mercer's supreme value lay in offsetting risk and carrying the costs of production until he found his client. His was no longer a trade, it was now a profession. It is no surprise that during Whittington's first fifteen years in London we see not only the formalisation, codification and segmentation of his profession but also its diversification out of wool and cloth into a much broader range of luxury goods, into wine and foodstuffs, into shipping and export, into housing development and rental, and even into high-profit industrial staples such as coal and iron.

* * *

From the start of his apprenticeship Whittington would have known from the merchants and the craftsmen with whom his master traded in towns like Bury, Norwich, Winchester, Gloucester, Oxford and Coventry, and from stories that were commonplace about radical new ideas abroad in the ports of Southampton, Lynn, Bristol and Chichester, that traditional guilds in which the craftsman was also the merchant were rapidly giving way to a division of roles and the onset of specialisation. There were exceptions, of course, and in some areas this onset was either delayed or diverted. In London and other large towns, commercially minded craftsmen chose their own route, opening shops to market their goods directly to the public, charging more for the privilege, and dispensing with the traditional form of sale from the backrooms of cramped workshops. Most, however, for reasons of pride in their craft, or because they were made offers that guaranteed them continuity of work, or because they preferred a simple life, succumbed to the charms, pressures and greater confidence of those who had the resources to buy up materials, purchase stock, and introduce new business on a much greater scale—and make it pay handsomely. This was the type of mercer that Richard Whittington would become.

While the pitch to craftsmen rested chiefly on the delegation of risk, mercers also spoke confidently of their commercial knowhow, of excelling in understanding and securing best value. They might well buy low and sell high, but the promise they offered was of assured satisfaction. If the customer was not content then it was they who would make the reparation, not the craftsman, though no doubt they would take up the matter privately. This relationship between risk and reward was also used to explain away the exclusivity that the Mercers' Company would bring to membership, particularly after its charter was secured. The argument ran that to assume the scale and complexity of risk that many of its members took required considerable wealth and a capacity to withstand the unforeseen. A leading mercer therefore had to have the confidence and status to move comfortably in the highest circles and acquire the social and cultural skills necessary to win the favour and recommendation of leading figures at court. They needed the resources and standing to entertain and play host to their patrons and enjoy the esteem of those who desired the very best, wanted it quickly, and expected it to be without fault. This would be the template adopted, 'stress tested' and refined by Whittington from the mid-1380s.

London was notable in having an influential group, supported by a small number of associates in Bristol, Coventry and York, who had access to the Palace of Westminster and who individually and severally could underwrite the considerable risks of high-value imports from Italy, Germany, Spain and the Netherlands. In an age of mushrooming international trade channelled through London, Bristol and Southampton, and ever-closer business dealings with alien merchants and their captains, it was essential to insure against threats to mutual interests posed by theft, piracy and seizure under war, by weather and by poorly constructed shipping. Only a select few, acting often in consortia, could bear these costs and would continue to bear the risk of doing so because they saw the opportunity and had the resources and knowhow to turn calculated endeavour into spectacular profit. If things went wrong, they alone lost their investment. It was all a matter of risk and reward, but one that was increasingly tested, measured, segmented and shared.

Midsummer's Eve, 23 June

The life of an apprentice was not entirely nose to the grindstone; there were plenty of feast days and religious festivals, sporting events, street entertainments, river-based activities and grand occasions for civic and military pageantry to divert London's apprentices, not the least of which were hard-fought guild rivalries embracing football, archery, swimming, wrestling, bowls and early versions of cricket and shinty. If he had arrived at Leadenhall by the spring of 1370, then Whittington's first experience of London's pageantry would have been the preparations for the celebration of Midsummer's Eve on 23 June.[2] Like most young boys he would have been drawn to the daily preparations in Lime Street ward, avidly following the checking, adjustments and approvals offered by its aldermen and by those who had contributed to the effort to make their neighbourhood stand out. In the days leading up to the celebration, the citizens of London's wards might have been engaged directly in the preparations or simply content to observe their aldermen and the constables affirming the safe construction of the bonfires, ensuring that the usual fire precautions were in place, and putting the torch-bearers and escorts through their paces. Whittington would have seen for the first time the part played by London's mayor in overseeing the city's reputation for pomp and pageantry and might have been instructed to take a special interest in John Barnes, one of London's leading mercers, now in his second year of office. Barnes had received much acclaim for his general good works but also as a benefactor of St Pancras, a modest church located on the corner of Needlers Lane, an area which housed many workshops associated with the cloth trade. This year Barnes had caught everyone's imagination with his latest charitable gesture, the donation of a chest bearing three locks and containing 1,000 marks, which he held 'therein to be lent to young men upon sufficient pawn, and for the use thereof, to say *de profundis* or *pater noster* and no more'.[3]

Had Whittington been present at the briefings given to the mayor, he might have been surprised to find the focus placed firmly on the logistics, funding and practicalities of the celebrations: how high the Corporation's main bonfire would be, which ward would lead off the procession, who had been selected to hoist the cresset, which bannerets would be represented in the rows just behind the king's vanguard, which individuals and guilds had contributed most, who had failed to contribute sufficiently, whether there was anything the mayor still required help with, and where one might procure good seats for guests. During Midsummer's Eve and the Eve of St Peter and St Paul on 28 June, it must have seemed that every man, woman and child had gathered in the narrow confining streets around St Paul's, where each year the crush of the crowds would trample at least a dozen people under foot before they surged into Little Conduit, down Cheapside and Cornhill, and on to Aldgate then worked their way back again to Cornhill via Fenchurch and Gracechurch Street. From here the leaders and their vanguard would quicken the pace and urge momentum as they closed in on the broad sweep of Cheapside, where many in the vast throng would fall upon the cook shops, food stalls and hawkers and London's ubiquitous taverns and drinking dens. It was a tradition for some groups of men from Farringdon Within to drink themselves into a stupor before cramming into the wherries anchored near the mouth of the Fleet to finish their merry-making in the libidinous 'Stews' across the river at Southwark.[4] There were always a few reckless enough to lay wagers on 'shooting the starlings', the pillars and rapids beneath London Bridge. Each year a few poor fools would deprive themselves of celebrating the next.[5]

In preparation for the celebrations every alderman would have been instructed by the Corporation to recruit robust and dependable men from their ward who could lead the way, marshal the crowds, deter troublemak-ers and help to keep the procession moving and the peace intact as the assembly shuffled raucously through its area of jurisdiction. These were the men of the 'watch party', an honourable duty often performed by veterans of the war with France. Alongside them, minstrels, lutists, jugglers and acrobats would play to the crowd. Astride an armoured destrier, a tower-ing knight dressed in a flowing red cloak embroidered with the Plantagenet lions bore aloft the cresset beacon, lit to announce the mayor's arrival. Each time he rounded into the next street the crowd would surge forward to catch the scent of rosin that burned in the metal cup. In his wake fol-lowed the mayor's attendants, members of his guard, his swordbearer and, immediately behind them, the mayor himself, flanked by footmen, torch-bearers and more of his guard. Close on their heels, the city's aldermen would jostle and manoeuvre, each competing unashamedly for position and advantage, bobbing up and down in a sea of mink-trimmed scarlet cloaks. Cries of recognition and territorial solidarity went up as each passed through his home ward: a salutation to London's innate tribalism that could be called upon for a relatively modest offer of coin to support the most divisive and self-interested parties, regardless of moral worth—provided they were local, 'of the ward', perceived variously as both the root of and the solution to London's perpetual factionalism. Later, the crowd would rush to the crammed expanse of Cheapside where a dais was erected for the comfort of the king and queen and their party, to preside over the highlight of the day, a rumbustious tournament.

In recent years, the procession had acquired a more profound purpose, gradually evolving as an opportunity for old soldiers and comrades to meet and for their efforts and sacrifices to be acknowledged. Most within the long tail would be veterans of France and Scotland, a sharp reminder that war and service were never far away. Among the soldiery were archers and infantry, knights and pages, captains and sergeants, and a multitude of ensign bearers. The injured and those missing limbs were transported in small carts and makeshift barrows. Many wore the insignia, an armorial bearing or some other attachment representing the companies and bannerets under which they had served. There would be loud, resonating cries of salutation and recognition as men announced their names, their company and their renown to the throng who lined the route. The noise from the crowds and from the trumpeters and buglers, the rhythmic pounding of the drummers, and the shrill pitch of the fifes would be thrilling and good-natured. A young rural lad new to the city and to the scale and richness of this spectacle would surely be enthralled to witness London in such finery and good heart. As he looked about him, he would see fathers explaining the meaning of military dress, pennants and insignia to their wide-eyed sons—a powerful tool for enlistment. At the margins, jugglers, jesters, acrobats and actors dressed in wild and vivid costumes would vie for the attention and amusement of the crowd. Beggars would work their way between the tight rows of onlookers, doing their utmost to draw on the general sense of joy and goodwill; some would leave with their pots full, others no doubt would be cuffed about the head for daring to demean the great pageant. It would be 29 October before Londoners assembled in such numbers again, on this occasion for the mayor's formal election on the Feast of St Jude. This was Richard Whittington's first experience of what the mayoralty meant to the city and to its people.

16

FROM GOOD TO BAD

A Marriage in the Household, 1372

By the turn of 1372 Whittington was probably in the second year of his apprenticeship and aged about thirteen. It would prove a momentous year in personal terms, opening in January with Sir Ivo Fitzwarin's marriage to Maud (Mathilde), one of three daughters and co-heirs to the enormously wealthy John d'Argentine.[1] Later in the year Whittington would suffer the first of three significant personal blows in his life with the death of his mother Joan, thirteen years after her husband Sir William and three years after her youngest son had departed for London.[2]

We know little of the impact that the Hundred Years War would have had on the household, but the national mood took a turn for the worse with the defeat of an English squadron at La Rochelle on 23 June by a Castilian–French fleet supported by Owain Lawgoch, claimant to the title of Prince of Wales.[3] It was a serious reversal for Edward III's ambitions and a blow to England's national pride. After the humiliation and terrors of the Black Prince's recovery of Limoges in September 1370, the French were once more in the ascendancy and regained control of Poitou and Brittany in what became over the next few years an alternating pattern of invasion and retreat. On 16 June 1373 a treaty was signed between England and Portugal establishing a series of renewed perpetual friendships, unions and alliances between the two nations which have since survived as the world's oldest active treaty. In August 1373 it fell to John of Gaunt to reinvade France and to relieve Aquitaine with a mounted force of 9,000. His ill-fated *chevauchée* between August and December, which stretched across 600 miles, resulted in a hopeless and tragic waste of England's thinly stretched resources. Huge numbers of men and horses succumbed to French attacks, to starvation, sickness and exhaustion, to the onset of a severe early winter, and eventually to demoralisation and desertion.[4] By the time Gaunt's forces arrived in Bordeaux on Christmas Eve 1373, only one-third of those who had set sail in August remained. A similar number had died in action, and another third had been lost to disease. Worse was to come as they found Bordeaux in the grip of bubonic plague. By April 1374 Gaunt's forces were so decimated that the campaign was abandoned with nothing to show for its costs, its ambitions or its great loss of life and spirit. For England's economy and for London's merchant community a period of huge uncertainty now loomed.

At home, a few developments were momentarily diverting. On St George's Day, 23 April 1374, London's great and good celebrated the achievements of Geoffrey Chaucer, whose works were recognised by Edward III with the grant of a gallon of wine a day for the rest of his life, an appropriate gift perhaps for someone whose father had been one of London's leading vintners and who had grown up on Thames Street, the centre of London's wine trade.[5] He continued to collect his gallon a day until Richard II came to power, after which it was converted to a more conventional form of liquidity in the shape of a monetary grant on 18 April 1378.

Chaucer was something of an enigma, an engaging, complex figure with interests far wider than the poetry and writing for which he is best known and celebrated. At the time of his birth in 1343, his family had been vintners in London for two generations and before that they were merchants in Suffolk. Throughout his life he sustained an interest in both. His fondness for wine may have been purely social but his interests in trade were entirely commercial and provided him, along with timely sinecures from the state, with the financial security he needed to pursue his writing. As a young man he had been brought up as a page in the household of Elizabeth de Burgh, Countess of Ulster, wife of Edward III's son Lionel, Duke of Clarence.[6] His service in their household brought him into the sphere of the English court and effectively prepared him for and launched him into a diverse career, much of which was in service to king and state as courtier, diplomat, administrator and, in 1389, eccentrically as clerk to the king's works. His role as an envoy may well have masked his true mission as an 'intelligence gatherer'—in short, a spy. After all, he was known to have all the necessary attributes: he knew the machinations and social mores of the English court; he had brief experience in 1360 of military service before managing to get himself captured during the Siege of Rheims and freed for a ransom of £16; he was cultured and widely travelled; he was graced with exceptional knowledge and intelligence; and he was reputed to be conversant in Spanish, French, Italian, Flemish and Latin. In 1366 he strengthened his association with the court through his marriage to Philippa de Roet, lady-in-waiting to Queen Philippa of Hainault, wife of Edward III, and later became closely associated with their son John of Gaunt. In a further twist much later in 1396, Chaucer's sister-in-law Katherine Swynford would become Gaunt's third wife. Whether he was an envoy or on some occasions a 'secret agent' in the service of the English state, his talents and his connections were no doubt perceived as essential assets for either role.

* * *

In March 1375, then aged sixteen and halfway through his apprenticeship, Richard Whittington learned that his middle brother Robert was among the Gloucestershire esquires about to embark for Brittany in the retinue of Edward, 1st Baron Despenser, eldest brother of Henry, the Bishop of Norwich, and a friend and patron of the French chronicler Jean Froissart. Edward died in the November, but Robert maintained his relationship with the family.[7] John of Gaunt was taken up with Aquitaine again this year during the conference with Philip II, Duke of Burgundy, called by Pope Gregory XI to try to settle the long-running war between the two countries. Negotiations foundered on who should retain the fiercely disputed sovereignty of Aquitaine. Unresolved and barely patched together, the resulting Treaty of Bruges was little more than a fig leaf, an uneasy postponement of the issue, and a deferment of hostilities which, despite its renewal in 1376 and the death of the talismanic Black Prince—Sir Ivo Fitzwarin's liege lord—in June of that year and the death of his father Edward III almost exactly a year later, still resulted in a resumption of the war in 1377.

Chaucer reappears about this time, dispatched in the final months of Edward's life on a series of naval expeditions to France and to Flanders which appear to have been directed either to intelligence gathering on French preparations for the resumption of hostilities or, more likely, with the elderly king's health failing and his warrior son no longer available to succeed him, to exploring the diplomatic back channels for extending the uneasy peace until England was ready. On 12 February he had been issued with Letters of Protection, intended to serve him until the end of September, to ship abroad in the king's service. On the 19th of the month further letters instructed the payment of expenses to be forwarded to Chaucer and his superior, Sir Thomas Percy, who were referred to as being 'on the king's secret affairs' in Flanders. Five days after Edward's death, on 26 June, Chaucer was dispatched again, this time to Paris, Montreuil and 'elsewhere' on state business.[8] Froissart suggests that Chaucer had been instructed to deploy his diplomatic talents in arranging a marriage between the future Richard II, not yet eleven, and a French princess with the intention of ending the war between England and France. However, there was no wedding and the war continued unabated.[9]

From Good to Bad, 1376

After not having met since November 1373, deferred by Edward's fears that it would be a lightning rod for social and political unrest, Parliament was finally reconvened on 28 April 1376, remaining in session until 10 July, England's longest Parliament to that date. While Edward and his advisers sought to avoid an assembly at all costs, the perennial issue of an empty treasury rendered its convention as essential. The king needed to replenish his war chest, but there were deep concerns in the City about his ambitions and his financial needs, and the authority of his government was already in question. When it convened, the 'Good Parliament'[10] was intent therefore on exposing and rooting out corruption in the Royal Council and on curtailing the dismissive overbearance of the discredited and highly unpopular Gaunt, Edward's fourth son, who had stepped into the vacuum as England's de facto ruler as the health of both his father and his elder brother waned. Parliament was outraged by Gaunt's efforts to impose huge increases in taxation to fund his failing campaigns. It didn't help that he also refused to brook criticism or engage with opposition from London's merchant class. With Gaunt isolated and badly out of step with an angry public mood, Parliament pressed its advantage, adamant that if there was no reform and no dismissal of incompetent or corrupt chief officers of state, then there would be no funds for war. Many among the Commons and a small number among the Lords were determined to go further, however, placing charges of misgovernment, fiscal mismanagement and widespread corruption among the ruling class at Gaunt's door. His wealth and arrogance were held to intense scrutiny and sustained ridicule. Hopes for reform had rested fleetingly with the Black Prince, by now mortally ill, who would die soon after on 8 June, yet for a moment it seemed that the Parliament would succeed. However, its eventual defeat would be self-inflicted; it would press too hard, go too far. Even after their demands for reform and dismissal were largely won, the Commons continued to refuse funds for war, alienating those among the Lords who had initially supported them. The tide turned in Gaunt's favour and he wasted little time in dismantling Parliament's efforts and removing its leading figures. The other focus of his suspicion and distrust, the City and its merchant class, was firmly in his sights.

17

INTEREST GROUP POLITICS

The political turbulence of 1376 spilled over into the first half of 1377. Gaunt now used the Good Parliament's successor not only to dismantle prospects for fiscal, political and administrative reform but also to imprint his own manifesto for governance. The so-called Bad Parliament sat for the first time on 27 January 1377 and immediately set about undoing the work of its predecessor, famously introducing a deeply unpopular poll tax to finance the war against France, before being dissolved on 2 March. On 22 May 1377, Pope Gregory XI issued five papal bulls condemning John Wycliffe's view that Catholic priests should follow the example of Jesus' twelve disciples by living a life of poverty.[1] Four decades later, Richard Whittington would be instructed by Henry V to lead an inquiry charged with identifying and seizing the property of those Lollards who continued to follow Wycliffe's teachings.[2]

The Boy King

On 21 June 1377 the death at the age of 65 of the once imperious Edward III ended a tumultuous fifty-year reign, handing the succession to his grandson Richard II, a boy of just ten years, and ushering in a period of great political uncertainty and social turbulence. On the face of it, his young successor started with many advantages. His grandfather had re-established the authority of the English Crown and asserted its military prowess on the Continent while his father, the legendary Black Prince, had triumphed at Crécy and Poitiers and had 'left a great legacy of goodwill towards his infant son'.[2] However, he would also inherit the fault lines and partisanships that characterised the final years of his grandfather's reign. His uncles, John of Gaunt, Duke of Lancaster, and Thomas of Woodstock,

1st Duke of Gloucester, were to rule on his behalf during the period of his immaturity. War with France remained England's chief preoccupation, yet a more proximate distraction was intensifying in London itself, a struggle for supremacy between the capital's leading guilds for the king's ear, with control over trade and oversight of the city's governance being the chief prizes. In March 1377 the conspicuously ambitious Nicholas Brembre replaced the deposed mayor Adam Stable, affirming the ascendancy of the 'victuallers' interest' which would come to have increasing sway over the young king.[3]

By the late 1370s London was as well marked for its monopolies, self-perpetuating interests, and economic and political corruption, which often went hand in hand, as for its undoubted enterprise and energy. At the time of Edward's death, the capital's economy was populated by as many as 88 trade guilds. As commerce expanded and diversified, it was these guilds rather than their handicraft counterparts which assumed a greater importance, both commercially and politically. The aspiration to expand their influence can be seen throughout the course of the 14th century, not least in their pursuit of royal charters. At the forefront were the goldsmiths, the skinners and the merchant taylors, each of them essential links in the royal supply chain, and each of which secured their charter in 1327. In 1351, this growing political importance was affirmed in the invitation to the thirteen leading guilds to form the Common Council.[4] The mercers were among the principal cohort, comprising the grocers, drapers, goldsmiths and vintners, and had secured an interim charter of sorts in 1347, but would not receive the formal recognition that their de facto status demanded until 1394. Meanwhile, they must have looked on with puzzlement and envy as their close fellows, the drapers, together with the fishmongers and vintners, were awarded their royal approval in 1363 and 1364. It was this group, with the grocers foremost, which in 1384 brought its influence to bear in restoring election to London's wards and which went on to dominate the Common Council for much of the next fifteen years, with the grocers only occasionally interrupted by the mercers and drapers. AR Myers writes that 'by 1400 London had a firmly established merchant oligarchy'.[5]

The alliance of grocers, vintners and fishmongers and their acolytes was unlikely to be deflected by those it regarded as being of lesser status, lesser wealth and lesser account. Any attempt or aspiration towards governance by the lesser trades was viewed as inimical to the interests of what had become a powerful and, at times, a single-minded elite. The alternative was to control London's 24 wards by 'wealth', and this meant 'citizenship'.

London at this time has been described as a city 'firmly in the hands of an oligarchy closely connected with moneyed coadjutors abroad. Its members monopolised the offices of mayor and aldermen; they monopolised the supply and sale of foodstuffs. They bribed the king himself with a succession of loans, and with only infrequent interruptions became the virtual rulers of England.'[6] The reference to 'ruling' England is somewhat overblown, but there is little doubt that London's economy and its civil governance were in thrall to the six most powerful guilds—mercers, drapers, fishmongers, grocers, vintners and goldsmiths. Among the most prominent 'power players' were the grocers Nicholas Brembre and John Philpot, the fishmongers Walter Sibil and William Walworth, the draper John Hende, the goldsmith Adam Bamme, and the vintner Henry Vanner. Mercers had been influential at the beginning of the decade, with John de Bernes serving two terms and John Pyell holding the mayoralty after him, until September 1373. But from October 1373 until September 1388 the often disparate and competitive interests of what might be loosely termed London's 'victualler trades' were, when threatened or united to single purpose, the dominant force in London. During these fifteen years the grocers held the mayoralty for seven years (Nicholas Brembre on four occasions); the fishmongers for three years (Sir William Walworth once and Nicholas Exton twice); and the skinner Sir Adam de Bury for one year. The mercer Adam Stable held office for a single term and the draper John Northampton for two. The early 1390s followed a similar pattern. The grocer William Venour opened the decade in 1389 and two others of that guild, William Staunton and John Hadley, followed in 1392 and 1393. It was only in the figures of John Fresshe in 1394 and Richard Whittington in 1397 that mercers took the mayoralty. Although mercers would go on to hold office in 1401, 1405 and 1406, in the ten years from 1397 to 1407 they could not match the dominance of the 'victuallers' in the 1370s and 1380s. The grocers, goldsmiths and drapers each held office twice, and the fishmongers for a single term.

* * *

The Ties That Bind

The associations and networks of these influential figures and their trades went far beyond their economic ties, as they were closely connected also by marriage. The vintner Henry Vanner, for example, was married to Margery Stodeye, the daughter and heiress to one of London's richest men, John Stodeye.[7] Another of Stodeye's daughters was married off to Brembre, and a third, Margaret, took as two of her four husbands Adam Bamme and John Philpot. Both men were closely involved with Vanner as partners in property deals. On Stodeye's death in 1376 three of his executors were revealed as Vanner, Brembre and Philpot. The commercial relationship between Vanner and Brembre largely developed after the summer of 1379 and centred on property development, lucrative land management, and rents and lending. In September and November 1387, shortly before his downfall at the hands of the Lords Appellant, Nicholas Brembre would convey much of his London and overseas property and chattels to Vanner.[8] Henry Vanner was later an associate of one of Whittington's closest friends and business partners, the mercer John Shadworth. On 25 June 1392, having been elected as sheriffs and believed to be behind a wider refusal by the City to accede to Richard II's demands for further loans, both Vanner and Shadworth were summoned to appear before the king at Nottingham and were imprisoned at his leisure.

By the early 1390s leading figures in most of the pre-eminent guilds or companies can be seen to have moved beyond and even rejected the parameters and constraints of their traditional trades, operating instead as sometimes closed and at other times fluid syndicates that shifted their interests across commerce, investment and politics with relative ease and with the facility of knowing that for the most part their enterprise would produce gains for the Crown. This 'mutuality' of interest suited both parties. For much of the period before Richard Whittington first assumed the mayoralty, a mutable coalition of grocers, fishmongers, vintners, brewers and outlying supporters was at the forefront of a self-interested drive for power over trade, regulation and control of London's governance. In his later terms of office, Whittington would become locked in a recurring and robust struggle with the grocers and fishmongers, but it was to the brewers he would become an implacable adversary.[9]

* * *

Vying for Position

Richard's accession to the throne in July 1377 coincided with the resumption of hostilities with France and with Spanish naval raids on

England's south coast, which exposed the vulnerability of her defences and posed a potentially existential threat to maritime trade. By 1379 the Exchequer found itself once again short of funds to finance both offence and defence. Gaunt's influence was waning and any prospect that he might continue as regent to the young king sat ill with the three interests capable of rescuing the national finances—the senior clergy, London's merchant class ('the City'), and the Commons in Parliament, each of which resented his autocratic manner and his presumption of power. His patronage of John Wycliffe had also succeeded in alienating the leading bishops; he aggravated them further in his impeachment of William of Wykeham, and he had made clear his distaste for the Church's influence in the management of the state.

It is during this period of flux—a 'changing of the guard'—that we see the emergence of a figure around whom a popular campaign against corruption would converge over the tumultuous course of the next seven years and who would become the lightning rod for protests directed at a cabal of powerful London figures largely drawn from the victualling guilds and determined that they alone should have the young king's ear. John Northampton had been a voluble critic and at times a physical adversary of those victualler trades he had accused of raising the true cost of food imports, restricting supplies and forcing up prices. He was a supporter of Wycliffe and was held also to enjoy the patronage of Gaunt himself.[10] In March 1377, he had influenced the compilation of the 'Jubilee Book', a set of ordinances that pressed for free trade and that took aim at the restrictive practices of the victuallers.[11] What may have begun, before the young king's coronation, as a combination of economic and social protest quickly developed into an intensely political contest after it.

Myers describes Northampton's opponents as better organised, better resourced and better placed in their counter-effort to turn the tables on his closest supporters—chiefly drapers and mercers—by railing instead against *their* restrictive practices and by whipping up the underlying prejudices of many Londoners against those who traded with foreigners and encouraged their settlement in their city, allegedly at their expense.

However, the sticks and stones hurled in the skirmishes over food supply and price regulation were a sideshow to the far more consequential main event—a power struggle for influence over the governance of London and of England itself during Richard's immaturity. The opportunity to court the favour and shape the interests of the young king was seized by the leading figures in the victualler guilds, notably the fishmongers Walter Sibil and

William Walworth and the grocers John Philpot and Nicholas Brembre. Brembre was one of London's richest men and had accumulated a fortune as a grocer, wool merchant, landowner and rentier. His great wealth, and a determination to deploy it for political gain and influence at court, were not lost on an adolescent and later spendthrift king. His first civic office in 1372 was as alderman for Broad Street and sheriff of the City of London, and he became mayor of London in March 1377.

1378

In March 1378 Nicholas Brembre had a fierce and public confrontation with the goldsmith Sir Nicholas Twyford, which caused the celebrated merchant Adam Bamme to stand surety for his friend Twyford.[12] Bamme had a substantial pedigree: he was one of London's richest and most influential figures, an exceptional goldsmith and jeweller, and a long-standing supplier to the household of John of Gaunt. He was later married to the notably wealthy and well-connected Margaret Stodeye. Later, in the 1390s, he was closely associated with a fellow goldsmith, Drew Barantyn, notable as one of Richard Whittington's own circle. Bamme served as London's mayor in 1390–1 and again in 1396–7; his death in office caused Richard II to 'impose' Richard Whittington in his place. However, it is Bamme's support for Twyford against Brembre that is of present interest. It is likely that by 1377

> he had already joined his friend, (Sir) Nicholas Twyford, in offering support to John of Northampton, who had by then placed himself at the head of a 'non-victualling' party intent on reducing the power of merchant capitalists such as Brembre. Bamme and Twyford were far wealthier and better respected than Northampton's other supporters, and undoubtedly used their influence to secure his re-election for a second term as mayor in October 1382.[13]

August 1378 marked the next misadventure of John of Gaunt, before the walls of St Malo. His 'great expedition' of mounted knights and a fleet of warships rigged to seize Brittany and intimidate the French failed miserably and stood in risible comparison with the exploits of the swashbuckling John Philpot, who had become something of a national hero. If Philpot's adventures annoyed Lancaster's party, then his achievements enraged them. Here was a fellow, they charged, who flaunted his wealth and wielded undue influence without responsibility. In truth it hardly mattered, for Philpot was a close intimate of the two most powerful men in

London, Walworth and Brembre, and would soon succeed the latter as mayor. He was, to all intents, their populist right arm and they basked in his popularity. In France, Gaunt was on the back foot, his siege abandoned, the campaign over: another ignominious misfortune.

At home, Gaunt once more turned his attention to domestic politics. He had already formed an 'alliance' of sorts with John Northampton, which produced its first fruit in October 1378 when he prevailed upon Parliament to remove Walworth and Philpot from their offices as war treasurers and introduce a statute that pronounced free trade in all food-stuffs except wine. The result was that Gaunt himself now became a target for the victuallers, who charged him, as they had done with the drapers and mercers, with direct complicity in undermining the freedoms and ancient trading privileges of Londoners and affording these to foreigners. Again, they succeeded through better organisation and a populist and base appeal to racial and economic prejudice, a theme that Whittington himself would have to contend with time and again throughout forty years of commercial and civic venture. The victuallers flexed their political and 'street' muscle, marshalled a vociferous section of public opinion, and seized the mayoralty. It was a swift and powerful riposte to Gaunt in particular. In October 1378 Philpot, recently deposed by Gaunt, succeeded Brembre as London's mayor. The next year the mayoralty fell to another victualler, the pepperer John Hadley, and in 1380 to another, a fishmonger, none other than Walworth himself.

Newgate, 1378

In 1378 it was announced that London was to have a 'reformed' prison system. This system had its base in the overhaul of English common law and the establishment of a new assizes structure between 1166 and 1176 by Henry II, which required that gaols be constructed throughout the country to enable the king's peripatetic judges to dispense he justice.[14] The diseased and filth-ridden hole of Newgate, in which the unfortunate poor were incarcerated for the slightest misdemeanour, was one product of this 'gaol delivery'. By 1337 conditions were so dire and so reviled that one of England's leading figures, the wealthy Sir John Poultney, established an annual contribution of 4 marks to the relief of its prisoners, setting a precedent for support and reform that Whittington and his friend and co-reformer, Sir Thomas Knolles, would develop much further.[15] In 1378 it would be the primary destination for serious criminals while Ludgate would be reserved for freemen of the city, an absurd contradiction surely, and for those among the higher clergy who had been both licentious and incautious enough to be apprehended for their greed and corruption. Time spent at Ludgate would be brief and relatively comfortable. What were Londoners to make of it? Was this the moment when, like many of his fellow citizens sickened by the circumstances in which the destitute and the vulnerable found themselves imprisoned in London's infamous hell-hole, and now affronted by this deepening of their isolation and the separation and cushioning of the better-off and better-connected, Whittington initiated a lifelong interest in Newgate, which would survive him in the provisions of his will more than forty years later?

More to the point, who had conceived this proposition to offer more hospitable circumstances to their friends who had fallen foul of the law? None other than London's incumbent mayor, Nicholas Brembre. A binary prison system was now established in which the inmates of Newgate would suffer acutely while those confined to Ludgate would be seen to accept some measure of chastisement, but also serve their time in a far more leisurely and agreeable fashion. At the Stocks, Londoners had already coined a suitable aphorism, 'Freeman's leisure, Brembre's pleasure'.[16] Brembre, a figure some today might describe as somewhere between driven, singular and even Machiavellian, would prove himself the most astute of operators: he knew both the value of political debt and how to trade on its repayment.

In October 1378 London saluted its new mayor, John Philpot, less than a month before an outbreak of plague was confirmed at York, where it would take a heavy toll on children and on military recruitment in the North.[17] Travellers and pedlars arriving in London reported that the town had closed its gates, and gravediggers were excavating deep pits and lining them with faggots and kindling, burning the bodies of whole families. It had not yet broken out of the town and the burghers had moved firmly to contain it. Households suspected of harbouring the pestilence had been daubed in red so all would know not to venture nearby. Those where it had already claimed lives were scourged with fire. In London, some took confidence that a harsh winter would kill it off, and as late as March 1379 London was still not free of a prolonged freeze that had gripped it since December 1378. Snow remained thick on the ground. Under Philpot's direction London proved to be remarkably effective in both its precautions and its vigilance. His officers reported that, during the winter, the city had sustained less than three dozen deaths resulting from a combination of boils, vomiting and 'the shits', which at first appeared to resemble the pestilence. The few remaining physicians and apothecaries who had survived the horrors of 1348 concluded, however, that none matched the severity or the contagion of that time. It was no more than one of the many routine maladies that daily afflicted this over-crowded and breathless place.

18

ARRIVAL

Having completed his apprenticeship and no doubt immersed himself in Fitzwarin's business, Whittington chose, or more likely was encouraged, to 'announce' himself in January 1379. The previous year had seen London gripped by significant unrest, partly a consequence of rumours of French preparations for invasion and of the likely cost to the public purse of expensive defences. At the same time a new and heightened threat was posed to London's trade and to political relations with 'the City' by the decamping of part of the court and many of its free-spending barons from London to their country seats. One might hardly have noticed elsewhere the founding of New College, Oxford, by William of Wykeham, who, as Chancellor to Richard II in 1389–91, Whittington would come to know well.[1] Diversions were, after all, plentiful, not least the free-spirited initiatives provided throughout the course of 1378 by Philpot, who after his election as mayor continued to enthral and bemuse Londoners in equal measure. The very happenstance that he succeeded his close political ally and business confederate, Nicholas Brembre, suggested that London was in for an even wilder ride in 1379. Both had eluded the fallout from their association with Adam de Bury, during whose mayoralty in 1373 they had served together as his sheriffs and whose own involvement in corruption, malfeasance and speculation had resulted in his impeachment by the Good Parliament of 1376.[2] Philpot had the ability, however, to smartly capture and channel the spirit of England, and was singularly effective in deploying his considerable wealth and his crowd-pleasing talents in not only articulating what many Londoners wished to hear but in creating a populist vision for them to follow.

He would certainly leave his mark on the city, on the citizens and on Parliament in an eventful year which saw him funding almost single-handedly the fitting out of a fleet to be sent to the assistance of the Duke of Brittany against the King of France.[3] In London itself he made clear his determination to tackle the appalling effluence that had built up in the city's streets and watercourses and that slopped along its ugly route towards the Thames, where it aggregated an even greater excrescence on the banks of the river. London now had a man at the helm who would have the city ditches excavated and cleansed, funded by a rate of fivepence charged upon each household. As a result of his adventures and his willingness to fund the city's defences, and in an evidently persuasive democratising of responsibility and cost, Philpot commanded sufficient general popularity to get away with it. For a short time, his influence was also felt in Parliament where he was able to kill off a bill considered deeply inimical to the privileges enjoyed by the City.[4]

Making His Mark

The circumstances of Richard Whittington's 'arrival' as a figure of note, and the earliest record we have of his 'emergence' in London, lay in the City's need to fund urgent works and to offer an incentive to attract back 'the great lords of the realm' in order to restore their custom and favour. The proposition took the form of a somewhat pandering solution—the raising of a 'gift' of £600 in January 1379 to encourage their return. Whittington was one of the 200 citizens who contributed, in his case the significant sum of 5 marks. It was his first public act and was almost certainly designed to attract attention. The question is why.

> The name of Richard Whityngton first appears in *Letter-Book* H. fol. 110 a (as Richard Whytyngdone) in the 2nd year of Richard II (A.D. 1379) where he contributes 5 marks towards a loan to the City authorities; about four-fifths of the subscribers contributing the same, which is the lowest figure among the contributions: John Philpot, the Mayor, giving the largest sum, 10 pounds; William Walworth, Nicholas Brembre, and others, 5 pounds, and Nicholas Twyford 4 pounds.[5]

Given his relative youth and inexperience and the likelihood that most donors were exhorted by the City and by their guilds, and individually invited, to contribute to the loan, Whittington's involvement may have been tantamount to a 'statement', an initiative perhaps by Fitzwarin and other influential merchants to promote his name, effectively marking him as a 'rising star'. Lysons suggests that Whittington was already a substantial

London citizen by 1379, but there is little evidence for this, and he was aged only twenty or twenty-one at this time.[6] What we do see throughout the second half of the 14th century and the first quarter of the 15th, by which time Whittington had become one of the most influential figures in London, is a widespread and well-established pattern of facilitation in which small groups of wealthy and influential merchants not only combined to spread the risk of their investments but also followed the practice of their companies in sharing opportunities with and taking a punt on enterprising and youthful upcomers in their ranks. In Whittington's case it amounted to both an initiation and a presentation on the London stage.[7] This was arguably a highly suitable initiative for a future pantomime star.

While Whittington's contribution to the City's gift is generally held to mark the outset of his commercial career, the device of a gift also established welcome parameters for what could be reasonably expected of London's common folk and poor. The size, purpose and consequences of the gift shaped how London's merchant class would in future deploy their own wealth to make provision for the poor and underwrite the cost of civic works. One cannot imagine its triple purpose—enticing the barony back to London to boost trade, thereby raising taxation without increasing the price of food, and funding infrastructure and repairs—would escape the attention of a progressive mind. Although it is true that the poor could not escape their tax burden, it is notable that 'A few wealthy citizens left money for the relief of poor taxpayers, and others made handsome bequests to the city … Although extraordinary expenses were still met from household levies and assessments of chattels as well as by income tax, there were attempts to make the rich shoulder a greater share than in the past.'[8] Whether the 5 marks contribution helped or not—and it seems likely that it did since the evidence suggests that Whittington's career took off almost immediately—his gesture was noticed and valued. At the least, it was intended to announce that he was now a freeman of London, with ample resources and backing, ready and equipped not just to initiate his career but to accelerate it. The aim was to make himself known quickly and with something of a splash. It did so.

To establish himself at this time, Whittington would have needed a reasonable stock of goods, either his own or access to those of a partner or investor, and a small reserve of liquid capital, the size of which would depend on the quality of introductions he sought to make or, more likely, which were made on his behalf, together with an evident confidence in his own abilities. It is likely that some of this funding, despite the limitations

151

on her resources, would have been placed in trust by his mother at the time of his departure from Pauntley. It is conceivable that Sir Ivo Fitzwarin had 'invested' and grown it on his behalf for the day when he was ready to announce himself as a fully indentured mercer. He may even have supplemented it, perhaps in the form of a deferred loan, on condition that the boy would 'reward' his confidence as his career developed. Might he also have furnished his protégé with at least part of his 'start-up' stock or provided a line of credit for him to acquire it? Given the common practice of merchants collaborating in small consortia, it is possible that some of Whittington's funding may have come from Fitzwarin's own mercer associates, keen but also professionally disposed to support the endeavours of a young and favoured player from within their ranks. There was little risk in doing so. If Whittington succeeded there would be gains for all, while the prospect of failure was hedged by a system of relatively assured introductions to tried and trusted patrons whose needs offered a high certainty of 'closure'. In any case, such introductions by their very nature made it likely that Whittington would be chaperoned in his early dealings with wealthy clients, whose business was far too important to place at risk with a novice, however impressive or well regarded he might have been. Business was business. We can imagine Whittington in the early years of his enterprise working primarily with and on behalf of Fitzwarin and his associates. Later, as he made his mark, he would build his own networks and make his own arrangements, while still drawing on and rewarding, as long-term 'investors', those who had helped launch his career. We should not underestimate the extent to which this support model was practised by London's merchant class. New entrants to the guilds meant renewal of their ranks; they offered opportunities for older heads to partner in and profit from the energies of 'new blood'; they created possibilities for laying off part of their own business burden to someone younger and willing to work hard for long hours to sustain it, take it in new directions or, in due course, buy it outright; and young, successful merchants from good families were also a fine catch to assimilate into the family through a well-matched marriage. Each of these would feature in Richard Whittington's own pathway. Later, as an employer of apprentices and a three-time warden of the Mercers' Company, he would sponsor or broker such arrangements himself.

* * *

Within three years Whittington is recorded as supplying velvets, silks and damasks to early clients among London's nobility and at court, some of whom quickly took on the role of patron, recommending him enthusiastically to their circles. It is interesting that he should be associated with so-called luxury goods and so early in his career. We don't hear of him as a run-of-the-mill mercer plying a lower quality of goods or travelling to the small country towns and regional fairs to eke out a subsistence living. He is never described in this way. Rather, he was received from the outset as one of a new echelon of mercers (and embracing merchants from other trades, to whom he was naturally drawn) bent on building their enterprises, investing their wealth and diversifying their interests, and in some instances resembling 'merchant adventurers'. While, like any ambitious mercer, he contracted with proven suppliers and manufacturers in the key centres of the Cotswolds, in Herefordshire and Yorkshire and at Coventry, and would later employ agents to undertake his work much further afield, including abroad, Richard Whittington was very much embedded in London and drawn to its burgeoning overseas trade and opportunities. Just two or three years after his 'arrival' and probably in his mid-twenties, we find him trading in cloths and in circles more typically associated with a long-established senior London mercer—a fellow who would deal in a range of fine cloths, including silk, linen, fustian and worsted, and who could also procure those luxury small goods and what we refer to today as 'accessories' so sought after by the English court. This suggests that not only did he rise very quickly, probably with the benefit of sponsorship and shared investment, but he had access almost from the outset to higher-level markets and more rarefied suppliers, likely to be Italian, than many of his much longer-serving competitors. Whittington would trade the very best that England could offer but he quickly recognised not only the interest shown by the Venetians, Genoese and Milanese in the purchase and import of fine English wool and cloth but the exceptional quality and design of the 'luxury' goods these centres could provide to him in return. In his dealings with the Italians and the Flemish he would draw on the energy, endeavour and enterprise of Europe's great cloth-manufacturing centres, described as 'pockets of capitalism in a pre-capitalistic world' whose great guilds 'bore no resemblance to the small associations of equal masters in towns, or crafts working for a limited market'.[9]

We might also venture the proposition that in Whittington's case his youth—and one assumes his energy, sharp-wittedness, focus and drive— were advantages and were perceived as such. His youth was not a 'barrier to entry' nor an impediment to his rapid advancement. He seems to have exuded confidence and capability, and to have had this spotted by those who took him under their wing, and was evidently trusted for his efficiency, engagement and discretion in his dealings at court. He was an exception in his youth and continued to be so throughout a forty-year commercial and civic career.

* * *

The king on whom he would make such a strong impact was even younger of course, by ten years or more, would not reach his thirteenth birthday until the following January 1380 and was still reliant on a system of advisory councils to lead his government. In October and November 1379 Richard II had convened Parliament at Whittington's home town of Gloucester, lodging his court in the abbeys of Gloucester and neighbouring Tewkesbury. Parliament met in one of the few places outside London which could accommodate its numbers and provide the setting and gravitas it required—the great guest hall of St Peter's. Given the new king's age, it was not all hard work and serious matters of state. As one writer puts it, 'The place was more like a fair than a house of religion, and games were played on the cloister garth.'[10]

Whittington would go on to become neither an 'equal master' nor someone who confined himself to the limitations of a single enterprise or market. He was fortunate to emerge and evolve as a product of an age which had access not only to what were now industrial-scale raw materials at home but also to expanding markets abroad for finishing and sale and the large-scale finance necessary to unlock them. Access to this wealth—both in the form of investors and customers—was almost certainly influential in his arrival and early progress. The great wealth accrued by English financiers in the early part of the 14th century had been instrumental in laying the foundations for the evolution of the merchant adventurism of the late 14th and early 15th centuries, and it also had a redistributive effect which widened not only the pool and enterprise of merchants but also their customer base:

> it was the expanding wool trade of the thirteenth and early fourteenth century which gave birth to the great capitalist financiers whose speculations reached highest in the syndicates which financed the Hundred Years' War. But ... the effect of the staple monopoly in the fifteenth century was to prevent the emergence of the great financier and to establish instead a large and substantial middle class.[11]

Of course, the efforts of these predecessors were foundations, not the finished edifice; the building blocks of a new and increasingly international capitalism were still under construction. The ingredient required to connect and synergise them, at times spectacularly, was the entrepreneurial vision and drive of outward-looking merchants and investors like the young mercer from Pauntley. The formerly self-contained and geographically disparate sub-economies of sheep rearing, wool production and fine cloth manufacture[12] had, by the time of Whittington's first business ventures, begun to converge and integrate with their 'connective tissue', the intensely entrepreneurial businesses of import–export, port development, ship design, cost-efficient transportation, and quayside storage and distribution, which hitherto had been the preserve of particular and often insular interests, trades and even nationalities. Whittington worked himself into the vanguard of a merchant elite that transformed the reach, scale and diversification opportunities of sheep farming in England's rural hinterland into a sophisticated international trade which opened the port and city of London to an ever-wider range of economic activity, and which helped make England's capital for much of his life one of the foremost economic engines of Europe. Yet this relentless progress could hardly disguise some of the acute structural social, economic and judicial casualties of wealth polarisation.

In March 1379 reports from London's infamous prison of Newgate indicated that as many as three times the number from the previous year had died since Easter 1378 in squalid conditions, most likely from want of clean water and food not yet condemned for swine. More deaths would follow as the deep freeze of February 1379 took its toll in the spring. In August, Whittington was given a sharp reminder of death closer to home, with that of his frail eldest brother, William. It seems that the family estates had achieved some measure of recovery under the more direct hand of the middle brother, Robert, long before William's demise, though even under his direction Pauntley rarely yielded anything more than a modest income. That said, he would later advance both Pauntley's and his own circumstances when he successfully contested the manor of Staunton in Worcestershire, winning his claim to be the kinsman and heir of Robert Staunton.

In September, John Philpot completed his eventful tenure as London's mayor and was succeeded by another grocer, John Hadley, who offers some parallels with the journey into which Whittington was now entering.

19

REVOLT

Connections at Court

On 16 January 1380 Parliament declared Richard II of age to rule. Within three years Richard Whittington was established as a supplier to influential figures at court, his route almost certainly secured as the beneficiary of Sir Ivo Fitzwarin's productive social and military connections. Following his father's death in 1361, Fitzwarin was a ward of Edward III's wife Philippa of Hainault. Declared of age in 1369, able to recover his father's lands, and knighted sometime before 1371, he was almost certainly instrumental in providing introductions and arranging access for his young protégé. Among Whittington's earliest clients was Thomas of Woodstock, 1st Duke of Gloucester and Earl of Buckingham. Fitzwarin had served with his banner and pennon in Woodstock's retinue at the Siege of Nantes in 1380. Woodstock's connections were impeccable: he was the youngest child of Edward III and Philippa of Hainault, brother to Fitzwarin's liege lord, Edward the Black Prince, and to John of Gaunt, another commander under whom Fitzwarin had served, and each of them uncles to Richard II. Whittington probably first supplied luxury cloths to Woodstock sometime around 1381 and continued to do so well into the 1390s, and may well have been a supplier to Woodstock's son Humphrey, later a ward of the Crown. Even more strikingly, we find John of Gaunt, Duke of Lancaster and one of England's richest men, among Whittington's patrons by the mid-1380s. The young mercer also made an early impression on Gaunt's teenage son Henry Bolingbroke, to whom he too became a supplier of fine goods and who, in 1400 as Henry IV, appointed him to his King's Council. Robert de Vere, Duke of Ireland and a close intimate of Richard II, is another who features prominently among the young mercer's rarefied clientele in the mid-1380s, as does Humphrey de Bohun, Earl of

Hereford, with whom Fitzwarin had served at sea about the time Whittington arrived at Leadenhall. Sir Thomas Beauchamp, Earl of Warwick (d. 1401), another person with whom Fitzwarin campaigned during the early years of Whittington's apprenticeship, also stands out as an early noted client. He is not to be confused with the similarly named Sir Thomas Beauchamp of Whitelackington (d. 1444), for whom in 1414 Whittington took a personal and very public risk in standing bail in the sum of 1,000 marks when Beauchamp was implicated by Henry V in the unsuccessful Lollard uprising inspired by Sir John Oldcastle. While Whittington successfully nurtured these introductions, Fitzwarin appears to have pressed on with his military career, taking up a series of related official appointments during the early years of Whittington's mercery. In 1381, in the tumultuous aftermath of the Peasants' Revolt, we find Fitzwarin appointed to his first royal commission and two months later as a commissioner with powers to proclaim against and prevent unlawful assemblies. By the end of August, he had been elevated as keeper of Mere Castle in Wiltshire, built originally by Henry III's brother Richard, Earl of Cornwall.

From Subversion to Charter

In his early twenties and with his career beginning to unfold before him, Whittington, like many of his fellow citizens, must have imagined that first London and then perhaps England at large would descend into political and economic anarchy during the events and aftermath of the summer of 1381. Yet, having dealt with the populist threat, England's new king and his partisan advisers were both confident and determined to focus on what they deemed to be a greater threat to their interests, the very quarter in which Whittington hoped to thrive. In the months following the Peasants' Revolt, Richard II, barely into his teens and just four years into his reign, was more convinced than ever that the City and its leading guilds were a material threat both to his personal and to national security. The mercers were among the increasingly powerful guilds whose numbers and resources had grown both before and after the confrontation of 1381. Though professionally and socially cohesive, as an organisational entity the mercers lacked a clear administrative and legal structure by which the Crown could bring their activities and interests to account. Formally at least, they held no property, no dedicated meeting hall and no licence to operate as a legal body; they adhered to a relatively vague and untested constitution, were unable to identify let alone list the entirety of their membership, and, most tellingly, a matter of great concern to themselves let alone the king and his ministers, they lacked the status and 'legitimacy' of a royal charter.[1] It would be another ten years before the formal process to secure this fundamental objective would gather any impetus. Meanwhile, the figure who may have been instrumental in getting it over the line was still two years away from commencing his second career as one of England's most influential 'lenders' and three years from embarking on his civic career as the common councillor for Coleman Street on 31 July 1384.[2] The years 1380–4 would prove enormously influential in Whittington's commercial career and civic outlook. The period was marked in 1380 by a public mood increasingly hostile to price fixing in the supply of food; followed by the ground-shaking events of the Peasants' Revolt in the summer of 1381; leading in turn to the knighting of William Walworth and Nicholas Brembre and their consolidation at court and at the centre of national politics. Two years of social and political upheaval then followed as the mayoralty was snatched by John Northampton, the charismatic draper and supporter of the Lancastrian faction, who subsequently fell from grace in 1383. That year heralded Brembre's succession as mayor. Brembre was victorious in reinstating the election of aldermen by wards, allowing them to stand in successive years and in effect depriving others of their right to direct election.[3] Meanwhile, Whittington's breakthrough in supplying goods to leading figures at court was also turning his mind towards politics. In October 1383, Northampton was effectively outmuscled, politically and physically, by a resurgent Brembre. Many saw the contest as one of 'dispossession' brought about in part by Northampton's alienation of his own supporters following his pronouncements on the Peasants' Revolt and their fear that he was disposed to revolution. It was the end of his mayoral ambitions.

> He held it for two years, partly by means of influence at court, partly by strategy in appealing for popular support and partly, his enemies alleged, by keeping armed men at hand on his second election day. He used his power with unflagging energy in the enforcement of price regulation and in attacking profiteers and usurers. This unfamiliar zeal soon aroused fears of social revolution.[4]

Yet it was clear from the way Brembre had conducted himself and his campaign that the prospect of his returning to office was by far the greater threat to political and social progress. Infamously, Brembre had stiffened the Guildhall with armed supporters who drowned out or beat down any opposition to their man, a disturbing portent of what was to come if he won the day.[5] Brembre was not someone who let dangerous adversaries slink off to lick their wounds. The reaction was forceful and intimidating when it arrived. On 7 February 1384 Northampton was arrested on a trumped-up charge of sedition, which in turn caused his supporters to take to the streets, serving only to confirm to those interests who had withdrawn from him that he was indeed a potential spark for political upheaval and social revolution. Following the affray, his kinsman John Constantine was identified as a ringleader and executed. Northampton himself and two of his associates, John More and Richard Norbury, were arrested and summarily sentenced to death, later commuted to ten years' imprisonment. Each of the three was to be held in a separate prison at least a hundred leagues outside London. The Cornish judge Sir Robert Tresilian intervened on Northampton's behalf, directing his confinement to Tintagel.[6] It would be two years before Richard II pardoned Northampton, while still upholding his banishment from London, and he would wait until 1395 for full restoration of his citizenship.[7]

20

AT COURT

November 1382 saw the death of John d'Argentine, father of Sir Ivo's wife Maud, already one of the wealthiest women in England, with significant landholdings throughout the south and south-west. His co-heirs were his three daughters and their issue. The Fitzwarins were sumptuously rich and their daughter Alice, now ten years old, was assured of a striking inheritance. Richard Whittington, at 23 some 13 years older, was by this time perhaps overseeing the Fitzwarin business, possibly still conducted from the Fitzwarin home. Leadenhall was conveniently close to the large community of drapers who populated much of Cornhill, Candlewick Street and Cheapside. Their mystery still pledged to the church and parish of St Mary Bethlehem, home to the hospital Whittington would have encountered on his first day in London had he entered the city through Bishopsgate.[1]

Permeation

In pursuing his early career at court, Whittington was following his commercial nose and stepping into a long and well-established tradition of commercial service to the Palace of Westminster that offered to the most successful merchants wider rewards on behalf of king and state. These included civil and port administration, the collecting and farming of taxes, acting as a contractor to the king's armies, managing specific aspects of the royal supply chain, acting as an adviser on overseas trade, and in some instances presiding in the king's name over public inquiries and the regulation of goods, services and measures. Whittington would eventually have a role in each. The provision of loans rather than goods, however refined or coveted, was the key to these opportunities. But, first, he would make his mark as a mercer. By the early 1380s he had firmly established himself as a supplier of luxury velvets and gold cloths to Richard II's favourite courtier and confidant, Robert de Vere, 'a glittering young noble, a few years older than himself ... for whom he had conceived a strong affection, lavishing on him every favour',[2] procuring goods worth a prodigious £2,000, and to the king's cousin, the Earl of Derby, Henry Bolingbroke, later to become Henry IV. The key to this rapid accrual of elevated clients, and a further reflection of the high-level military circles in which the Fitzwarins moved, was the 'moving spirit' and acting chamberlain of the royal household, Sir Simon Burley, Richard II's military tutor and a former servant of his father, the Black Prince.[3]

In 1383, Whittington is recorded as having been paid £80 for goods and services to Hugh, 2nd Earl of Stafford, and to the 3rd Earl, his teenage son Thomas. He would go on to supply the comital household for at least twenty years, sustaining his relationship with the 5th Earl, Thomas's youngest brother Edmund. It is probable that his service to the Staffords continued with Edmund's son the 6th Earl Humphrey, 1st Duke of Buckingham.[4] There was an unlikely though not unusual connection. On Thomas's death, his younger brother married his childless widow. As the eldest daughter of Thomas of Woodstock, Duke of Gloucester, and Eleanor de Bohun, and a first cousin of both Richard II and Henry Bolingbroke, Anne of Gloucester was an important catch.[5] Woodstock was the key accelerator here. As one of Whittington's most important customers, he recommended the young mercer among his inner circle. The question is: how did Whittington find himself introduced in the first place? This throws up an intriguing and somewhat convoluted backstory, in part connected to both Sir Ivo Fitzwarin and to his father Sir William. The latter had a distinguished record of military service and a close association with the court. He had served as a commander with both Edward III and the Black Prince, was elevated as a Knight of the Garter, and held the formal position of 'knight for the body' to Edward's queen, Philippa of Hainault, in effect her 'bodyguard'.[6] His son had followed in his military footsteps and in 1380 served in Woodstock's retinue at the Siege of Nantes, pointedly adopting the swan crest in honour of his patron. A minor at the time of his father's death in 1361, Sir Ivo Fitzwarin was for a time 'at court' under the oversight of Queen Philippa. He remained close to Woodstock, to the Staffords and to the de Bohuns. There are suggestions that the house at Leadenhall may have been rented from the last-mentioned or from another of his father's military connections, the Nevilles. Woodstock's wife Eleanor was the sister of Mary de Bohun, the first wife of Henry IV and the mother of Henry V, who died in 1394 before her husband came to the throne. Whittington continued to develop his relationship with each of the leading families introduced by his mentor. Nor did he forget the influence and access they gave him, later making provision in his will for Woodstock's soul and for that of his elder brother, John of Gaunt, and Gaunt's son Bolingbroke. It was chiefly through these initial introductions that he extended his remarkable networks and came to acquire such great wealth and influence.

Loans at Court, 1383

This advancement turned not only on his merits as a mercer or on the quality of his cloths and luxury goods but also on his commercial instincts and ability to make money and, most importantly, to save it and keep it 'liquid'. Whittington also possessed another quality of great value: he was exceptionally discreet and this, combined with his financial resources and a sharp sense of 'opportunity', made him a perfect source of high-level borrowing. He was astute in modulating his interests between cloth, wool, lending and what might be termed 'adventurer' investment, later in his career spotting money-making opportunities which may have had relatively little direct connection with his early interests in mercery and wool. The trick was to remain commercially flexible, financially agile, while all the time retaining a strong degree of liquidity that enabled him to become almost indispensable to the English monarchy during the reign of three kings. His agility and his spread of interests ensured that he would ride out the troughs and the swells of economic and political turbulence over a period of more than thirty years from the mid-1380s to the glory of Agincourt in 1415. Fluctuations and opportunities in the wool trade would play an instrumental part in building his fortune and embedding him at the highest level. Against a backdrop of semi-continuous war with France, disruption to the European economies and, in London itself, a series of often volatile confrontations between City and king, he somehow managed to navigate what Power describes in this period as first raising up a class of great capitalists but 'then … levelling down the peaks'. Whittington was ever ready to lend but also ever careful not to exceed his limits—financial and good sense.

> The whole age is that of merchants tuned to a lower scale. The greatest of all—those of whom most is known, like Whittington and Hende—seldom exceed £3,000 in outstanding loans to the crown, a puny sum beside its

liabilities to de la Pole and Picard, or beside the dealings of a contemporary great landlord and bishop, Beaufort, who may at certain times have advanced to the crown, and had owing to him, sums exceeding £15,000.[7]

Loans to the court and to England's kings were nothing new and had been a characteristic feature of the dealings with leading merchants and the City for over a century. Typically sought and offered in a spirit of mutuality, they were, as May McKisack points out, when sought at the 'corporate' or 'City' level, often a source of tension, sometimes wilful belligerence.[8] Individually based, however, they were a fast track to offices and sinecures dispensed by the Crown and in some instances to political influence. In the early years of his career Whittington would become aware of figures such as Nicholas Twyford, Adam Carlisle, Nicholas Brembre, John Hadley, John Philpot and the discredited Richard Lyons actively proffering loans in return for commercial gain, political influence or social advancement.[9] However, even these 'lenders', their successors and later Whittington himself rarely exceeded a ceiling of £3,000, a paltry figure when compared to the sums made available by William de la Pole, who is recorded as having lent Edward III as much as £100,000 between the months of June 1338 and October 1339 and who at one point provided a single loan of £18,000.[10]

By comparison, during his early career Whittington was focused primarily on making a success of his nascent enterprise and was trading at a level of about £1,000 a year with the Great Wardrobe.[11] In due course, he would also become a frequent supplier to the King's Wardrobe, and to the Queen's Wardrobe in Tower Royal, and almost certainly a familiar at the 'Prince's Wardrobe', a favoured hostelry and place of business for London's leading mercers. Similarly, the King's Weigh House, the repository for the Crown's weights and measures, was a natural destination for someone who would come to act for the Crown in the regulation and accounting of the wool custom at Westminster and at Calais.

Initially, he was content in supplying the king and court with fine cloth and making money rather than seeking sinecures or political influence. The passage of his early career suggests that he was excited by politics but more as an observer than as a player. Until 1397, his interest lay chiefly in being close to the exercise of power by others rather than wielding it himself. However, making money, and in turn making it available to his patrons at court, produced a virtuous circle that made him wealthy and positioned him well for other openings. After he had proved his worth, this relationship quickly extended to the king himself. Not surprisingly, this enhanced his standing and produced further opportunities to enlarge his fortune. Caroline Barron notes: 'that the crown on its own played a large part in the creation of Whittington's wealth appears undeniable'.[12] For the moment, his interest in politics and 'reform' would remain subordinate to royal favour and his mushrooming enterprise. As Sylvia Thrupp puts it:

> The merchant did not aspire to a political career. The tangible favours for which he looked were in the shape of business for the royal household, military victual contracts and minor offices of profit. While still a young man, Richard Whittington was supplying the Great Wardrobe with quanti-ties of cloth of gold, embroidered velvet, and other valuable mercery, running to well over a year.[13]

First Civic Steps

Yet, for all its vivid excitement and consuming distraction, when he placed his enterprise in the context of City rather than court, Whittington recog-nised that in order to safeguard the conditions in which his business could flourish, untrammelled by those with little love for mercers and keen to exclude them from London's governance, it was in his own self-interest, and expected of him by his guild, that he enter local politics to promote and defend their common ground. On 31 July 1384 Richard Whittington was put forward and elected for a term of two years as a common council-lor for Coleman Street ward, the first step in a civic and largely reformist career that would extend for 36 years and see him become the alderman for Broad Street ward in 1393, transferring to Lime Street in 1398, serv-ing a part term as London's mayor in 1397, and re-elected for a full term later that year and again in 1406 and 1419.[14] His interest in enterprise, however, remained primary and he appears to have started investing in other opportunities at this time, acquiring his first London property, a row of tenements and shops at Castle Baynard, in the same month. During the next fifteen years his endeavours would, for the most part, synchronise with but occasionally run contrary to the ambitions of the monarch, with whom he was developing his business relationship.

Located near London Wall, Coleman Street's chief landmark was the ancient church of St Stephen, which, as a chapel to St Olave Jewry, had between 1171 and 1181 been granted by the Dean and Chapter of St Paul's to the prior and abbot of Butley in Suffolk. It is said to have func-tioned first as a synagogue, then as a parish church, and latterly as a chapel to St Olave's. Stow tells us that Coleman Street itself was named after

'Coleman, the first builder and owner thereof', who had the honour to give his name to one of the then 24 wards of the City of London.[15] During the course of the Civil War its popular tavern, 'The Star', became a favourite haunt of Oliver Cromwell and his party. Today it beats ever strongly as an integral and significant part of the City of London's commercial district. 1 Coleman Street is the eye-catching headquarters of one of the world's largest insurance companies, Legal and General. The St Stephen's that Whittington would have known so well was eventually destroyed by the Great Fire of 1666 and was 'meanly' rebuilt by Sir Christopher Wren in the 1670s. The few monuments that survived are attributed to the haberdashers, not the mercers.[16]

In 1384, the 'party' representing the interests of the fishmongers, grocers and vintners finally achieved the objective denied them eight years earlier by securing election to the Common Council by representatives of the wards, their chief power base.[17] Significantly, the new arrangements also extended to the election of the mayor and aldermen by the Common Council 'with as many sufficient men of the city as they might think necessary'.[18] Thus, whoever held sway in the Common Council would arguably control the city, and from this date both the council and the mayoralty were dominated by the most powerful guilds—these three and their 'competitors', the mercers, drapers and goldsmiths. These leading six were more consolidated, better resourced and characteristically organised on competitive lines. Relatively small cadres within this group of six would, almost exclusively, return London's mayor until the middle of the 17th century.

We know little of Sir Ivo Fitzwarin's own business at this time, but his personal wealth, his wife's recent inheritance and Whittington's striking progress—including perhaps managing Fitzwarin's commercial interests—must have been influential in allowing him to indulge his wish to return to soldiery. He appears to have 'attended' John of Gaunt throughout the course of 1385 and in July 1386 he joined his expedition for the recovery of the estates and inheritance of his wife Constance of Castile and León.[19] As for Whittington, he is recorded during 1385 as supplying the household of Henry Bolingbroke with expensive velvets and damasks.[20] The following year we hear of him, possibly for the first time, involved in a transaction with his family in Gloucestershire, in this instance lending a large sum of money to his uncle Philip Maunsell, his mother's brother. In February 1394 he would lend him the further sum of £500, but Maunsell defaulted upon his obligations and subsequently conveyed his manor at Over Lypiatt to Whittington by way of settlement.

Lender to the King

Whittington's most celebrated impact as a lender, however, was at the court of Richard II. Initially he confined his loans to a relatively closed circle of trusted clients who sought cash in hand, a line of credit, the resettlement of an extraneous debt, and Whittington's discretion. Of course, this had the dual merit of placing the borrower in his debt and of furnishing him with the means to purchase his goods. As these arrangements developed, they were sought by the higher echelons of Richard's court, providing him with access to a superior level of clientele than might have been the case had he confined his services and his ambitions simply to mercery and the sale of fine cloths. Here was an opportunity to be influential and become something of a stakeholder in the plans and prospects of others. That is not to say that he entered the role of lender with this intent; in fact it was more likely that the request was difficult to rebuff and the consequences of doing so would almost certainly have damaged his budding business. After all, if he didn't make the loan then somebody else surely would. There were good reasons to follow this course. First, the very request for a loan from a figure significantly above his social and economic station meant that they were in difficulty, foolish or errant. In helping to extricate them or simply sating their expensive lifestyle, he sought repayment through commissions, recommendations and opportunities otherwise denied to him. Second, those making the request clearly saw him as exceptionally trustworthy, and it was *they* who beat a path to *his* door. We encounter this estimation of him time and again in his dealings as a man, as a mercer, as a civic leader, and as a servant of the Crown—conscientious, stolidly moral and, above all, dependable. Third, his shift into lending in the mid-to-late 1380s is evidence that Whittington recognised that he had already outgrown mercery. It would continue to be an essential part of his business arrangements and it would remain at the heart of his social and political connections, but it was no longer his singular or his preferred path. An excellent way to make money, certainly, and he excelled in doing so, but there were far more interesting ways to mobilise and deploy his wealth. Not for him the conspicuous consumption that characterised the lifestyle of so many of his contemporaries; instead his money would be deployed to gain 'position', secure influence and widen his horizons. Fourth, it was known that Whittington's wealth was 'liquid'. It wasn't tied up in convoluted investments, in distant plots of land or in the construction of fine houses. It was readily available. There was also a fifth factor at play which became apparent only as his lending arrangements expanded: Whittington would not levy interest or necessarily press for like-for-like reimbursement. Rather, he looked instead for more imaginative forms of repayment. For the most part, eminent clients such as Sir Simon Burley, who had facilitated his earlier arrangements with Robert de Vere, and who borrowed 400 marks from him in 1387 against two coffers of jewels, or John Beaufort, Earl of Somerset, and Sir Thomas Talbot who borrowed 1,000 marks and £100 respectively to finance their military endeavours, each understood the quid pro quo of these arrangements. They were assured that they would never be pressed or chased for repayment; it was simply understood that they would make good their debt in good time and in various ways. It was a template which the king himself would exploit for his own purposes, and for the most part it would suit the lender.

> His increasing preoccupation with the demands of royal finance led him to take less interest in the mercer's trade through which his fortune had been made, and to concentrate upon the use to which his capital could be put. From 23 Aug. 1388 to 23 July 1422, he made *at least* 59 separate loans to the Crown of sums ranging from £4 to £2,833.[21]

Wonderful and Merciless

Yet, before this relationship was initiated, the court, London, and England itself would be racked by controversy and upheaval. Among the casualties were some of Whittington's chief patrons and one of his guild's most intractable adversaries. In November 1386 the new parliamentary session, the so-called Wonderful Parliament, had seized on the growing unpopularity of Richard II and laid the blame for recent military failures and misadventure on his inner coterie of advisers, accusing them of misappropriating campaign funds and embezzlement. The powerful and overreaching Sir Nicholas Brembre was now firmly in its sights. His gradual eclipse had also affected the improbable figure of Geoffrey Chaucer, who had been drawn too near to Brembre's now declining sun.[22] Parliament appointed a commission of leading nobles, the so-called Lords Appellant, to intervene and act as the king's regents. Among their number were Thomas of Woodstock, the king's uncle; Thomas Beauchamp, Earl of Warwick; Richard Fitzalan, Earl of Arundel and Surrey, and subsequently Henry Bolingbroke, Earl of Derby, and Thomas de Mowbray, Earl of Nottingham. Richard rejected their authority but lacked the means to resist them. He sought instead to mobilise his allies and in June 1387 to negotiate a secret and deeply controversial treaty with France so that he might direct his entire resources against his domestic opponents. This involved ceding all of England's possessions in northern France, including the great and symbolic prize of Calais, in order to contrive a peace. In turn, the French agreed to restore most of the Duchy of Aquitaine provided the English king paid homage to Charles V. Richard's enemies had wind of the accord and moved against him to abort it. In August, the king effectively forced his superior judges to rule that the Appellants had no legal authority and were themselves guilty of treason, and demanded their arrest. What must Whittington have thought as four of his most esteemed clients were denounced as enemies of the state? And what of his mixed loyalties, for it was none other than Robert de Vere who raised an army in support of the king but was defeated on 19 December by Woodstock at Radcot on Thames? The king barricaded himself in the Tower and was forced to surrender on the 27th. Initially, the Appellants threatened to execute him for his dealings with France but they were cautioned against it, forcing him instead to convene Parliament.

On 3 February 1388 'the Merciless Parliament' commenced session, acquiring this sobriquet for its ruthless pursuit and execution of its targets. Among them were de Vere and Brembre. Charges of corruption, betrayal and treason were levelled directly at the most senior figures among the king's circle and supporters. His opponents included some of Whittington's most notable patrons—Woodstock, Beauchamp, Bolingbroke. They assailed Richard and his close supporters with largely contrived charges of surrender in France, corruption and embezzlement, but the charges cut to the heart of Richard's ruling cadre. Michael de la Pole, 1st Earl of Suffolk; Brembre; de Vere, Duke of Ireland and Earl of Oxford; Alexander Neville, Archbishop of York; and England's Chief Justice, Robert Tresilian, were found guilty of 'living in vice, deluding the said king … embracing the mammon of iniquity for themselves'.[23] Neville was spared execution but was exiled, while the rest were sentenced to be drawn and hanged. De la Pole 'had a history' and had been impeached in 1386 by the Wonderful Parliament on charges of embezzlement and negligence, the first English official to be removed by this process. He continued to enjoy Richard's favour, however, and was a natural target for the Appellants. He escaped to Paris and remained in France until his death in September 1389.[24] De Vere, so prominent and influential as an early Whittington patron, also fled to France and would die there in a hunting accident in November 1392. At the time of his death, he owed Whittington the sum of £1,903 16s 5d.

The debt was eventually extinguished on the instruction of the Crown ten years later following the sale of de Vere's forfeited assets.[25] Richard's Chief Justice, Tresilian, and Nicholas Brembre were put to death. Four other knights and members of Brembre's household were also hanged.

There was a further sting in the tail for Whittington. The distinguished Burley, Lord Warden of the Cinque Ports, Constable of Dover Castle, Knight of the Garter, a campaigner with the Black Prince and for a time head of Richard II's household, and an influential figure to whom Whittington had lent 400 marks just a year earlier, was impeached for treason and executed. Parliament was dissolved on 4 June, and by the time of its recall at Cambridge in September 1388 it was the Lords Appellant who were unpopular, under duress and on the back foot, accused by many of pursuing a vendetta against the king and his supporters rather than occupying themselves with good government. Richard finally secured his convenient peace with France in the Truce of Leulinghem, while at home he was bent on revenge. Woodstock, 1st Duke of Gloucester, Whittington's first significant client among the nobility, was exiled to Calais and murdered there in September 1397.[26]

Business as Usual

Though not politically active or involved in the events that preceded or followed the two Parliaments, Whittington had well-known patrons among the adversaries and the 'casualties' on both sides. Yet his business and standing appear to have come through unscathed. Indeed, he looks to have prospered despite what at times had the hallmarks of a prospective civil war. On 23 August 1388, shortly before the Cambridge Parliament at which Richard II recovered ground against his opponents, he took the path that would eventually mark him as one of the most influential of English 'lenders.' 'Preference' in the wool trade was the price offered by the king in return. In 1389, Richard II purchased two cloths of gold from Whittington in the sum of £11, which he presented as gifts to emissaries from Scotland, marking a step change in his supply relationship, though there was an element of 'what the king giveth ...' since the mercer was prevailed upon to contribute to the Chamberlain a surety of £10 for the defence of London. Overall, between 1388 and 1422 Whittington made seven loans to Richard II, amounting to over £2,000, and he later made a further 51 loans to Richard's great adversary and successor, Bolingbroke, totalling about £30,000. In some transactions Whittington was assigned part of the wool tax collected at the staple ports in lieu of direct repayment, a prelude to October 1401 when he was appointed collector of the wool custom in London. The year 1388 saw the beginning of a relationship in which Richard II would spend freely on luxury materials and finished goods, setting a pattern of ostentatious consumption which was not lost either on the court or on London's wealthy merchant class. Whittington had worked himself to the centre of an intense if short-lived 'consumer boom', led by the king himself, which underscored the integral duality of 'borrow to spend', with Whittington a 'supplier' on both counts. Within four years his account at court would stand at nearly £4,000.

The elevation of Richard Whittington as a preferred lender to Richard II was good for business, existing and new. The king's favourites and other notables within his court approached the mercer for what might be termed 'small loans', and Whittington appears to have been able to accommodate them from his own resources, suggesting not only that his mercery business was doing well but that his facility and willingness to lend were inextricably linked. In some cases, the loans were the means that enabled the borrower to purchase his goods; in others they were a facility drawn on to meet other needs or exigencies. This did not mean that Whittington dispensed with 'credit', though he minimised it, and later in his career he acquired the deeds or mortgage rights to the properties of borrowers when they were unable to repay him by conventional means. Given the close affinities he enjoyed with a coterie of close friends and business partners, it is conceivable that he was also able to draw on the combined resources they could make available. However, this would have muddied his personal relationships with and influence over his borrowers (whom he viewed as patrons and 'friends' reliant on his personal attention), so resort to the 'collective pot' was almost certainly reserved for business ventures and investments. From what we can piece together of Whittington's character, behaviour and resources, we have a picture of someone determined to confine his lending within one-to-one financial relationships, treating these with utmost discretion, and who was sought out for doing so, and relatively relaxed about how these loans were repaid. Where cash was not available, he was content to accept a mutually beneficial 'like-for-like'. This may have been a sinecure, an office which brought financial and social capital, perhaps a valued introduction or the cession of a property or some other entitlement. Whittington saw both opportunity and safeguard in not diluting or sharing his services; he alone would be the *négociateur* and the provider.

21

MERCER RISING

Whittington's relationship with the king would strengthen further in the 1390s, reaching a personal culmination in his installation as mayor of London in the summer of 1397, by which time Richard II was ready to strike at those who he held had conspired against him. On 10 July he closed in on Gloucester, Arundel and Warwick, intending to arrest them at a banquet to which he had invited them. Only Warwick fell into the trap. Whittington could hardly have imagined that just five weeks after becoming mayor he would find himself caught up in the reprisals. 'On the same night, 10th July, with a contingent of City militia led by the young acting mayor, Richard Whittington—the famous Dick Whittington of popular legend—the king galloped thirty-five miles through the night to Pleshey Castle in Essex where he arrested the second of his two intended guests and victims, his royal uncle the duke of Gloucester.'[1]

Yet what is most striking about the period following the parliaments of 1387 and 1388 is a growing personal isolation, a neurosis, in the king's behaviour and outlook. The events and psychological impact of 1387–8, including the personal devastation of Sir Simon Burley's execution, are seen by some as triggering Richard II's downward spiral towards 'tortured instability' and 'paranoia' in the final weeks of 1399. Anthony Steel observes Richard slipping away from his earlier disposition as a 'passionate and loyal friend and husband' into 'the unbalanced widower, half-hearted autocrat and pitiful neurotic of the later years'.[2] Steel suggests that after the death of his queen, Anne, in July 1394, the day-to-day challenge of those around the king may well have been to keep him sane. He was certainly dependent on close friends and stable voices in his circle, Whittington among them. Steel concludes that by 1397 his 'neuroses' had deepened further and he had entered the last stages of his illness and that by August 1399 he had become a 'mumbling neurotic, sinking rapidly into a state of acute melancholia'.[3] Nigel Saul believes that Richard had become unpredictable and showed signs of instability, concluding that his character and judgement were determined by his narcissism, his subjective convictions, his physical isolation and his detachment from reality.[4] McHardy writes that such a condition 'detaches its victims from reality so that they become cocooned from the outside world by groups of yes-men and by physical isolation'.[5] This raises the question of whether Richard Whittington, a figure who became the king's banker, his close friend and quite probably a source of counsel on matters beyond trade and court–City relations, was one such 'yes-man' and whether his installation as mayor was a demonstration of that. At the turn of the decade, it was plain to see that Richard II could not sustain his military campaigns without frequent resort to direct taxation, a prospect that grated on the City, the shires and the commonalty alike and did little to temper, let alone reverse, his unpopularity. It was therefore imperative to secure 'lenders' who could contribute to the Exchequer or at least support his personal and court expenditure, which might otherwise have been a bridge too far had he imposed it as a further burden on his subjects.[6]

The new decade had begun with a spat over the mayoralty which laid bare the continuing divisions between those still wedded to the victuallers' interest and those who had been close to John Northampton. It was claimed by the latter's supporters, among them goldsmiths, drapers and mercers, that Adam Bamme, himself a goldsmith, had gained the greater number of votes over his rival William Venour, with whom he had been in sharp dispute following a personal slight attributed to Venour during his tenure as sheriff the previous year, and had been manipulated out of his 'victory' in October 1389. Barron describes Venour's election as 'the occasion of some contention'.[7] An accommodation was reached with both sides accepting the need to put an end to their divisions and agreeing that Bamme should succeed the following year. By 1391 London's growing reputation as a hub for investment, enterprise, and high fashion and luxury goods did not sit well with the fetid reality of its choked watercourses and filth-strewn streets, now so overwhelmed by rubbish and effluent that Parliament finally rose to action, outlawing the dumping of any waste, excrement, rubbish or offal into any street, ditch or conduit, on penalty of fine or imprisonment.[8] In the same year, it also acted to remove the staple from Calais to England, resulting in a sudden brake on the exportation of wool and a sharp fall in price.[9] The most notable events, however, were the interventions of king and mayor to address the shortage and sharp rise in the price of wheat and stave off the prospect of starvation and civil unrest. On 4 February 1391 Richard II suspended the collection of duties on grain and other foodstuffs transported on the Oxford to London road until the next harvest. The duties had been intended to pay for its repair and upkeep. His intervention was cited as *pro republica et relevatio populi*—in mitigation of the Commons.[10] The imperative was to get grain into London as cheaply, quickly and abundantly as possible. While the king was removing the impediment of duties, London's mayor, supported by his aldermen, was more direct in his measures to address the fundamental issue of scarcity. Serving the first of his two terms, Adam Bamme led the way in unlocking the means to purchase much-needed imports. 'On 8 Feb 1391 Richard Odyham, city chamberlain, with the agreement of the aldermen, gave £400 from the Orphans Fund to mayor Adam Bamme, goldsmith, to buy grain from overseas.'[11]

There was more to come. The chronicler Henry Knighton reported that in addition to this sum, London's 24 aldermen 'each contributed £20 to make similar purchases for fear of famine in the city'.[12] In an unusually progressive act, the grain was stored and made available to the poor 'at a fixed price enough to sustain their families' and, for those without the means, a pledge to repay the following year was deemed sufficient. Meanwhile, England's spendthrift king continued to indulge himself and his court, quite oblivious to or simply uninterested in the abject poverty of his subjects, lavishing what was left of his non-existent private means and an exhausted public purse on as many as 6,000 courtiers, employees, servants and jobsworths attached in one way or another to the fantasy factory of the Palace of Westminster.[13] Richard II's Olympian effort to 'spend for England' could not sustain itself and in 1391 he found himself once more seeking to borrow from the City and from those he knew could afford to extend him large and flexible lines of credit and be discreet about it. Whittington figured prominently; his rise through the ranks of the king's lenders had been meteoric, and by 1390 he was among the leading group to whom Richard regularly turned, in some instances for loans, in others for extended credit, for which there was a reducing prospect of payback. After 1389, the principal focus of English trade was the Low Countries and Italy. Like many of his peers, Whittington was immersed in both, the former providing the volume of London's foreign trade while the latter, to which he increasingly gravitated, had seized the high ground in the trading of luxury cloths and goods. In transacting with the merchants of Genoa, Venice, Florence and Milan, there was not only the attraction for all parties of making a good profit from the sale of expensive Italian merchandise to a receptive London market but the prospect also of purveying 'flagship' goods to an English court obsessed with an extravagance bordering at times on the hedonistic. Now 30 years of age, Whittington was once more in the right place at the right time and equipped to exploit the opportunity presented by a loosening of tensions with France and Spain after 1388. London was able and ready to deepen its commercial traffic with the Low Countries and Italy.

Winter, 1391–2

Historically, London's mayors and sheriffs frequently found themselves at odds with the monarch and his view of what he had entitlements to or held the primary rights over. The relationship with Richard II not only affirmed the pattern but frequently extended and aggravated it. In November 1391, for example, Richard asserted that it was he, the king, who enjoyed superior rights over parts of the Thames and therefore had a financial interest in the vessels and trade that passed through or anchored there. It was a purely manufactured and sweeping attempt, and was received as such, to squeeze London's merchants and the shipping that docked on the Thames for revenue already levied through taxation. The claim fell within the mayoralty of the wealthy draper John Hende, who instructed his sheriffs to rebut it, countering that it was to the City and not the monarchy that the 'franchise' for the Thames fell legally and through historical precedence. Hende himself was caught up in another dispute with the king some weeks later in January 1392 when he asserted, contrary to the view of the King's Council, that no one might be arrested within the confines of the city without the assent of the mayor or his sheriffs. The definitive outcome is unknown, but the requirement that Hende and his sheriffs must report to the King's Council daily for a period of eight days, and that each of them must pay £1,000 in what was effectively a fine for standing their ground, suggests that the mayor may well have prevailed and was penalised for having done so. Three months later Hende was arrested and deposed from office, and London was under the oversight of a 'royal warden', Sir Edward Dalyngrigge. These events were also a reflection of Richard's impatience and later his outright horror that the City would neither bow to him nor, more to the point, provide loans to him, and hadn't done so since March 1388.

The king was also struggling to raise loans on a one-to-one basis. Barron tells us that personal loans totalling over £1,500 were granted by six Londoners in 1388, with eight lenders providing just a third of that figure in 1389, and the amount halving again in 1390 from just four lenders. There were no loans from Londoners in 1390 and just one in 1391.[14] Any dismissal of his needs or unwillingness to support the Treasury, real or imagined, was perceived as a 'political' challenge to his sovereignty. Barron notes that Richard was 'irritated and annoyed' by the Londoners' refusal to provide him with money, and he had 'extravagant tastes and grandiose schemes' that needed to be underwritten. It seems clear that this failure to obtain funding from the City corporately, and from London's merchant class individually, not only rankled deeply but was also a source of humiliation. We see here a very thin-skinned figure, frequently anxious or uncertain about his authority and his ability to make it stick. His behaviour in penalising the City, in contesting its rights, in depriving leading figures of office, and in imposing fines on and even imprisoning them during the early 1390s is a direct reflection of this indignity. What must have rankled most was the fact that he knew the money was available and the tap had simply been turned off. 'The king knew that Londoners could, even if they would not, lend him the money when he required, and, in these circumstances, he could only transform requests for cash into inescapable demands by a judicious use of the royal power and prerogative.'[15]

Salvo against the City, May 1392

Barron's excellent résumé of Richard's case and action against the City and mayoralty is unlikely to be bettered, so what does she make of the events of May 1392? He was, she observes, skilful in choosing his moment, the time when he was ready to unleash an accumulation of his grievances and bring down the full force of royal power upon the recalcitrant and the naysayers.

> When the king decided to move against the citizens he had much which he could throw into the scales against them: the injustices done to John Walpole; the butcher's nuisances; the detaining of royal deodands; the intransigence of civic custom; the lack of financial support and the general lawlessness. In the face of a campaign which had been devised over a period of months, if not years, and which was sprung upon them by surprise attack the Londoners were helpless. For their recent stubbornness and financial stringency, Richard made them pay remorselessly with their pride and their pockets.[16]

The detail of what followed is well documented and does not concern us here, but what we may see in the events of May–July 1392, when Richard effectively turned the tables and brought the City to heel and also embarrassed and humbled some of its most influential figures, are the seeds of his installation of Richard Whittington as mayor four years later. By the spring of 1392 Whittington was a leading figure in the City. He had served as a common councillor, he had been a favoured supplier within Richard's court since 1383, and he was appointed to the king himself by 1390. In the years 1392–4 Richard II would spend nearly £3,500 on merchandise bought from the mercer. He held him in high estimation, and it helped that Whittington was not in office at this time and not caught up in the polarising events of that summer. Moreover, Whittington was one of the tiny handful of Londoners who had made loans to the king during the period since 1388, the first provided in August of that year. Just eight months after Richard II had assailed the City, Whittington resumed his civic career as alderman for Broad Street ward. It is unlikely that this escaped the watchful king's attention. Both men had seen the retribution and instability that could ensue when the two main centres of power in London found themselves at odds. When relations soured again in the mid-1390s and a vacancy for mayor arose unexpectedly, one can't but wonder whether the 'script' had been considered, if not plotted, after the events of 1392 when John Hende and his sheriffs Henry Vanner and John Shadworth were removed from office and dispatched to prison. Whittington may have distanced himself from the fray, but he was most certainly an acute observer. He must have had torn loyalties. Close to the king, trading regularly with Hende and Shadworth and well known to Gilbert Maghfeld, appointed as one of the two new sheriffs, he can hardly not have absorbed the lessons of 1392, nor drawn on them to sharpen his own political senses. In the meantime, there was an opportunity and business to do at court. An ambitious mercer was hardly likely to turn either away.

Despite his personal attachment to Richard II, Whittington continued under Henry IV to provide luxury goods for the use of the court, although never on the same scale as he had done during the 1390s. His increasing preoccupation with the demands of royal finance led him to take less interest in the mercer's trade through which his fortune had been made, and to concentrate upon the use to which his capital could be put. Barron tells us that from 23 August 1388 to 23 July 1422, he made at least 59 separate loans to the Crown of sums ranging from £4 to £2,833 11s. Several leading public figures were also in his debt: Burley had borrowed 400 marks from him at some point before 1387; at a far later date he lent John Beaufort, Earl of Somerset, 1,000 marks and Sir Thomas Talbot £100 to finance their military operations. As late as 1411 Sir William Bourchier, Count of Eu, was still paying off an advance of £200 from the mercer. This is hardly surprising when we examine their mutual connections. Whittington's relationship with king and court continued to deepen throughout his career, the 'soldiers' network' remaining as productive as ever, but the difference was that they now approached him. Thus, it was Thomas of Woodstock, Duke of Gloucester, who first brought him to the attention of William Bourchier, the grandson of Robert Bourchier, England's first lay Chancellor. The young Bourchier served under Woodstock in Ireland in 1392–3 and was retained by the duke for the duration of his life with an annuity of 50 marks. In 1405, Bourchier would become the third husband of Anne of Gloucester, Countess of Stafford, the product of Woodstock's marriage with Eleanor de Bohun, elder daughter and co-heiress of Humphrey de Bohun, 7th Earl of Hereford. Their second son, another William Bourchier, would later become the 9th Baron Fitzwarin in right of his first wife, Thomasine Hankford, daughter of Elizabeth Fitzwarin, 8th Baroness Fitzwarin, none other than the sister and heiress of Sir Ivo's relative Fulk, 7th Baron Fitzwarin. Albeit distant, this was one connection that really was 'in the family'.

Yet for all the introductions and the benefits to his business of client 'recycling' and interconnected marriages, it must have been difficult at times for Whittington to manage his relationships with two powerful men who had become such sworn enemies—one, Thomas of Woodstock, the leader of the Lords Appellant, the other his king and the object of his discontent and revolt. Somehow, he succeeded in manoeuvring between two figures he clearly held in the very highest regard, so much so that he described them in his will as 'the particular lords and patrons of Richard Whittington' and made provision for prayers for the souls of both and for their wives. Jean Imray refers to them as 'his special promoters'.[17]

Whittington not only saw but quickly seized the opportunities afforded him. The sharp growth and increasing affluence of his business can be seen in his employment of five apprentices during the year 1391–2. Taking on an apprentice was an expensive business for mercers, requiring a fee of 20 shillings for their admission to the Mercers' Company. The cost for admission to the lesser and less status-conscious guilds was significantly lower, in the case of the carpenters as little as 1 shilling. On completion of a carpenter's apprenticeship a payment of 3s 4d was due; just a sixth of that was due for a mercer. If ever any assurance or affirmation was required, the disparity must surely have underscored the superior status and the material advantages of becoming a mercer.[18]

By the early 1390s Whittington was supplying goods to king and court of the highest value, contributing about a quarter of Great Wardrobe expenditure in this period, second only to that of the financier and draper John Hende, then reputed to be London's richest man. Hende, however, was too conspicuously wealthy for his own good, and while he may have justifiably stood his ground against the king's whims and artifices, he was dogged by whispers and accusations of financial manipulation, fraudulent trading and corruption, which famously caught up with him in the early months of his first term as mayor. It was a salutary lesson for those wealthy enough to lend and even more so if they harboured ambitions of political office. He was replaced by the royal warden, Sir Baldwin Radyngton.[19] Caroline Barron speculates that Richard II's 'wild spending spree' during this period may have been funded from the £10,000 worth of loans he had squeezed from the citizens of London by February 1393. Robbing Peter to pay Paul springs to mind. Whittington's ascent was not without its own reversals. This largesse had been extracted aggressively and wilfully by the king following his summoning on 25 June 1392 of London's 24 leading commoners, Whittington among them, to attend him at Nottingham, a deliberate manoeuvre to remove the proceedings, where he railed against alleged malpractices in the City, from opposition and scrutiny. It was a familiar Ricardian attempt to impose control and extract revenue, this time under real threat of contrived prosecution and imprisonment.

> The city had refused to lend the king the sum of 1000 pounds and they had compounded his ill will by failing to control a series of disturbances in which first a Lombard who had offered to make the loan instead was attacked and beaten for undermining the city's stance and then in separate incidents a servant of the Bishop of Salisbury had been attacked and the gates of the Bishop's residence in Fleet Street stormed by a mob. Richard saw these as attacks on himself and the city must pay for the assaults and the affront. Accordingly, it 'was thought proper to punish these enormities in an exemplary manner.'[20]

29 May 1392

Mortimer notes that, in the words of one chronicler, the writ Richard II served on the mayor and his aldermen on 29 May 1392 was 'so fearsome and utterly hair-raising as to cause the ears of whosoever heard it to tingle'.[21] It also ran the risk of drawing into the argument his uncle John of Gaunt and Gaunt's son Henry Bolingbroke, who 'were patrons of several of the implicated London merchants'. 'In particular, Henry had close links with Richard Whittington … and John Woodcock.'[22] This suggests that Whittington's fears in 1399 that Henry IV would think badly of the strong relationship he had enjoyed with Richard II were almost certainly misplaced. Both kings came to view him not only as a valued supplier of luxury goods and even more so as a ready and significant lender but also as a friend and wise counsellor in matters of trade and City governance. Regardless of his summons to Nottingham, Whittington was held in the highest regard by Richard II and, despite his proximity to the Ricardian court, was similarly valued after 1399 by his successor, to whom he continued to provide loans and luxury goods, 'although never on the same scale as he had done during the 1390s'. The funds extracted by Richard II from London's leading merchants in 1392–3 may well have financed the erection of two self-proclaiming stone effigies of himself and his queen, Anne, installed in the tabernacles of the great stone tower of London Bridge sometime in 1393. These no doubt served as a reminder of his power over the City, and his wilful determination to secure the means to proclaim his majesty.

Election of Whittington to the Shrievalty

Meanwhile, Whittington was also raising his own profile. In March of 1393 he was chosen as alderman for Broad Street ward, a natural progression for a common councillor who had served neighbouring Coleman Street from 1384 to 1386 and was now ready to resume his civic career.[23] What is more, the ward was home to many of London's drapers.[24] Acknowledged as an influential, non-partisan figure untainted by the squabbles and upheavals of the previous fifteen years, he saw his star was rising at court, within the City and within his own guild. We can imagine that he was pressed hard to reinstate himself in London's civic politics.

There is no firm evidence that he harboured or had declared ambitions for the mayoralty. Even with Brembre, Walworth and Philpot long dead, London's great prize still lay with a loose coalition of 'victuallers': the grocer Sir William Staunton, buyer for the king's household, won office in 1392 and was followed by another grocer, John Hadley, in 1393. What might have piqued Whittington's future interest was his concurrent tenure in 1393–4 as sheriff of London and Middlesex. While the position was historically subordinate to the mayor, there was a long-established tradition that service as London's sheriff was tantamount to 'qualification' for the higher office. As recently as 1385, this 'expectation' had been entrenched in the stipulation of the Common Council that every future mayor should 'have previously been Sheriff so that he may be tried as to his governance and bounty before he attains to the Estate of Mayoralty'.[25] The list of those attending Whittington's election as sheriff provides a striking insight into the self-perpetuating elite that not only dominated the senior political and civic offices of the City of London but was also formed by small groups of associates and friends, often fluid in both their social and commercial interests, who came together to support and promote each other's candidacies.

> On Sunday, the Feast of St Matthew the Apostle [21 September], in the 17th year etc., in presence of William Staundone, Mayor, Adam Bamme, William Venour, William More, Henry Vannere, John Fraunceys, Adam Karlille, John Walcote, William Sheryngham, Roger Elys, William Bramptone, William Evote, William Parker, Thomas Knolles, John Cosyn, Aldermen, and Gilbert Maghfeld, one of the Sheriffs, and Alderman of London, and of very many Commoners of all the Wards of the City aforesaid, for the election of Sheriffs in the Guildhall of the said city summoned; the said Mayor chose Richard Whytyngdone, Alderman, and the aforesaid Commonalty chose Drew Barentyn, to be Sheriffs of London for the ensuing year.[26]

The roll call not only captures the names of individuals who populated London's elite across a quarter of a century of great economic and social change, but also sheds light on Whittington's own diverse circle, among them the grocer Thomas Knolles, the mercer William Parker, the draper John Walcote, the merchant adventurer Gilbert Maghfeld, and the goldsmith Drew Barantyn, the last-named serving as his fellow sheriff. It would be with Knolles that Whittington would later campaign vigorously for the rebuilding of Newgate. Knolles had been warden of the Grocers' Company (1387–8) and was now embarking on his own civic career as the representative for Dowgate ward in the year Whittington took on Broad Street, serving there until 1397, and thereafter as the representative for Cordwainer until his death in 1435.[27] He would follow his friend as sheriff a year later and as mayor in 1399–1400, taking the office again in 1410–1. Both men, though Whittington only fleetingly, served as members of Parliament for London in 1416. The mercer William Parker took up the tenure of Bishopsgate, serving from 1393 until 1403, and left his role as sheriff of London just as Whittington became mayor for the first time. He would later serve as a member of Parliament for London in 1402 and died in 1403.[28] In March 1394 the number of wards was increased from 24 to 25 by the division of Farringdon into 'Within' and 'Without', both seats falling to goldsmiths. John Fraunceys, who had been alderman of the undivided ward since 1383, was chosen for the outer division and Drew Barantyn for the inner.

* * *

Here is evidence perhaps that if Whittington had not actually planned to become London's mayor, he had at least ensured that he was both qualified and positioned to do so. The period after March 1393 suggests that he may well have been setting out his stall for higher office. In April 1394 he was appointed a commissioner for London able to make arrests. It was a useful and 'knowing' move: the route to mayor was signposted, well established, almost formulaic. An example is provided by the figure who claimed to be the only royal supplier to out-supply Whittington himself. John Hende had joined the civic roundabout five years earlier than Whittington in 1379 and he too had contributed to the civic gift of that year. Hende's journey began as alderman for Candlewick ward in 1379–80, serving again in 1381–2 and subsequently from 1384 until 1392. He had been sheriff for 1381–2 before being first elected and then deposed as mayor during his term of office in 1391–2, and subsequently imprisoned. Presumably his wealth and the arrival of a new king helped to smooth his way to office once more in 1404–5. Where Hende presents as something of a 'chancer', Whittington was more the assiduous 'planner'. By 1393, he was ready to resume his civic path; his transformation from mercer and supplier of luxury goods to royal lender was largely accomplished, and he may have tired of and outgrown it. In the second half of the decade a new and transforming opportunity beckoned, and he would begin to lend heavily and frequently. Barron describes him developing an 'increasing preoccupation with the demands of royal finance', which would lead him 'to take less interest in the mercer's trade through which his fortune had been made, and to concentrate upon the use to which his capital could be put'. It is hardly a coincidence that the escalation of his lending from 1397 onwards coincides with his installation by Richard II as London's mayor.

In October 1393, the Common Council elected the grocer John Hadley as the city's new mayor to succeed William Staunton, who, for most of

1392, had shared his oversight of London with two royal wardens, Sir Edward Dalyngrigge and Sir Baldwin Radyngton, installed after Hende's removal. Their imposition constituted the most formal reminder yet from Richard II that London was his to rule and that 'the City' was allowed its freedom of governance only by his grace and discretion. He drove home the lessons of Nottingham from the previous year. London's merchant elite would be reminded, when he chose, of 'some misdemeanours committed in the city', the crux of which had always been money. Richard's need to raise revenue and to restore relations with the City would create a playbook in which Whittington became a leading character.

22

THE COMPANY

The Mercers' Charter, January 1394

Whittington must have watched with great interest the achievement in February 1393 of Adam Bamme, the man who had saved London from famine, his brother Henry and one of his own circle, Drew Barantyn, in securing for the goldsmiths their new charter from Richard II.[1] For Bamme the achievement was striking, as just eight months earlier he had been one of the 24 summoned to appear at Nottingham and among those required to give evidence on 18 July at Eton and, four days later, fined a total of 3,000 marks for certain undisclosed offences. He had joined with three others, including John Shadworth, a leading mercer later very close to Whittington, in acquiescing in the king's 'displeasure' with the City by providing sureties of £1,000 on behalf of its two sheriffs, one of whom was his brother-in-law. Bamme's exposure to the king's political and financial pressures endured until October 1393, a full fifteen months after he had been humiliated at Eton and eight months after he had formally affirmed the status of the goldsmiths as one of London's leading 'companies'.[2] It raises the question of whether the king was simply messing with heads, continuing to exploit the City's fear of its loss of liberties. Otherwise, what are we to make of yet another twist at the end of November 1393 when Bamme and fourteen other aldermen remitted to the Chamberlain of London the sum of £11 6s 8d? Almost certainly it was yet another concession or bribe demanded by the king as the price of his continuing favour.

Arguably, this presaged the conditions in which Richard II could impose his own mayor when the need or opportunity arose, as it did in June 1397 up on the untimely death of Adam Bamme, the central figure in the events of five years earlier. The 18th-century London topographer

John Noorthouck has described threats to seize the City charter or place its authority or legitimacy in question as a never-failing expedient by the king to 'extort money from the corporation', particularly on those occasions when its leading figures attempted to publicly withstand the royal pleasure. Certainly, Richard was adept at extracting gifts or contributions in exchange for the restoration of liberties he had curtailed or threatened in the first place.[3] Despite the king's haranguing and humiliation of him, Bamme was made of stronger stuff, and his success in securing the goldsmiths' charter paved the way for the mercers to follow. In the early months of 1393 the master of the Mercers' Company, William Sheryngham, pressed their case 'for the ease and common profit of the fellowship'. A deputation to the king urged that the mercers 'might have a perpetual community of themselves with power to choose for themselves yearly four Wardens to govern the mistery and license to purchase lands to the value of £20 a year for the maintenance of a chaplain and for the alms of the mistery to the honour of God and the relief of their distressed poor'.[4] They were treading an established path, and Richard II was quick to recognise there was something in it for the Crown; after all, a content and status-conscious trade was likely to be ever more industrious, ever more productive, and ever more successful if its self-worth was elevated in this way. In turn, this made a newly minted 'company' an even better source of tax revenue and more susceptible to requests for loans. Three years earlier, in 1390, the merchant taylors had also secured a charter which affirmed their rights of assembly and allowed them to make ordinances, hold feasts and sport an exclusive livery. The goldsmiths followed in February 1393, seeking to extend and formalise a loose template they had first established over fifty years earlier in 1341, and it was the refreshing of this updated charter that accelerated the mercers' own ambitions. The goldsmiths' privileges allowed them to purchase and hold tenements and rents to the value of £20, to be used for charitable purposes, including the relief of infirm members and those injured during their trade, and support for the poor.[5] The mercers' charter of 13 January 1394 went further, declaring its basis in overseas trade. Its representatives remarked that 'many men of the mistery of the Mercery of the City of London oftentimes by misfortune at sea and other unfortunate casualties came to such poverty and want that they had little or nothing whereon to live unless of the alms of other Christian people pitying and assisting them from charitable motives'.[6]

This long-sought royal affirmation of the status and worth of the mercers was only secured at significant cost. The proposal to make financial and spiritual provision for these 'casualties', including the appointment of a chaplain to celebrate in perpetuity divine service for the king himself, was eventually extracted on the payment of 110 marks, a punitive sum for a company whose total assets were less than £400. To some it must have looked as if Richard was making a point, extracting yet another pound of flesh. It certainly demonstrated that royal charters could be purchased under the present king if the price was right. Yet it was a price worth paying, giving London's mercers the *de jure* status they had sought for so long. Henceforth the company would annually elect four wardens to govern their number; it could purchase lands and tenements, and raise rents to the value of £20 annually in both the city and its environs. These were to be held and dispensed to meet the material needs of the poor men of the company and their families, and to fund the cost of the chaplain to celebrate divine service for the monarch and his family, and for the estate and souls of 'all the faithful dead' of the mystery.[7]

Whittington had most likely played a part. He was an influential voice and his activities at court had brought him directly into the king's orbit. He was among the leading cadre of mercers who recognised the value of having a royal charter and understood the commercial and political benefits it would bring. Regardless of the outer trimmings of status, position, recognition and esteem, and even the progressive initiative to underpin the welfare of the company's less fortunate members, the securing of the charter was ultimately a financial transaction, bought and sold for a price acceptable to both parties. In the year following the grant of its charter, Whittington was elected for the first of his three terms as one of the four new wardens of a resurgent Mercers' Company. Buoyed by its royal status and with a bullish confidence in its immediate future, the company admitted 90 new apprentices that year.[8]

The aspiration to secure a royal charter was in fact just one—albeit the most desirable—of three aspirations intended to elevate and consolidate the status of the company. The second was the search for a meeting place with sufficient presence to match the mercers' newly won status, and the third, which would become increasingly important in the first decade of the 15th century, was the creation of livery, emblems and heraldry intended to confirm and remind those who enjoyed its membership of their privileged worth. Such devices would also erect a barrier to those unable to afford the benefits of membership and exclude those deemed unworthy or of insufficient standing: in short, they were barriers to entry, pointers to a valued scarcity.

Long before its incorporation, the fraternity had assembled in the hall and worshipped at the Church of the Hospital of St Thomas of Acon, situated in Cheap.[9] Watney tells us that records for 24 June 1390, the Feast of St John the Baptist, record a meeting 'en la Sale de Seynt Thomas d'Acres' on that day, describing this as an assembly of 'toutz les bons gentz de la Mercere', at which the wardens were chosen, and the accounts of their predecessors audited and admitted. As noted, the mercers were also accustomed to meeting at a favoured hostelry in Old Jewry known appropriately as 'The Prince's Wardrobe'. Later, even after the Mercers' Hall was completed, members of the company would congregate at other hostelries or at the house of a warden for business meetings and feasting.[10] The accounts for 1407 and following years refer to a chapel, part of the hospital church, and a small room, 'la sale de Mercerie', having been purchased and granted to the company.[11]

The terms granted to the mercers, goldsmiths and saddlers between 1393 and 1395 went much further than the charter granted to the taylors. The right to establish a 'perpetual community' and to hold lands 'corporately' was a significant material and political advance. The effect on other guilds was immediate and transforming. A royal charter had been awarded by Edward III to the vintners as early as 1363, but it was the charters awarded by his grandson which effectively consolidated the commercial, social and political superiority of those companies which traded and distributed on a greater scale as 'wholesalers' and which were likely to have more diverse interests, economic and political, than the smaller traditional craft guilds. Thereafter, 'it became the ambition of all the greater guilds to be incorporated'.[12] The ensuing incorporations included the fishmongers (1399 and 1537), cutlers (1416), grocers (1428), brewers (1438), drapers (1438), cordwainers (1439), leathersellers (1444), haberdashers (1448) and armourers (1453). 'The fifteenth century thus saw the working out of tendencies which were already apparent in Chaucer's day. The great trading companies fortified their position by royal charters and drew apart from the lesser companies.'[13]

From the outset of his career, Whittington had carefully conserved his wealth as cash, and on those relatively infrequent occasions when land and buildings fell into his hands, they largely did so as a surety or as the means of wiping out a cash debt. Many were already mortgaged or had been pledged previously as earlier-stage collateral for the payment of debts. As we have seen, one of the most notable examples fell much closer to home, and it provides an illustration both of his accessible wealth and of his lack of sentiment in what he clearly saw as a business transaction. In February 1394 he provided his uncle Philip Maunsell with a sizeable loan of £500 on which the latter would later default, obliging him to convey his manor at Over Lypiatt, Gloucestershire, formerly held by the de Bohun family, to his nephew as settlement of the debt.[14]

Fitzwarin, at the King's Service

Maunsell's fortunes, both literal and pecuniary, contrasted sharply with those of the man Whittington probably regarded as his closest 'family'. Sir Ivo Fitzwarin was also strengthening his ties with Richard II at this time, and in the early to mid-1390s we find him taking on various commissioner roles in the counties in which he and his wife Maud held large landholdings, partly to protect his own interests but also because he was authorised by royal command to supervise local infrastructure, act for the courts in matters of insurrection and concealment, serve as a justice of the peace, make arrests and determine sentences, and preside over appeals. The most eye-catching of these appointments was surely that of keeper of Whittington Castle in Shropshire in February 1394, an entitlement which he held until 1407 and which appears to coincide with the minority of his young kinsman Fulk Fitzwarin, the 6th Baron, who died in that year. As the grandson of the celebrated Fulk Fitzwarin III, who had presided over Whittington Castle until his death in 1349, Sir Ivo now found himself overseeing one of the two principal estates—the other being Wantage, to which he and Maud already devoted much of their time and where they would eventually be buried—that so described his family's history. In June 1395 Richard II granted him the sum of £40 from the annual rent of £60 due to Whittington Castle, effectively retaining him for life in the service of the king, a benefit that would continue under Henry IV from 1399.[15] This trust between Richard and Fitzwarin was a natural consequence of the latter's military service to the king, which reached back to the first months of the young monarch's reign in October 1377 when Fitzwarin had served under John Arundel, Marshal of England. As a knight of the royal chamber, he was awarded in June 1385 an annual fee of £22 by the Crown to retain six men at arms and six archers, ready at any time to come to the king's aid. Now, from September 1394 until April 1395, in the months preceding the grant of rent from Whittington Castle and his instalment for life in the service of the king, he would serve under Richard II himself in Ireland. The soldier who accompanied Richard in battle was the same fellow who had first introduced him to his favourite merchant and lender.

Warden of the Mercers' Company, 1395–6

Richard Whittington's own growing standing was acknowledged formally by his peers on 24 June 1395 when he was elected a warden of the Mercers' Company. He held office again in 1401–2 and 1408–9. He was already a favoured supplier and had made his mark as a lender to Richard II, but his elevation must surely have alerted the interest of a king troubled by and impatient with a recalcitrant City. The man to whom he looked increasingly for cash and for credit, and perhaps for 'advice', was now one of the most influential voices in the very estate that most challenged and troubled him. It is not inconceivable that Richard considered that his recent grant of the Mercers' Charter and Whittington's election as one of its principal officers provided a political as well as an economic 'opportunity'. If so, it would soon be tested.

> Election to office as a master or warden in any of the city companies was also an honour, its importance varying with the size, wealth and influence of the company. By the middle of the fourteenth century these officials wielded a formidable complex of authority. In matters concerning supervision of their particular branch of manufacture or retail trade in the public interest they were agents in the city's system of economic administration. After election they were supposed to take an oath before the mayor and aldermen, binding them to be loyal to the king and the city, to be honest and impartial, and to administer all approved craft ordinances 'and noon other'.[16]

Among the warden's responsibilities lay other considerations which helped to form Whittington's own social instincts. Chief among these were the touchstones incorporated in the company's new charter, those of fraternity, fellowship, and the welfare and sustenance of its members and their families. By the 1390s London's most prominent companies and guilds were restating and recalibrating their early principles as parish-based 'mysteries', moving on to embrace mutual aid and self-help and developing a basic social paternalism that extended beyond their inherent economic self-interest. It was the emergence perhaps of an early form of corporate social responsibility. This resonated with Whittington's own moral outlook. Here was an opportunity to seek ways in which the direction, activities and charitable works of the companies and their wealthy members could be more consonant with the public interest. This recognised that the support of the commonalty was essential in securing support on the streets, in the workshops, at the markets and on the quays for a company's political interests, not least in contesting civic office; that there was a common bond between self-interest and public good. Arguably the outlook of the Mercers' Company and the authority of its wardens drew strength from resolving the contradictions of inclusivity and alienation. Members were kept in line by threat of expulsion but also by the prospect of economic reversal as beneficial 'connections' contracted, by the professional and public humiliation that would follow, and ultimately by the horror of imprisonment. 'The powers of company wardens were supported by the sanction of the individual's inner fear to displease established authority and by additional persuasion from the secular arm of the law.'[17]

So, what might Whittington's role have been? The duties of warden have been described as 'fairly exacting'. In fact they were rather more than that and included having authority over the searching of shops; presiding over the purchase of cloth for liveries; an important 'gatekeeping' role as the leading companies increasingly differentiated and distinguished themselves by the pomp, quality and markings of their regalia, the cost of which also served to reinforce their exclusivity and effectively preclude membership of the poorer craftsman; determining the distribution of alms; ordering the assessment and advance of loans to members; the arbitration and settlement of disputes and complaints; the bringing forward of new members; and the disciplining of those deemed to have breached the letter and spirit of their constitution.

If Whittington found any of the above prosaic in their intent or mundane in their execution, he could take comfort that administrative support was available from the company's scriveners and, in any case, counsel was always at hand from other wardens, past and present. Being a warden of the Mercers' Company was also hugely educative, an excellent preparation for his unexpected installation as London's mayor two years later. The social and spiritual responsibilities of office were even more compelling. As a warden he would assume 'the responsibility of numerous trusteeships in connection with chantries and charitable foundations'. Indeed, it is in his role as warden, in this first term and subsequently, that we see

Whittington absorb the progressive instincts of like-minded peers and develop the libertarian outlook that he would later invest in his social reforms and public works. In the spiritually powerful environment of the Mercers' Company, he was able to refine and test his ideas and draw others to support him in their implementation. It was here too that he built on the power base that would support his mayoralties. The provisions of his will nearly thirty years later make clear that the Mercers' Company was not only a compelling and enduring influence in both his day-to-day life and his wider outlook but also the vehicle for continuing his work after his death. Of course, wealth was essential to his endeavours, and by the time he first became warden he was among London's richest men. Wardenship added to his status and amplified his influence, not least because he had about him, both within the sanctum offered by the Mercers' Company and within the progressive circle of friends he had cultivated outside, other wealthy self-made men who saw the rewards in this life and the next of improving the lives and circumstances of the wider community. As Sylvia Thrupp observes:

> Only men who were well established in business could afford to hold the senior offices, and even they often hesitated. In the greater companies it was not the policy to allow such men to serve continuously for more than a year or two at a time, but after an interval they would be brought back. In the circumstances the wealthier and more successful men of each company tended to have an option upon office. This contributed greatly to their status, for it meant that they were potentially invested with authority and could command ... respect ... In merchant companies it became the custom to address veteran wardens as Master not only while they were presiding but for life.[18]

The Path to Mayoralty

At the commencement of his first term, the buoyancy of Whittington's own business was such that he was able to increase further the number of apprentices he employed. A year later he had at least seven apprentices under his tutelage. Looking back, the intense and unsettled period from 1391 to 1397 can be viewed as the defining watershed in both his influence and prospects. He had made huge strides across five areas. He had achieved a striking breakthrough in his service as a royal supplier and lender, building credibility, influence and obligation at court. In turn, this powered an accumulation of capital which, against prevailing fashion, he retained as liquid cash available for the loans that he would use to build his political influence. His reputation for competence and his influence within his trade were evident in his efforts, with others, to secure the Mercers' Charter and were recognised in his subsequent elevation as warden of the Mercers' Company. He had resumed his civic career, taking on Broad Street, serving as London's sheriff, and making his first forays into social reform. And in June 1397 he would go on to assume the role that would define him in popular history, his first tenure as London's mayor. By the autumn of 1397 it must have seemed that he had 'made his name' and reached the pinnacle of an already illustrious career. In truth he had barely started.

23

THE MAYORALTY

> The most dangerous and the most imperative duty of Mayor, Sheriffs and Aldermen was the firm maintenance of those privileges against the encroachments of the Crown and the Court. And the careful and ceaseless watch for such opportunity of further extension as the necessities of the king might allow.[1]

The office of mayor was created in 1189 as one of the first acts of Richard I's reign, reflecting an institutional response on the part of the Crown to better frame and more efficiently divert towards the Exchequer its claims on London's prosperity, to simplify the political and fiscal interface between the monarchy and the City, and to hold the latter to more effective account. It would develop as a device by which the king and the treasury could shuffle off financial responsibility for the upkeep of London's infrastructure and the safeguarding of its clamorous citizens. It crystallised the shift in the relationship between the English state and its most wealthy sector, London's merchant class. Most of all, it was intended to provide the means for an English king to extract and legitimate the taxation and 'gifts' he required to finance his campaigns overseas, notably in France. Two hundred years later Richard Whittington found that very little had changed, except that the demands of the Crown were now more excessive, and, in balancing the interests of the City and citizenry with those of the monarchy, the office of mayor was more complex, and at times more treacherous, than its first incumbent could ever have imagined.

Henry Fitz-Ailwyn was a prosperous manufacturer and trader in cloth, widely respected as a leading figure in London's commercial community by the time he christened the office in 1189.[2] Over 700 mayors have followed him since, yet he remains the only incumbent to have served for life, holding office until his death 23 years later in 1212.[3] From the outset it was clear that he was expected to act as both an intermediary and a fixer in the fractious relationship between the king and the City. Richard I's demands for increased taxes and loans from London's merchants to pay for the war in France resonate time and again during Whittington's mayoralties with the sweep of expectations and demands insisted upon by Richard II, Henry IV and Henry V. So, too, do the sinecures, offices, sureties and autonomy proffered to lenders in return for their fiscal acquiescence and their largesse. The quid pro quo for this 'autonomy' was the creation of the mayoralty, superseding the position of the portreeve, whose authority as an officer of the Crown had been drawn directly from the king. After Richard's death in 1199 his successor King John granted further powers of self-rule to the City. The mayor's purview extended much further than simply acting as a conduit for revenue raising. It was Fitz-Ailwyn, mindful of the infernos which ravaged London in the 11th and 12th centuries, who established the mayor's responsibility for the safety of the city and its citizens.[4] It was Fitz-Ailwyn also who first introduced measures for settling boundary disputes between neighbours and who imposed regulations requiring the use of stone in buildings as a means of firebreak. Whittington and his predecessors owed much to the first of their kind, a far-sighted figure who set out not only the regulations defining the construction, materials and siting of walls, gutters, privies, windows and pavements for a safer and more ordered townscape but also the procedure to be followed at assizes for punishing breaches of those regulations.[5]

For the first ten years the relationship between king and mayor went well, such that in 1200 John felt assured enough to authorise the establishment of a 24-strong Court of Aldermen intended to strengthen the relationship between monarch and City further. Ten years later the goodwill had soured and evaporated as resentment raged over the king's imposition of extortionate taxation and levies. In 1212 the unimaginable damage to the recently completed London Bridge, 33 years in the rebuilding, consumed by yet another horrendous fire, was a fateful moment in the relationship. Over 3,000 people lost their lives and countless small businesses, already dangerously squeezed by the king's relentless pursuit of revenue, were swept away, shrinking even further the city's and the nation's tax base. By the end of London's *annus horribilis* the king's reliable and judicious emollient, its mayor Henry Fitz-Ailwyn, was also gone. London was adrift, England's revenues exhausted, and its king not for turning. It would fall not to the city's merchants, then a relatively weak force in London's governance, but to the traditional brake on overreaching kingly ambition to check John's high-handedness. On 17 May 1215, with the support of a city faction and the agreement of the then mayor, Serlo le Mercer, London's gates were opened to the barons and at Runnymede on 15 June, King John was forced to sign the 'Articles of the Barons'.[6] On 19 June the Magna Carta was agreed upon in its final form. At this momentous gathering there was a single signatory or 'enforcer' to the 63 articles who was neither a noble nor a senior clergyman: the vintner William Hardel, London's fourth mayor.[7]

> His inclusion affords clear proof of the key role which London had played in the rising that brought King John to the negotiating table in 1215 ... The Londoners' reward for their backing of the rebellion came in clause 13 of the Charter, which said, albeit without much precision, that the city was to have all its ancient liberties and free customs both by land and by water.[8]

Henry III, 1216–72

The relationship between the monarchy and the City fared little better under John's son Henry III (1216–72). A spendthrift with little understanding of his country's shallow and precarious finances, Henry pursued a reckless foreign policy and respected the constitution only when it suited him. Worse still, he alienated the City by allowing Italian merchants and investors opportunities to infiltrate and appropriate English trade. 'Convinced of his countrymen's inexhaustible capacity to replenish his needs and to bend a compliant knee, Henry sought to recover financial ground through exactions on his own church, upon the citizenry, upon England's wealthy Jewish community, and upon what the Papacy clearly regarded as the golden goose, London itself.'[9] For Pope Innocent IV, Henry had opened the door to 'a garden of delight: it is an inexhaustible well abounding in good things'.[10] Henry's gross extortion of the City in 1242, and his painful and discriminatory exactions from London's Jewish community following a wilful and irresponsible extravagance, evaporated any residual goodwill towards the monarchy.[11] Enmity on both sides deepened further with the English king's persistent demands that London and not the Crown or his Exchequer should bear the costs of the construction of Westminster Abbey.[12]

Despite resentment that the king continued to treat it as little more than a cash cow, London went about its business and enjoyed twenty years of prosperity. By the time Thomas Fitzthomas, a wealthy draper from Cornhill and associate of Simon de Montfort, assumed office as London's 25th mayor in 1261 for the first of his four terms, at the end of which he would be deposed and imprisoned, trade was again flourishing, the city's merchant community was resurgent, and London's infrastructure had been renewed. However, a gust of political change was once more sweeping through the relationship between the king and the barons and within the city's trades, where the craft guilds were in the ascendancy. At the London Parliament on 2 April 1258, the discontent of England's magnates and of the City had been so overwhelming that Henry III and the future Edward I were forced to agree to scrutiny of royal supply and finance. At the Oxford Parliament of 11 June, led by de Montfort, the king accepted the 'Provisions of Oxford',[13] through which authority was to be invested in a Privy Council of fifteen members reviewed by a Parliament that would meet three times a year.[14]

In 1261 an invigorated City pressed the advantage, the mayor Fitzthomas embodying both the shift in political initiative and the changes under way in his own back yard. Fitzthomas was not unusual in flexing and manipulating the scope of the mayor's powers to anticipate and respond to an increasingly noisy and influential 'electorate' and a wider commonalty determined to have their say and proclaim their rights. The City knew and could articulate its evident economic and political worth and it behove those elected for short terms or installed precariously to pay heed to what it had to say and to the disruption it could bring if ignored. In some instances, London's mayors were not simply content to ride the clamour for change but were themselves active and leading instigators of demagoguery, rabble-rousing and sectarian violence.[15]

During the ensuing crisis of 1263, it was again Fitzthomas and his predecessor as mayor, the grocer John Gisors, who took the lead in rallying the support of the Commons behind de Montfort and the barons. The Commons prevailed, the barons entered London, and, in one of the city's most shameful episodes, many in the Jewish community were slaughtered. De Montfort's radical call for a directly elected Parliament haemorrhaged support, leading to his rout and death at Evesham. The vicious punishment inflicted on London by Henry's son Edward, who sustained a lifetime contempt for the City, led to the imprisonment and impoverishment of Fitzthomas and many of his circle. For a time, London's mayoralty looked to be at an end. Henry imposed his own man, the Constable of the Tower, as warden of London. Elections were set aside, then restored in 1270, only for the first two mayors to be denounced as 'reformers' and removed from office. This presaged future instances in which a king at loggerheads with City and Commons would stoop to the same tactic. Edward I was received with even greater trepidation. Consumed by his father's disdain, he revelled in destroying his opponents in the City and, if anything, deepened his sour distrust of London's merchant class and its political ambitions. The threat posed to the mayoralty was now truly existential.

Henry le Waleys, 1273

Yet the office of mayor would be saved and reinvigorated by a figure very close to the royal family, who happened to be neither a Londoner nor an Englishman. Henry III's former vintner Henry le Waleys has been cited as either a Gascon or a Welshman, who had become a Londoner by 'naturalisation' and through his service to the court. He certainly nurtured very close connections with France and in 1275 served at the request of Edward I as mayor of Bordeaux, the city where he had accumulated much of his fortune. From time to time he also represented the king as his 'ambassador' to France.[16] His impact on London, however, was greater by far, for he served as mayor on three occasions spanning seven years, first in 1273 and then from 1281 to 1284 and latterly from 1298 to 1299. Henry le Waleys had gained local popularity for his efforts in establishing the covered Stocks Market adjoining St Mary Woolchurch, which became a 'backdoor' means of raising rents, and therefore revenue, for the public works for which he as mayor now had responsibility. He was close to another mayor, his fellow royalist and the court goldsmith Gregory de Rokesley, whose seven years of office separated le Waleys's first and second terms. The two men had been appointed together as sheriffs of London in 1270 and would go on to control and reshape the mayoralty for an unbroken period of twelve years between 1273 and 1285 before le Waleys took up his fifth and final term in 1298.

For the formative years of his reign Edward could take comfort that the mayoralty was largely in his pocket. Both men had a strong part in the reform of London's coinage, both were involved in the regulation of overseas trade, both were drawn into Edward's circle as advisers—not only on London's economy and governance but also on England's ambitions abroad—and both acted in a number of capacities as his 'agents'. Their careers offer some parallels with that of Richard Whittington. As sheriff, le Waleys found himself frequently having to intervene against the victualler trades—the bakers, butchers and fishmongers—in the flouting of regulations, the manipulation and adulteration of measures, pricing irregularities and bribery, and the setting up of 'fast-food' cook shops and stalls in locations that blocked important thoroughfares.[17] De Rokesley, also like Whittington, was known for retaining strong liquid funds that enabled him to establish himself as a successful lender and banker. As for Edward, there are parallels with Richard II and Henry IV, in having mayors who were seen to be close to the monarchy but who also had a detailed understanding of enterprise, trade and the interests and instincts of London's merchant class. Both le Waleys and de Rokesley were instrumental in imposing the king's will on the City and his stamp on the mayoralty. They were 'cosmopolitan', each having a good knowledge of Europe and of France in particular, their value evident in their accompanying of Edward on missions to Paris and Montreuil in 1274. They were also exceptionally rich, which, for a king short of money and ever focused on where the next mark would come from, insulated them from his bouts of rage at the City. He could also rely on their influence as leading figures within two of London's wealthiest guilds, the vintners and the goldsmiths. De Rokesley had the additional merit, as Whittington did much later, of being influential within London's wool trade.[18] Their part in helping an English king to raise from the City in 1282 the sum of 6,000 marks towards his military campaigns (in this instance against the Welsh) has parallels with Whittington's periods of office. Overall, they are perhaps best described as accomplished wheelers and dealers on behalf of the king. One can imagine, for example, de Rokesley's usefulness as a prominent goldsmith and the man closest to the king's ear. 'The Crown, in the interests of its coinage, if of nothing else, needed the goldsmiths as an organised body. Before the modern ubiquity of officialdom, measures affecting a whole craft or trade could seldom be operated save through the trade concerned.'[19]

By 1294 the wave of lending, trading and preferment that the great Italian banking houses and their affiliate merchant community had enjoyed for twenty years at the expense of their English counterparts was ebbing as the English king contemplated the size of his foreign debt and his unwillingness to repay it. Ironically, his position was stiffened by the very group whose interests he had so often ridden roughshod over. It was the City's rising protest against their loss of rights and profits to 'aliens', in a few instances spilling over into violence and the murder of Italian merchants, that helped bolster his resolve, and no doubt provided the 'legitimacy' he sought for dispensing with his long-time lenders. Edward now had the comfort of knowing that if he did default on his debts and send the Italians home, effectively bankrupt, there was very little they could do other than protest at the sheer injustice of it all. The Bardi, the Frescobaldi, the Cerchi and the Falconeri were uprooted from their assets, expelled from their lucrative offices in the Royal Mint, and summarily dispatched home. This was no irrational fit of pique on the king's part. He knew, not least from the services provided to him by le Waleys and de Rokesley, that there were wealthy and politically ambitious Englishmen ready to take their place. By this summary act of expulsion Edward could have it all ways: he would be free of an enormous debt and obligation; he could recoup goodwill in the City that would translate as revenue; he would dismiss, in a single stroke, the recurring protest that foreigners were acquiring English assets, leaching English profits, and colonising valued parts of London's trade; and he would pave the way for new and imaginative means of financial engagement with his subjects, opening a door that Whittington would walk through almost exactly a hundred years later.

Two other events, one centred on enhancing representation, the other on eradicating it altogether, were also accelerating opportunities for wealthy natives and consolidating the influence of the City. The barbaric expulsion of the Jews in 1290 ranks as one of the most deplorable acts of religious persecution and racial exclusion perpetrated by any English monarch. A community which had first established itself after the Norman Conquest was systematically reviled, attacked and, in numerous instances, violated and murdered for its enterprise, its practice of usury, its perceived religious peculiarities, and its social and cultural separation. Suspicion, distrust, ignorance and envy had fuelled a gathering and deeply obnoxious anti-Semitism since 1218 when Henry III issued the Edict of the Badge, which required Jews to attach an insignia to their garments that 'marked' them as such. Despite having effectively extorted over 200,000 marks from the Jewish community between 1219 and 1272, Henry elevated racism to a new level in 1275 in a Statute of Jewry which outlawed all forms of usury while effectively directing the charge at a single embattled community. Besieged and outcast, Jews, who had known no other living or trade and were already barred from entry to most of the guilds, were summarily given fifteen years to establish an alternative living or face expulsion.[20] In 1290, in one of the most deplorable acts of the Middle Ages, at least 2,000 Jews, generally held to be a conservative estimate, were removed forcibly from England's shores.[21]

In 1293, as John le Breton, another mayor of French extraction, commenced the second of his seven terms as royal warden, it was made clear that London's electoral college would comprise a narrow elite drawn from the wisest and wealthiest from London's wards and would, on the face of it, be the sole determinant of the City's choice of mayor. In 1315 this 'representative' base was narrowed further by a writ from Edward II, who succeeded his father in 1307 and who now confined the franchise to those he had summoned to attend. Despite repeated complaints and periodic outbursts of organised protest, the principle of having been 'summoned by the monarch' remained intact until 1346 when a new arrangement allowed between six and twelve representatives to accompany their alder-men to the election of the mayor. In 1350 the number was reduced to just four, and in 1370 the size of the complement was abandoned and electors were once again summoned to their duty on the basis that they were deemed to be citizens of appropriate and superior background or, to put it more concisely, 'sufficient of wealth'. By the time that Richard Whittington returned to the mayoralty for his second full term in 1406, his third period of tenure, the pendulum had swung once more and a new protocol was in place: it was now stated definitively that members of the Common Council would attend the election.

24

SELF-PERPETUATION

Interest Group Politics

Between 1189 and 1300 at least 35 candidates were invested as mayor. For 93 of these years the office was shared between just thirteen men. If we set aside the unique case of Henry Fitz-Ailwyn, who remained in office 'for life', some of his successors also held the mayoralty for long periods, twelve serving four terms or more, among them Serlo le Mercer (five terms), who has been described as 'the archetype of the late twelfth-century mercer who made good ... a man who created his own fortune and thereby earned a byname, "le Mercer"'.[1] Arguably, it is Serlo's impoverished background, his rise to the pinnacle of his trade, and his service to London as mayor for five terms that better fit the popular mythology that has developed around the pantomime character of Dick Whittington. Ralph de Sandwich served London for an even longer period of nine years, de Rokesley served for eight, and John le Breton and Andrew Buckerell for seven. Together, these six men oversaw the affairs of London for 60 years, at times subject to considerable interference from the monarch. Setting the time frame slightly differently, we find that in the 123 years from 1300 until Richard Whittington's death in 1423, London had at least 77 mayors but that the arrangements for their election, their lengths of tenure, the likelihood of multiple terms, and the intervals between those terms were coming under closer scrutiny as the City's relationship with the Crown ebbed and flowed, as the burden of administering London and representing its interests to the king became more demanding, and as the office of mayor itself became increasingly a proving ground for the competitive interest group politics of London's guilds and emerging companies.

During the early part of the 14th century, tenure often extended for more than one year, but from about 1350 and during the first quarter of the 15th century a consensus emerged that mayors should serve one year only and that a reasonable period should pass if and before they served again, partly to prevent manipulation by the more powerful guilds and companies or by self-perpetuating groups of aldermen, but also because of the sheer volume of responsibility and the burgeoning complexity and expectations associated with the office. At first glance it seems ironic that it was not until 1424, the year after Whittington's death, that the Court of Aldermen extended the interval between repeat tenure to seven years and stipulated that henceforth no one should serve more than two terms in all. This timing may represent a courtesy to Whittington, whose health had been failing since the completion of his final term in 1420 and whose multiple terms, while admired and lauded, were already seen as a thing of the past and no longer suited to the changing circumstances of London's governance. 'The decision may have been provoked by Richard Whittington's third term of office in 1419–20. It was certainly unusual, by this time, for a man to serve three times' and (with a nod to the popular pantomime version of his tenure) 'hence the extraordinary message that Dick was supposed to have heard the bells of London: "Turn again, Whittington, thrice Lord Mayor of London."'[2] For some in the City, it must have been fresh in the mind that Whittington's career and those of members of his close circle had been much favoured by their occupancy of the mayor's office; and, to put it bluntly, others wanted and expected 'their turn'. His enemies would also recall his crusade against usury—despite his being among London's most prominent lenders—and what appeared to many as an increasingly personal feud with the brewers. The brewers and their acolytes, London's innkeepers, had been a thorn in the side of London's mayors since at least 1331, when an inquiry was established to investigate the malpractices of the innkeepers. A statute of that date empowered the mayor of London to search all malt brought to the city and to prevent and punish the frauds of the country maltsters, so that the purchaser might have the full measure and value of clean malt.

This shift to single-year tenure, greater intervals between repeat terms, if a second proved desirable, and a determination to afford opportunity and better regulate manipulation of the electoral process had been making its painstaking course, often deflected and sometimes reversed, throughout the entire period since 1300. London at the beginning of the 14th century has been described as being 'governed by a highly privileged oligarchy of 24 aldermen ... Neither individually nor collectively were these men responsible to the citizens, nor was there any effective popular control over the filling of vacancies in their number'.[3] Among this narrow self-perpetuating group, the mayor was effectively *primus inter pares*, holding at least nominal sway over an increasingly politicised office fought over and driven by the tribalism, exclusive privileges and ingrained self-interest of London's most powerful guilds and their allies. That they were also frequently at odds with the revenue-driven mindset of the monarch merely added to the sense of turbulence. By the turn of the 14th century, London was a highly diverse, competitive and often combative arena in which a wide range of interests were played out in politics, in commerce and in the city's evolving social and labour relations. Ruth Bird describes the emergence of the 'victuallers', who assumed their 'characteristic form' at this time and became 'a storm centre of city politics'.[4] They were not alone, and other interests organised themselves to counter and contest them. The events of the final quarter of the century in Parliament, at Blackheath and Mile End, in the confined spaces of London's back streets and alleyways, at the Guildhall and across the Channel in northern France demonstrated that while the city's mayor and aldermen, and even the merchant community that formed 'the City', may have claimed to speak for London, a far more layered pluralism was emerging in which even those who held the greatest power and wealth recognised that their own interests depended on forming a variety of social and political contracts with those who did not. The infrastructure that drove London's economy and that shouldered much of England's tax burden was inextricably interconnected with the interests and aspirations of its ordinary citizens. Some leaders recognised this more than others, a few engaging the commonalty in progressive terms, others merely manufacturing populist engagement when their own self-interest demanded a superficial show of responding to expectations. Caroline Barron notes:

> In fact there was a plurality of voices [in which the ruling elite and aldermen may have dominated but which also included the city's merchants and artisans, the households who exercised a voice at ward meetings] and then there were the unenfranchised, the women, aliens, clerics (of whom there would have been thousands rather than hundreds in London), members of the numerous aristocratic households in the city and, of course, boys and girls who often formed an important part of the workforce, but had no say in how their craft or trade or household was run, let alone in the government of the city.[5]

By the end of the 14th century, not only were the process and structure of London's governance increasingly polyarchical,[6] but the gradually irradiating pluralism which had developed within and outside the primary centres of interest and influence 'determined the character of the response to the social problems created by urban life'.[7]

Mayoral Affinities in Richard Whittington's London

Year	Mayor	Profession	Year	Mayor	Profession
1369–70	Sir John Chichester	Goldsmith	1397–June/Oct.	Richard Whittington	Mercer
1370–1	Sir John de Bernes	Mercer	1397–8	Richard Whittington (2nd)	Mercer
1371–2	Sir John de Bernes (2nd)	Mercer	1398–9	Drew Barantyn	Goldsmith
1372–3	John Pyell	Mercer	1399–1400	Thomas Knolles	Grocer
1373–4	Sir Adam de Bury (3rd)	Skinner	1400–1	John Fraunceys	Goldsmith
1374–5	Sir William Walworth	Fishmonger	1401–2	John Shadworth	Mercer
1375–6	John Warden	Grocer	1402–3	John Walcote	Draper
1376–7	Adam Stable	Mercer	1403–4	William Askham	Fishmonger
1377–8	Nicholas Brembre	Grocer	1404–5	John Hende	Draper
1378–9	John Philpot	Grocer	1405–6	John Woodcock	Mercer
1379–80	John Hadley	Grocer	1406–7	Richard Whittington (3rd)	Mercer
1380–1	John Northampton (2nd)	Draper	1407–8	William Staunton (2nd)	Grocer
1382–3	John Northampton	Draper	1408–9	Drew Barantyn (2nd)	Goldsmith

1383–4	Nicholas Brembre (2nd)	Grocer		1409–10	Richard Marlowe	Ironmonger
1384–5	Nicholas Brembre (3rd)	Grocer		1410–11	Thomas Knolles (2nd)	Grocer
1385–6	Nicholas Brembre (4th)	Grocer		1411–12	Robert Chichele	Grocer
1386–7	Nicholas Exton	Fishmonger		1412–13	William Walden	Mercer
1387–8	Nicholas Exton (2nd)	Fishmonger		1413–14	William Cromer	Draper
1388–9	Sir Nicholas Twyford	Goldsmith		1414–15	Thomas Faulconer	Mercer
1389–90	William Venour	Grocer		1415–16	Nicholas Wootton	Draper
1390–1	Adam Bamme	Goldsmith		1417–18	Richard Marlowe (2nd)	Ironmonger
1391–2	John Hende	Draper		1418–19	William Sevenoke	Grocer
1392–3	William Staunton, Sir Edward Dalyngrigge and Sir Baldwin Radyngton	Grocer		1419–20	Richard Whittington (4th)	Mercer
1393–4	John Hadley (2nd)	Grocer		1420–1	William Cambridge	Grocer
1394–5	John Fresshe	Mercer		1421–2	Robert Chichele (2nd)	Grocer
1395–6	William More	Vintner		1422–3	William Walden (2nd)	Mercer
1396–June 1397	Adam Bamme (2nd)	Goldsmith		1423–4	Sir William Cromer (2nd)	Draper

Alan Myers writes that by the early 14th century the power of the craft guilds had developed to such an extent that in 1311 'a reforming mayor', presumably the pepperer Sir John Gisors, as his predecessor, the mercer Sir Richard de Refham, had been deposed, was obliged, or simply thought it to be in his own good interests, to grant rights of self-regulation to many of the crafts and was supported in doing so by his aldermen, many of whom were leading lights in their guilds. But a sea change was on its way and this concession was no longer adequate to placate rapidly escalating political as well as long-standing commercial aspirations. In Myers's words, 'the craft guilds wanted a share in the city's government, and they began to get it. They wanted rights of citizenship to be protected against immigrants and other non-freemen.'

Demands for citizenship necessitated the formalisation of social and political obligation. Representation required order, proof of identity, formal registration and the means to pay for it. The guilds also had to get organised if they were to influence the governance of the city, and that meant affirmation and proof of citizenship. 'Improved records and a more efficient bureaucracy enabled them to make a drive to ensure the registration of freemen and payment of taxes; over nine hundred men were enrolled as citizens between 1309 and 1312.'[8] And to consolidate and safeguard their status—and also assure himself of a steady flow of funds into the Exchequer through registration and through the benefits that would flow from it—Edward II ruled in 1319 'that no stranger should be admitted to citizenship unless his claim was supported by six men of the same craft he wished to follow; the same charter enacted that the mayor and aldermen should be annually elected.'[9] The wealthiest and most influential actors here were mercers, drapers, grocers, fishmongers, woolmongers, skinners and goldsmiths, who would later formalise their dominance of London's civic, political and economic arrangements as the vanguard of the twelve great livery companies. In 1348 it may have seemed that membership of a craft guild was firmly established as the chief route to political influence through the Common Council. However, even as they applauded their progress, the influence of the crafts was already being eclipsed by the greater resources, organisational consolidation, and more overt political ambitions of those guilds driven by trade rather than craft; and their route to even greater wealth and influence was not the secondary byway of the Common Council but the fast-track power and status of the royal charter.

During the 234 years that passed between the appointment of Henry Fitz-Ailwyn in 1189 and the death of Richard Whittington in 1423, the tenure and the 'constituency' base of London's mayors underwent a series of changes. The period is notable for the domination of five of these guilds—the drapers, grocers, mercers, fishmongers and goldsmiths. It is the constituency—the guild or mystery—from which the incumbents were drawn and which was typically instrumental in propelling them to office in often fierce, occasionally violent, struggles that remains of most interest here. During the period it is the drapers, traditional 'trade allies' of the mercers, who are the most recurring office-holders, with twenty-two different incumbents holding the mayoralty for a total of 67 years, although 24 years fell to a single individual, Fitz-Ailwyn, and a further 7 years to John le Blund. Mercers fall second with eighteen mayors serving a total of 33 years. Richard Whittington's four terms (his first partial) are outmatched only by Serlo le Mercer's five. The next largest group are the pepperers, represented by eleven of their number in office for an aggregate 23 years. In fact, their grip on the mayoralty was much greater since, in 1373, they were reconstituted as 'the grocers', and under their new structure from 1374 a further ten of their number were in office for a combined total of 16 years. Overall, the two groups lay claim to twenty-one office-holders serving a total of 39 years, placing them ahead of the mercers on both counts. From the 1370s there is an adversarial relationship between the grocers and the mercers, which spills into commerce, civic life and political ambition. Typically, they constitute the two cores around which a range of other interests and trades coalesce. The fishmongers had to wait until 1319 to return their first mayor, Hamo de Chigwell, who held office for a total of 7 years. Overall, they returned nine mayors occupying office for a total of 16 years, among them Sir Nicholas Exton, and were the trade most closely associated with the grocers, forming the core of 'the victuallers' interest'. Both groups were the subject of civil unrest and political redress directed at hoarding, abuse of weights and measures, and price fixing. These produced particular challenges for 'mercer mayors', Whittington prominent among them. The vintners, also associated with 'the victuallers', were arguably the most influential of London's smaller guilds, enjoying well-established access to court and the wider nobility, and were closely interconnected with many of London's port trades. In all, six vintners served the city for a total of 11 years, their most prominent figure being the five-term le Waleys.[10] The goldsmiths, wealthy, influential and generally 'free-floating' in their affinities, returned seven mayors totalling 19 years, the long-serving de Rokesley accounting for 8 years and Nicholas de Farndone a further 4. Of the remaining office-holders, the skinners (formerly 'furriers'), an ancient guild which dressed and traded furs, had long enjoyed the favour of the Crown and the nobility, recognised in the grant of a royal charter as early as 1327. Control of their manufactures had formed an essential cog in the Sumptuary Laws of the 1330s and 1363. Yet we do not encounter one of their trade as mayor until 1347 in the person of Sir Thomas Legge, who served a second term in 1354. Better known, but for the wrong reasons, their second incumbent, Sir Adam de Bury, in 1364 brought the guild into disrepute following his impeachment in office but was enabled to return for a second bite at the cherry in 1373. The guild's reputation was recovered in full by their third mayor, the distinguished Sir Henry Barton, purveyor of furs and pelts and skinner to the king's household from 1405 to 1433, who held office for two terms in 1416 and 1428. The only other guild to reach the mayoralty during this extensive span was the ironmongers, their candidate, Richard Marlowe, an associate of Richard Whittington, serving in 1409 and 1417. Taken together, these eight guilds held office for a total of 193 years.

These episodes of tenure reflect the eruption of social issues, prevailing political currents, the strength of commercial forces, and the adversarial nature of caucus interests as well as their abilities to marshal support and resources for a tilt at London's great prize. But what of the remaining terms: who governed the city during the 41 years when these interests were not in the driving seat? We find two other guilds briefly playing their part and some years when there are joint tenures. For 34 of these years, we have the name of the mayor but not their guild. There is an explanation for this: 30 terms fall between 1216 and 1266 when the office of mayor was still in its infancy and when the relationship between the guilds and the mayoralty had not been formally or fully established. For the most part the mayor was the individual appointment of the king, following a template established by Richard I. Mayors had to be figures of considerable wealth, confident and influential within the City, with a demonstrable ability to get the king's business done. They were also favoured for their political fealty. Henry Fitz-Ailwyn, Roger Fitzalan, Serlo le Mercer and William Hardel each met these requirements.

Presumably the grocer Andrew Buckerell, who served for seven years from 1231 to 1238, was installed for similar reasons. The trade of the remaining incumbents is either not known or not recorded, and from 1265 the arrangements and trade attributions are distorted in any case by the installation of a 'royal warden' in place of a mayor. During the entire 234 years royal wardens were in office for 19 years, arriving first in 1265 when three shared the office in that year and with the last two holding office in 1392 in the persons of Sir Edward Dalyngrigge and Sir Baldwin Radyngton, who would later provide a vignette in Richard Whittington's story, and who shared the office later in the year with the grocer William Staunton. There was good reason for their appointment. 'Following the removal of the government to York in May 1392 and the suspension from office of the mayor and aldermen of London a month later, Sir Edward was chosen to act as warden of the City.'[11] As Richard II's conflict with the City deepened, it became clear that he needed a skilled administrator with a judicial background to take on the task of imposing his will and reordering his relationship with London. Dalyngrigge fitted the bill, and his reassignment also allowed the king to bring in the no-nonsense Radyngton. 'He was replaced by Sir Baldwin Radington, the controller of the Household, by all accounts a rigid disciplinarian. It was rumoured that the King had found Dallingridge to be "too gentle and tender with the Londoners", but it seems more likely that it was Richard's intention to release him to act as a free agent in the complicated negotiations between the Crown and the City which were to follow.'[12]

While the great majority of mayors would serve either for one term only or for two or three punctuated by those of other candidates, a number remained in office uninterrupted for long periods. Arguably the inaugural arrangements, the breaking of new ground, and the uncertainty about the relationship between City and Crown go some way in explaining why Fitz-Ailwyn could hold on for nearly 24 years. It is also the case that many of the costs and interventions associated with the office then, and for some time after, were laid at the mayor's own door. Ground-breaking incumbents like Fitz-Ailwyn and le Waleys set examples that Richard Whittington would later follow, not least in his determination to rebuild Newgate from his own resources. These men not only had to be willing but also possess the financial wherewithal to discharge some responsibilities by their own means or else command sufficient support from the wider economic community to persuade it that the burden should be shared. We might then ask, if the intention of Richard I was to reduce civil and financial pressures directed at the treasury, why rock the boat with regular elections?

From 1300, there is greater evidence of candidates achieving office because of their affinity with a guild or 'company'. Competition for the mayoralty intensifies and becomes far more partisan. Office is pursued as a prize that confers authority, status, political influence and commercial leverage for the sponsoring trade. Yet even the most powerful and wealthy guilds recognised that they needed to support a leading figure from within their ranks, or else one from an 'allied' guild, capable of commanding both partisan and popular support in the City and able to hold his own in the City's frequently tense relationship with the monarch. Individuals emerge throughout the course of a disrupted and turbulent 14th century in each of the leading guilds capable or popular enough to win multiple terms. The goldsmith Sir Nicholas Farndone commenced the first of his four terms in 1308; Sir Hamo de Chigwell, the fishmonger, embarked on the first of his seven terms in 1319; and the entrepreneur and banker Sir John Poultney, widely regarded as the Croesus of the age, completed four terms in 1337. In the second half of the century 'politics' intensify and we see the emergence of figures who cross the line between public service and financial self-interest or who pursue power for power's sake and beyond the confines of the mayor's office. Examples include the skinner Sir Adam de Bury and the controversial, polarising Sir Nicholas Brembre. One of the latter's close acquaintances, the enormously wealthy but disgraced draper Sir John Hende, served a partial term in 1391, interrupted by his deposal and imprisonment, yet still managed to return in 1404. In the dying light of the century it was the turn of Whittington to take his first steps as London's mayor, in line with both the early template of Richard I and the 'competition model' that superseded it. In the 25 years that followed, no one other than Richard Whittington served on more than two occasions.

25

EYES ON HEAVEN

Greyfriars Tradition Set by London's Mercers

In office, Whittington would follow the example of civic works and social reform overseen by some of London's most celebrated mayors, sustaining and enlarging the efforts of his own company and of his associates in the dispensing of charity, the patronage of education, and the endowment of religious institutions and good works. A pattern for the last-mentioned had been set in the regular provisions made by London's mercers for the city's Greyfriars community since its establishment in 1225 close to St Nicholas in the Shambles.[1] It was the London mercer John Iwyn who initially purchased the site in the 'old butchers' quarter' and in 1228 another, Joce Fitzpiers, donated property in Stinking Lane to accommodate the community's expansion. These individual acts by members of London's mercer community encouraged Henry III to provide the oak from the royal forests needed to construct the friars' house. Its first chapel was funded by another merchant in luxury goods and cloths, William Joyner, mayor of London in 1239, who also acted as an occasional 'banker' to the king. By the early 14th century, the Greyfriars demesne incorporated one of London's largest churches, an extensive library of theological and philosophical texts, and a *studium*, or 'religious university', that placed it as a leading centre of higher study second only to Oxford and ranked co-equally with Cambridge.[2]

For London's mercer community, involvement in the Greyfriars project over a long period of time was a combination, as were many 'good works', of charitable instinct, political nous and commercial self-interest. For many, however, the principal driving force was a belief that good works in this life would enhance their prospects of salvation in the next. Having been involved from the outset and continuing to remain among its primary supporters, they were, of course, *seen* to support the needs and aspirations of London's leading religious community, which in turn impacted beneficially on the perceptions of many ordinary Londoners. But this was only part of the 'goodwill capital' accrued; there was far greater political and commercial leverage in being seen to actively support the involvement of the monarchy in the very early days of Henry III's interest but, most significantly, during the further development of the site in 1301–2 by Edward I's second wife, Queen Margaret.[3] Completed in 1348 as the second-largest church in medieval London, Greyfriars would attract both the spiritual and the worldly interests of London's merchant class, becoming a much sought-after place of burial for people of rank, wealth and position and a centre for scholarship and the promotion of social reform. It was not the first church to attract the endowments and interest of the city's merchants, but its association with two queens and the prominent roles played by mercers and others in its development demonstrated the multi-layered value and opportunities that could be drawn from the endowment of religious 'projects'. During the forty years in which Whittington developed his career, there is little doubt that politics, religion and commerce were even more inextricably linked. Charity was good for the soul but also for one's business and advancement. Yet few would accuse Whittington of mixing business and charity for his own ends. In 1411 his personal contribution to Greyfriars amounted to £400 of the £456 required to build and stock a library there.[4]

The Civic Good

As with any age, the aspirations or purposes which drove the attainment of high civic or political office were variously populist, partisan and personal, and sometimes a mixture of all three. For the guilds, the reasons for propelling their own man or mobilising their support behind the candidate of a kindred trade or ally were characteristically rooted in self-interest: promotional or defensive or, more often, both. For some candidates the mayoralty was little more than an opportunity to further their own political or commercial ends, while others saw it as a celebration of their personal standing, content to sustain the principle of 'Buggins's turn'. Even for the well-intentioned majority, the prospect of establishing a legacy that served the interests of Londoners at large was likely to be slender. Annual election promoted short-termism. Yet there is abundant evidence that despite the challenges and turbulence that dogged London's mayoralty,

many of those who sought one of Europe's great civic offices did so precisely because they *did* wish to bring about an improvement in the lives of
their fellow citizens and hoped to be remembered for it. What united
them, almost without exception, was a belief that God himself had played
a hand in the events which brought them to office. They were spiritually
and morally bound to acknowledge this through good governance and, in
many instances, in the form of private endowments and charitable works.
Of course, there were those who translated this duty to their Maker as
ensuring that the laws and trading conditions of the City enabled *their*
'party' or the wider merchant class to prosper and profit. After all, would
not the freedom to create personal wealth also produce benefits for the
common weal in the form of gainful employment, an improvement in
living standards, food on the table, and the easing of taxation on the poor?
For the more administrative-minded, good governance might amount to
the complex challenge of keeping London in good physical and social
order, a significant consideration when England was at war and the king
and his Exchequer regularly drained the country's tax resources. Others,
almost certainly more than records show, were determined to use their
moment of authority to implement social reform, make provision for
better health and sanitation, introduce opportunities for education, and
enable self-improvement. Every mayor also had to represent London in its
dealings with the king, often the most challenging of his duties and relationships. As mayor, he might find himself pressed by the king to rally the
City and to raise loans and grants for war, to underpin national solvency,
or simply to satisfy the monarch's wilful personal consumption. He might
respond pragmatically, treating loans as 'goodwill capital' that the City
might draw on to win important concessions elsewhere, or with weary
resignation, treating them as the price to pay for London being able to go
about its business, a tax in lieu of interference.

What the most influential mayors recognised, Whittington among
them, was that in addition to being harangued by the king to raise loans
from the City as its representative, they were also, in their capacity as
private individuals, expected by the public at large, London's commoners,
and by the church to endow, to enable and to improve. There was a fine
line, and frequently none, between public duty and *noblesse oblige*. Funding
good works and charity from the Corporation's own coffers was the official face of leadership, but it was common for mayors to set a personal
example in leading their aldermen, the city's merchant class, wealthy
members of the barony, London's leading guilds, and their own friends and

associates to do the same from their private means. This extended to the encouragement of faith-based works, including endowments and repairs to churches, chapels, chantries, choirs and colleges, most of which were provided at the request of or initiated by individuals themselves for their own and their family's salvation.[5] The provisions of Whittington's own will is an exemplar here. Throughout the 200 years before Whittington took office, London's mayors played an essential part in promoting a climate of beneficence in which this culture could develop, in both the civic and private spheres. Most of these initiatives reflected this dual purpose, serving the public good while making a personal or familial preparation for the afterlife. To take one example, the endowment of churches, typically in the form of improvement and repair, we find a distinct pattern of charitable giving in the period 1225–1409 by wealthy members of London's merchant class, many of whom also served as mayor.

Notable Church Endowments, 1238–1409

- 1239 William Joyner (Mercer), Mayor of London in 1239 was a principal donor to the Greyfriars project during the period 1238–43 providing the sum of £200 towards the construction of the chapel and funds to acquire additional land and buildings for Greyfriars' later expansion
- 1274 Henry le Waleys* (vintner) built the nave of the Greyfriars church
- 1274–80 Gregory de Rokesley* (goldsmith) funded St Paul's chapel, St Mary's Woolnoth, All Hallows, Greyfriars
- 1298 William Kingstone (fishmonger) sold his tenements to fund St Peter's Cornhill
- 1337 Sir John Poultney (draper) gave funding for St Paul's church
- 1348 Sir Walter Manny supported the foundation of Gonville College; in 1349 he acquired land at New Church Haw, Smithfield, to create a cemetery for plague victims; in 1371 he funded and was buried at the Carthusian monastery, the London Charterhouse
- 1360s John Lofken* (fishmonger) endowed St Michael's in Crooked Lane
- 1370s Sir William Walworth* (fishmonger) funded a college of priests at St Michael's

---

- 1370s John Barnes* (draper) endowed St Thomas Apostle
- 1379 John Hadley* (grocer) gave land for a cemetery to St Pancras
- 1390s Adam Bamme* (goldsmith) gave funding towards the edification of St George Botolph Lane
- 1398 Drew Barantyn* (goldsmith) gave funding for St John Zachary
- 1405 Sir John Hende* (draper) built St Swithin by London Stone
- 1409 Richard Whittington* rebuilt and extended St Michael Paternoster, which later became a college for priests and a set of almshouses

(*London mayor)

The funding methods for such works varied according to the need of the building itself, the requirements and aspirations of the clergy and the parish, and the personal preferences and conditions attached by the donor, his family and, in some instances, his guild. The churches of St Botolph, St Magnus, St Peter and St Mary, for example, had their roots in the fishmonger community, came to be regarded as the churches of that guild and were endowed by its members. The principal means by which individuals and the guilds funded London's churches included donating sites, assembling the capital for their initial construction, setting aside funds for or contributing along the way to their future repair and maintenance, providing religious works and ornaments, purchasing books and relics, meeting the cost of stipends for chaplains and tutors, and making provision for food, clothing and furnishings. Support also extended to generating income through the 'purchasing' of benefactions and the establishment of chantries for the singing of Masses, which dovetailed with the wills of many of London's richest merchants. Not every act was entirely philanthropic. In many instances the affluent were simply endowing the very churches and chapels in which they and their family would later come to rest. There were instances too of land and buildings being donated to a church which were due for demolition in any case, which were blighted in some way, or whose relinquishment had rather more to do with avoiding taxation. There were those who believed that such initiatives would also help to damp down the prospect of social unrest. They were a hedge against the disruption of their business. But for the great part these acts of donation and endowment were well intentioned and well received.

Their outcomes produced a proliferation in the number of London's churches and chapels as well as improvements in their design, construction and ornamentation, and in the associated development of colleges and libraries. Elsewhere, we also see the commissioning of hospitals and alms-houses, improvements to water supply and hygiene, and the creation of open spaces and amenities. Richard Whittington and Thomas Knolles would prove to be notable standard-bearers for such improvements. The beneficiaries were their parishioners, the poor and the mendicant, veterans of the war with France, young children, the clergy and monks, the guilds and the great companies, and of course the individual donors and their families. For London this brought significant changes. This continuing programme of endowment, investment, development, improvement and ongoing repair, and the related works and infrastructure it produced, mopped up labour, created new employment, sponsored apprenticeships, and generated demand for a range of skills. It was sustained further by the parallel development of fine houses and mansions that this same wealthy merchant class jostled to construct on sites often adjoining the very churches they had funded or helped to repair. By the time Richard Whittington arrived on the scene at the end of the 1370s, the newly acquired power, wealth and influence of London's merchant class in bringing about improvement to the city's built landscape were already an established *sine qua non* in the political platform of its mayors and in the expectations of their electorate and the wider commonalty.

In short, mayors were expected to 'give a lead' and, to do so, they or their inner circle had to be wealthy. In turn, the guilds and companies that supported them had begun to develop, alongside their traditional self-absorbing interests, a genuine benevolence and concern for the less fortunate. This recognised that faith and philanthropy were closely linked to personal redemption. There was also the ever-present shadow of the plague and a sense of 'there but for the grace of God'. Wealth, corporate and personal, was by now an instrument for 'social insurance'. In the last quarter of the 14th century, we see a shift in the culture of the wealthiest companies towards using some of their largesse to provide for those within their ranks, and their families, who had encountered great adversity or were experiencing hard times and, in the wider community, a much greater willingness to invest in charitable works and social improvement.

Yet for all their diverse responsibilities, personal munificence and many good works, London's mayors were reminded always that much of their role lay in managing the perpetual and often aggressive conflict of London's many interest groups, frequently driven by the quest for control of the mayoralty itself. They were expected to navigate and mediate the ever-present underlying tension between City and Crown, which broke through so spectacularly during the reign of Richard II. Mayors were ever watchful to keep on the right side of the king. There was a 'chronic fear of incurring the royal displeasure through failure to maintain high enough standards of law and order' because such failure brought the very real and punishing prospect of a 'consequent loss of the city's liberties'. In this regard the mayor, his two sheriffs and his 24 (later 25) aldermen 'were like the rulers of a nation engaged in a war for existence, who dare not throw any controversial issues open for public discussion lest disagreements should weaken the unity that is for the moment so vital'.[6] Above all, maintaining and being seen to maintain this unity was both a political and a moral imperative for London's mayor. Place this in jeopardy and he placed himself there also. Whittington's closest friend and executor, John Carpenter, author of the *Liber Albus*, wrote in 1419 that the electoral college from which the mayor drew his support and earned the confidence of the Crown was essential to this unity. The proposition that councils should be elected directly from self-interested misteries would only alienate the citizenry and increase this jeopardy.[7]

26

TWICE MAYOR

By the late 1380s the ostentation and louche tendencies of Richard's court were being openly remarked upon. The Benedictine chronicler Thomas Walsingham famously wrote of men who were apparently most interested in their appearance, their romantic pursuits and fashion that they presented as 'knights of Venus rather than Mars' and were 'more active in the bedchamber than on the battlefield'.[1] In contrast to some representations of Richard as tyrannical, neurotic, tortured and vengeful, Sylvia Federico tells us that at heart Richard II was rather a generous and peaceful figure 'known for his lively court', a place given to frequent feasts, games, entertainment and music. This may explain why, in her words, 'in large part, a chivalric knight in Richard's court was not an accomplished English warrior' and instead 'the king surrounded himself with his young friends and favourites'.[2] She notes further that the Monk of Evesham wrote that Richard was 'prodigious with gifts, extravagantly ostentatious in his dress and pastimes'.[3] EW Stockton prefers to rely on the observations of the contemporary poet and friend of Chaucer John Gower, who famously encountered the king by chance on the Thames quayside and was invited to converse with him aboard the royal barge; during this time Richard commissioned what would become the *Confessio Amantis*.[4] Gower would later describe him as the 'most beautiful of kings and flower of boys', noted for his taste in fine clothes and his attention seeking.[5] In addition to his ostentation, his expensive taste for fine goods, and his extravagant partying and entertainment, Gower portrays Richard as an uncertain and insecure figure who sought close friends (many no more than hangers-on) and kept them close. He was far more likely to place his trust in his personal acquaintances than his formal advisers or those in institutions for which he held little regard, including the City of

London. As noted, Whittington first supplied fine cloth and other goods to Richard's court in the early 1380s and among his first patrons had been the king's great favourite, Robert de Vere; Sir Simon Burley, under-chamberlain of the king's household for life; and, of course, Richard's uncle, the formidable John of Gaunt. In this inner group Whittington captured the attention and patronage of the three figures with the most direct influence over the impressionable teenage king. It can hardly have escaped Richard's notice that Whittington too was relatively young, and that he was already highly regarded, trusted and valued by members of his inner circle. The fast development of their relationship from the early 1390s, when it came to embrace lending, wise counsel, the principal civic responsibility in England, and what certainly became a 'close friendship', was rooted therefore in Whittington's early service to the Ricardian court some ten years earlier.

Whittington's independence from the general hurly-burly of guild politics and his perceived detachment from what the king saw as the effrontery and impertinence of London's governing class, together with his capacity and integrity as a 'banker', gradually came to supersede his earlier purpose as a supplier of fine goods. By the mid-1390s this suited the interests of both men, and their mutual trust is evidenced in the provisions of Whittington's will. By the early 1390s Whittington had already made his first fortune and built up a significant reserve of liquid capital; much of this had been accumulated through his service to the king. Caroline Barron's survey of the account roll of Richard Clifford, the keeper of the Great Wardrobe during the early 1390s, who went on to hold the post until 1397, reveals that Richard II spent over £13,000 on saddlery, skins, drapery and mercery during the years 1392–4 and that 'Of this £13,000 about 90% went into the pockets of London merchant suppliers of whom the two most prominent were the draper John Hende, the imprisoned mayor of 1392, and the young and rising mercer, Richard Whittington'.[6]

Richard's infatuation with fashion and luxury goods is evidenced not only in the scale and quality of his purchases but also in the exceptionally close interest he took in the day-to-day operation of the Great Wardrobe. It is reported that during Clifford's keepership he would even sometimes dine in this place 'where he had chambers; a trestle table and cupboards and standing chests were kept for use during his visits'.[7] For his part, Whittington had begun to shift his primary interests away from mercery to lending, and by now had consolidated his position within the mercer community, playing an influential part in elevating their de facto status as

London's leading company to a formal recognition of their ranking and prestige. What he could not have anticipated was the sudden and transformative change in his civic interests and responsibilities. In London the new decade had opened with a sharp public outcry on the state of the city's streets and its inadequate infrastructure. Midway through 1397 Whittington would find himself quite unexpectedly in the hot seat as London's mayor, charged with remedying its built and environmental deficiencies, and managing the needs and expectations of a population that had recovered to and probably surpassed its pre-Black Death level of 50,000.[8] London's mayor also had to ensure that its commerce and prosperity would continue, oversee the regulations on weights, pricing and the quality of goods and services, and ensure that the city was secure and well policed. Most challenging of all, he would find himself charged with negotiating an increasingly fraught accommodation between the escalating demands of a king who may have considered him 'in his pocket' and the interests of a City and electoral college which had played no legitimate part in his appointment.

Indeed, this was the very point: he had been installed as the king's man rather than elected from the jostling and accommodations of the City's chief interest groups. Yet Richard II was prescient in identifying the right man for the job. From what little we know of him, Whittington was not someone who would have regarded himself as captive to politics or as the representative of one faction against another. Rather, he presents as someone who saw himself as above the day-to-day partisanship of guild and city politics, free to exercise his own judgement and to demonstrate his independence. His interest lay in a higher game, and it was imperative that he distance himself from anything that would alienate a volatile and often vengeful king. What we see in Whittington is someone clearly fascinated by the levers of power, not least those wielded by the monarch himself, and he was evidently willing to trade his financial facilities to be closer to the action. He was neither a supine nor a disinterested lender and is notable for trading his affluence, not simply for the opportunity to create further wealth, but instead to play some part in influencing events. It might be ventured that, far from being a sudden surprise, his installation as mayor was a collusion between a wealthy, ambitious and resourceful 'operator' and a needy but ruthlessly single-minded king. We find Whittington more of a conductor and broker of interests, aiming to 'manage' London's governance and its relationship with the monarchy through skilful engagement, reconciliation and inclusion rather than stoop to threats, stand-offs and bare-knuckle politics. These would come later in his confrontations with the fishmongers and the brewers, but for the most part deed, example and reputation mattered more than mobilising supporters to occupy the streets.

Destined to be a watershed in Whittington's career and in his broader journey, the year 1397 had begun inauspiciously. Around February he found himself caught up in the first of a series of diverting property disputes that offered an unwelcome reminder of home. The first related to property on the Gloucestershire–Oxfordshire border apparently 'belonging' to Richard Monmouth and to James Sparsholt, the legal title for which was held by Whittington. Presumably, he had sought to retain his hold over the property until the two men fulfilled the financial and statutory obligations he had set them. Sparsholt appears later at the periphery of another property dispute which erupted in 1397, concerning ownership of the Frampton estate, which rumbled on to a protracted conclusion in 1408. Originally owned by the Cauntelo family, the Frampton manor had passed to the Clifford family in whole or in part.[9] In 1397 John Clifford of Daneway, part of modern-day Bisley in Gloucestershire, died while holding his lands 'of the king', Richard II. On Clifford's demise Whittington and another local landowner, Hugh of Bisley, asserted that Clifford's other landholdings formed part of *their* respective manors of Lypiatt and Bisley, and that the Frampton estate was in fact in the ownership of John Clinton of Temple Guiting. John Clifford's heirs were his daughters Elizabeth and Alice. Elizabeth took as her husband John Staure, and later, in 1401, Whittington and Hugh would bring a complaint that Staure and Clifford's cousin James Clifford had ejected them from John Clifford's estate.[10] This had ramifications at Bisley manor, part of which had been owned by the powerful de Bohun family. Roger Mortimer, Earl of March, had died in 1360, having granted Bisley to several beneficiaries, the most notable of whom was the Bishop of Winchester. In turn, the partition of the estate collided with Whittington's own claims on Tunley, more commonly known as Daneway, which he and others regarded as part of the fee of his own estate of Over Lypiatt, held from Bisley manor by his mother's family, the Maunsells. The Cliffords had been 'tenants in fee' of Daneway manor since at least 1338 and had remained so until John's death in 1397, when his estates were appropriated by the Crown. However, the escheat was contested by Whittington and Hugh of Bisley, and in 1398 the Crown gave Whittington, and subsequently in 1401 Hugh also, leave to hold their estates until the matter was decided.[11] In London, it is likely that Whittington would have been involved in a quite different property event in April 1397, the acquisition by the Mercers' Company of a licence in mortmain for three shops and three messuages in St Martin Outwich. With a royal charter in its hands, the company had been actively searching for investments and opportunities that would bring it a sustainable income.

The King's Lender

What we don't know is whether Richard II played any part in the decision by the Crown's escheator a year later to support a reversion of Over Lypiatt, but by then Whittington had successfully completed his first tenure as mayor, had been 're-elected' and had for a time eased the relationship between the monarch, the Corporation and the City. It is noteworthy here that when a property did fall into limbo on the demise of its legal or putative owner, the act of escheatment enabled the Crown to consider its options. Escheatment could be deployed as a convenient means of transferring the asset to a supporter of the king, providing a means also to accumulate fees for a year and a day until conferment on the succeeding owner and to reschedule the level of fee thereafter. In short, it was a useful ruse for raising revenue.[12]

The year 1397 was also the moment that Whittington began lending heavily and regularly to Richard II. He was not the only wealthy merchant willing to extend significant credit to the king when opposition to him intensified in the second half of the 1390s, but he was clearly Richard's preferred choice. By now, Whittington had been a discreet and trusted supplier to the Crown and to Richard's inner court for over a dozen years. Outside Westminster he was regarded by many of his peers as beyond reproach, above politics and not given to partisanship. For a hard-up, embattled king, frequently at odds with London's merchant class, Richard Whittington must have seemed a safe bet for mayor should an opportunity arise. Even so, Whittington was realistic enough to know he was not safe from the political undercurrents that could drag him down if he extended his financial support to such an increasingly unpopular and divisive figure. Indeed, we gain a strong sense of this just two years later during the upheavals of 1399 following the death of John of Gaunt and the subsequent seizure of his estates, with Richard's dethronement by Gaunt's son Bolingbroke. That Henry IV later reached out to Whittington in 1400 was not only a formal acknowledgement of the mercer's value, reputation and great wealth, but also a recognition that Whittington may have considered himself in limbo and been fearful for his security given his support for Henry's predecessor. On the other hand, he had the safety net of having also been for many years a favoured supplier to both the new king and his father. Within Henry's circle there would have been some who considered that the mercer's vast wealth and his ability to fund Richard II must have contributed in some part to the unwelcome prolongation of the king's position in the late 1390s. Furthermore, this proximity was evidenced in a particularly, perhaps uniquely, favourable relationship: a contract of sorts which saw most of Whittington's loans to Richard repaid in cash rather than by the route usually favoured by the Crown of Exchequer assignments. Henry was not slow in recognising this, acknowledging that he too would need to draw on the mercer's deep pockets and to rely on his astute commercial judgement. Whittington may not have realised it prior to Henry's accession, but with hindsight there was never a likelihood that he would suffer for the financial facility he had provided for Richard II. Both Henry IV and Henry V would require it and become even more reliant on it, though they would vary the terms and format. Henceforth, their loans would be secured against future revenues, largely generated from the wool custom, in which Whittington had an ever-greater role and from which he accumulated a second fortune. Repayment typically took the form of a licence enabling him to export wool free of duty. However, we are running ahead of ourselves here. Richard II's downfall was still over two years away, and it is to the events of June 1397 we return, events which established Whittington as a significant political figure. A combination of extraneous circumstances, perverse fortune and political exigency favoured London's most celebrated mercer.

Imposed as Mayor

On 6 June 1397, eight months into his second term, London's acclaimed incumbent, the goldsmith and property dealer Adam Bamme, collapsed and died in office. A description of him as 'one of the wealthiest and most influential Londoners of his day' who 'owed his success to a striking combination of shrewd political sense, business acumen and good fortune' might just as readily have been applied to Whittington himself.[13] He had recently completed a term as collector of the wool custom in London and was buried in the church of St George in Botolph Lane.[14] *The Chronicle of the Greyfriars* records that on 8 June 1397 Richard II 'decided' that

Whittington would replace Adam Bamme as mayor and should occupy that position until St Edward's Day, 13 October 1398. It appears, though, that Whittington was 'approved' by Londoners when the official end of Bamme's foreshortened term came around in October 1397.[15] Clearly, to step in for just three months would have been disruptive to London's stability, and any attempt to remove Whittington and insist on a formal election would amount to an open challenge to the king's intention that he should serve the remainder of Bamme's term of office and then show what he could do in a full term. In any case he had already won the doubters over by the end of October 1397.

This virtuous circle was completed on 13 February 1398 when Whittington inherited Lime Street ward, where Bamme had been alderman since 1393. Whittington would go on to hold it until his death in 1423. Bamme had also served as a member of Parliament for London in 1388. In the joint endeavours that characterised much of London's luxury goods trade, both men shared common business partners, including the mercer John Woodcock, one of Whittington's closest friends and business associates, the highly enterprising John Shadworth, and the wheeler-dealing ironmonger and general merchant Gilbert Maghfeld, who enjoyed similar relationships with Bamme and Whittington.[16] Both men were also close to the goldsmith Drew Barantyn. In 1396, shortly before his death, Bamme had established a joint venture with Woodcock in the collection of duties on wool and leather in the port of London. Whittington would find himself effectively imposed on the City and thrust upon London's citizenry at a moment already turbulent before Bamme's sudden demise. The decision meant that he would be perceived as the 'king's man', and this can have done little initially to assure his good health or augur a successful term of office. Compounding the king's tense relationship with the City and the febrile state of London generally, Richard II was also adrift on a personal front. He was by now 29 years old and had lost his wife, Anne of Bohemia, to plague in June 1394.

On 31 October 1396, he sought to strengthen ties with France by arranging a contentious marriage to Isabella, daughter of Charles VI and his wife Isabeau of Bavaria. She was six on her marriage to the English king and widowed at ten. Their union was intended to bring England and France together and to nurture a new period of friendship. If money was the measure of good intent, then Richard appears to have got off to an extraordinarily fortuitous start, his child bride bringing a breath-taking dowry of 800,000 francs, equivalent to £130,000. The chief players in this surreal event, Richard and his younger father-in-law, had met on 26 October near Calais, where Isabella was handed over. The English king opted for a display of great ostentation, spending as much as £15,000 on the event.[17] We can only imagine that he had laid off the cost with his English lenders or had hedged against the enormous bounty promised by his French counterpart. Either way it was an expensive affair.[18] The marriage ushered in a long truce between the two countries and provided a great, if temporary, relief to the Exchequer. Yet with war postponed indefinitely and the dowry providing an enormous net surplus on the wedding cost, Richard still managed to get himself into financial straits in the year that followed. He would fall out yet again with the City, intervene in its electoral process, and install Whittington as 'his' mayor. This was the year, according to observers, in which Richard's 'tyranny' is reckoned to have commenced, the February Parliament being 'rocked, after a number of years of comparative calm, by Richard's reaction to criticism of the government of the realm'.[19] Apparently, the king had got wind of a particular, and clearly sensitive, item of discussion to which he took a personal offence, 'that the great and excessive cost of the king's household should be amended and reduced'. Mention was made of 'a multitude of bishops ... and their hangers-on' and 'also of various ladies and their hangers-on who stayed in the king's household at great expense'. The king was said to be greatly aggrieved at what he regarded as a gross impertinence.[20] So much for hopes of stability in the year ahead.

One of the first tasks he assigned to the new mayor was to tackle the overcrowding and disease-ridden conditions in London's notorious prisons and determine 'how the city could be delivered of new gaols'. The shocking condition of London's prisons had been brought into sharp focus nine years earlier when in November 1388 a tailor, John Walpole, complained publicly about the inhumanities and malpractices inflicted on the inmates of Ludgate Prison by its feared keeper, a nefarious thug named John Bottesham. Walpole's case against Bottesham was subsequently quashed, but the outcry lingered and the charges finally prevailed.[21] Demand for reform was building. Whittington's chief attention, however, was directed towards the replacement of a far more notorious and reviled London landmark, the heinous Newgate, the object of simmering social and political discontent.

Richard II knew from his own dealings with the mercer and from the testimonies provided by courtiers and leading figures in the city that, although he had imposed him as mayor, disregarding process, risked further deterioration in his relationship with Londoners and placed his appointee in an invidious position, Whittington was arguably the outstanding candidate in any case. It helped too that he was well connected and enjoyed a reputation for unshakeable integrity. If the king was going to set aside rights and protocol and expect the Corporation to cave in, then Whittington was probably his best option. Despite the difficulties they would share over the next two years, the bond they developed was powerful and respectful enough for Whittington to salute the king in his will and make bequests available for Masses to be said in his name. He was discreet and amenable to the needs of the monarch and, despite the suddenness of his instalment, he must have been confident that he could rebuild Richard's fractious relationships with the Corporation, the City and London's commonalty. Naturally, Richard was determined to ensure that Whittington remained 'onside' and, within a matter of weeks, he surprised the mercer by reimbursing him in the sum of £1,903 16s 5d 'by assignment' for goods he had provided to the king's favourite, Robert de Vere.[22] It was a shrewd move on Richard's part, settling a substantial debt, consolidating Whittington's confidence, and perhaps, with some insight, effectively bundling repayment of a third-party debt into his much more important and evolving political 'contract' with the mercer. It was a demonstration that the king had the ability to make selective repayments, when it suited him, by robbing a less important Peter to pay a more important Paul. Whittington would also take comfort from the election of his close friend John Woodcock as alderman for his old stamping ground of Coleman Street. One of the leading voices who got behind him as mayor, and his successor as warden of the Mercers' Company, Woodcock would become an even more significant cheerleader for his friend when the opportunity to run for mayor next caught Whittington's eye in 1406. It helped to have influential friends.

While the installation by the king of his own favoured choice as mayor may have been new in its particularity, it was not an isolated example of Richard II's abrogation of civic or political protocol. In the Parliament of January 1390, his dismissal and subsequent reinstatement of his ministers had made clear that he reserved the right to remove and create his officers and councillors by his own choice whenever he judged it necessary. There is no hard evidence to determine that Whittington's installation was foreplanned, and his appointment is generally accepted as a king's urgent response to an untimely and potentially disruptive event. Even so, his arrival at the Guildhall presents as an opportunistic episode in Richard II's otherwise planned and long-standing effort to ensure that the Corporation, City and Commons bent the knee. Bamme's death was a convenient windfall in the king's persistent determination to impose his will, already evidenced in the events of 1387–8, those of January 1390, and his head-on collision with the City in June and July 1392 when he angrily denounced 'notorious defaults in the government of London'.[23] By September 1397 Richard was ready to move. Whittington's installation was the icing on the cake, a topping to a far greater political prize, the king's subordination of Parliament.[24] As Dodd notes:

> Not only did the crown dominate the legislative programme, but it had also secured an unprecedented grant of the wool subsidy for life ... the Commons were also remarkably partisan; over half the knights of the shire were either the king's retainers or servants, associates of the Counter-Appellants or were directly implicated in the proceedings of the assembly itself ... It was, perhaps, a measure of the support Richard received in this parliament that only four of its members were subsequently re-elected to the first parliament of Henry IV's reign.[25]

New Broom

So, what of the mayoralty itself? It is widely understood that the Corporation, the City and the Commons were in too vulnerable a position to oppose Richard's disregard of protocol. There were murmurs, of course, and the barons of the Exchequer were said to have refused to take Whittington's mayoral oath, leaving the king, apparently, to perform the task himself. Yet there was acquiescence, too, in having as mayor someone who enjoyed the king's estimation. The new mayor could have hardly imagined, however, that almost the first responsibility pressed upon him by the king during the Parliament of September 1397, which saw large numbers of the barony flood into London, many openly opposed to Richard, was to oversee personally the keeping of law and order in the city. For a novice, he made a good fist of it. According to one account, he 'ordeined at euery yate and yn euery warde strong wacche of men of armez and of archers, and prinspally at euery yate of London duryng this same parlement'.[26] His actions in safeguarding London's citizens, preventing outbreaks of factionalism and random violence, and his assured management of the City's frayed relationship with its unpredictable king went some way in demonstrating to Londoners of all classes that he deserved to be freely elected when his 'imposed' mayoralty concluded in October. He had made an effective start, and when he stood for re-election, his candidacy was approved largely unopposed. Now the real challenge began with just a year to make his mark. It helped that the early 1390s had seen a partial economic recovery driven by wool and cloth and that London was at the heart of it. 'In the framework of later medieval European trade, England was part of a North Sea–Eastern Atlantic economy which, from the fourteenth century, was linked to the Mediterranean world by direct sea routes. England's most important market in the period, both for wool and cloth, was Flanders and the Low Countries.'[27]

Bolton provides a fascinating map of London's strengthening position as an entrepôt for these towering centres of trade. From western Europe the cosmopolitan mercantile centres of Antwerp, Utrecht and Bruges exported into the Thames a range of manufactured goods, linens, finished cloths and endless trinkets for London's markets at Cheap, the Stocks and Leadenhall. They were essential, too, in meeting London's irrepressible demand for fish, unloaded at wharves near Billingsgate, just a couple of years away from receiving its royal charter in 1400. From Lübeck and Bergen in the north came furs for London's skinners, timber, flax, copper and potash. From the Rhine, the Hanseatic city of Cologne shipped steel and other metalwares into its appropriately named outpost on the Thames along with fine thread for London's drapers, embroiderers and seamstresses employed in the workshops around Threadneedle Street. With the sophisticated city economies of Venice, Florence, Milan and the port of Genoa triangulating with the ports of the Low Countries, London traded English wool and cloth in exchange for gold and silver, luxury goods and fabric, fashionable clothing and what we might today term 'accessories', along with haberdashery, fish and basic raw materials. From Iberia, Spain and Portugal were sources of iron ore, oil, soap, dyes and even exotic fruits like oranges and lemons.

On the streets of London, the civic challenges and day-to-day responsibilities Whittington found at his door can be broadly summarised as improving and maintaining the city's infrastructure, its roads, bridges, toll gates, public buildings, historic gates and walls. There were matters of health and hygiene to consider, the improvement of living conditions, the alleviation of poverty, the provision of charity, measures for the containment of plague and disease, intervention 'in the market' against food hoarding and price rigging to address hunger and the prospect of starvation (the efforts of Adam Bamme in using city funds at an earlier time to purchase foreign wheat were the most notable), and the supply of fresh water—a particular interest of the new mayor and even more so of his friend the grocer Thomas Knolles.

Then there were matters of judicial oversight, security and confinement, defence of the city, the raising and funding of yeomanry and constables, and the maintenance of London's gaols. And, of course, there was the regulation of trade, competition, pricing, weights and measures, in the city's workshops, in its breweries and taverns, and within the waters and boundaries of the Thames, and the prevention of usury. It was trade, commerce and the economy that surely gripped Whittington's professional interest most. In this regard he and other London mercers had much to thank his predecessor for. In the year before his death Adam Bamme had been instrumental in persuading the city's aldermen to purchase Blackwell Hall, a building close to the Guildhall, from which Whittington would oversee the establishment of a designated centre or market clearing house where all merchants not citizens of London were now required to bring their cloths for sale.[28] Henceforth all trading of cloth by mercers and drapers who were not freemen of the city would be conducted here under regulation. The initiative would go a long way in addressing the complaints and, at times, violent opposition of domestic merchants to the infiltration of their markets by 'aliens'. Although Blackwell Hall was also intended to curb, illuminate and apply much greater scrutiny to trade by non-Londoners (including merchants from other English towns), arguably its real purpose lay in curtailing the business of 'foreign', principally Italian, merchants and their encroachment on English markets. It was intended to give their London counterparts the upper hand and a superior market edge. Presumably the city's mercers were delighted to see it established by one of their own. The outcome would be to give Whittington's own community control not only over the London wool trade but over that for England at large. The facilities created at Blackwell Hall for storage, for workspace and for collaborative enterprise ensured that it would become England's principal trading and pricing floor, the national centre for distribution via the Thames. However, the restrictions were far less punitive than might have been hoped for. While many saw it as the means to stifle and even eliminate foreign traders in the London market, the reality was that many English merchants, including Whittington himself, relied on the financial benefits of the close ties they had fashioned with their foreign counterparts, especially for luxury goods and the finessing of English wool. Indeed, Blackwell Hall is said to have centred and intensified foreign trade in a commercial hothouse where the Venetians, Genoese, Florentines and

Milanese, and the German and Polish Hanseatic merchants of London's Steelyard, together with the Flemish and Dutch, could rub shoulders with their London counterparts.[29] Superficially, alien merchants were *seen* to be regulated to a greater extent than hitherto, but one can't help wondering whether they and their London partners were bound to profit further from being obliged to concentrate in this way and with the incentive of a ready and very focused market. Of course, the establishment of a national trading floor for cloth and related goods also boosted tax revenues. Arguably it was a win all round. Yet through the commercial hubbub Whittington had seen that the wider economy was already on the slide, and by the time he completed his second term as mayor on 13 October 1398 he had begun to reduce his reliance on mercery in favour of lending, investment and what might be described as 'political opportunism', no better illustrated than in his later appointments as collector of the wool custom and mayor of the staple at both Calais and Westminster. Whittington's installation as mayor was rare but not unique. Just five years earlier, Richard had enforced his authority by removing the mayor John Hende and his two sheriffs when the City had last dug its heels. On that occasion he had appointed a royal warden until he was ready to allow the return of a mayor by free vote. Much earlier, his grandfather Edward III had deposed London's mayor on two occasions but without preventing or interfering with the free election that followed. Richard's intervention in June 1397 was characteristically different, appointing his own man, over the heads of the electorate, in breach of a right established in 1215.[30]

While it is true that Richard himself appointed Whittington, it is presumed that he had first approached the barons of the Exchequer, who were responsible for swearing in London's mayor. They had declined to do so because of the king's infringement of the right to free contest.[31] It was therefore on their refusal that the king is believed to have administered the oath personally. The fact that there is no formal record of Whittington being sworn in in June 1397, but there is in October of that year, when he was freely elected, is held to confirm the king's breach and the barons' defence of right. The king's installation of a figure he held in great trust and whom he may have regarded as a friend and useful ally proved to be something of a masterstroke. Barron describes Whittington as someone who 'rose to prominence and wealth in the sunshine of royal favour'.[32] Whittington not only slipped easily into the vacuum created by Bamme's death but skilfully calmed the tensions between king and City, managing to balance the interests and ease the rancour of both. His achievement is evidenced in his negotiation after just two months of a loan of 10,000 marks from the City to the king by which the former secured their full and perpetual liberties from the latter. During this hectic abbreviated term of three months, he would diffuse tensions in the City, the Corporation, Parliament and the streets, keeping London safe and peaceful at a moment when a wider confrontation loomed. It was no surprise that he was subsequently freely elected as mayor for a full term.

Matters Personal

Regardless of the progress he had secured, Whittington soon found himself on the wrong end of the king's escalating financial exactions. Besides sealing a blank charter on behalf of the City, effectively an open cheque book on which the king might draw or from which he more likely used the threat of withdrawal to lever 'freely given' gifts and loans, Whittington was among the 28 'distinguished persons' summoned before the Royal Council in April 1398 to place their own personal seals on similar documents.[33] We may never know whether this came as a complete surprise or if his inclusion was engineered to demonstrate that the king had no favourites and that anyone with a fat purse fell within his sights. Including Whittington may well have been the means to leverage others. It would have conveyed that he was no longer the 'king's man'. It raises the question: did Whittington collude in this?

Away from his mayoral distractions Whittington received news from Pauntley that his eldest brother William had finally succumbed to the frailties that had dogged him for much of his life. There is no record that they had kept in touch since the younger brother's departure nearly thirty years earlier or that Richard attended Pauntley to mark William's death. He died without issue and the estate passed, as intended, to their middle brother Robert, who for some time had been the effective master of Pauntley and whose own descendants still hold land in the county today. There were developments too in Whittington's 'adoptive family'. By now Alice Fitzwarin was 26 years of age, and it is possible that she and Whittington were already married or were intent on union. We have no record either way. The first indication that they may have joined as husband and wife does not surface until 1402 when Alice's father remade arrangements to his will and Whittington raised cash from the sale of some London properties to fund a significant acquisition elsewhere. We will come to this shortly but turn first to Sir Ivo Fitzwarin himself, now somewhere around

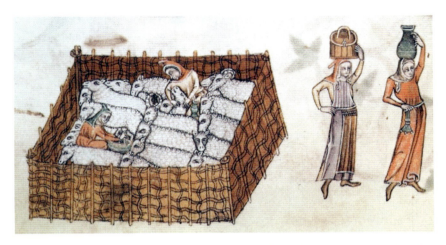

1. Medieval representation of a sheep pen in the Luttrell Psalter commissioned by Sir Geoffrey Luttrell (1276–1345), Lord of the manor of Irnham in Lincolnshire. Acquired by the British Museum in 1929 and now in the collections of the British Library.

2. The Norman church of St John the Evangelist at Pauntley. Neighbouring the birthplace of Richard Whittington at Pauntley Court and where he was probably baptised.

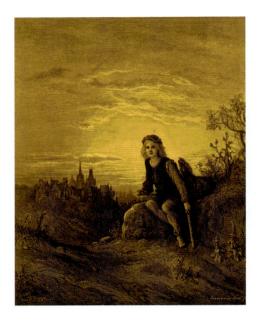

3. 'London, a Pilgrimage' by Gustave Doré and Blanchard Jerrold, 1872. A romantic representation of Richard Whittington supposedly at Highgate in 1375 within sight of a golden-skied London. One of the few that eschew the company of his cat.

4. Two years after Whittington had 'announced' himself by contributing to the 1379 gift of the city to the barons, London was thrown into turmoil by the Peasants' Revolt in 1381, which resulted here in the smiting of its leader Wat Tyler. In the forward party are the 14-year-old boy king and three of the most influential figures at court and in the city. William Walworth, John Philpot and Nicholas Brembre, each knighted for their services in putting down the rebellion.

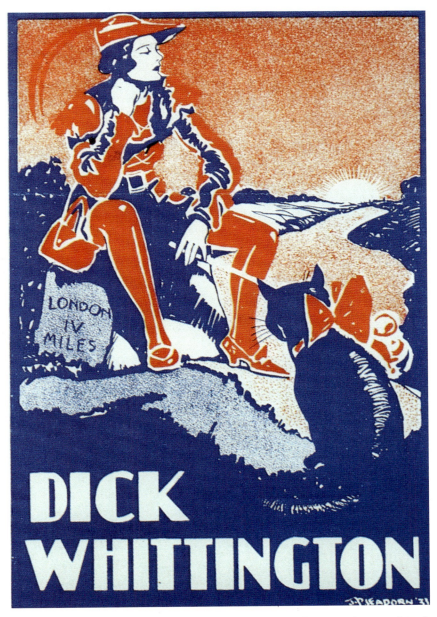

5. No poor boy on his way to make his fortune here! The sharply attired Dick Whittington having a deserved breather with his bow-tied feline companion, free of dust, absent of perspiration and with not a semblance of fatigue having travelled over 120 miles by rough road and dirt track to the very edges of London. And in those shoes!

6. Statue of Richard Whittington and his cat outside The Guildhall Art Gallery, which houses the art collection of the City of London. The historic Guildhall lies adjacent on Basinghall and Gresham Streets. Construction of the present-day Guildhall commenced in 1411, transforming it from what was described by the then Mayor, Thomas Knolles, as 'a small cottage' into 'a great house'. It was completed in 1440. Whittington contributed funding to its early development. The Guildhall Library at Aldermanbury was originally founded in 1420 and was funded in large part by Whittington under the provisions of his will.

7. The Corporation of the City of London's commemorative plaque outside 'Whittington's church' at College Hill and St Michael Paternoster Royal is what the modern Londoner might term 'a bit previous' given that Richard Whittington died in March of the following year, 1423. Perhaps it is another example of those uncertainties that characterise Whittington's timeline.

The Death of Whittington.

8. *The Death of Whittington.*
   from the Ordinances of Richard Whittington's Charity.
   (*Mercers Company*) Wellcome Library, London http://wellcomecollection.org/works/wwsbgcgc

   Richard Whittington on his death bed in March 1423, attended by his four executors, John Colop, John White, William Grove and chief executor, John Carpenter. The other figures most likely represent some of his beneficiaries. The image also shows a physician examining a sample of his urine.

9. St Michael Paternoster Royal: Alice Whittington was buried here in 1409 and her husband Richard in 1423. The St Michael Paternoster 'project' was a joint vision and would lead, under the provisions of Whittington's will, to the establishment of a perpetual college of five secular priests in honour of The Holy Spirit and St Mary and an almshouse for thirteen poor citizens of London. After the death of Whittington's executors, supervision of the college was vested in the wardens of the Mercers' Company and the Mayor of London. Whittington was buried on the south side of the altar next to his wife. His body was later dug up during the reign of Edward VI (1547–53) and stripped of its lead shroud by the rector of the church who believed the grave contained the mercer's treasures. A later attempt in 1949, after the Blitz, to find Whittington's grave failed to discover his body… but did produce a mummified cat!

10. The Steelyard and surrounding neighbourhood, 1540 (from Van Wyngard's plan taken for Philip of Spain). A late medieval drawing of the '*kontor*' or trading base of the Hanseatic League in London, with the Thames in the foreground.

11. A Whittington triptych: the representation, the real thing and the latter-day admirer.

12. *Wittington's Ghost…* here tonight, live on stage at The New Blanchard Theatre, Covent Garden, 1807. Still searching for his long-lost cat. Was she too merely an apparition? In the writer's own words… *Good people don't think it's strange. That Wittington's ghost should appear. And throughout the City should range. For the Cat that he once loved so dear, Her, he lov'd more than some love their Wives…*

13. *He's just heard the church bells and glances back...* A more recent take on Richard Whittington at St Michael Paternoster Royal on College Hill (EC4R 2RL) by the artist and glassmaker John David Hayward, depicts him at Highgate Hill. Here he appears in the reliable company of that well-travelled cat. Jack Kerouac would have been proud.

14. Whittington commenced his civic career in July 1384 as Common Councillor for Coleman Street Ward, serving until 1386. Today, the ward adjoins the boundary of the Borough of Islington. Its name is believed to derive from it being known for its charcoal burners. The cockerel is the ward's emblem. John Stow remarks in 1598 of nearby St Margaret's church that 'There be monuments in this church of Reginald Coleman, son to Robert Coleman... (who)... may be supposed the first builder or owner of Coleman Street'.

his 50th year, whose political antennae mark him as a bellwether for the events ahead. In the spring of 1398, we find him taking personal precautions, with one eye on stirrings of revolt against Richard II, with whom he and his protégé were so closely identified, and his other on the growing support for Gaunt's son Henry Bolingbroke, to whom they were also both connected. On 3 May Fitzwarin secured a general pardon for any crimes he may have committed before 31 January of that year, the last day of the Parliament held at Shrewsbury. His intention was clear: to wipe the slate clean. During the months that followed he gravitated ever closer to Bolingbroke, certain that Richard's end was near. During the second half of 1398 he either chose or was actively encouraged to edge closer to the camp of the usurper. By October of the following year, Richard II was deposed, Henry was on the throne, and Sir Ivo Fitzwarin was a few months away from becoming governor of Southampton.

27

CIRCLES

London's Elite

Whittington chose his friends and associates well, and they him. While he appears to have collaborated regularly with a small core of leading mercers and investors, favoured *ad hoc* dealings with a secondary group of similar numbers and been supported by a close-knit team which included some of his former apprentices, he cultivated friendships and business with prominent figures across a wide arc of London's merchant class—goldsmiths, drapers, ironmongers, cordwainers and even grocers and vintners. These were men often linked to the mercers in their manufacturing and distribution interests or free-spirited investors, adventurers and risk-takers who looked beyond the confinements of their trade, who were inherently entrepreneurial and who saw merit and opportunity in pushing or dismantling boundaries. Others were drawn into his orbit and he into theirs through shared social, civic and cultural interests. A pious man, religion, duty and charity played a significant part in defining Whittington's outlook and his relationships. Close to mercers such as John Woodcock and John Shadworth, he numbered within his circle the goldsmith Drew Barantyn and two of the leading grocers of his generation, Thomas Knolles and Robert Chichele, both frequent lenders to Richard II and Henry IV. With Knolles, he shared a long and determined interest in rebuilding London's gaols. Men like these formed a fluid and overlapping professional elite whose individual and at times collectively focused wealth and stature could be used to influence and bring about social improvement. It is important not to lose sight of scale; the numbers involved and the interconnecting concentric circles that characterised London's social, economic and political structures rendered self-and group interest inevitable. Even by 1400, London was still a small city in comparison to its European neighbours. The city's 25 aldermen, their associates within the wider electoral college and in the newly established House of Commons, numbering perhaps another 250, together with other influential figures within or connected to London's most powerful companies probably didn't exceed 350. For most, their overriding attachment was to the trades in which they had been apprenticed or invested and through which they had made their lives. They socialised with each other; struck marriages between their families and close friends; acted as executors to each other's wills; formed mutually advantageous investment and business partnerships; and sponsored and cleared a path to follow for their proteges. During the last quarter of the 14th century, we see a growing number of partnerships and 'accommodations' led by like-minded individuals rather than conditioned by their trades. Within these progressive circles was a fluid elite, Whittington among the most prominent, who were often the king's 'chosen men'. These were the men he preferred to do business with and seek loans from and whom he would commonly reward by offering sinecures, commercial opportunities and social advancement. Whether Whittington set about actively to form his own inner circle is arguable but his purpose, character and ability to make his mark at trade and at court commanded the attention of his peers and attracted their interest. Had he not developed some form of power base, he would not have been able to win two further terms as mayor in 1406 and 1419. The conjoining of individuals with shared commercial interests and common social aspirations was characteristic of London's merchant class and even more evident in its political formations. At times, this led to the confluence of curious bedfellows. Clementine Oliver cites the example of Nicholas Brembre as a centrifugal force in the 'Ricardian faction' favoured by Richard II and perpetuated by their mutual self-interest:

> the crown typically granted the appointment to members of London's political and mercantile elite, and it was not unusual for the post to be occupied by an individual who might, at one time or another, also occupy the office of mayor. Indeed, Nicholas Brembre, collector of the wool custom and subsidy at London throughout much of the 1370s and 1380s, was just such an individual.[1]

There was a compelling and mutually rewarding *quid pro quo* for these arrangements: 'those appointed to collect the wool customs and subsidy received their positions in reward for personal and financial service to Richard II'. As of course did Whittington, and again during the terms of

Henry IV and Henry V. The reasons cited during Brembre's time were essentially those exploited almost serially by Whittington from the mid-1390s. Oliver's subject is Brembre, but her words resonate for both men. Though their characters differed sharply, their good fortune

> was because (throughout the 1380s) the crown typically used the revenue from the wool customs as security against which to raise cash, and loans made to the crown by both the city of London and by individuals were thus repaid out of customs receipts.[2]

There were others, of course, who fell in with the *quid pro quo* of the Ricardian system and who at times fell out of it.[3]

The Mercer Caucus

Of all Whittington's relationships, outside of that with Sir Ivo Fitzwarin, his close friendship with the mercer John Woodcock was perhaps the most durable. They had been close from at least May 1382, when they were called upon to value jointly a cache of pearls produced in evidence before the court of the Mayor of London, a recognition of their competence, integrity and growing standing in the City. Their friendship, careers and progressive interests were bound closely over a period of nearly 30 years until Woodcock's death in 1409. Like Whittington, Woodcock was a supplier of luxury goods to Richard II and a member of his court, making his first sales to Henry, Earl of Derby in the autumn of 1387. He also followed the well-established civic path, elected as a common councillor for Cripplegate ward in August 1388. In 1392, both men were among the 24 leading commoners summoned to Nottingham by Richard II during his escalating quarrel with the City. Both shared a powerful and life-long commitment to their formative roots as mercers, Woodcock serving as warden of the Mercers' Company in 1390–1, 1397–8 and 1407–8; Whittington in 1395–6, 1401–2 and 1408–9. Woodcock was less successful in recovering the full extent of debts owed to him by Richard II but in 1401 appealed successfully to his former patron Derby, now Henry IV, to restore much of what was due to him from the Royal Wardrobe.

> Perhaps Woodcock's previous association with the house of Lancaster led the new King to look upon him with special favour. At all events, in November 1401 he was awarded a royal annuity of 40 marks for life from the issues of London; and when, seven years later, the money could not be found because of over-assignment, instructions were given for him to be paid directly from the Exchequer.[4]

The successes of both mercers in retrieving the greater part of their outlay, while many of London's merchants did not, goes some way in demonstrating their financial nous and political value as lenders to the crown and as what we might today term 'influencers' within the City. Within two years of Henry's accession, Woodcock had supplied the royal family with fine merchandise worth over £2,300, scheduled for repayment chiefly through the proceeds of the wool custom. Appointments to oversee the custom were intended to increase the volume and efficiency of revenue collection and carried the incentive of a handsome payback. Woodcock served as collector of the wool custom for London 1399–1400, the year of Henry's enthronement, having oversight of the bustling wool trade between Gravesend and Tilbury. By 1405 he was owed more than £3,000 by the king.[5] This rising debt, and Woodcock's enduring position as a preferred supplier, brought other royal appointments including Commander of Gaol Delivery for London, reflecting Woodcock's passion for prison reform, shared with Whittington and Thomas Knolles. In 1406, we find Woodcock and Knolles rescuing the king with a timely loan of £200 to fund the Good Friday alms. Alongside Woodcock, John Shadworth ranks as one of London's most enterprising and influential mercers.[6] Older than Whittington, he would also outlive him by seven years. By 1379, he was already 'farmer of customs' for the money-making short haul trade between Dover and Gravesend and a contributor of 5 marks to the London gift of that year. He is noted two years later as a currency dealer trading in Flemish coinage. He has been described as 'at various times a party to conveyances made by or for the most eminent Londoners of his day, being on particularly close terms with the mercers John Bosham, Richard Whittington and John Woodcock (the last of whom also made him his executor).'[7]

Having established his commercial credentials with the Gravesend custom, in January 1384 Shadworth was assigned 500 marks by the Crown, in a joint endeavour with John Philpot and William Staunton, a leading grocer and buyer for the king's household, to arrange for the shipment of wool and other goods to the Middelburg Staple. In three remarkable months, Shadworth obtained royal licences to export at least 155 sarplers of his own wool from London to Calais.[8] His skills, enterprise and interests in Flanders, Middelburg and Germany also opened opportunities for trade with the Steelyard and a relationship in London in which he would effectively become the unofficial 'alderman for the Hanse', energetically promoting their trade and acting as their defender and advocate. In 1389, like Whittington, he too was providing credit and loans to the Royal Wardrobe. The relationship would not last, Shadworth being one of those who fell out of the 'Ricardian system'. Unlike Whittington, Shadworth would become overt in his support for Richard II's overthrow by Bolingbroke, though both were later appointed to Henry IV's Council. Both men were active in promoting the interests of the Mercer's Company and in 1396–7 and again in 1403–4 and 1409–10 Shadworth succeeded Whittington as Warden. Both had been involved in intense efforts to secure the Company's charter and in the acquisition of property on its behalf. Between 1409 and 1411, with Whittington perhaps acting as his 'proxy', Shadworth was foremost in making the case for the City of London to acquire Whittington's first home in London, Leadenhall. Without heirs on his death in 1430, Shadworth left the greater part of his estate 'for the performance of pious and charitable works'.[9]

The wealthy mercer and civic leader John Bosham also appears as an early influence on Whittington. Bosham was already a well-established figure of ten years or more when he and Whittington both contributed to the 1379 'gift'. By then, he had already accumulated service as a tax collector, auditor, trier of usury cases, commercial adviser and alderman for Cheap ward from 1377 to 1380. The two mercers would later meet more frequently as part of the October 1384 intake of common councillors and through Bosham's role as warden of the Mercers' Company 1384–5, a time when Whittington was making his first breakthrough as a supplier at court. Earlier that year, Bosham had been cited by the Common Council as one of the 'best and wisest men in the City.'[10] Bosham traded extensively with the wool centre of Coventry where he and his wife were members of the Trinity Guild. In November 1385, he famously sued 22 of his clients for default on repayment of loans and lines of credit, their far-flung dispersal across the Midlands, Yorkshire and the South and East coasts suggesting 'that he did business on an impressive scale'.[11] His death around December 1393 bears some parallel with Whittington's own demise three decades later in the extent, provisions and beneficiaries of his will. Also striking is his closeness to the two other senior mercers who figure prominently in Whittington's life, Shadworth and Woodcock. Although they were business partners first and foremost, Bosham was also engaged by both men as an adviser and trustee in their affairs. If the young Richard Whittington did have a small group of experienced and well-connected mercers in his corner, both at the start and during the formative years of his career, figures known for their commercial nous and their ability to facilitate introductions and who saw merit in encouraging and supporting his progress, then, alongside Sir Ivo Fitzwarin, the most likely names are those of Shadworth, Woodcock and Bosham.

The Wider Circle

Described as 'a citizen of London of the better sort', the leading grocer Thomas Knolles embarked on his career with the benefit of inherited wealth and quickly proved proficient in accumulating a great deal more. So much so 'that it is evident that he was able to invest large sums of capital in his various enterprises, albeit sometimes with little hope of immediate repayment'.[12] Later a celebrated MP, he held office as sheriff in 1394–5 and served as alderman for two of London's most prominent wards, Dowgate 1393–7 and Cordwainer Street in the early part of 1398, also acquiring experience as auditor of London on three occasions: 1393–4, 1395–6 and 1398–9. He followed another of Whittington's wider circle, the goldsmith Drew Barantyn, as mayor in 1399–1400, returning for a second term in 1410–1.[13] By then, Knolles's interest in social reform was gaining pace; he shared with Whittington a fierce determination to demolish and rebuild Newgate and, for his own part, to bring sanitation and improvements in hygiene to London. His physical legacy would also include his work alongside Whittington and others in rebuilding the Guildhall and his establishment of fresh water supplies to Newgate and Ludgate. Like his friend, he was a regular lender to Henry IV, providing as many as 15 loans to the king between July 1400 and June 1410, frequently secured against the London customs for which he was collector 1400–1.[14]

Knolles was also one of five so-called 'war treasurers'—Whittington was another—appointed by Parliament in 1404 to raise taxes for Henry IV's campaigns. Later, in 1417, he was a significant contributor to Henry V's second expedition to France. A leading member of the Grocers' Company, he served as warden in 1387 and again, a remarkable 44 years later, in 1431 when he would have been in his 70s. A frequent developer and acquisitive property owner, Knolles used property to further his social ends, bequeathing his family home at Watling Street to the Grocers' Company on his death in 1435 to fund relief of the poor. It is here that he was closest to Whittington, sharing a common purpose and drive in social improvement and civic renewal, most notably in their endeavours to reform and improve conditions in London's hellish prisons; they were implacable in their joint determination to demolish and rebuild Newgate.

Knolles has been described as 'on a par in terms of his influence and wealth with contemporaries Richard Whittington and Robert Chichele, and—like them—a long-liver.'[15]

Knolles was almost certainly even closer to his fellow grocer Chichele, later strengthening their ties through the marriage of his daughter to Chichele's nephew. Both were closely associated with the 'grocer's church' of St Antholin's which fell within Knolles's remit as alderman for Cordwainer ward and was redeveloped at his expense. Unlike Whittington and Barantyn, who had childless marriages, Knolles and his wife are reputed to have produced as many as 19 children, though only five survived.

Whittington's association with London's most fashionable goldsmith Drew Barantyn probably commenced in the early 1380s. They shared similar backgrounds, each arriving in London from the shires to take up an apprenticeship with someone known to their families. Barantyn's people were wealthy Oxfordshire landowners, and he was apprenticed in 1363–4 to the well-known goldsmith Robert Oxenford, also of that county and later MP for Wallingford. Barantyn was sharp and talented and rose quickly, becoming a freeman in 1370 and going on to employ his first apprentice in 1379. He was evidently strict in the terms he set for his young proteges, as Sylvia Thrupp makes clear:

> The indentures drawn for a Cirencester boy who was apprenticed to Drew Barentyn, wealthy goldsmith, in 1382, specified that he should not commit fornication either in his master's house or elsewhere, that he should not marry, and that without his master's permission he should not even become engaged. Nor was he to play at tables or chess or other forbidden games or to go to taverns except on business for his master.[16]

Elected as a warden of the Goldsmiths' Company in 1380 and again in 1385, Barantyn was slightly ahead of Whittington in becoming a common councillor, later establishing a power base at Aldersgate in 1392–3 and then for Farringdon in 1393–4, the year in which he served alongside Whittington as sheriff of London. Their mayoral careers were also interlinked, the goldsmith succeeding the mercer as London's mayor for his first term in 1398 and serving shortly after him again in 1408 for his second. Both men traded in luxury and ostentation. In July 1387, a cup made by Barantyn, or under his supervision, was presented by Richard II to an emissary from Duke John IV of Brittany. By 1393 he and his partner, John Doubler, were regular purveyors of exceptional jewellery and gold to the royal household. One of Barantyn's gold cups was gifted by Richard to the queen of Sweden in May 1394. Barantyn's influence at court almost certainly assisted his endeavours on behalf of the Goldsmiths' Company. In February 1393, the Company was awarded a licence to hold land and rents worth £20 a year and Barantyn and his fellows Henry and Adam Bamme were foremost in securing the royal consents. His growing wealth and stature were consolidated further through his position as 'court jeweller' during the reigns of Richard II and Henry IV and through his extension of credit and loans to both kings over a long period. Having quickly amassed a fortune as a goldsmith, Barantyn began investing more widely in the import and export of luxury goods, a niche in which Whittington excelled. They were often cited as the two wealthiest men in London: 'Barantyn was probably the only goldsmith of his day who could match men like the mercer, Richard Whittington, in wealth and influence.'[17] Like Whittington, he married late and was childless. Each made notable bequests to support the poor of London and left to their company significant endowments, including property and income from rents. He also made bequests to religious orders and to his favoured church St John Zachary, the parish in which London's goldsmith community was established and where in 1339 the first Goldsmith's Hall had been erected. Barantyn would fund the building of the second Goldsmiths Hall there in 1407. He has been described as 'a pattern of the active Londoner building up a flourishing business and investing its profits in civic office, city properties and manors within easy distance of London.'[18]

In 1401, Barantyn and Whittington were chosen as men of status and wise judgement in their joint appointment as commissioners to determine an appeal against the decision by Henry, Earl of Northumberland, Constable of England over the ransom of the Count of Denia, captured by the Black Prince. In 1404, we find him pressing once more the interests of his trade at court, persuading Henry IV to grant an updated and wider-ranging Goldsmiths' charter that would encourage other companies to follow.

A business partner of Thomas Knolles and associate of Richard Whittington, Robert Chichele was the brother of Henry, Archbishop of Canterbury and is thought to have arrived in London about 1390. In 1414, he found himself working alongside a deeply uneasy Whittington, who had been appointed in January as a Commissioner to arrest 'Lollards at large.' Both men were placed under intense pressure from Henry V to locate and bring to justice the remnants of Sir John Oldcastle's final Lollard revolt. Four years later, in July 1418, Whittington was instructed further by Henry to recover Oldcastle's properties and possessions. Chichele rendered loans to both Henry IV and Henry V. He followed Knolles as mayor in 1411 and served for a second time in 1421, two years after Whittington's final term.[19] He was succeeded by another mercer with close ties to Richard Whittington, William Walderne. Although there were probably earlier ventures between the two men, Walderne's relationship with Whittington comes into view in 1416 when the pair, together with William Cromer, were partners in receiving from nine Italian merchants an assurance of repayment of a debt of £2,666 13s 4d which presumably related to their joint supply of goods. In 1417, with three other aldermen, they also acted as brokers in the financing of Henry V's forthcoming French expedition. Walderne had strong links with the Florentines, with the Coventry mercer Ralph Garton and with one of Whittington's former apprentices, Thomas Faulconer. A year after Whittington's death, Walderne was installed as mayor of the Calais staple, a mere month after being made mayor of the Westminster staple, holding both posts until his death a short time later.[20]

William Babington doesn't appear in any notable way in Whittington's life until it has almost run its course. The two men were, however, well known to each other by 1419 when Babington was Chief Baron to the Exchequer before becoming Chief Justice in 1421. Born in the year Whittington arrived in London, he was aged about 53 at the time of the mercer's death and expired at the impressive age of 85 in 1454. Babington was well regarded by Whittington and was present at his deathbed, chiefly in his formal capacity as England's Chief Justice to pay his personal respects and those of the king and government, but also as a close friend appointed specifically by Whittington to act as 'supervisor' to his executors.[21]

Whittington's relationship with the ironmonger Gilbert Maghfeld[22] is more curious and less documented, but Maghfeld's approach to investment and lending is worth citing as it throws light on a less formal, less structured approach to loans and repayment. As a collector of tonnage and poundage in London from 1388 to 1391, and as a collector of the cloth custom, Maghfeld traded extensively with London's mercers. He soon acquired a reputation as someone able to procure almost anything, when required and at the right price.[23] He attracts our attention when, as one of two 'replacement sheriffs' installed under the Royal Warden Sir Edward Dalyngrigge (interim 'mayor' of London) no 1 July 1392, he furnishes Dalyngrigge on that very day with a loan of £20 and a succession of £10 loans for a period thereafter. Like Whittington, he was someone to whom Richard II could look for help when money was tight, providing a loan to

the king's chamberlain of 40 shillings towards the cost of Christmas celebrations at Eltham Palace and further small loans at a time, 1392–4, when
the Royal Wardrobe was spending far beyond its means—in part resulting
from Richard II's significant purchases of merchandise from, among others,
Whittington himself. In December 1394, Maghfeld increased his facility to
the king, contributing the sum of £50 towards the City's loan of 10,000
marks for Richard II's unexpected expedition to Ireland. A politically astute
lender, characteristically Maghfeld offered finance on credit. As Bolton
remarks, 'indeed his unique ledger reveals that he conducted more than
75% of his business on credit.'[24] This enabled him to move his money
around, to flex payments in and out of his business and to offer 'easy terms'
to attract clients who preferred to pay later when their particular ship came
in. At the heart of these transactions was the facility to charge interest. Yet,
when his borrowers stalled or were unable to transact in this way Maghfeld
found other means. Even the inventive Whittington might have drawn the
line at loans made to the clerks of St Giles Hospital secured against church
vestments and chalices but often repaid in wheat, in which London had a
vigorous 'black market'.

* * *

Among other names that feature either intermittently or in brief moments
of intensity in the Whittington story are William Bury, a well-known mercer from Suffolk who would make a good career for himself in London but
eventually fall foul of the law and find himself hauled before Whittington
during a period when the latter was instructed by Henry V to oversee an
investigation into usury; Richard Clifford, keeper of the Great Wardrobe,
Bishop of London 1407–21 and a driven promoter of clerical education,
who encountered Whittington regularly in the mercer's role as a preferred
supplier of luxury goods to the royal household; and the grocer William
Staunton, who served as mayor during the transition from the Royal
Warden Sir Edward Dalyngrigge in 1392–3 and followed Whittington as
mayor in 1407–8. Staunton was appointed by Richard II as commander for
gaol delivery at Newgate in 1392–3 and for London at large in 1407 during
Whittington's third mayoralty. The two men had first met during Staunton's
tenure as 'buyer for the King's household' and their interests overlapped in
the wool trade. 'In common with other leading members of the Grocers'
Company, Staunton made a considerable amount of money out of the wool
trade.' A regular business partner of John Shadworth and Thomas Knolles,

both men would act as his executors. It is noted that 'Never one to miss the opportunity for a quick profit, Standon [Staunton] dealt in a wide range of commodities, often as an agent for others'.[25] In February 1409, he acted with Whittington and others in acquiring Leadenhall on behalf of the City of London. Mention should also be made of John Colop. A grocer by trade, Colop features in several of Whittington's property transactions and financial distributions. He was an active advocate and funder of so-called 'common-profit' volumes and 'lay learning' which capitalised on the growing interest in the circulation and availability of written works. He is also noted for working alongside Whittington and John Carpenter in the early development and stocking of the Guildhall Library.[26]

His Master's Apprentice

Among Whittington's 'students', Thomas Roos may have been his first apprentice in 1391–2. He succeeded well enough in business to be elected a warden of the Mercers' Company in 1401 and again in 1410 and is recorded in the year of his master's death contributing a gift of £3 6s 8d to the Company under the same entry as a contribution of £13 6s 8d from Whittington's executors John Carpenter and William Grove.[27]

Among the half-dozen early figures closest to Richard Whittington, Thomas Faulconer's relationship with the mercer also derived from being one of his first apprentices and he remained throughout his life part of Whittington's trusted inner circle. Faulconer followed in his master's footsteps in representing Coleman Street ward from 1402–14, before taking on Cheap in 1415–6. As mayor 1414–5, his tenure was squeezed between those of the drapers William Cromer and Nicholas Wootton. He was elected warden of the Mercers' Company four times, the last in the year of his mentor's death. Immersed in the wool and cloth trades, he, too, built a reputation for dealing in luxury goods, at times quite likely in joint endeavour with Whittington himself and with Italian merchants. As with other members of the mercers' circle he was called upon by Henry IV and Henry V for loans and he followed Whittington and John Woodcock in developing close connections with the mercery and draper communities of Coventry. Stow remarks of him:

> I find that Thomas Falconer, mayor about the year 1415, the third of Henry
> V, caused the wall of the city to be broken near unto Coleman Street, and
> there built a postern, now called Moorgate, upon the moor side where was

never gate before. This gate he made for ease of the citizens, that way to pass upon causeys into the field for their recreation; for the same field was at that time a parish.[28]

Though we know far less about Henry London, he too is associated closely with Whittington after 1400–1 when he is recorded as being apprenticed to the mercer. A few years later the faint picture we have of him is as someone elevated to run his master's household, serving him domestically as his steward and personally as his friend and counsel. Five days before Christmas 1410, we see him appear at court with Whittington and John Chamberlain to receive the delayed royal licence that would finally give his master the authority to grant the land at St Michael's to John White. Whittington was exasperated to discover that, given the waiting list, it would take up to a further two years to make the grant and conclude the legal contract.

William Cavendish was only briefly associated with Richard Whittington. In his case, strings were evidently pulled to get him into Whittington's much prized employ. The grandson of Chief Justice Sir John Cavendish, murdered during the Peasants' Revolt in 1381, there were sound reasons for accepting him, and Whittington was well compensated with a substantial premium to take the boy under his wing. Doing so offered Cavendish immediate status as part of the celebrated mercer's 'stable' and, by association, presumed to open and accelerate opportunities on completion of his term. Cavendish is of more interest, however, as an illustration of how Whittington's apprentices and backroom team developed their own endeavours, in his case in 1415 acting as a valuer of fine bedding and jewels for an Italian merchant from Lucca. He also provides an example of how young mercers from the same stable continued to work together as feoffees, executors or business partners. Two of Cavendish's feoffees were other Whittington apprentices, Thomas Roos and John Wells.

His Trusted Executors

Arguably, in the last two years of Whittington's life those closest to him were the executors of his will. John Coventre was the man who may, as his name suggests, have introduced Richard Whittington to the town of Coventry or else been talent-spotted by him during his business dealings there.[29] It was customary for leading mercers to recruit 'agents' to handle their business interests outside of London and it is likely that Coventre was one such figure. Admitted to the Mercers' Company in 1401, later becoming its master in 1417 and again in the year of Whittington's death, 1423, Coventre was a regular partner in his friend's wool ventures and someone who, together with his wife, also Alice, was close to the Whittingtons socially and in business. Both couples were members of the Guild of Holy Trinity at Coventry, where they held extensive interests in the cloth and wool trades.

The cleric John White had probably first developed a close relationship with Richard and Alice Whittington as their parish priest. It was logical therefore that he should be chosen in 1409 as the inaugural rector of their 'project' at St Michael Paternoster and he is likely to have been in attendance during Alice's illness and death. In 1417, he was championed by Whittington in his appointment as master of St Bartholomew's Hospital—the modern-day 'Barts'. During the writing of Whittington's will, White was awarded the not inconsiderable sum of £13 6s 8d 'for his labour' in acting as one of the four executors. He resigned from St Bartholomew's on 18 February 1423, taking up residence in Whittington's house, having probably been requested to oversee St Michael's during the final weeks of the mercer's life.[30] The strong social and moral bond between the two men is evidenced in Whittington's bequest of 100 shillings to him 'so that he may pray for my soul and the souls of the others mentioned' in his will. White ended his days at St Michael's.

Having arrived in London, apparently from Oxford University, keen to practise in the fast-developing specialism of commercial law, William Grove had been introduced to Richard Whittington by John Woodcock in March 1404. Whittington must have taken to him immediately because he features in his employment from that time and is frequently mentioned alongside two of the mercer's other acolytes, Thomas Roos and Henry London. He appears to have been included as Whittington's fourth executor by virtue of his drafting and legal skills, receiving a payment of £10 for his labours. Jean Imray notes that Grove is also named in the Husting Rolls as a Scrivener in several deeds relating to Whittington's estate.[31]

* * *

By 1400, Richard Whittington had established himself as one of England's foremost mercers and entrepreneurs. He had laid the foundations and begun to reap the rewards of his skills and influence at court, in the City, within London's domestic and overseas trade, and in the overlapping spheres of politics, administration and social reform. He was aided in this by well-placed and well-cultivated networks, by common interest and shared values. Despite his characteristic singularity of purpose and his preparedness to follow his own path, sometimes to the point of self-containment and aloofness, Whittington was universally regarded and trusted as a mentor, adviser, partner, friend and figure of wise and proven counsel. He chose his friends and colleagues well. His circles radiated from four, in part overlapping, groups: those who were leading mercers and merchants of the day, with whom he shared other interests; those with whom he conducted business as a royal supplier or in his capacity as civic leader; his relatively unknown and unsung, at times fluid, 'back-room team', who were often essential in freeing him to concentrate on developing his mercantile, social and political interests and lastly, but in many ways foremost during the last quarter of his life, those he trusted most with the vision he had for his great project at St Michael Paternoster and with the provisions of his exceptional will. These were his innermost circle of trusted advisers and executors: his wife Alice who predeceased him, John Coventre, John White, the former rector of St Margaret Lothbury Roger Hunt and William Grove. There is one figure missing from the list whom he had yet to engage—the man who would become his greatest friend, his most trusted confidant and his chief executor, John Carpenter. He would come later. First there was the highly unsettling prospect of Whittington's transition under England's new king.

28

NEW KING, NEW CENTURY

By 1399 Parliament had been transformed to serve Richard II's will and needs. One writer describes this *regimen parliamenti* as effectively determining both Parliament's legislative and its financial agenda. It had become little more than 'a tool of royal power'.[1] Yet power could only be exercised with money, resources and popular support, and each fell away sharply as the year progressed. The Exchequer was empty, the Crown was broke, and large sections of Parliament, the City and the country had been alienated beyond recovery. Even those close to the king had been ground down by his financial demands and extravagance. His time as England's king was coming to an end. On 1 October 1399 Richard II was deposed and on the feast day of Edward the Confessor, 13 October, Henry Bolingbroke was crowned Henry IV of England. Richard remained in the Tower until he was removed from London to Pontefract Castle shortly before the end of the year. When news broke that a group of earls favoured by Richard and distanced from Henry were mobilising to restore the former king, his time was up. The so-called Epiphany Rising flickered, spluttered and failed. Richard died in captivity around 14 February 1400, his body displayed at St Paul's three days later before its removal for interment at Kings Langley on 6 March. As for Whittington, even though he had known Henry as a patron in the 1380s and had served his father, there were grounds for the mercer to fear that the new king or his most zealous supporters might wish to do him harm. For some there may have been good cause. While many of those present at the recent Parliament had called for Richard to be put to death, 'many more wanted those who had benefitted from his reign to be punished as traitors'.[2] Indeed, the Speaker had requested that all of Richard's 'evil counsellors' be arrested, and there was loose talk of revenge and reprisal against those who had Richard's ear or had been close to him in some way. It didn't help that Henry's reign commenced, and would continue to be dogged, with rumours that Richard had somehow survived, had amassed a large force determined to reinstate him, and had spies and confederates everywhere, and that those who had been closest to him remained under suspicion and, at worst, would be vigorously pursued by his successor.

If Whittington had any doubt about his own personal safety given his proximity to Richard, or about his usefulness to Henry, his mind was quickly put at rest. On 6 October 1399, a week before the coronation, Thomas Arundel, now restored as Archbishop of Canterbury, proclaimed the new king to Parliament as one who 'wished to be ruled and advised by the wise men and elders of the realm, for his own advantage and assistance and that of all his realm'.[3] It appeared that loyalties and services afforded the previous king might well be forgiven provided the 'guilty' party could render the same to his successor. Whittington was certainly a 'wise fellow' and long recognised as such, and could undoubtedly provide the 'advantage and assistance' that Henry sought for himself and for 'all his realm'. The king's first initiative was to repay the mercer the £1,000 owed by the Great Wardrobe at the time of Richard's abdication, a significant sum used largely to fund his spending sprees between 1392 and 1394. The keeper of the Great Wardrobe during much of this time (1390–8), and well known to Whittington, was Richard Clifford, who had become Lord Privy Seal in November 1397 and who would continue to preside before resigning on 4 November 1401 to become Bishop of London. Clifford's interim presence, with that of other figures familiar to him, provided the reassurance that the mercer must have hoped for. He need not have worried; he was far more useful to Henry than he could have imagined. Whittington's dual value to Richard had been as a source of finance and as an influential figure within both the City and the Corporation, able to mobilise support, acquiescence and funding. Henry valued him for the same reasons. Retaining Whittington's role would serve the new king's need to replenish England's finances and smooth his transition with those who opposed him in London. There would, however, be changes in the way loans to the Crown would be 'managed'. From the outset we see a revision in the repayment methods adopted by the two kings. While Richard had generally repaid his loans in cash, often fitfully, partially and on deferred terms, Henry favoured repaying the lender by swapping debt for 'Exchequer assignments' or 'royal goods', usually small items of jewellery and plate. He also adopted a more manipulative course by offering his lenders the temptations of office,

sinecure and profit share in lieu of repayment. With an Exchequer to refinance and a war to pursue, Henry recognised the importance of the advantage that Whittington could provide—liquidity. Less evident about
Henry's attitude to money, though there were clues enough in his youth
and in his more recent past, was that England would be ruled by yet
another king who sought and would squander a fortune on a wilful, lavish
lifestyle. While his predecessor could claim that much of his expenditure
reflected his cultural and aesthetic interests, Henry's fixation was rooted
in his cavaliering experiences in camp and campaign as a young soldier,
many of them in eastern Europe.

> In short, Henry of Derby was brought up amongst rich and restless travel-
> lers and acquired their tastes at an early age. To these men foreign countries
> were not places to be understood but enjoyed and used. They were at home
> almost anywhere ... It was a man's world in which slight discomforts and
> occasional dangers were as nothing against the comradeship and startling
> luxuries of the officers' mess.[4]

While Richard II has drawn a mixed reception from historians, he does
have his admirers, some of whom explain his expenditure within the wider
context of his higher regal aspirations. 'The period of adult government by
Richard II is notable as a self-conscious and highly sophisticated attempt
by a medieval king of outstanding intellect and sensibility to achieve real
power—not only for himself but for his legitimate successors. Richard
was alarmed at the threats which, from several quarters, menaced the
institution of kingship in England.'[5]

In November 1400, Henry offered a striking public acknowledgement
of Whittington's continuing usefulness in his appointment to the Royal
Council, the body intended to manage the 'transition' from the monarch he
served so well to a successor who intended that he should reprise that role.
He would attend from 1 November 1400 until 18 July 1401, long enough
to allay his fears. Perhaps an even more striking acknowledgement of the
mercer's worth was demonstrated in the matter of his eligibility for military service, though he had by now turned 40 and had no experience of
martial life or war. But Whittington was nobody's fool, and even if he had
harboured some anxieties about how Henry would treat him, he was also a
shrewd businessman confident of his skills and value. Thus, in 1400, when
the new king was urgently seeking financial support to underpin his household and fund his campaigns, he granted Whittington exemption from military duty, keeping him close at hand and freeing him to provide a more vital

financial service instead. The mercer was therefore not 'drafted' under the letters of Privy Seal which required that every person holding a fee under the king should present themselves for service in the borders of Scotland. The importance of Whittington's other 'gifts'—in both senses of the term—was acknowledged, and he was among a select group of wealthy lenders exempted by the King's Council on 15 June 1400.[6]

Henry's estimation of those whom he could trust and who offered a tradeable value also extended to the figure to whom Whittington was perhaps the closest, the man to whom he owed so much for his early life and career. Sir Ivo Fitzwarin was also set to prosper under the new king by virtue of a relationship founded on long-standing military ties, family connections and shared networks. He was well known to Henry and was someone he could trust and for whom plans were already in motion. The two men had been the co-feoffees of certain estates within the liberty of Tyndale, held to the benefit of Henry's retainer, Sir Hugh Waterton, and there was little doubt that 'Fitzwaryn was unquestionably useful to Bolingbroke, who brought him from local to national importance'.[7] Fitzwarin must have thought that his opportunity to join the king's circle had passed. Just a few months earlier he had missed out on being chief cup-bearer at Henry's coronation because of a long-standing dispute with his wife's family. But in January 1400 he was appointed governor of Southampton and tasked with readying the town for a rumoured invasion.[8] If that was a welcome surprise, he must have been quite taken aback a few months later to find himself at Bourbourg representing his new king in one of his first embassies to the French. And in July, despite having had to withdraw through illness from the king's expedition to Scotland, he was held in sufficient esteem to be invited to sit on the Royal Council that autumn, about the time that his protégé was being withdrawn to concentrate on the king's financial needs. 'Family' connections took a rather more unexpected turn after the collapse of the Epiphany Rising in January 1400 when Henry also made a surprising overture to Whittington's elder brother Robert, who had carved an impressive career for himself as a judicial and administrative figure in Gloucestershire. Already a king's esquire, the elder Whittington was granted by Henry the life custody of Corse Chase, six miles north of Gloucester and part of the manor of Tewkesbury. Both had belonged to the Earl of Gloucester, the traitor Thomas le Despenser, executed at Bristol on 13 January 1400. For good measure, he also received a fee of £12 a year from the manor of Stoke Orchard. Robert had served in the retinue of Gloucester's father 25 years earlier. Surprisingly, his earlier allegiance with the Despensers was set aside. Whether this windfall was a product of Henry's wish to keep Whittington close to him or a reward for his own part in the suppression of an earlier Despenser revolt, Robert profited handsomely from Henry's favour and in August 1401 was summoned as one of five Gloucestershire representatives to attend the Great Council.[9] If this was a 'backdoor' bid to bind Richard more closely to him, then Henry had overestimated the proximity of the brothers' relationship. Richard required neither personal inducement nor fraternal preferment to hitch his wagon to the new king: it was plainly in his interests to do so.

Even so, he continued to nurse other relationships, his standing within the Court of Aldermen being one example. While he recognised that his immediate objectives and the opportunity for far superior influence resided elsewhere, it was important to attend to his duties as the representative for Lime Street and to continue to cultivate support among his peers. He knew that he would need the support of his fellow aldermen should he wish to stand once more for the mayoralty. Having held office twice, he recognised that he would need to enter the race again if he was to achieve other objectives. Nothing was left to chance. It seems surprising that at the close of the 14th century the seniority arrangements of the Court of Aldermen ranked him only tenth among their number. Yet three of his closest friends, among the most influential men in London, were also ranked behind him: Drew Barantyn at eleventh, Thomas Knolles twelfth and John Woodcock seventeenth. Only John Shadworth, a more industrious figure within the court, ranked higher at sixth.[10]

The rankings reflected a combination of time served, the strength of one's guild or company within the Court of Aldermen (rather than outside), and the extent to which an individual was active in pursuing aldermanic interests and fulfilling various offices. Whittington remained active and visible on the court's behalf, but his singular interest and influence lay at a far higher level. In repaying his predecessor's debt to the mercer, and so quickly, the new king had signalled that Whittington's access and value would continue. Whether Richard Clifford had played a part in encouraging the repayment to Whittington is not known, though he may well have been consulted, but it was a clear sign that business would carry on as usual. Almost as significant was the manner of repayment: the sum was not reimbursed in cash but in the form of an opportunity—an office or a contract to oversee the king's business or some other mutually satisfying quid pro quo. Though Whittington's resources must have been depleted by the loans and goods he had previously supplied to the Crown, he was willing to set aside like-for-like repayment in favour of recovering the debt, and more, by exporting wool from the port of London without having to pay the subsidy. In demonstrating his flexibility, he made himself more valuable to the king and more likely to accrue the commodity he now elevated above wealth—influence. Henry had established a new game and Whittington was keen to play.

Barron writes that fifty years after Edward III is said to have accumulated the names of around 170 wealthy figures he could resort to for loans and other financial easements, by 1400 a London merchant might be contributing to royal finances in a number of ways: through the custom duties levied on their imports and exports; through parliamentary taxation on their assessed 'moveable goods'; and through loans offered to or demanded by the Crown and provided either as an individual or corporately as a constituent of 'the City'. Despite this frequently dispiriting burden, and the tensions and disputes it generated, Barron notes that 'there is none of the bitterness that characterises the financial relations between London and the Crown in the thirteenth century'. And the reason for this absence of rancour was the replacement of arbitrary royal tallage by parliamentary taxation.[11]

Both Richard II and Henry IV were able to exploit the aspirations of London's merchant class for status and self-improvement. Like Whittington, many had already made their fortune and were open to forms of 'investment' other than commerce or property. The prospect of becoming a royal creditor, ideally by choice, offered opportunities and rewards beyond mere financial gain. Whittington was one among a small group of particularly wealthy figures in the City whose wealth and largesse increased further through their close association with the Crown but who also saw that lending led to influence and offered excitement over the mundane. This inner elite were essentially self-selecting because of their early dealings at court, among them some of Whittington's closest associates, Woodcock, Barantyn, Henry Barton, John Whatley and the royal embroiderer Robert Ashcombe. Both Richard II and Henry IV actively cultivated this self-interest and traded it outright for loans or for lengthy deferment of repayment such that 'suppliers of the Lancastrian household ... found that, despite the length of time that they might have to wait for repayment, their connexion with the Court brought many real advantages'.[12]

Business as Usual

Myers writes:

> By 1400 London had a firmly established merchant oligarchy. In theory its
> control was subject to the concurrence of the Common Council, in which
> the interests of the minor guilds could find a place, and there could at times
> be clashes within the dominant class ... But until the eighteenth century
> the fundamental control of the merchant oligarchy over the city's govern-
> ment was never seriously challenged after the reign of Richard II.[13]

Henry moved quickly to build bridges with London's wealthy merchant
class. In October 1399 he relaxed the conditions under which merchants
traded, encouraging Parliament to enact new laws favouring the City of
London.[14] On 25 May 1400 he went further, granting a new and wide-
ranging charter that gave the City custody over the gates, and therefore
the tolls, at Newgate and Ludgate and over the gathering of tolls, customs
and tronage in the markets at Cheap, Billingsgate and Smithfield. This gave
the city responsibility for and an income from the weighing of lead, wax,
pepper, alum, madder and other similar wares. Due to these economic
concessions there could be no excuse later when the Exchequer demanded
higher tax contributions and the king himself summoned individual merchants to dip into their pockets and provide him with loans. Theoretically
at least, all parties shared a mutual interest.

Whittington had first established his relationship with Henry in the
mid-1380s and the introduction had almost certainly come from
Fitzwarin. Like Richard before him, Henry had an irrepressible appetite
for luxury, and this ensured that Whittington would be in his sights. In the
spring of 1400 Henry moved to Eltham Palace and established it as his
favoured residence and as a temple to conspicuous consumption. No
expense was to be spared in making his life as comfortable and ostentatious as possible, and who better to call on than London's most illustrious
purveyor of luxury goods and its most notable lender? Mortimer describes
an extensive remodelling of Eltham that saw the addition of new rooms,
including the king's personal study and great chamber, extensive and
expensive redecoration and refurbishment, the commissioning of exotic
stained-glass windows, new fireplaces, and the construction of two fine
desks and a spiral staircase leading to a newly created private oratory.[15]
The Lancastrian motto, *Souveignez vous de moi*—'Remember me'—would
not have been lost on his favoured merchant and banker. Henry's seemingly endless taste for the very finest things in life would alone have

guaranteed Whittington's usefulness. That Henry would also require him to contribute funding for rather more exacting needs, home and away, made him essential. His need in May 1400 to raise loans to fund a campaign in Scotland was an early case in point.

Lending against the Wool Trade

Whittington's lending arrangements with Henry were closely interlinked with the wool trade. In December 1400, short of capital for the first time because of expenses he had to meet in order to export wool, the Crown granted him assignments on the wool custom in several English ports. In some ways this resembled a medieval version of the modern 'futures market', with loans secured against the Crown's prospective revenues and drawn on the wool taxes levied in ports specialising in that commodity. Instead of repayment by cash, the Crown granted Whittington a licence to export wool free of duty. This presented him with an exceptional opportunity to make a second fortune by establishing himself as a leading player in England's lucrative wool trade. Within a year he was regularly shipping wool both independently and with associates from London and from the less tax-burdensome backwoods port of Chichester. His later appointment as collector of the wool custom for London, from 6 October 1401 until 5 November 1405 and again from 20 February 1407 until 26 July 1410, helped to confirm him as one of the two or three richest men in London and certainly one of the most influential. His oversight of the wool trade gave him preferment over less influential royal creditors. As his opportunities and wealth increased, so, too, did his value to the king. In turn, this brought about a striking mutual dependency. Having been given the opportunity to exploit England's wool trade and to make the collection of tax revenues more efficient, Whittington could hardly complain when Henry came calling, and, in any event, their interests were rapidly converging. 'Whittington was almost certainly motivated more by a desire to influence matters of policy than the wish to make a financial profit out of his loans to the Crown, and there can be little doubt that he used his position as a royal creditor to achieve such an end.'[16]

Whittington's star was in almost uninterrupted ascendancy from the moment he made his first loans to Richard II in the early 1390s, and by 1400 it was evident that it would rise even higher under Henry. Over the next dozen years his role as the king's lender, even 'banker', would evolve further, requiring him to get Henry out of a hole whenever the king found himself in financial straits. This included having the wherewithal to 'gift' expensive cloths of gold, silk and damask for the weddings of both of Henry's daughters and effectively funding the wedding arrangements for the younger Philippa and Eric of Pomerania in their entirety. In something of a virtuous circle—or perhaps 'convenient mutuality'—he also lent regularly to the Great Wardrobe, enabling the royal household to make purchases from him and from other suppliers, and continued to fulfil his reputation for discreet loans to courtiers, further underwriting trade and dependency at the court of Henry IV. His standing was such that few among the cognoscenti would have batted an eyelid when two clerks of the Privy Seal sought to advance one of their own candidates as gaoler of Newgate and judged that the two most influential people in London to approach on his behalf were the Archbishop of Canterbury, Thomas Arundel, and the mercer Richard Whittington. But before all this, there is the matter of his introduction to the King's Council in the autumn of 1400. Why was he called?[17]

29

PULSE OF THE NATION?

The King's Council

The King's Council was charged with the most pressing matters material to Henry's needs and ambitions, including finance and fundraising, public order, England's foreign relations, military preparedness, and lines of supply. Its members included the Chancellor, the Treasurer, the Keeper of the Privy Seal, and those among England's judges, senior clergy and barony that the king or his advisers considered useful to invite. These numbered influential members of London's merchant class. Apart from a small core of the key offices of state, its membership was fluid, determined by needs and events and by finance. It was intended to be purposeful and practical, focused on strategy and task, with no pretences about 'representivity'. Henry wanted thinkers, influencers and doers. Above all, he favoured problem solvers and those capable of 'delivering'. Whittington fitted the bill. EF Jacob writes:

> For Henry IV they must be men he knew very well. That was why in the early part of his reign Henry relied ... mainly on the professional administrators like John Scarle (chancellor, formerly master of the rolls), John Norbury (treasurer, previously a duchy administrator), Bishop Thomas Langley (keeper of the privy seal), Sir Thomas Erpingham (the king's chamberlain) ... The addition, on 1 November 1400, of three citizens of London—Richard Whittington, John Shadworth and William Brampton—indicated the king's need to get the maximum help from the city.[1]

Henry may have seen something else in Whittington, reflected in Arundel's statement that the new king wished to be 'counselled and governed by the *honourable, wise* and *discreet* persons of his kingdom' and 'to ensure that all liberties and franchises should be respected'.[2] The archbishop had also spoken of restoring confidence in the Crown and of replenishing the nation's finances. Who better fitted the picture than Richard Whittington? Had these words been spoken today, it would seem that Henry was seeking a 'PR coup'.

Pulse of the Nation, January 1401

If Arundel's speech had offered optimism, realism and encouragement, this quickly evaporated. By the time of Henry's second Parliament in January 1401 he had already reneged on his promise that he would not raise taxation unless England was at war. Assailed on all sides for the growing national debt and his demand for further taxation, he would not retreat. He played to the gallery: were there not large bills to pay for defence at home, for safeguarding the realm against revolt, and for ensuring that Calais was readied for war if it should come? The Commons had already made clear that it would not tolerate further taxation, the non-repayment of existing loans or the extraction of new. For his part, Henry was insistent that Parliament must raise the money he needed and meet the reimbursement of loans he had already signed off. Both parties had marked their ground, the Commons intransigent in its resolution not to raise money except in the imperative of war, the king implacable in his demands for the resources to rule and defend his kingdom and to extinguish costs and debts incurred to date. Just fifteen months in, he was already in deep financial straits, having spent as much as £60,000 in his first year, much of it on his campaigns in Wales and Scotland.[3] This was of a piece with the wild profligacy of his youthful excursions in Prussia and elsewhere, where he had relied on his hugely wealthy father to underwrite his adventures and simply wipe away his extensive debts and fanciful expenses. Here, for some, is the making of the financially reckless and fiscally unreliable Henry IV.

Of his youthful extravagance and waste, Du Boulay writes that the man who would become the impoverished king of England spared himself nothing in maintaining his life of luxury. The listing of his expenses and his apparently inexhaustible 'supply chain' is revealing. What Henry wanted he made sure he got, whatever the cost, whatever the source, regardless of distance or inconvenience to others. There was always someone on hand to meet his needs and he, or rather his family, friends and funders, would dutifully pay up. Take the simple matter of food and drink. Du Boulay writes that 'When the household officers wanted to know where to buy, local officials and merchants were there to tell them. Germans, English, Prussians and Lithuanians were engaged in the victualling trades, and transactions could be made even in the Wilderness'.[4] As for entertainment: 'Henry's chief indoor amusements were listening to minstrels and dicing to which he had been addicted since early youth. Lengthy treatments for ill health and to cure his contraction of the "pox" never deterred him from games, gambling and the tourney.'[5] Perhaps the most revealing insight into his priorities was his elevation of personal wants, for which he first and later sought the services of Richard Whittington, over his apparent disregard for public need. 'His wardrobe accounts constantly betray in Henry a taste for luxurious equipment and "subtleties" no less than that for which Richard II is famous. In contrast with his personal spending his almsdeeds were derisory.'[6] Here we are talking about Henry in 1391–2, eight years after Whittington was first favoured as a preferred supplier. Now, almost a decade later, he had come to rely on the mercer's services again. As Du Boulay notes, hitherto 'his business with merchants was confined to his private advantage'. Now he was king of England. While finery and luxury were ever present in his wants, his greatest need was money, cash to run his government, his campaigns and his court.

Henry signalled his confidence in the mercer by appointing him on 6 October 1401 as collector of the wool custom for London, an influential and potentially highly remunerative position that he would hold until 5 November 1405 and for a second term from 1407 to 1410. Later in the year Whittington would become warden of the Mercers' Company for the second time. The remit and importance of both positions had transformed in the thirty or so years since his arrival in London. In May 1369 the city had shipped just a third of the national wool export, but by 1400 more than half was shipped almost exclusively by London-based merchants. During these three decades Whittington had personally gained from a process of rationalisation, specialisation and, latterly, outright exclusion of smaller craftsmen and their craft guilds, which had been left in the wake of powerful individuals and corporately driven livery companies that now controlled both London's and much of the nation's overseas trade. Whittington's appointment as collector was in some ways a 'deed of convenience', accelerated by Henry's inability or unwillingness to reimburse him by the normal means. Perversely, what resources the Exchequer did have at its disposal were derived in some part from loans and cash injections contributed by Whittington himself and lenders well known to him such as Woodcock, Shadworth, Knolles and the rehabilitated John Hende.

Henry IV or his advisers—and Whittington may have had a part in helping to formulate the arrangements—calculated that in awarding tax-raising offices and offering a share in profits and 'efficiencies' in lieu of formal loan repayment, lenders would exploit the opportunity to make themselves and the Crown even more money. Investing status-conscious merchants with the challenge of creating wealth for themselves and for the Crown would motivate them to create more than they were owed. In this way Henry would either have no debt at all or else, if he did, then such arrangements would ensure it simply fell away. Whittington features as a 'stand-out' figure in these arrangements and in Henry's public estimate of his worth: the king allegedly once described him at court and before Parliament as 'the pulse of the nation', though we struggle to reference this. Whittington had an additional value, of course: the influence he could bring to bear on his peers in the City. Henry knew, and the evidence supports it, that where Whittington took the initiative, others would follow. Valued for digging into his own pockets, he was remarkably persuasive in encouraging others to do the same.

In this way Whittington fashioned with England's new king a virtuous arrangement that, for the most part, worked well for both parties. His appointment as collector of the levy ensured that his licences to export wool, without paying customs duty, would be obeyed to the letter by those known and unknown to him alike. He had secured for himself a first-hand opportunity to see that assignments made on the customs revenue for the repayment of his own outstanding loans would be given priority. In addition, he stood to make a handsome profit far above the value of his loans because the opportunities afforded him and his ability to make the collections far more efficient, most notably in improving the accuracy of weighing and reducing evasion of payment, enabled him to do that. As collector, he would know precisely what quantities and quality came in and out and from whom, and could regulate them accordingly.

This placed Whittington in an exceptional position to ensure that in future the Crown would have the wherewithal to repay what it already owed him. With those loans repaid and Whittington's income ever increasing, Henry would have no inhibition in calling on him for further financial support. He was placing one of his most valuable sources of revenue in the hands of London's most capable and least corruptible man. Further, his capabilities and status were also acknowledged by leading members of the City and the nobility. He was one of two reputable and influential Londoners, the other being Barantyn, who were appointed with two doctors of law, three bishops, two knights of the realm and five others to a Crown commission to determine an appeal against the decision by Henry, Earl of Northumberland and Constable of England, over the ransom of the Count of Denia.[7]

March 1401

At the beginning of 1401 Henry is thought to have required at least £140,000 to finance the costs of England's administration and defence. The true figure was probably far in excess of this and excluded costs associated with his adventures in Wales, Ireland, Gascony and Calais, not to mention the repair and maintenance of England's threadbare navy. The real income of the Exchequer at this moment was barely £90,000, perhaps less. The king's capacity to raise finances was not helped by a slowing in the wool trade, the Tilbury–Gravesend revenue declining to about half of what it had been just five years earlier.

Henry wasted no time in testing Whittington's goodwill or in gauging his resilience. In March 1401 he sought to strengthen his position in England and announced his intention to make gains in Europe by arranging the marriage for July 1402 of his eldest daughter Blanche to Louis of Bavaria, son of his ally Rupert, recently crowned 'King of Germany' in January 1401. Through this strategic marriage the English king would acquire new allies in Europe while Rupert hoped that England would become a bulwark against the House of Luxembourg. It was a bold and far-reaching move certain to demand even further investment when Henry's real intentions became clear. The marriage contract was signed early in the month and the bride's dowry was fixed in the amount of 40,000 *nobeln*. Whittington's own part in the arrangements began gradually, almost fitfully. Most likely he would have been approached by representatives of both the Exchequer and the Great Wardrobe to test his willingness before it was announced at court that 'he had been honoured by the king' to provide the cloth of gold from which his daughter's trousseau would be fashioned. However, the speed of events and Henry's numerous obligations elsewhere meant that the king needed an 'advance' and quickly. Ready money was required to meet various expenses associated with the wedding arrangements and gifts. Given his entanglement with the King's Council and as collector of the levy, Whittington was in no position to refuse a substantial request that hardly appears to have come out of the blue. Whether or not he had seen this coming is unclear, but he was snared like a rabbit in a trap. How could he not help? We can almost visualise the process. A clerk would have been sent to his home, requested that he place his mark on a contract for the loan and seal the undertaking, and then been off like an arrow before the wax had set. Thus, we find him supplying ten cloths of gold to the value of around £216 for Blanche's trousseau. However, the loan was later determined a 'transaction' and was reimbursed to him some time after the wedding by Blanche's own treasurer, who, in turn, recovered it on her behalf from her father's Exchequer. It was a convoluted form of recovery, but the mercer was repaid in full for his timely support. As for 'spending money', Whittington ended up providing the further sum of £258 towards Blanche's travelling expenses to Germany. It is not clear if this was dealt with in the same way.

We may wonder how the spiralling calls on their funds and goodwill were discussed privately by the likes of Whittington, Shadworth, Woodcock, Knolles and Hende, five of London's richest men, each a former mayor and each conflicted by a wish to assist a new and apparently more even-tempered king while still fearful that he might repeat the profligacy and antagonisms of his predecessor. We might have found them ruminating over whether they were right to offer a continuing line of credit without the proper scrutiny and formal safeguard of Parliament. Whittington's relationship with Henry IV provides a revealing insight into the borrowing of the Crown from a relatively small, affluent group of native lenders who had, over the course of his time in London, completed the displacement of the historical reliance of English kings on the great Italian banking houses, which had reached its fateful zenith in the 1340s. By the time Whittington arrived in London in 1369–70, England may still have lacked the overarching and culturally steeped banking structures of the Florentines, Venetians or Genoese, but Englishmen were already well established as the Crown's primary lenders.[8] Throughout the late 1380s and 1390s Richard II demonstrated once and for all that the Crown looked to the country itself and to the City for financial services, and there were many willing to fill the Italians' once fashionable shoes. By 1400, the English lender was almost exclusively the first and preferred port of call for a hard-up monarchy and depleted Exchequer. Here Henry IV and Richard Whittington were at one. Wool provided an enormous and everready source of revenue for the Crown, whether its circumstances were hard pressed or expansionist. Its sheer scale and relative liquidity enabled an ambitious king with covetous eyes on France to mobilise his revenues. Administered by the Company of the Staple, the 'staple' itself was a fixed location through which the export of wool was conducted. Established by Edward I, it had been adapted further by Edward II and by Edward III to suit their own political and revenue needs. Effectively, it presented an English king with a cohort of like-minded merchants galvanised by the incentive of a monopoly which rewarded them handsomely for generating revenues the Crown could draw on for loans and for credit.[9]

During the first quarter of the 15th century the wool trade remained the chief source of loans throughout the time that Whittington was associated with it. To some extent, he followed in the footsteps of those earlier English merchants and lenders who had made their fortune through wool. Yet Whittington's control over the trade and his personal influence with the king may well have exceeded those of his predecessors. By July 1402 he was well established in shipping wool from Chichester as well as London, export through the smaller port proving more flexible and evidently lucrative. His direct access to England's king, his influence within the City, his imprint upon London at large, and his foresight in looking beyond it were second to none.[10]

Right Place, Right Time

Once again, he was in the right place at the right time. Even before he had contributed his 5 marks to the city gift in 1379, the staple was, as Power notes, already firmly established as 'an instrument of monopoly connected with royal finance in the Hundred Years' War'. In the preceding twenty years the hold of foreign merchants over England's wool trade had largely been extinguished, and the Company of the Staple exercised a virtual monopoly from the early 1360s. Now it had developed further into the Company of the Staple of Calais, a means by which Henry could raise or extract loans to fund his continental ambitions. Whittington's appointment as mayor of the staple at Westminster followed in July 1405, and from December 1406 until July 1413 he would also oversee the Calais staple. Clearly, he was both encouraged by and well disposed to the instrumentalism offered by the wool trade in furthering his own interests and those of the king.

In the 15th century the principal source of England's finest wool was the very area from where Whittington originated, that northern part of the Cotswolds where it meets Herefordshire and embraces the Welsh Marches. Is it serendipitous or emblematic that his wealth, status and social achievements should derive in large part from his circumstances as

a child in Pauntley nearly forty years earlier, when his family and neighbouring estates saw what was happening in the Ryelands and in
Herefordshire and sought to recover their fortunes by shifting from arable
to sheep rearing? And was it serendipitous that his family reduced their
domestic costs by dispatching him to London, where he joined the household of someone who could tutor him in the arts of mercery, causing him
to complete this circle? In the 16th century William Camden described
Cotswold sheep as having 'the whitest wool, having long necks and square
bodies', and in the 15th Michael Drayton's poem *Poly-Olbion* (1612) eulo-
gised the whiteness of the Cotswold breeds and their fleece as 'staple deep
and thick on a large body'. This was 'Cotswold, that great king of shep-
herds', while the renowned Herefordshire breeds produced an even finer
wool, superior even to that of Gloucestershire.[11] It cannot have escaped
Whittington, even as a young boy, that his family's estates were in or
adjoined areas where wool already reigned supreme. His route to London,
then, and a good deal of his trade later in life, passed through huge tracts
devoted to sheep farming that stretched through Gloucestershire and
Oxfordshire, and that were marked by the wool centres of Northleach,
Witney and Oxford.

Thus Whittington fell, mid-career, into a dynamic and booming industry that had first begun to expand with great speed in the 12th and 13th
centuries, an industry centred at that time in the Low Countries and Italy,
Florence in particular. It was an increasingly 'trans-European' enterprise
which generated demand for English wool and which could convert it to
expensive luxury cloth, something Whittington had already developed a
speciality in, trading as a mercer and as a supplier of luxury goods to
court. It was an industry driven by the adventurism and expertise of
Flanders and the Low Countries, and the infrastructure of the Scheldt, and
it was dominated by the three great producing centres of Bruges, Ypres
and Ghent, all less than a day's sail from England's eastern ports and its
wealth-hungry capital. This too offered vital lessons. By the start of the
Hundred Years War in 1337, and throughout its course, the industry of the
Low Countries was virtually dependent on English wool. Many of Italy's
fine cloth manufacturers were reliant on their English supply chain, with
London and its merchant entrepreneurs at its pulsating centre. This had
transforming consequences for London's economy, not only bringing the
city and its pre-eminent traders huge wealth but also placing them firmly
in the sights of four successive kings, each of whom saw in wool the
opportunity to extract the ever-mushrooming tax revenues that would

enable them to pursue their ambitions abroad and keep opposition in check at home. Indeed, the Ordinance of the Staple in October 1353 referred to wool as 'the sovereign merchandise and jewel of this realm of England'. Ten years later the merchants from the staples of York and Bristol established a new staple across the Channel at Calais. A new trading centre for wool was created at Bruges, intended to promote 'freedom of trade' in cloth to Flanders.[12]

The immense impact of wool lay in its becoming the currency of politics. It was a tap to be turned on and off as the king willed; it formed a means and an end in English foreign policy; it was the engine of England's domestic economy; and her kings relied increasingly on its investors and entrepreneurs to finance their policies at home and abroad. Wool was knitted through England's constitutional arrangements, and it shaped its political settlements.[13] The development of the wool tax and revenue collecting are also intimately linked with the evolution of Parliament and the Commons. Eileen Power observes that the struggles between king, Commons and merchants ended in a compromise which left the monarch in possession of a very high subsidy on wool, Parliament in control of taxation, and the Company of the Staple with a quasi-monopoly on the trade. She remarks that even the peasantry at this time was 'intensely wool-conscious'. Reviewing the century that ended with the death in 1377 of Edward III, she could just as accurately be describing the forty or more years that would end with Richard Whittington's death in 1423.

> The trade which gave England her key position was bound to dominate the domestic scene: her commerce and her politics alike were built on wool. When her kings got themselves taken prisoner, like Richard I, the ransom was paid—with grumbling—out of wool. When they rushed into war with their neighbours, like the three Edwards, the wars were financed and allies bought—with more grumbling—out of wool ... At home honest burgesses climbed upon wool into the ranks of the nobility, only to be outstripped in their progress there by the dishonest ones.[14]

When Whittington took up Henry IV's offer to become collector of the wool custom, he stepped into a favourable wind blowing in London's direction. Flemish hegemony was at an end, and the manufacture and finishing of cloth at Florence were in decline and assailed by competition from England, Burgundy and Castile. He came into an industry that for much of his term held its ascendancy. Henry's early attempts at running the country have been described as treating it 'as if it were a large extension of the duchy of Lancaster', in which men who had been loyal and long-standing comrades in war were invested with civil and governance responsibilities, essentially 'a personal form of government'.[15]

Finance and Government

It soon became clear that in order to ensure financial stability and efficient government, the new king would have to recall some of the same men who had advised his predecessor. Parliament insisted on it. Figures close to Henry such as Thomas Erpingham and John Scarle were obliged to make way. It was the influential Scarle who made the approach to Whittington. Richard II's Lord Chancellor, Edmund Stafford, Bishop of Exeter, was reappointed, and two other Ricardian stalwarts, Thomas More and Thomas Brounflete, were recalled as treasurer and controller of the royal household. Parliament was calling the shots, but across the kingdom Henry encountered violent resistance to his urgent efforts to gather taxes, resulting in the murder of the royal collectors. By Christmas 1401 any hope that Henry would create in his own image the glorious kingship of Edward III was effectively sunk. It didn't help that he continued to prioritise the comforts of his court as the prospect of famine loomed darkly in the countryside. For many, he had fallen at the first hurdle, either oblivious to or simply unable to anticipate the failure of successive harvests in 1400 and 1401, with the result that the price of wheat doubled. 'He was under pressure in almost every area of his responsibility. Bitter feelings about him were spreading as food became increasingly scarce and purveyors continued to requisition food for the royal household.'[16]

Abroad, following a sharp slump in revenue from its wool exports in 1401, England's foreign earnings had also fallen short, down by a sixth from the 'high' achieved under Richard II, from £47,000 to £39,000. If the impact of poor harvests fell most heavily on the commonalty, the loss of wool revenue hit the king much closer to home. The community he most relied on to help fund his domestic needs and his military adventures was now much less able to pay. England's wool merchants were hardly on their uppers, but their ability and willingness to fund court and campaign were severely diminished. Worse still was the unfolding reality that Henry's Exchequer was already overburdened with loans and overcommitted to their repayment. He had already misjudged Parliament with demands for excessive levels of taxation at a time when much of the country remained divided over the circumstances of his coup and the legitimacy of his position.[17] At the beginning of 1402 the king's financial situation was so parlous that he was unable to pay the army stationed in Ireland and faced desertions in France. In April, the King's Council went as far as urging postponement of the prospective marriage of his daughter Philippa to the King of Denmark. He refused. Overall, 1402 would prove something of an *annus horribilis* for the Crown, dominated by England's costly policing of its troubled borders with Wales and Scotland, which required huge mobilisations of men, the funding of extensive supply chains, and the expense of fortifying its remote and costly defences in the Marches. It was bound to get worse. Towards the end of June, Sir Edmund Mortimer was captured by the Welsh leader, Owain Glyndŵr. Following Henry's rejection of ransom, Mortimer turned about, inverted his loyalties and married Glyndŵr's daughter. It wasn't until September that the king's fortunes finally turned with the sweeping defeat of the Scots at Homildon Hill. But war, pursuit or defence, meant finance, and that meant trouble. Effectively bankrupt, he summoned a Parliament on 30 September so that he might set out the extensive threats to the kingdom and his desperate need for more money to extinguish them.

> The parliament of 1402 was not nearly as bruising as that of 1401. All the same hard questions were raised about finance. The commons asked where had Richard's great treasure gone? John Ikelington, Richard II's clerk and the custodian of £44,000 of the hoard, was examined and acquitted. The money, it turned out, had been given to the Percy family to defend the Scottish border. Another tough question was why Henry had appointed his personal friend, Henry Bowet, as treasurer.[18]

Rebuked that he was reverting once again to his former preferences for 'personal government', he dismissed Bowet and was obliged to bring in yet another Ricardian, the Bishop of St David's. Henry was finally granted his taxation in the dying moments of the Parliament on 25 November. The year ended as dolefully as it had begun, with Sir Edmund Mortimer proclaiming his nephew Edmund as the rightful heir to Richard II.

30

MARRIAGE

Whittington had now made his mark as a mercer, importer-exporter, financier, civic leader and lender to two kings, and had given early glimpses of the social reformer he would eventually become. Henry's decision to place him at the centre of England's wool trade was, in modern parlance, a 'no-brainer'. At home, Whittington presided over a wide network of business associates, while abroad his interests flourished through the supply relationships he had nurtured with Flemish, Venetian, Genoese, Spanish, German and Milanese merchants and their captains. In partnership with others, possibly Woodcock and Maghfeld, he had begun to expand his interests in the Baltic and northern Europe, where the Hansa had traditionally held sway. Though London remained the fulcrum of his activities, he also traded through the provincial ports of Bristol and Southampton and regularly through the smaller facilities of Chichester and Lewes, Colchester and Lynn, and, when it suited, at tiny Essex harbours that were little more than remote timber-boarded jetties. He was active in Gloucestershire, Herefordshire, Oxfordshire, Worcestershire, Northants, Herts, Devon, Coventry and Leicestershire, using a web of trusted agents to handle his business in each location. His connections with Sir Ivo Fitzwarin suggest he may also have had interests in Dorset and perhaps in Berkshire. No longer the singular mercer of the 1380s, Richard Whittington was now in both spirit and accomplishment one of England's, perhaps Europe's, leading merchant adventurers—one of those outward-looking entrepreneurs whose commercial nous, access to markets, and approach to risk and capital and to the accrual and deployment of wealth were also elevating their social and political status. Even so, Whittington ensured that he remained close to the helm of the Mercers' Company. Thus, on 24 June 1401, the feast day of St John the

Baptist, we find London's pre-eminent company assembled in their traditional meeting place, the hall of St Thomas of Acon, where John More
moved the election of Richard Whittington as one of four new wardens
for the following year. Among the others was Whittington's former
apprentice and long-term associate, Thomas Roos, elected by his pro-
poser, William Marcheford.[1] The interconnectedness of London's merchant elite was in further evidence on 13 October, the feast day of St
Edward, at which the Company saluted the outgoing mayor, John
Fraunceys, and his successor, John Shadworth. The names of those in
attendance at this 'immense Commonalty' constitute a roll call of
London's most influential figures at the opening of the 15th century,
many of whom had already been or would become mayor themselves.[2]

The year 1401 is significant for another reason: it marks the end of
Whittington's employment of apprentices. He is believed to have enrolled
a total of nine by the end of 1400–1, but after this, aside from one exceptional case, there appear to be no further additions, and as these came of
age their numbers would have begun to decrease in any case. There are
two obvious explanations. The first is that these young men were already
beginning to make their mark, having completed their term, and—in the
case of Thomas Roos, apprenticed in 1391–2, and Henry London, apprenticed more recently in 1400–1—would continue to be closely involved as
employees or associates of Whittington until his death.[3] The second is that
mercery was no longer the centrifugal force in Whittington's life: he had
moved on, or at least diversified, from his chosen trade and therefore from
the need to nurture further associates or successors. With his wider interests firmly established, a considerable fortune at his command, and his star
on the rise with another of England's wilful, profligate kings, he was at last
beginning to contemplate his personal needs and who might share his life.
An altogether different journey now lay ahead.

Marriage

The completion of his apprenticeship obligations was among the events
that point to 1402 as the most likely moment when Whittington entered
into marriage with Alice Fitzwarin, the daughter of his own former master, Sir Ivo Fitzwarin. Someone he had known from her birth, Alice was
now 30, and both clearly judged it was time. There is no record that they
married earlier, but given the remarkable intertwining of their lives since
1372 it is reasonable to assume that they were 'expected' to marry and had

been betrothed formally for some time. The substantive preparations for marriage appear to have begun in December 1401 when Whittington put in hand a reassignment of his London properties. He had held tenements and shops at Castle Baynard from as early as July 1384 and later acquired tenements in the parish of St Michael Bassishaw and other properties in the parish of St Botolph without Bishopsgate.[4] With the help of those close to him, notably William Hedyngdon, chaplain to the Mercers' Company, and three of his former apprentices, Thomas Roos, Thomas Faulconer and Henry London, his assets were incorporated in a deed eventually dated 3 August 1402, which conveyed them jointly to both 'Richard and Alice Whittington', affirming their marriage had taken place sometime in the months before. Preparations were also evident six months earlier on 22 February when, with the help of the same group, Whittington had acquired a house from his friend the knight Sir Baldwin Berford, a relative of Alice's mother Maud Fitzwarin, one of several of her outlying kin who hailed from Bedfordshire. Berford may have served as the member of Parliament for the county, and in London he appears to have been something of a 'fixer' in the city's lively property market. It may explain how we find him selling his house, apparently formerly owned by Sir Nicholas Brembre, to the newly wed Whittingtons. The house was not intended simply to fulfil the couple's domestic needs, though it boasted the status, proportions and features sought by and expected of a man of Whittington's standing and appropriate to the social status of his wife, one of the richest women in London.[5] Rather, what mattered most to the Whittingtons was its location, its extensive demesne, and its potential to meet a much more pertinent objective—the fulfilment of a radical joint 'vision'. Standing close to St Michael Paternoster, the house held both a strategic and moral imperative. Whittington was already thinking ahead, though it would not be until April 1409 that he would eventually acquire the land adjoining St Michael's and so develop the project through which he and Alice intended to realise their vision. This would require still more land, the securing of licences for its development, and of course investment. It may explain why Whittington's regular backroom team, Roos, London and Faulconer, and Hedyngdon, the chaplain to the Mercers' Company, were involved in progressing the purchase. The house formed the greater part of the large tenement that the Whittingtons would live in while they steadily accumulated adjoining land and planned their reconfiguration of St Michael Paternoster. To the west the site was bound by Paternoster Lane, a popular spot for the sale of rosaries, so-called saintly relics, other artefacts and general religious 'tat'. To the south ran Church Lane and immediately below lay Thames Street, the bustling gateway to Vintry ward and the street where Chaucer had been raised. To the east, the site was framed by Walbrook. Within this rough rectangle the main house spanned the entire width of the upper third of the site, more than doubling its footprint as it stretched from west to east. In the middle of the site overlooking Paternoster Lane were three small tenements which produced a modest rent and to their east a group of low utilitarian buildings which had evidently set Whittington's mind racing. A narrow passage separated the house from the church of St Michael Paternoster Royal, derived from its early associations with a vintner community whose forebears hailed from La Riole in Bordeaux. The project would be visionary and transformative in other ways. Jean Imray describes the rebuilding of the church of St Michael Paternoster as 'the earliest recorded instance of Whittington's public generosity'.[6] It would lay the foundations for yet another remarkable phase in Whittington's life, and hand down many of the legacies we associate him with today.

To the immediate east lay the churchyard, leaving in the south-eastern corner of this *territoire* a sizeable plot of land that offered a range of possibilities to test the Whittingtons' imaginations. Socially, the site offered within a fifteen-minute walk everything they needed, both then and for the future. To the north, it led almost directly onto Londonstone and its perimeter stretched towards the shops and churches clustered around East Cheap. Crossing Londonstone and heading north, they could trace the Walbrook to Cheapside, Poultry and Cornhill. From here they could make their way onto Lothbury and from there into the heart of Whittington's political base in the wards of Coleman Street and Broad Street. The house lay to the immediate north of what later became the almshouses site, which in turn adjoined the church of St Michael Paternoster. Imray sets out the detail of the plan, and it is worth repeating it here. If one views the site clockwise, the house lay at the top, the almshouses just below, then the site of the college of priests. To its side, bound by Church (Elbow) land lay the churchyard of St Michael's and the church itself. Above, bound by College Hill, lay the tenements which would later become part of the almshouses and the mercers' school.[7] Twenty or so years later, in January 1424, Thomas Roos and Thomas Faulconer would find themselves involved with the Whittington home again when, under the terms of their former master's will, they were tasked with isolating it from the St Michael's project, eventually selling it the following year. An attempt by the Mercers' Company to reacquire the building forty years later proved unsuccessful.

Whittington was clearly not deterred by the putative identity of its former owner. The quality of the house at College Hill and the opportunity to develop his wider ambitions for St Michael's were irresistible and suited both the moment and his future aspirations for his life with Alice. While the purchase of the house points firmly to their marriage at this time, an even stronger indicator lies in their joint partyship to deeds in which Sir Ivo Fitzwarin granted them the reversion of manors and land in Somerset and Wiltshire on his death. These stated that if Alice should predecease her father without an heir, then the entirety of his property in Somerset, Wiltshire, Dorset, Berkshire and elsewhere would fall to Alice's sister Eleanor and her husband John Chideock.[8] From this, we conclude that Richard and Alice were married shortly before or during the early spring of 1402, at a moment when Whittington's stock was rising but England itself was slipping towards war and uncertainty. As Whittington contemplated his domestic arrangements, it seemed that events elsewhere would deflect him. In the month that he acquired the house, Henry IV announced the first tranche of loans he had called for to fund the preparations for his forthcoming campaign in France. An initial £700 came jointly from William Parker and Thomas Oyster, and on 28 February the Bishop of Bath and Wells lent the sum of 1,000 marks, creating pressure and raising the bar for others to follow. The draper John Hende, then thought to be the richest man in London, trumped him by committing £2,000. The City of London contributed its customary corporate loan, in this case the sum of £1,353 6s 8d, and Whittington pitched in with £1,000. The remarkable highpoint of the call came a few months later, in the second week of May, when no less than 61 separate loans brought in the extraordinary sum of £14,020.[9]

April–May 1402

For now, it was back to business, to wool and to the king's irrepressible financial needs. In April, Henry renewed John Shadworth's oversight of the wool tronage, enabling him to prosper even further from the trade, so much so that his warehouse at Dowgate was now popularly referred to as the 'wool wharf'. Meanwhile, Whittington was asked again to plug the gaping holes created by the king's reckless expenditure. In May 1402 he was caught up with preparations in every direction, personal and political, and was appointed on 7 May as receiver-general in England for Edward, Earl of Rutland, also finding time to complete his duties as warden of the Mercers' Company before completing his term in June. At home, he was preoccupied with the need to address the terms of Sir Ivo's prospective will and commute the deferred promise of Alice's inheritance into something that could be capitalised far sooner. Neither wished to be encumbered with crumbling manors and rural estates or to be made responsible for the welfare of far-flung households. Whittington would have been aware, in any case, that land and estate values had long since fallen away from the peak demand that followed the years after the Black Death. By 1400, rural estates were exposed to the twin torment of sharply falling prices for their produce and steep rises in agricultural wage rates. It would not have mattered in any case, for the Whittingtons saw their life together building and expanding at College Hill, and cash in the hand was a far more powerful asset than a distant and dilapidated rural seat. Hadn't the king himself made this clear? He wanted Whittington on hand, in London, providing ready access to the mercer's liquid resources, not wasting his time, energy and money chasing a bucolic dream. Together, the Whittingtons chose to set aside such encumbrances and to surrender Alice's claims there and then if Eleanor and John Chideock offered them a suitable level of 'compensation'. It was a practical solution for both parties. The Chideocks were given certainty of ownership and assured the immediate use of valuable assets in return for a very modest cash sum. For their part, the Whittingtons 'commuted' distant assets they neither sought nor needed into the means for further development. The settlement amounted to 460 marks. Whittington met with Chideock and agreed three-stage payments. The first instalment of 260 marks was paid to him and Alice on 9 May 1402; the second instalment of 100 marks was agreed for 15 May 1403; and the final payment, also of 100 marks, was scheduled for 26 June 1406.[10] Chideock had his much-coveted estate and the Whittingtons the promise of cash to use as they pleased. Elsewhere, Whittington hardly seems to have paid notice to the appointment of his brother Robert as sheriff of Gloucestershire, the first of five terms.

The loan provided by Whittington to the king in February 1402 formed only a small part of his wider lending to Henry between 1400 and 1408. Jacob notes that the peak years of borrowing by Henry IV were between 1400 and 1402 and during the year 1407–8, and that the greater part of the sums received from London came from a group of wealthy mercers, 'one of whom, Whittington, had already begun to be active before 1400 and contributed two-thirds of the whole effort'.[11] Whittington found himself in 1403 in much the same position he had occupied on Richard II's removal, with Henry owing at least £1,238 for goods he had supplied to the Great Wardrobe since 1401. This sum was set against 'Exchequer tallies', effectively a receipt or proof of payment owing by the king, which, incidentally, Whittington had still not been able to encash by 1405, at which time the Exchequer was finally instructed to repay him in full or agree new assignments to him.[12] Just a year after he had wed Alice, marriage was in the air again and Whittington was destined to play no small part in it.

7 February 1403

On 7 February 1403 Henry IV married Joan of Navarre, occasioning yet another burden on buckling resources. The wedding feast alone required an outlay of over £520 while the king's personal gift to his bride, an extravagantly inscribed jewelled collar, cost £385. It was no more than a momentary distraction from the persistent drip of bad news that continued to threaten his monarchy, the most troubling of which was the disclosure that Richard II's great 'war chest', amounting to £40,000, had ended up in the hands of his great enemies, the Percys. Worse was to follow: in July the Percy family joined forces with Owain Glyndŵr and his new son-in-law, Sir Edmund Mortimer. The two principal forces of opposition were now a unified whole, strikingly well-funded, and a formidable constitutional and existential challenge. In London, the Parliament of January 1404 weakened Henry's parlous position, conceding a measure of taxation which fell so far short of his needs that he was unable to honour annuities promised to his own household. Wherever he looked, Henry found himself having to capitulate to constraint, pass around the proverbial begging bowl, and simply accept what was given: a humiliating experience.

Later that year, Whittington was also caught up in events, though minor by comparison, which brought him rudely back to earth. In October 1404 he brought forward one of the few lawsuits of his career, other than those in which he later appeared alongside his brother. This centred on the disputed non-payment of arrears owed on a Whittington property by the litigant John Hert and his future wife Joan. Whittington won the case, and the litigants were bound by statute of the staple of Westminster to remit to him the sum of £651 within four months. The Herts simply played on Whittington's goodwill and ignored the ruling, presuming that someone so wealthy and so preoccupied with matters elsewhere would not find the time to pursue them. This was a misjudgement that fell considerably wide of the mark. Whittington considered John Hert's behaviour immoral and a blatant abuse of the trust and goodwill he had shown him, a far greater injury than any material threat to his income or property. Had Hert followed Whittington's career, he would have discovered that the mercer was characteristically wont to teach a lesson where he believed it was due. In his view, he had treated Hert equitably, had fulfilled the contract requested of him, and had allowed him with all consideration to occupy his premises. After a great length of time and many wild and public accusations that impugned his reputation, Whittington still awaited the sum he was owed. Indeed, it wasn't until eleven years later that he finally recovered the debt, though he was by then in legal possession of the house on London Bridge.

June 1405

In June 1405 a far more serious challenge to the king emerged, presenting an altogether different existential threat. Henry was stricken by the first of a series of debilitating attacks which traumatised his gut and constitution. Further episodes would follow in April 1406, in June 1408 and throughout the winter of 1408–9, leaving him dangerously depleted. If this was not dispiriting enough, he also developed a deeply distressing condition, which may or may not have been related, in the form of a disfiguring skin disease, diagnosed by modern writers as leprosy or something akin to it. Later, this caused him to hide himself away and refuse to meet people, and it must have affected the orderly performance of his duties. He seems to have recovered quickly from the initial abdominal attack in June, sturdy enough a month later to appoint on 3 July Whittington as mayor of the staple of Westminster, an office he went on to hold until his death in 1423.

Underwriting a European Union

Throughout 1405, Whittington was caught up in Henry's convoluted arrangements for the marriage of his second daughter, Philippa, to Eric of Pomerania on 26 November. The principle of the union had been fermenting since at least 1401. Henry had come to the English throne determined to fashion a wider continental alliance that would extend his influence in Europe beyond the historical parameters of England and France. In the first year of his reign, he had proposed to Queen Margaret I of Denmark, Norway and Sweden that an alliance be formed between England and the Kalmar Union, over which she presided, by engineering a double wedding between Philippa and Eric of Pomerania, heir to the Nordic thrones, and between his son, the future Henry V, and Eric's sister Catherine.[13] The latter never materialised, but Philippa's marriage to Eric was settled by proxy in November 1405, enabling her formal proclamation on 8 December 1405 as Queen of Denmark, Norway and Sweden. The wedding eventually took place on 26 October 1406, the month that Whittington became mayor of London for the third time. The marriage is said to be the first documented in which an English princess wore a white wedding gown, lavished with a tunic and cloak of white silk bordered in squirrel and ermine. The 'agent' of this spectacular trousseau was none other than Richard Whittington, her father's 'banker', who supplied cloth of gold, silk and pearls to the value of £248 for her memorable outfit.

31

THREE TIMES MAYOR

An aggressive thirst for trade and new commercial outposts would develop further during 1406, the year that Whittington took on the office of mayor for the third time. Fourteen years after Richard II's government and the Teutonic Order had first intervened to improve relations between England's merchants and the Hansa, the English found themselves denounced once more as the rougher and less honourable of the two great competitors. 'To the Germans the English were still in 1406 (and despite Henry IV's rapid confirmation of their privileges) a perverse nation, lost to all honesty and truth and steeped in trickery, treason and venomous lies.'[1] Perhaps this perspective was occasioned in part by the successes of John Woodcock. In the early months of 1406, still only halfway through his term as mayor, he had startled the entire City, and perhaps the Hansa too, in breaking all export records by shipping to Calais 21 sarplers of wool in a single day. That alone would have been reason enough for Richard Whittington to meet up with his friend; after all, Woodcock had himself served as collector of the wool custom for London and had taken on similar duties for the stretch of the Thames from Gravesend to Tilbury and more recently at Ipswich. Both men had lent heavily to Richard II and were now regularly extending credit to his successor. By the summer of 1402 Woodcock had already provided the king and his family with goods worth almost £2,330. Henry had agreed that half of the debts were to be repaid out of the wool custom and, in Woodcock's case, to be siphoned from the levies at Ipswich. Similarities and common interests abounded, but the two men had other reasons for meeting regularly at this time. The first was Woodcock's wish to introduce changes to the way the election of London's mayor was administered and celebrated, and he intended Whittington to be the first beneficiary. The second concerned another matter of joint interest—Newgate. In January, Woodcock had been appointed as commissioner for gaol delivery in London, with responsibility for the refurbishment or replacement of London's decrepit, disease-ridden prisons. Whittington's own ambition to raze and rebuild Newgate was well known and shared with another mutual friend, Thomas Knolles. Whittington would have his ears burned by Knolles's indignation at the king's latest scam, the raising of a £200 loan from prosperous citizens to fund, apparently, the distribution of Good Friday alms to the poor—another dereliction by the monarchy of the social good and effective sub-contracting of it to the City's would-be reformers. Whether Woodcock made any material progress with prison reform remains unclear. He appears to have devoted much of his time in the second half of his mayoralty to reordering its electoral arrangements and paving the way for Whittington as his successor. Perhaps that was the plan, connecting the loose ends and preparing the groundwork for a programme of prison reform that his friend, not he, would see through.

Second Election as Mayor, 13 October 1406

On Wednesday, 13 October 1406, the Feast of the Translation of St Edward the King and Confessor, Woodcock summoned London's aldermen and a large body of the city's most substantial commoners to the Guildhall to elect a new mayor, instructing that first a Mass of the Holy Spirit should be celebrated with 'solemn music' in the adjoining chapel. His intention was that this assembly, by the grace of the Holy Spirit, would convene to nominate two able and proper persons to be his successor and that the circumstances in which London's succeeding mayor would draw his authority would be characteristically different.[2] From the appearance of this sumptuously clad gathering, it must have seemed that through this quasi-religious device they were no longer simply a civil electoral college but a congregation of pious, reverential brethren. Their gathering in this place, in a ritualistic manner, clad in robes more ecclesiastical than secular, was intended by Woodcock to prompt a transformation in the king's perception of the City and Corporation, and to instil in the assembly itself a deeper sense of its own spiritual status and moral obligations.[3] Casting his eyes over this well-dressed 'congregation', Whittington would have seen on the faces of those about him the realisation that a profound change was taking place in the way that London's mayor was now being chosen. The election was being consecrated and the incumbent was being anointed. The 'solemn music' requested by Woodcock, the hymns, the incense, the investment of the proceedings by the highest order, higher even than the king himself, gave the election a strikingly religious gloss. Gathered in exceptional finery, the participants looked what they now were, not simply electors but celebrants, London's civic elite drawing their authority from God and investing their choice with His guidance. In Whittington's midst stood his friend and fellow contestant Drew Barantyn, his promoters Thomas Knolles, John Shadworth, Thomas Faulconer and William Staunton, the grocer John Hadley, the prior of Holy Trinity who served as alderman for Portsoken, the outgoing sheriffs, the drapers Nicholas Wootton and Geoffrey Broke, and the prominent fishmongers and general merchants William Brampton and William Askham, with whom London's foremost mercers, Whittington, Woodcock and Shadworth, often communed. Askham, too, had been a regular lender to Richard II and Henry IV and had served as a buyer of food for the royal household. His interests went far beyond fish, as he traded extensively in the export of cloth and the import of wine. By the late 1390s he was one of London's leading wool merchants and had recently completed terms as mayor of the staple of Westminster (1402–5) and mayor of the staple of Calais (1403–6). A beneficiary of Woodcock's will, he acted as attorney to the mercer's wife Felicity. Askham and Brampton were close friends and business partners, and would have approved the religious infusion that Woodcock introduced to the mayoral ceremony. The pair had been prominent in funding the foundation of the perpetual fraternity and guild of St Peter in the church of St Peter Cornhill in 1403. In October of that year Askham had commenced his only term as London's mayor. Later, in May 1411, he would be another among the group of friends that assisted Whittington's ambition to settle upon the commonalty of London the manor of 'Le Ledenhalle', the place where he had first resided and made his mark on London. Almost inevitably, his co-trustees in this matter were Hende, Shadworth and Whittington himself, among the most powerful men in London.[4] Brampton's pedigree was no less auspicious. With Askham he was instrumental in breaking down the at times intractable and adversarial interests of the mercers and fishmongers. He too was an estimable figure, notable for his successful trading relationship with the Hansa. He served as governor of the staple of Middelburg, as mayor of the staple of Westminster (1397–1402), and alongside Whittington as one of Henry IV's 'wise men' in the king's first Royal Council.[5] Led by Woodcock and his departing officials, the entire body of aldermen made their way from the chapel into the chamber of the mayor's court at the Guildhall, where the nominations for the two candidates were counted, enabling Woodcock to declare that by the guidance of the Holy Spirit, Richard Whittington had been chosen by his fellows as London's next mayor and that his successors would each be 'ordained' in this way.

> And hereupon, the Mayor and Aldermen, with closed doors, in the said Chamber chose Richard Whytyngtone aforesaid, by guidance of the Holy Spirit, to be Mayor of the City for the ensuing year; after which, the Mayor and Aldermen, coming down from the Chamber into the Hall, to the Commoners there assembled, as the custom is, notified by the Recorder unto the same Commoners, how that, by Divine inspiration, the lot had fallen upon the said Richard Whytyngtone ... And hereupon, the Mayor and Aldermen, by assent and consent of the said Commoners, did ordain and decree that every year in future a solemn Mass with music shall be celebrated in presence of the Mayor and Aldermen.[6]

Perpetuation

Self-perpetuation had prevailed again. In the previous eight years Whittington had served twice, Barantyn had followed him in 1398–9, and Knolles had succeeded in 1399–1400. In 1401–2 it was Shadworth's turn and in 1404–5 John Hende returned for a second term. The year 1405–6 fell to Woodcock and that of 1406–7 to Whittington again, followed in 1408–9 by his defeated contestant Barantyn and latterly by Knolles in 1410–11. This narrow recurring cycle was not confined to the Court of Aldermen, the Common Council or the close-knit cartels that engineered much of the city's commerce.[7] Figures in each of these, including Whittington and probably Woodcock too, were associated with the English Company of Merchant Adventurers, which obtained a charter from Henry IV in 1407 during Whittington's mayoralty. Its conferment awarded neither wide-ranging oversight nor exclusive powers but did invest the organisation with an authority that mattered deeply to its entrepreneurial members—the means to regulate their business and the right to choose a 'governor' who would vigorously promote their interests. When Whittington resumed office in October 1406, London's merchant adventurers were actively trading throughout northern Europe in the Baltic, Prussia and Scandinavia, where Henry had extended the reach of the English royal family.[8]

The Appointments of November and December 1406

On 8 November 1406, in almost the last act of significance before it adjourned for Christmas, Whittington summoned a meeting of the Council. He had news, exhilarating news, to impart to them, which probably only Knolles and Woodcock knew beforehand: the king had finally conceded the need to rebuild Newgate anew. Whittington had been instructed to establish and lead 'a Commission for Gaol Delivery for Newgate' and to select up to five aldermen to join him. There was no shortage of candidates. William Gascoigne, William Thynning, John Cockayne, William Rykhill, William Haukeford and John Preston were among those who stepped forward to offer their services.[9] All were committed to wider social improvement, were regular visitors to Newgate and Fleet, and had campaigned to improve conditions at both. Four weeks later, Whittington was summoned to the Exchequer, expecting to hear that the king required further loans or else that he had had second thoughts about the commission. Once more Henry surprised him: he was to act as mayor of the staple at Calais as well as Westminster, and his appointment as collector of the levy was to be extended until 1410. His mission was clear and conveyed with great urgency: to help reflate Henry's fast-sinking reserves. If successful, he would have the gratitude of the king and would accrue the resources needed to fund Newgate.

He was in place as mayor of the Calais staple by 25 December 1406. Its location had the advantage of not being tied to a producing centre on the English mainland, thereby removing the objection that by siting it in England one centre of production or export would be favoured and would profit unfairly over its competitors. John H Munro notes that placing it across the Channel also precluded the cartel practices and price fixing associated with the great Flemish centres; these had effectively sabotaged the Bruges staple until its gradual replacement by Calais after 1348.[10] There was also a historical context for its location here. The Company of Merchants of the Staple, through whom this trade was conducted, is thought to have been started by a group of 26 wool merchants in the late 13th century, making it one of the oldest mercantile corporations in England. Active in Bruges by 1282, it was unusual in being 'of England' yet not bound to or constrained by ties to any English city or municipality. Granted charters by the dukes of Burgundy and the counts of Flanders, the company was trading at Antwerp by 1296 and at St Omer by 1313, and effectively controlled the export of English wool to the Continent from

1314. Its authority and rights to trade were increased by the grant of a charter by the Duke of Flanders to English merchants in 1341.[11] Its commercial hegemony grew further with the establishment in 1348 of the staple at Calais as the chief centre for controlling the wool export to Europe. It now fell to Whittington to maintain impetus and squeeze more from its tax pool. As overseer of the staple, serving both Henry IV and later Henry V, Whittington proved an inspired choice. He was expected to be an example to and an orchestrator of England's merchants in their financial dealings with the Crown. His brief was to make far more efficient (and profitable) the collection of, and therefore the tax revenue derived from, England's primary trade at a time when its volume was already in decline. His contacts and influence made him best placed to encourage personal lending by his peers to the state.

The year 1406 closed with another reminder of Whittington's residual ties to Gloucestershire. On 14 December, in return for the payment of 200 marks, James Clifford, a relative of the main family which had held the prominent estate of Frampton manor at Frampton on Severn since the Conquest, was pardoned of various outlawries and debts. A condition of his pardon was that he would formally renounce his persistent claims to various properties whose ownership he had fiercely disputed, and this required him quitclaiming to Richard Whittington the manor of Over Lypiatt. There is no further mention of the manor until after Whittington's death, when his brother Robert and nephew Guy claimed that he had left the manor in trust for them.[12] However, there was no provision for this in Whittington's will and the claim was contested by his surviving trustee, Thomas Roos, who refused to grant it to them. We hear no more of the claim, but at some future date Robert or most likely Guy must have been successful, as by 1457 it had passed to the latter's son Thomas, and in 1505 it descended to the ownership of his grandson Robert Wye.[13]

32

PESTILENCE AND ICE

In the course of Whittington's third term as mayor a violent plague raged in England, swept away vast numbers of inhabitants of its metropolis and obliged the king to remove his court to Gloucester.[1]

October 1406

From the start of his tenure at the end of October 1406, it is possible that Whittington had to deal with what some writers describe as a further visitation of plague, said to have gripped London during the period 1405–7 and reported to have led to many deaths. The evidence that London continued to function and prosper during these two years suggests that if this was plague, it was certainly not a recurrence of the Black Death. As its disruptive effects on the city's economy and the scale of its casualties are barely recorded, it seems to have been much less serious and resulted in far less loss of life than the episodes of 1348, 1361 or 1369. The nature and extent of this latest pestilence are much disputed and have produced altogether different views on what really happened. In his seminal history of the bubonic plague, John Shrewsbury summarised the competing assessments:

> To return now to records of pestilence, Short affirms that London sustained a death toll of 30,000 of its citizens from pestilence in 1406 but Noorthouk transfers this figure to 1407. Creighton and Vine cite Walsingham for the report that 30,000 people died of plague in London sometime between 1405 and 1407, both dates inclusive. Grafton declares that 'the plague of pestilence'—by which phrase he meant Bubonic Plague—'reigned so sore' during the summer of 1405 in London and the surrounding country that Henry IV dared not reside in his capital.[2]

In his own sweeping and detailed history of the plague, Charles Creighton observes that 'The first great outburst of plague in the fifteenth century falls somewhere between 1405 and 1407. "So great pestilence," says the St Alban's annalist, under the year 1407, "had not been seen for many years." In London "thirty thousand men and women" are reported to have died in a short space.'[3] Creighton supports the view that it was extensive and threatening enough to force the king to take safety in the countryside: 'But it is under the 7th of Henry IV (1405) that Hall's chronicle narrates how the king, to avoid the city on account of the plague, sailed from Queenborough to a port in Essex, and so to Pleshey, "there to pass his time till the plague were ceased".'[4] Other writers place this outbreak in the summer of 1406, saying that 'London was afflicted synchronously with Bordeaux, Aquitaine and Gascony with a deadly epidemic of malignant dysentery in 1406'. If this is so, then it would have visited in the closing weeks of John Woodcock's mayoralty, but there is no recorded evidence of this, and it certainly did not affect the mayoral convocation of 13 October when Woodcock handed over the reins to Richard Whittington. Nor is there mention of it during Whittington's term, which lasted until the end of September 1407. This suggests that it must have visited in 1405, in which case it had dissipated before Woodcock took office in October of that year. In 2008, Shrewsbury dismissed the contradictory assertions about the timing and precise nature of this outbreak of 'plague' as 'a chronological tangle and statistical absurdity'. Perhaps the real nature of the 'pestilence' lay, he suggested, in Macgowan's reference to dysentery, a relentless killer on the battlefield during the Hundred Years War—it was the cause of the Black Prince's death—and, at home, increasingly river-borne by the early 1400s. The cancellation of Parliament suggests that this 'plague' may have arrived on the lower Thames during the early spring of 1407 during the second half of Whittington's mayoralty. Wary of claims that its visitation may have resulted in as many as 30,000 deaths in London (out of a population which then probably did not exceed 55,000), Shrewsbury concludes that if a virulent disease had indeed befallen the city and its outlying areas during this period, then Macgowan may have it partly right: 'a water-borne epidemic of cholera or typhoid fever or an epidemic of malignant dysentery, could have killed that number further afield along the lower reaches of the Thames during a summer epidemic'.[5] Another chronicle says that 'the plague of 1407 was mostly in the West country. In that year, the 9th of Henry IV, there is a petition from Ilchester in Somerset for a remission of dues "because the town is so impoverished and desolate of people that the burgesses are unable to pay the said ferme", and for the cancelling of all arrears due since the 43rd year of Edward III' (1369).[6] The fact that London appears to have functioned as normal throughout 1406–7 suggests that a far-reaching episode of 'plague' or some other virulent contagion was not, after all, a substantial challenge that Richard Whittington had to contend with. But there were others.

Brewers, February 1407

During his third term Whittington not only acted in the governance of London and as the principal official conduit between the City and the king but was required to execute the formalities of other roles assigned him by the Crown and those informal 'assignments' given to him by Henry IV as and when circumstances demanded. On 20 February 1407, he was reappointed as the collector of the wool custom for London, an office he would hold until 26 July 1410. This was an appointment by the Crown and had little to do with his responsibilities as mayor, though even for someone of Whittington's energy and skills the expectations, if not the day-to-day duties, must have been a distraction, not least as he began to grapple in this month with a difficult assignment which would colour this and especially his final mayoralty of 1419–20. While, as mayor, he had some responsibility for setting and monitoring standards and for determining 'official prices' charged by the purveyors of ale, wine, meat and fish, including the authority to inspect goods and premises, he encountered an intractable obstacle in the form of one of London's most formidable and pugnacious commercial interests.

> The brewers, being independent, were not trusted at all. Ale-conners were elected in each ward, whose pleasant duty was to taste every brewing made for sale and to assign it to one of the grades priced by the mayor. Beadles checked the measuring vessels and were allowed to confiscate a third of any ale that was being sold dishonestly. Despite all these precautions, there were constant complaints that brewers and caterers sold above the official price.[7]

It was here that his role as mayor and the king's own financial interests converged and where Whittington found himself hard pressed on both counts. Henry had determined that Whittington was one of the few men he could trust to resolve the growing abuses within the brewing trade, which deprived him of revenue, and which provoked unrest among his subjects. The mercer had acquired a reputation for incorruptibility and fairness and conducted his affairs with a high order of morality. Now, in the early months of his term, he was instructed to investigate claims that the bulk import of barley for London's brewing industry had been rigged to avoid paying the full excise duty. Some of the consignments had been adulterated with other inferior grain, while quantities had been taken off the market and secreted for long periods to create scarcity and drive up prices. Lengthy storage also meant that it was likely to become riddled with vermin and contaminated by rot and mildew. Customers were paying through the nose for short measures and for dangerously adulterated sour ale likely to make them unwell.

Whittington knew that he would need to confront the brewers' leaders directly and in terms they understood. Severe penalties on or closure of their hugely profitable businesses, the impugning of their reputations, the repayment with interest of their skipped taxes, and the threat of imprisonment were among the chief options. Those closest to him would have counselled him against it, as the power and influence of the brewers were forceful and pervasive. When it came, his assault on their business dealings was received as an impertinent affront to one of London's most powerful and intimidating companies. They had not been questioned or assailed in this way before. It is likely that when he first summoned them to the Guildhall, they imagined that it would be for no more than a slap on the wrist; that they would be required to pay a small compromise figure or donate to the mayor's costs or to a nominated charity to buy him off. Through these emollients the whole affair would subside. However, the brewers dismissed the gravity of Whittington's mission, authorised directly by the king, and wholly misjudged his resolve to see it through, and in full. Settling the matter with a gentle reproval, accepting a gift as a measure of good faith or acquiescing in a shallow promise to do better next time was not Whittington's way, and he seems to have been particularly forceful in making clear that he would marshal the evidence required to enable the king to put the leaders on trial and send them to prison for malpractice. Making an example of them also removed the soft option of serving for a short time in the relative comfort of Ludgate. Instead, they would find themselves dispatched to the horrors of Newgate. They would hardly have believed their ears: some would have tossed the threat aside; others would have tried to buy him off. The prudent would have counselled their fellows to pay up for now, swallow their pride, and withdraw to fight another day.

The charges were undeniable—tax evasion, the corruption of goods, price rigging, and the dispensing of short measure. How would this look in London's watering holes? As he concluded his case, Whittington delivered the blow he had held in reserve: the king had instructed him to send in 'meters' to the brewers' tied taverns with the specific purpose of examining their measures and the quality of their ale. Those falling short now understood what to expect. At the time his victory must have seemed like the *coup de grâce*, but he would discover twelve years later that he had won only the first skirmish, not the ensuing war.

April 1407

At the end of February, the Exchequer had raised £25,000 towards Henry's needs at Calais, but the sum was still deemed insufficient. In March, further loans were called for, with Thomas Knolles finding £200 and the Earl of Westmoreland a similar amount. Arundel, now Chancellor, announced that the backpay owed to the Calais garrison, vital to Henry's defences and his ambitions for expansion, was seriously in arrears. Morale was draining, and the seizure of the wool staple by angry soldiers threatened the prospect of rebellion. Historically, part of the wool subsidy at Calais had been reserved for the garrison's upkeep and the remuneration of its complement, about 800 men apportioned between the town and its outlying defences.

> It had been the practice to earmark part of the subsidy in wool for the garrison, which was itself guarding the market where the wool was sold, so that by a simple operation of credit it had been possible to pay the troops at Calais with the cash received from the merchants. This system worked well enough if the exchequer had ample cash and credit for the king's current expenses in England: but this was not so now.[8]

The cost of maintaining the Calais garrison was estimated at around £17,000 a year, equivalent to about a sixth of the entire annual income raised by the Exchequer. The ratio was no longer sustainable, but the immediate concern was to quickly refinance Calais, address the grievances of its troops, rebuild confidence, and restore some semblance of normality. After a period of intense consultation in which Whittington was instrumental, it was announced on 29 and 30 April that London's mayor and incumbent mayor of the Calais staple would, with other merchants of the staple, provide an urgent financial fix in the form of a collective loan to the

Crown of £4,000. In turn, Henry undertook to repay the loans in full out of the first cycle of wool subsidies collected from certain English ports. The loan had the effect that Henry must have been relying on, the loosening of the purses of other English and alien merchants. John Hende pledged an additional personal loan of £2,500, secured against his 'keeping' of the cocket seal in the port of London, which gave him collection rights over customs tonnage and poundage. With Hende's contribution as the signal, the pledge quickly climbed to £12,000, though still far short of the cost of maintaining Calais for a full year, and was paid to the treasurer of Calais on 30 June 1407.

This and subsequent episodes demonstrated that Henry had not only come to depend upon, but was now dangerously over-reliant on, a small group of very wealthy Englishmen, mainly but not exclusively Londoners, and an even smaller self-interested group of senior churchmen, not only to periodically plug holes in the economy but arguably to keep it from drowning. Henry has been described by one authority as resorting far more than his predecessor to this very small group, prominent among whom were 'great capitalists such as John Hende, Richard Whittington or Thomas Knolles ... men who could wait some time for repayment'.[9] Another writer reports that 'the face value of worthless tallies cut by Henry's Exchequer was over three times as much as under Richard' and that there was an 'enormous increase in untrustworthiness and insecurity of payment under Henry'.[10] In yet another example of the intensely cliquish nature of appointments at this time, Henry announced in June that Richard Clifford, keeper of the Great Wardrobe during the period of Whittington's large sales to Richard II, had been appointed Bishop of London (1407–21). He was one of the few men for whom Whittington acted as executor. On 24 October, two weeks after he had completed his second full term as mayor, the 1407 Parliament opened in Whittington's home town of Gloucester. He would have been well acquainted with the new Speaker, Thomas Chaucer, son of Geoffrey.

An Arctic Weather Front, October 1407–March 1408

While a visitation of plague, or at least the precise date and extent of it, is much disputed, there is some reporting of an invasive event but one not, it would seem, of any significant or enduring impact on London. That would come instead from an entirely unforeseen and unexpected 'agent', the weather. Barely a fortnight after Whittington's term had ended, London found itself in the early stages of a hugely challenging and prolonged

Arctic front that held England and much of northern Europe in its grip from late October 1407 until March 1408. In London's case the glacial weather endured for fifteen weeks, the Thames froze over, businesses were unable to trade, and food was scarce and sold at a premium. The lives of the sick, the weak, the vulnerable and the hungry were lost. The city had last suffered a severe fall in temperatures during the same months of 1363–4, and some Londoners were old enough to remember the polar winter of 1353–4, which had torn through a population barely recovered from the ravages of the Black Death. Yet both are said to have paled in comparison with the onslaught of 1407–8, when an extreme and prolonged winter, described as 'one of the most rigorous on record', descended on England's capital.[11] Just a fortnight into William Staunton's term, the ground and the city's watercourses were already frigid, and by December the Thames was frozen solid to a considerable depth, producing the rare event of people and cart animals crossing the ice on foot. The 'first authentic report' of the Thames having been frozen over concerned the similarly severe winter of 1149–50 (or 1150–1) when the ice was also apparently thick enough to support men crossing the river on horseback. Londoners were able to cross the river in this way again during the winter of 1204–5 and during the harsh winter of 1309–10; 'dancing took place around a fire built on the ice and a hare was coursed on the frozen waterway'.[12] Where sport had shown the way, enterprise and entertainment would surely follow. In the early weeks of 1408, it was said that thousands of Londoners converged on the banks of the frozen river to view the extraordinary spectacle of a great frost fair. 'Thys yere was ordened the alay of golde. And the kynges sonnes beten in Chepe. And this yere was the grete frost and ise and the most sharpest wenter that ever man sawe, and it duryd fourteen wekes, so that men myght in dyvers places both goo and ryde over the Temse.'[13]

There is no reliable measure of how thick the ice was at this time, but if the Greyfriars Chronicle is accurate, then, having located its greatest depth, even those on horseback deemed it safe enough to cross. As in other parts of Europe, the freeze would block ports and slow trade, but only for a short time. Londoners had learned to become increasingly resilient and ride out whatever life might throw at them. In the middle of February, at snowbound Bramham Moor in frozen Yorkshire Henry IV would finally dispatch the rebellion of the Duke of Northumberland and break the power of the Percys; and Richard and Alice Whittington would surely have been deepening their plans to realise their joint vision.

33

LOSS

Whittington entered the new year re-elected as warden of the Mercers' Company for 1408–9, but it is not until 1409 that he comes once more into close view. A combination of reasons may explain this. He had just completed two of the most arduous years of his business and civic life. He would need time, like many merchants with strong interests in import–export, to reorder his trading arrangements after the disruption caused by the great freeze. He had accepted high-level offices and tasks from the king on which the Crown depended for revenue, and he remained a first port of call for private loans. He had completed an eventful third term as mayor and had taken up the difficult challenge presented by the brewers. These demands on his attention were surely enough to exhaust most figures, but Whittington was now confronted by events much closer to home which would impact on him deeply. He may have already anticipated what lay ahead as 1408 unfolded, uppermost in his considerations a growing concern with the uncertain state of his wife's health and a consequent urgency to accelerate their shared vision for St Michael's. The health of the king was also a matter of great personal concern. It was not until 1408 had passed and 1409 was ushered in that some of his hopes and fears would be better understood.

On 18 March 1409 he assisted in resolving a case brought before the mayor's court, presided over by Drew Barantyn, by agreeing under extenuating circumstances to take on Robert Steven, son of Laurence Steven, a mercer from Great Yarmouth, thereby providing under his aegis a solitary and unplanned opportunity for the boy to complete his apprenticeship following the imprisonment of his previous master, William Butte, for debt. Superficially, it was an example of the Mercers' Company looking after their own and accruing the 'social capital' provided by the generous intervention of the highly esteemed Whittington. AH Thomas writes that the boy was 'exonerated from his apprenticeship to William Butte, mercer, who was then in the Fleet prison and had ceased to instruct and provide for him. The apprentice was then committed by the court to Richard Whityngton, mercer, to serve the remainder of his term.'[1] There was, however, some 'history' to this. Butte had come before Whittington, then mayor of the staple, two years earlier on 11 February 1407 when he had been sued for debts of £1,000 owing to two other mercers, Roger Wringleworth and Richard Everard. It was reported at that time, somewhat quaintly, that Butte 'was not found in the bailiwick'. In modern parlance he had 'done a runner'.[2]

A month later it was back to business. On 18 April 1409, assisted by Henry London and the chaplain John Chamberlain, Whittington acquired from his friend the draper William Weston and his wife Joan a site in their ownership adjoining St Michael Paternoster church. It would be a further eight months before a royal licence was obtained on 20 December enabling the land to be granted to St Michael's future priest John White and his successors, with the intention of rebuilding the church. After a further delay, which offers some insight into the queues that had formed in seeking permission for acquisition, planning and development in London at this time, the granting of the licence to White was finally completed on 13 April 1411, while preparatory works at College Hill had almost certainly begun in the summer of 1409. The re-edification of the church of St Michael Paternoster Royal itself is likely to have been triggered by a rapid decline in Alice Whittington's health and her impending death. One of the immediate tasks was the construction of her tomb towards the end of July.[3] Before that, in May 1409 Henry IV appointed Whittington to supervise the collection in England of the papal revenues, Peter's Pence.

The Physician, October 1410

During 1410 Alice Whittington's already failing health was debilitated further by regular bouts of severe illness and increasing frailty. Her condition had probably first developed during 1409 or possibly earlier, perhaps harbouring the virus that had originated in the summer of 1407. Alternatively, like many Londoners, she may have developed something akin to pneumonia in the shockingly freezing conditions of the winter of 1408. If the latter, her respiratory strength may have been aggravated further by the invasive effects of the airborne dust and pollution that drifted upwards from London's industry and from its burgeoning domestic hearths, which deposited their poisons throughout the city's densely packed buildings and streets. By October 1410 her situation had worsened considerably and, judging by the events that followed, she must have already exhausted the remedies and expertise of the best English physicians that her husband could buy. Her life hung in the balance.

Whittington was desperate. In a remarkable and unprecedented approach to Henry IV, he beseeched the king to allow him to bring to England a physician of great repute, Master Thomas Sampson of 'Mierbeawe' (Mirabeau in Vaucluse). It was a last throw of the dice, a desperate attempt by a distraught husband to procure for his dying wife the finest expertise available. Bringing someone over from mainland Europe would have been complicated enough—the logistics alone would have been formidable at this time—but what makes Whittington's request so complex, so challenging and so controversial was that the physician was not only an 'alien'—and there were many even in his own rarefied circles who would have rejected the very thought of a foreigner ministering to the daughter of an English nobleman and wife of one of London's most unimpeachable figures—but an eminent Jew.

If the request and the identity of the physician were not exceptional enough, even more astonishing was Henry's assent, with the king granting Whittington the request as a mark of royal favour. It was a momentous episode in Whittington's relationship with his wife and with his king and in the conditions and circumstances of English statute, royal prerogative and social convention. Jews had been forcibly driven from England by the Edict of Expulsion imposed by Edward I in 1290, fifteen years after he had forbidden them to practise usury.[4]

At the time of Alice Whittington's illness, Jews were believed to have been removed entirely from England and were certainly no longer present to offer their essential medicinal services as apothecaries or physicians. Yet just forty miles away across the Channel such services remained in high regard and were widely sought. To an ordinary Londoner it would have seemed either a miracle or an unthinkable breach of statute that a Jewish physician could be found, engaged and transported to England at great cost and be admitted in direct contravention of one of England's most demeaning statutes to practise his skills on an Englishwoman, in the centre of London, in the home of one of its most eminent citizens, and with the blessing of its king.[5]

The procurement of Sampson of Mirabeau was one of the most exceptional of Richard Whittington's many achievements.[6] He was probably the only man in England, held in such high esteem and with sufficient sway over the Crown, who could dare to ask the monarch, in contravention of an ugly and divisive law that had stood for 120 years, to accede to such a deeply personal request. That Henry granted him his wish is either a striking reflection of his respect for Whittington or a measure of his reliance on the mercer's abilities. These were not easy times, even for someone of Whittington's prodigious resources, to get word to someone remote from England in every sense. How had he heard of this man and his reputation? The clue probably lies in his business relationships, his trading links throughout Europe and his access to agents, far-reaching networks and influential friends throughout the European mainland, including perhaps leading figures in the Hansa. As a merchant of great stature, he would have been well placed to advertise his needs and make discreet enquiries of those who might help him. Such a man would surely be in great demand among Whittington's counterparts in one of the ports which had a significant Jewish population and where the skills of their physicians were well known and highly regarded—Antwerp, Ghent, Bruges, even Paris. In the autumn he located one. Bringing him to London was another matter, but here again Whittington was well connected and well placed, able surely to procure a fast ship and a discreet captain to convey his charge to one of London's quieter quays, and from there a swift horse and cart to speed the man and his life-saving talents to Alice's bedside.

It was all about measuring risk. For his part, Sampson would need to be assured that he was accorded absolute safety of passage in travelling to England and the highest immunity when he arrived there. With papers sealed by Whittington or even by the king himself, there would still have been great uncertainty about what might lie ahead. What if he was compromised en route; what if his identity was discovered on arrival in England or advertised in London? What if he failed to save Alice Whittington's life—she was, after all, very seriously ill and he was her last resort? On the other hand, he had been granted permission by Henry IV, he was under the protection of one of London's richest men, and he was dedicated to his profession. He apparently decided to take his chances. For his part, Whittington appears to have disregarded the significant risk to his own position, a so far unimpeachable standing and reputation, assembled and polished over a period of three decades. His wife mattered more, and he was effectively setting Alice's health and his own ability to influence the king above all else. To his peers and to ordinary Londoners it would have seemed exactly as it was, one rule for the rich and influential and one for the rest. Whittington's love for his wife and his desperation to save her provide one of the few insights we have into his personal life. Her welfare produces the only known instance where he places his private interest above convention and statute. He not only enlists the help of the king in circumventing the law but consorts with someone whose presence and religious interests were bound to draw opposition and censure. The terms of Sampson's licence were that he was to attend Alice Whittington and confine himself to the Whittingtons' premises, and was prohibited from practising elsewhere, for a year. The last is an interesting condition because it implies that, having overcome the legal barrier, he would be able to remain and continue to practise in England.

There was, however, a further and unexpected twist: Henry IV's own health. A vigorous and sturdy figure at the time of his coronation in 1399, married twice and the father of four sons, Henry had experienced since the summer of 1405 frequent and startling episodes of ill health. In just five years he had undergone a significant physical decline for someone who, Ian Mortimer reminds us, was the only English king to set foot within the walls of Jerusalem, probably the greatest tournament knight produced by the English royal family, and an accomplished musician and scholar.[7]

These sporadic bouts of acute pain and illness occurred primarily in June 1405, April 1406 and June 1408, a period during which, as noted, contemporary chroniclers and modern writers have remarked that London was visited by a virulent epidemic. Was this the reason during the summer of 1405 that Henry 'dared not reside in his capital', in which 'plague' is said to have 'reigned so sore', and a clue to a condition which first appears in June of that year? Did he withhold himself from London because the city was indeed gripped at this earlier moment by a pestilence or because he already had a fearful condition that he did not wish to communicate? The answer is complicated by the fact that his next two 'attacks' also coincide with dates given for outbreaks of pestilence in London. Is it conceivable, given his own tribulations, that Henry felt such a deep empathy for Whittington's plight that his personal compassion caused him to flex his obligations as head of state? Or was there some other factor, something altogether different? Was this an opportunity to offer 'penance' for an act which he had come to regret, the execution on 8 June 1405 of Richard Scrope, Archbishop of York, for his part in the rebellion of the Earl of Northumberland? At least one contemporary writer, Thomas Gascoigne, was convinced that Henry's fearful collapse on the road from

York to Ripon 'with horrible leprosy of the worst sort', and at what he contends was the exact moment of the execution, was his punishment for taking the clergyman's life.[8] Was Henry minded later to 'repent' by helping to ease the pain and suffering of others close to him? Was this a factor in his decision to consent to a Jewish physician attending the wife of someone he held in such high esteem?[9]

On the other hand, in granting a licence to Sampson was Henry simply mindful of his own deteriorating health and the inability of English physicians to find a cure? Should Sampson prove successful, was it conceivable that he might then address the king's own needs? All this is supposition of course: we are not privy to Henry's precise motives and they are not recorded, if indeed he had any other reason than simply responding to Whittington's plea. As for Alice, Sampson was unable to arrest her decline and she lingered until her death the following summer. Her obituary points to her death on either 30 or 31 July 1411. The nature of her illness and the cause of her death remain unknown. Unable to cure her, Sampson returned to Europe sometime before October 1411 when his licence to attend her for one year would have expired. We do not know whether he could or would have remained in England had Henry granted him an extension. The granting of a longer period would have had far wider ramifications than allowing what could be presented as simply a 'one-off' arrangement, an eventual eight or nine months or so, which the English king might have justified as keeping one of his leading 'wise men' balanced and focused on the national interest. The fact that, in formal terms, the statute of 1290 was not effectively repealed until 1655 suggests that the licence granted to Whittington was the only one of its kind and was not repeated. However, this is not the case, and it was Henry himself who instigated further visits by Jewish physicians to England, specifically to attend to his own needs. A Weiner notes that in his younger days he had spent time in Italy and had visited Lithuania, Poland and Germany, where he had become familiar with the expertise and reputation of Jewish doctors, several of whom 'occupied eminent positions at the courts of his contemporaries'.[10] These included the courts of Henry III of Castile and Boniface IX. Furthermore, there is a suggestion that the king had brought to England his own Jewish physician in the year Whittington is believed to have recruited Sampson of Mirabeau. 'Upon these half-forgotten memories of his youth the king fell back in his time of need. In 1410 the king's illness had become so serious that foreign aid was necessary. The first of the newcomers was Doctor Elias Sabot the Hebrew, brought specially from Bologna.' Who came first is not clear, but Weiner infers that Sabot followed later and that, unlike the narrow constrictions of Sampson's licence, 'The royal protection was extended to Sabot and his retinue for two years with permission to practise his art unmolested in any part of the kingdom, provided they always showed their safe-conduct before entering any town, fortress, or camp of the king.'[11] And later still, having made little progress with Doctor Sabot, in the words of JH Wylie, Henry looked to Europe again and 'followed the prevailing fashion and called in the services of an Italian Jew, Dr David di Nigarelli of Lucca who remained in this country until his death in 1412'.[12] Alice finally succumbed to her illness at the end of July and was buried, as she and her husband had planned, in a tomb which he had built on the north side of the high altar in the church of St Michael Paternoster.

* * *

At the end of 1411 Richard Whittington was still providing small and probably long-term personal loans to a select group of notable clients. These included Sir William Bourchier, later Count of Eu, who is recorded at this time as paying off an advance of £200 from the mercer. However, these were now of minor interest as personal, civic and professional impulses drove him elsewhere. In 1412 Whittington began to develop what would be his most significant friendship and trusted relationship with John Carpenter, the great confidant and talented administrator with whom he would entrust the provisions of his will. Whether they were formally associated before 1412 is not certain, but given that Carpenter had by then been in the service of the City of London for twenty years or more, it is unthinkable that they would not have encountered each other before January of that year. The catalyst that drew them together in the early part of 1412 was probably Henry IV's choice of Whittington to lead an inquiry in London into the 'liability' of citizens for taxation. As Carpenter had been a close observer of the governance of the city since his youth, apprenticed to John Marchaunt, his predecessor as town clerk, we may assume that Whittington called upon his noted legal administrative talents during his inquiry. Brewer describes him somewhat excitedly as

> distinguished by his general attainments and learning; his knowledge of the laws customs and privileges of this city; his integrity of character, and universal benevolence. From his earliest youth he was devoted to the service of his fellow citizens, and throughout the course of his life proved himself a ready defender of their rights and a zealous promoter of their interests. He was

elected Common Clerk or Town Clerk of London AD MCCCCXVII and held that office for twenty-one years, during which period he compiled the valuable treatise still extant under the title of 'Liber Albus'.[13]

The two men found immediate common ground in their complementary interests and skills and in their origins. Carpenter's family hailed from Dilwyn, Herefordshire, close to where some of Whittington's own kin originated. Indeed, his relatives the de Solers had given their name to the neighbouring settlement of Dilwyn Solers.[14] Like John Woodcock, Whittington's new friend believed that a man's route to progress and status was to assemble as much property and land as he could, and they would go on to share a vision that men of their ilk should strive to improve the governance of their city, establish an ordered and lasting record of their efforts, and shape the regulations that would be necessary for them to do so. Of all his friends and associates John Carpenter would be the closest to Whittington and the confidant he chose to fulfil his legacy and the distribution of his estate after his death. In 1428 he was chosen as an executor for another of Whittington's circle, John Shadworth.

It was Carpenter alone whom Whittington consulted in 1421 on the content and purpose of his will and to Carpenter as his senior executor that he awarded its oversight and implementation. Here was a perfect match of foresight and capabilities, the entrusting of London's most gifted administrator with the posthumous ambitions of its greatest merchant and civic leader. It is Carpenter who is often cited as the single-minded driving force behind the deployment of Whittington's fortune in charitable and civic works. We come to this later. He was aged 40 when the two began to forge their relationship. His immersion in the intricate workings of London's interest groups and his knowledge of English and commercial law were valued highly. Apprenticed to the City as a young boy, he had acquired an unrivalled understanding of the complexities of civil administration and a mastery of legal contracts. Married to a Dutch wife from Zeeland, he also understood the essential relationship between trade and immigration. While it was not until around 1420 that Whittington began to work through the terms of his will, occasioning the moment when Carpenter really comes to the fore in this story, he had been selected— 'talent-spotted' perhaps—by the mercer long before then to act as his principal confidant, and we can imagine Whittington conferring with him over a lengthy period.

* * *

The Will of Sir Ivo Fitzwarin

In October, following the successive mayoralties of the grocers Thomas Knolles and Robert Chichele, another of Whittington's circle, the mercer William Walderne, stepped up for the 1412–3 term. He would later also hold the office at the time of his friend's death. For much of 1412 Whittington was most occupied by the provisions of someone else's will, and we hear little of him until November when he brought a lawsuit against one of his 'agents', a Thomas Chapman of Market Harborough, for failing to render an account. The episode presents one of those few, but revealing, instances where Whittington used the law to rebuke those who had breached his trust. It was no more than a momentary diversion from a far more important matter, one closer to home and a sharp reminder of his recent loss. Earlier in the year he had been appointed by Sir Ivo Fitzwarin as one of his executors, the only one named in the will written up on 6 November 1412. It must have provided something of a template for Whittington's own arrangements drafted with Carpenter in 1421. There are notable commonalities in their avoidance of ostentation and their insistence that their demise should benefit the less fortunate. Fitzwarin wished to return 'home' to his favoured place in Berkshire, instructing that his body 'be buried in the chancel, next my father in the parish church of Wantynge, on the north part of the aforesaid chancel'. His executors were to 'make no great expenses about my hearse for pomp of the world, but that they feed neighbours and other poor folk on the day of my burial, so that they pray for my soul.'[15] His assets were widely dispersed, chiefly to religious houses, the beneficiaries including the abbot and monks of Milton in Hampshire, the monks at Cerne Abbas in Dorset, and orders of friars at Bristol, Ilchester and Dorchester. Each was endowed to say Masses and pray for his soul and that of his wife Maud and his sister Philippa Fitzwarin, a nun at Wilton in Wiltshire. To the great church of Sarum, he gifted 'a great missal, covered with red and black bawdekyn' and he asked for them 'to pray for me and my ancestors for ever and to hold my obit yearly'. To the church and chapel of Caundle Haddon, a village closely associated with his wife's family, he left 'my best vestments of red silk gilt, of one suit, viz., a cope and a chasuble, with the tunicles and all their belongings', and he made similar gifts to his local parish church at Wantage. Of more interest here are his reference and bequests to 'Richard Whityngton, my son, a silver gilt piece, ywrite around, with a cover of the same make, and a pair [i.e. set] of paternosters of pure gold, enamelled with clear red, with gawds of pure gold enamelled with white in the form of a head of Saint John the Baptist'.[16] Whittington, his 'son', is the only named executor and is referred to with much resonance as 'Richd. Whityngton, citizen of London'. The one person not mentioned and whose omission must have caused great sorrow for both men is his daughter Alice.

* * *

A Royal Death, 20 March 1413

The death of Alice in July 1411 proved to be the first of three traumatic losses for Whittington. Her father made his will and withdrew permanently from London to what would be his eventual resting place at Wantage. His death, when it came, would be no surprise and his son-in-law was to some extent prepared for it. Fitzwarin would hang on for some time yet. It was a death outside the family, however, that would have the most unsettling impact, that of the man who had set aside the law to help Whittington's beloved wife. On 20 March 1413 Henry IV finally succumbed to a combination of conditions that had debilitated him since 1405. His life passed in the apt surroundings of the Jerusalem Chamber in the abbot's house at Westminster Abbey during a session of Parliament.[17] Whittington would find himself serving his third English king in the short span of fourteen years, one who made clear from the outset that he would continue the war with France and that he would require loans and hike taxes in order to do so. Unlike his relationships with Richard II and Henry IV, Whittington had no 'history' with this latest monarch other than being favoured by his father. Would that be enough? It didn't take long to find out that he was still valued, still of use, but that the extent of his service would expand into new and unfamiliar territory, some of it challenging, some deeply unsettling. He must have been taken aback to find himself appointed in the latter stages of 1413 as one of the supervisors and accountants for Henry V's renewal of work to the nave of Westminster Abbey, begun by Richard II, to which he himself had contributed funding twelve years earlier in 1401–2. His role this time would be as 'joint commissioner' to oversee the works to the great abbey, essentially administering the pricing and costs of building work—a far greater challenge than his limited experience at St Michael's allowed for. His responsibilities were quickly extended to approving all major building works in London and acting as the king's watchman for quality and expenditure while he was away campaigning. If the supervision of the king's building works was challenging and unfamiliar, Henry also had in store a position that would severely stretch Whittington's moral compass. It was also a test of loyalties. Following a revolt of Lollards on 9–10 January 1414 at St Giles's Fields, led by John Oldcastle, Whittington was instructed to lead a royal commission to identify and 'seize lollards at large', a group for whom he may well have had some sympathies. Oldcastle's revolt led to the capture and imprisonment on 23 January of Sir Thomas Beauchamp, a former retainer to Henry IV and a man well known to Whittington. Beauchamp was taken to the Tower and placed in chains. On 8 February, presumably with Henry's acquiescence, Whittington and three other influential Londoners agreed to stand surety in the sum of 1,000 marks for Beauchamp on his pledge that, freed of his chains, he would not try to escape and would be a 'true prisoner'. He would remain confined, however, until his release on 13 September. He was eventually acquitted on 26 October.[18]

So, what must Whittington have thought of his next task for Henry V, the recruitment in March 1414 of carpenters to accelerate reconstruction at the king's favourite project, Westminster Abbey? He would spend much of that month trying to remedy the shortage of skilled artisans needed for the abbey roof and having to source more labour generally to get the project back on schedule: all very distracting. What might have captured his interest rather more was the passing in April by Parliament of a statute for the reform of hospitals following evidence of corruption and the abuse of funds and manipulation of the foundations whose remit was to govern them. In 1410 the Commons had presented a petition to Henry IV, and now they presented one to his successor, urging both kings to examine the degradation of England's hospitals, essentially its almshouses for the poor, and to deprive those charged with their upkeep, particularly the Church, which had presided over an appalling decline of their assets. This formed part of a wider political assault on the temporal wealth of the English Church. The higher clergy had grown fat, corrupt and arrogant with wealth and property, and showed little interest in the poor or, for that matter, in their own rank-and-file priests and clerics. Events of 8 April 1414 brought matters to a head. The petition appealed to the generous spirit of successive English kings and the nobility in making provision for the poor, the pregnant, the infirm and the afflicted. While they had established hospitals and almshouses throughout the land from their own resources,

Now, however, most gracious lord a great number of the hospitals within your said kingdom have collapsed, and the goods and profits of the same have been taken away and put to other uses by spiritual men as well as temporal, because of which many men and women have died in great misery through lack of help, livelihood and succour, to the displeasure of God.[19]

Henry bought into the proposition, assenting to the petition, undertaking to instruct inspection visits of those which had been established by royal decree, and agreeing to establish royal commissions to bring them back to good order. He appointed Richard Clifford, Bishop of London, 'to enquire about the foundation, governance and estate of the hospitals within his diocese, and to certify in Chancery those being of royal foundation and patronage, and to make reform of others'.[20] The Commons wanted more, contending that appropriation by the Crown of the Church's temporal wealth could be put to better use—the alleviation of poverty, the improvement of degraded almshouses, the building of new facilities in every town, the commissioning of hospitals and, in a direct appeal to the king's favourite interest, the stripping of the Church's vast wealth to fund his armies. Contained in this was the ulterior hope that by focusing on the Church, it could shift the king's attention from exacting taxation from the City. For Whittington this was encouraging, progressive. It affirmed that his own vision for St Michael's, which he had initiated before the first petition in 1410, was consistent with and a potential exemplar for the emerging zeitgeist.

On 6 August 1414 there was a momentary diversion for the mercer, when he was proclaimed among his fellow aldermen Thomas Knolles, Richard Marlowe, Robert Chichele and Nicholas Wootton and alongside London's mayor, William Cromer, and the Chancellor of the Exchequer, Henry Somer, as being in receipt of a grant by Thomas Horsham and his wife Alice of all their tenements called 'le Barge' in 'Bokerelesbury', the former manor of the Bukerel family in the parish of St Stephen Walbrook, better known today as Bucklersbury, near the intersection of Poultry and Walbrook, and close to what is now Bank underground station. The relief was momentary. On 6 September 1414 the event that Whittington feared most finally confronted him, the loss of his father-in-law, the man who had been his mentor, his early sponsor, his introducer at court, and one of the principal guiding influences in his life. Fitzwarin's death was not unexpected: he had been ill for two years and had suffered the physical and mental wear and tear of many years of soldiering, and of time in governance and administration and in London's trade and enterprise. Sir Ivo

LOSS

Fitzwarin was buried in Wantage church against the wall of the north aisle, his life represented by a striking brass figure clad in full armour with the distinct and very rare feature of a moustache.

34

NEW PURPOSE

In October 1414 the draper William Cromer was succeeded by one of Richard Whittington's former apprentices, the mercer Thomas Faulconer, during a year that would advance further the status of London's mayor. The ceremonial aspects of the mayor's office had been gaining strength since Whittington's last term in 1406–7. Since then, the mayor's entry to office had involved quite lavish ritual and ceremony, leaving no one in doubt that after the king he was the centre of power in England's capital city. In 1415 his status strengthened further. At meetings at the Guildhall, it was the mayor who now took precedence over the king's kin, his archbishops and senior members of the nobility in the newly reordered seating arrangements. At meetings within the City, the perception was now reality: London's mayor was trumped only by the king himself.

Richard Whittington, meanwhile, discovered that bad pennies have a habit of reappearing. He can hardly have expected that his dispute of 1404 with the litigant and rogue John Hert would be reignited in 1415 by his formidable and troublesome future wife Joan. Ten years had passed since the pair, yet to be married, had pledged on statute to repay Whittington within four months the sum of £651. Yet here he was, a decade later, having already been ceded the mortgage on Joan Hert's house on London Bridge, still waiting for the full debt to be repaid. It didn't help that Hert also attacked Whittington's reputation by defaming him in the courts. It was Whittington, she asserted, who owed *her* money and recompense for subterfuge, and there were many among his enemies eager to believe her. Remarkably, it would take until June 1419 for his dispute with Joan Hert to be finally resolved. After fifteen years of wrangling, defamation and bouts of slander, the courts finally upheld Whittington's defence and removed the stain of Hert's assault on his reputation. She had proved to be a tenacious, vindictive and underestimated rogue.

27 May 1415

Happily, the king wasn't among those who doubted him. On the contrary, Henry was far more interested in extending Whittington's responsibilities further. The minutes of the King's Council held at the Tower of London on 27 May 1415 record Henry instructing that henceforth no buildings of consequence in the city could be demolished or erected without Whittington first viewing and approving the proposals on his behalf. Henry also made clear that on his return home from the war in France, he expected to find London in far better order than he left it. What had prompted this double-edged trust? In matter of fact, Whittington was rather well qualified. This included his proven ability to supervise projects and get things done: as a three-times former mayor, he had exercised considerable oversight over the city's buildings and infrastructure; his private interest in and financial support for the restoration and improvement of London was well established; he was a known and fierce opponent of graft and corruption; he had resolved the complex financing of repairs to London Bridge; and he had also endowed funds to maintain the bridge constructed at Rochester in 1391, to which both Henry IV and Henry V made contributions. Aside from this, Henry knew that this was not the first time a king had invested a well-known figure with such an apparently unusual responsibility. Hadn't Richard II appointed Geoffrey Chaucer in July 1389 as clerk of the king's works with a responsibility for the management of the Crown's building and repair projects, including oversight of Henry Yevele's work on the nave of Westminster Abbey and the construction of the jousting lists at Smithfield?[1] At least Whittington avoided another of Chaucer's one-time charges, the condition and cleansing of London's parlous sewers, though even here his curriculum vitae might have stretched a bit, having initiated a clean-up of the effluent-choked Fleet and Walbrook during his first two mayoralties. Yet Henry's true purpose, surely, was that Whittington would personally contribute or raise from other sources the funding for outstanding repairs and improvements deemed essential to those parts of London's townscape that he expected to gleam when he returned victorious from France. This was in June 1415, when the Great Wardrobe owed the mercer at least £600. That Whittington appears not to have pressed for repayment of what largely amounted to Henry's personal debts to him, and indeed would soon find the means to lend further to the king, suggests someone not simply able to extend credit and even write off large debts, but one excited by his 'proximity' to the irrepressible Henry, able to observe the political game at close quarters, and exert some influence over the king's economic and commercial ambitions.[2] A letter sent by the Duke of Albany, Regent of Scotland, to the Earl of Cambridge shortly before the latter's conspiracy against Henry V in July 1415 provides a useful measure of Whittington's standing. Albany had agreed to encourage the plot by releasing a 'pretender' to the English Crown claiming to be Richard II in return for a suitable hostage. Albany would accept any one of eighteen prominent Englishmen. Among the list of bishops and leading members of the nobility were two Londoners, one the wealthy goldsmith Drew Barantyn, the other Whittington.[3]

In contrast to the financial flexibility and leniency he reserved for king and court, Whittington was far less tolerant of those not blessed by title or privilege to whom he had made loans and who defaulted on their obligations—not least if he later suspected that they were 'playing a long game', as the Herts had done, hoping perhaps that he might not outlive or might even forget the arrangement. On 20 October 1415 he acceded to a request that would still occupy his estate ten years later. He had lent to a then unmarried woman, Eleanor Busshe, the significant sum of 600 marks, which neither she nor her husband Ralph Busshe had made any effort to repay by the time of his death in March 1423. This was an extraordinary amount to lend to a single woman, and perhaps the clue here is that she and her husband were from Caundle in Dorset, a place closely tied to Sir Ivo Fitzwarin and which features prominently in his will. Eleanor Busshe appears to have presented to Whittington an undertaking given to her by Fitzwarin before his death. Apparently, he had died before it could be contracted. Busshe may have presented this as an unfortunate default on Fitzwarin's part in which the family honour was at stake or else she was exploiting a situation in which Fitzwarin could no longer respond. Alternatively, it may have been an elaborate 'scam'. Given the sum involved, a housing or smallholding transaction seems the most likely purpose for the loan. Whatever the explanation, as his named executor, Whittington stepped in and made good Fitzwarin's allegedly unfulfilled 'undertaking'. A decade later the debt remained outstanding. The matter now fell to Whittington's own executors. In a case brought before the Hilary session of the Court of Common Pleas in 1425, John Coventre, John Carpenter and William Grove presented Whittington's will in court. They claimed repayment to his estate of a reduced sum of £200 and a further £20 for damages. The Busshes admitted the claim and their debt of 600 marks in the form claimed. Whittington's executors were authorised to recover the debt and the damages of £20 assessed by the court.[4]

Blackheath, 23 November 1415

Towards the end of October 1415 England received the momentous news that Henry V had been victorious at Agincourt, on St Crispin's Day.[5] For Londoners, his ceremonial return a month later was surely the most spectacular event of their lifetime and, for those old enough to have been present, the most memorable they had witnessed since the 14-year-old Richard II had ridden out to meet Wat Tyler 34 years earlier. On 23 November 1415 London was besieged by an altogether different populism heightened by the prolonged uproarious acclamation of the crowds, the endless extravaganza of the pageantry, the deafening cacophony of civic and military salutation, and the hypnotic moments of reverence, obedience and solemnity as its victorious king offered up his thanks to God and pledged his life to his subjects.[6] Had he returned home late that night to savour the day's memorable images, Whittington would have observed from the advantage of College Hill that, far from smouldering with ash, the braziers were still burning fiercely, drawing to their light and heat countless knots of citizens, heady with joy and cheap ale, still celebrating the return of their king and ushering in the first shafts of dawn. Many were relieved that their menfolk were now safe and well, either home already or on their way back from France. Whittington, a notable contributor of funds to Henry's latest campaign, would by now have received news that his own kinsman, his nephew Guy, had survived its horrors. Tens of thousands, not only at the centre of the revelry and thanksgiving, but throughout England during the celebrations that overtook every town and village, must have hoped that this was the culmination, the final closure of war with France—an end to the bloodshed, to bereavement, to husbands and sons returning deprived of mind or limb. Yet those acquainted with war and those engaged in trade would have been more circumspect. It was over for the moment; the two sides had simply exhausted each other. They would surely lick their wounds, assess their resources, and refuel their ambitions. Whittington may have reflected more soberly than most that this king was at heart a warrior and in mind an aggrandiser. The pattern and the ambition were as plain as day. He would raise taxation, assemble a new army and press again, further into France. It was simply a matter of time, after a suitable period of recovery. Then he would be knocking at Whittington's door again, asking for more, far more. After all, Henry had said it aloud and publicly: there was no man he trusted more or depended on so much to help fuel his financial needs.

He would be difficult to deny. More than 15,000 citizens had assembled in fields and lanes around Blackheath alone to await Henry's arrival and twice that number in the city itself. Beside the sumptuous awning suspended above the welcoming dais, strewn with flowers and set with thrones of red and gilt for Henry and his queen, were gathered by rank the mayor and aldermen, splendidly arrayed in fiery scarlet, and, beyond them, row after row of lesser citizens and officials in their red cloaks and red-and-white hoods. It was the largest assembly in London since the city had been occupied by the rebellious men and women of Kent and Essex in 1381. The waiting people were far from subdued by the grave loss of their menfolk, or by the threat to income, tenancy and survival their absence would bring. Indeed, the magnificent entry of the king and his queen at the head of cohorts of valiant and splendid knights, whose battered armour had already been beaten out and polished by their squires to minimise the evidence of injury and assault, seemed to galvanise hearts and minds.

The clamour would have subsided to a respectful hush when the heralds signalled to the king to kneel. After he had thanked God and the Church for England's victory, a deafening, widening roar would have erupted among those packed on the heath, and then in the surrounding narrows as he rose to acclaim the bravery of his troops and acknowledge with vigorous waves the raucous support of the crowd itself. One by one, for over three hours, beginning with the mayor and the council, he would have received a seemingly endless procession of senior officers of state and members of court, every bishop of consequence, notable parliamentarians, the noblemen of London and the barony of the shires, the leading commanders and captains of troops, assorted minor dignitaries and the holders of important sinecures, and other leading citizens not yet elevated to such appointments but hopeful still of the king's call, something this public display would certainly assure. Typically, a king would speak briefly to some, out of gratitude, special interest or fondness, but, for the most part, he would return a simple courtesy as each kneeled before him before rising and returning to their appointed place. The job done, each would remember and remind others of this moment, and Henry was well placed to remind them if he needed to.

Yet it was the Thames and its iconic bridge, the entry and gathering point for many of those involved at Agincourt and those now assembled to acknowledge their victory, the lung of this ambitious, indefatigable mercantile city—its conduit for both trade and war—that many would remember most this day. The structure was garlanded with so many flowers and lined so deeply on each side by a swollen press of citizens, barely kept in check by infantry and marshals from London's 25 wards, that many must have feared its collapse. The overhanging three-storey houses would have seemed more precarious than ever amid the relentless reverberations of the crowd and the thunderous rattle of armoured destriers, scores of horses and carts, and what then passed for 'carriages', appearing almost to totter as if the clamour would topple them into the river. The crescendo was so overwhelming that it drowned out the familiar roar of the water as its deafening rush was forced between the piers and starlings. Every citizen and office-holder of any worth had jostled for a precarious foothold on this narrow suspension over the Thames to ensure their own memorable place in England's history. Somewhere at the very front would have stood London's most acclaimed mayor, as consumed as any man with the magnificence of the victory and the splendour of the pageant, but perhaps nervous too that the repairs, improvements and approvals that had been entrusted to him would not meet his king's expectations.

The year 1416 proved to be a watershed in Whittington's outlook. He emerged from the debilitating personal losses of recent years and found a new energy and purpose in life. Over the course of the next seven years, we see him develop a prolonged burst of energy surprising for a man now approaching 60. He galvanised his interest in social and civic reform as if he were once again a young man with his life and mission before him, the Richard Whittington of those tumultuous years that bridged the old and new centuries. In 1419, at the beginning of his seventh decade, he embarked on his fourth and final term as mayor, attending all but two of the meetings of the Court of Aldermen.

A Matter of Reputation? 26 October 1416

In contrast to many of his contemporaries, Whittington had shown little interest in Parliament, having decided very early that the pursuit of business and trade was by far the best way of making his mark, recognising even as a young man that success as a well-connected mercer would gain him unprecedented access to court and government and bring the financial rewards he would require to pursue other interests. In any case, he had by 1384 committed himself to an alternative form of public service, continuing to dip in and out of civic life as a common councillor, alderman and mayor for the best part of forty years. Maintaining a distance from Parliament also made him an 'independent' choice to lead commissions and inquiries. His political 'non-partisanship' and his interest in practical improvements for the social good, which he was prepared to fund himself, allowed him to achieve far more than he could have done in Parliament, where he might easily have become embroiled in the adversarial politics of king versus Commons. His political sentiments lay far more in the efficient day-to-day administration of London than in the governance of England or the workings of the Crown. Though clearly excited to observe the Crown, he confined his involvement to areas where he was perceived to excel and was rewarded for doing so, the efficient management of trade, the regulation and collection of the wool custom, and the oversight of investigations and commissions. Occasionally, he was accorded responsibilities or issued instructions that were clearly political and partisan and that, given a free choice, he might have resisted—here, the 'seizure of Lollards' stands out. He was hardly likely to have been inspired during his formative years by the Good or the Bad Parliaments of 1376–7 and may have judged even then that a career as a member of Parliament was something of a health risk. Almost by definition, anyone committed to social, civic or ecclesiastical reform had a 'political' view; Whittington was careful not to make it too explicit. By the time of his first loan to Richard II in 1387–8, he had recognised that there were other ways of acquiring influence and gaining an insight into high-level politics without having to spend time on the benches at Westminster. Although he attended six of the parliamentary elections held in London between 1413 and 1423, he sat in only one session of Parliament during the entirety of his career—that of October 1416. The question is why?[7]

The Ordeal

In contrast to Whittington himself, his family had established a significant parliamentary pedigree long before he finally appeared for his one and only time at Westminster in October 1416. His grandfather William Whittington had sat in the Commons in 1327 and his father, Sir William, twenty years later in 1348. More recently, his eldest brother William had represented Gloucestershire in October 1377 and Whittington's surviving brother, Robert, whose own parliamentary business became enmeshed with Richard's only term, would become a regular attender of Parliament and play a leading role in the administration of their home county of Gloucestershire.

Whittington took up his seat as the member for the City of London on 19 October 1416, towards the end of a year when tensions with the monarchy had eased, when the city was quiet, and during which he made no loan to the Crown. It was a moment when probably for the first time a family issue diverted him from his usual preoccupations and brought a sharp and unwelcome reminder of his residual interests in Gloucester to his doorstep. That this episode coincides with his very short and uncharacteristic intercession with Parliament suggests that the two events became connected. The more likely reason for Whittington's brief attendance lay with his friend and executor John Coventre, who looked to him to assist in a serious dispute that the Mercers' Company had at this time with the master of the Mint. Here was the company's leading figurehead and perhaps the most influential man in London requested to attend, briefly, to defend its interests. This is the more compelling explanation for Whittington's appearance in the chamber. The other relates to the eruption of a family feud between his brother Robert and nephew Guy and a Gloucestershire ruffian and criminal, Richard Oldcastle, whose violence and activities Whittington's kinsmen insisted were a threat to the family's interests in the county of his birth. The dispute took a violent and potentially life-threatening turn on 26 October 1416, and it was this incident that brought the two men hurrying to London and to a Parliament that had commenced session, with Whittington already on its benches. Robert and Guy Whittington must have known that their influential kinsman was in Parliament for the first time and that the session had just three weeks to run before Parliament adjourned on 18 November. Robert was an experienced parliamentarian and would have been made aware of his brother's intention to sit, or else Richard had learned of the incident, judged that he could help, and instigated their dash to Westminster. Either way, father and son acted remarkably quickly, not least in recovering from their ordeal, organising an initiative to bring to Parliament, and getting there in time to make their case.

So, what was this ordeal, why did it produce this urgent race to London and why did it draw Whittington's participation when for forty years or so since the death of his mother, he had shown little interest in his birth family?[8] One week into his brief term, Whittington's brother and nephew were victims of a type of intimidation and crime that had begun to trouble many areas of the English countryside; in some instances the incidents had been associated with men returning from the war in France without the pay or other recompense they had been promised, without homes or families that had been lost to them, with no prospect of employment, and often brutalised and mentally scarred by their experiences. For some, there was no choice other than to survive by petty crime, by casual theft or, in more serious instances, by involving themselves in the rising tide of highway robbery, kidnapping and violent assault that had begun to afflict certain parts of the English countryside. This was a sharp and contemporary reminder perhaps of the need for protection and vigilance, which had been deemed necessary all those years earlier when, as a boy of ten, Whittington had been transported to his new life in London.[9] Some of these events were rooted in disputes over land, property and title, which had become areas of deep uncertainty and resentment since the Black Death. On 26 October 1416 the Whittingtons were victims of one such assault. It would become a *cause célèbre*.

In Gloucestershire, the family were doing very well. Robert Whittington was no stranger to Parliament and was probably far more acquainted with its ways and means than his more famous brother, having served as a member for Gloucestershire on no less than six occasions, most recently in April 1414. He knew his way around and how best to further his interests. In Gloucestershire a good deal of his time was centred on upholding and enforcing the law. As far back as 1382 he had been commissioned to suppress a rebellion in the county; he had served as a commissioner for the array of troops from the 1380s until May 1415 (and again in 1418 and 1419); and he was charged with imposing the law and punishing transgression in his responsibilities for policing the lordship of Newent, in overseeing land in the royal wards of Gloucestershire and on the property of Deerhurst Priory, and in his ownership of the manor of Kingsholme. He dealt with charges of trespass, poaching, assault, illegal entry, concealment, interference with weirs, and the intimidation of a jury. For good measure, he also acted from time to time as a tax collector, a justice of the peace, an escheator, a coroner, and a constable for the Forest of Dean, and as sheriff of Gloucestershire on five occasions. As one source puts it: 'there was scarcely a year between 1390 and his death in 1423 when he was not placed in some position of responsibility'.[10]

It is more than possible that he had alienated or ridden roughshod over some of his fellows and made enemies along the way. Robert and Guy were ambushed near the village of Mordiford by a large body of men, employed as servants to Richard Oldcastle. Taken by force to a place known as 'Dynmorehille' and deprived of their horses and armour, they were threatened with an even more remote abduction to Wales and with death if they failed to produce enough men to stand bail for them in the sum of £600. This was effectively a ransom and a rebuttal of any crime.

Robert, then aged 60, was held as a hostage while Guy was dispatched to raise the ransom. Under great duress, his father signed bonds for £111 and a general discharge of all actions against his captors. However, no sooner had the pair been released than they determined to condemn the bonds as unlawful and resolved to take their petition for redress to Parliament, applying to Henry V to abolish such bonds and covenants as unlawful. Their grant of application named eight servants of Richard Oldcastle and cited other miscreants, allied members of the 'gang'. It is likely that they were assisted in their petition by their influential brother and uncle, sitting very briefly as a member of the Commons. Whether Oldcastle and his men were ever brought to justice is unknown.[11] Robert would die just a few months after his brother Richard, probably in June 1423, and the family estates fell to Whittington's nephew Guy.[12]

London's Town Clerk

It was in the spring of the following year, 20 April 1417, during the mayoralty of the esteemed skinner Henry Barton, more properly 'purveyor of fine pelts and furs' to the royal household, that Whittington's impending chief executor, John Carpenter, finally broke through to significant public attention in his election as common clerk of the City of London. Whether or not Whittington assisted him formally is not known, but had his opinion been sought we can imagine that he would have generously proclaimed Carpenter's unassailable qualities and suitability. He would, in effect, become London's first town clerk. On 3 December of the following year, in recognition of his new duties and his evident skills in discharging them, Henry V exempted him 'for the whole of his life from all military and civil duties whatsoever, which included election as a Member of Parliament and receiving the Honour of Knighthood'.[13] He would, in fact, later serve in Parliament from 1425.

Meanwhile, Henry needed all the friends and expertise he could muster. He readied his troops and the nation for his controversial return to France in 1417, instigating a campaign that would commence with the savagery of the Siege of Rouen and end in 1420, encompass his marriage to Catherine de Valois, daughter of the French king, and assert his right as heir to the French throne. It was estimated that the combined cost of maintaining the prized port of Harfleur, financing with King Sigismund the costs of the Treaty of Canterbury, and meeting the huge expense of the earlier naval expedition to France in 1416 and the flotilla which followed in 1417, would place the Exchequer in deficit by at least £40,000. Characteristically, the king turned to wealthy lenders to bear the burden. Of the £31,595 produced by no less than 286 separate loans, Henry Beaufort contributed nearly a half, £14,000; the city of Bristol raised £1,000; London raised a very modest £1,860, reflecting a growing distrust of Henry's warmongering; and Richard Whittington contributed £1,333, a sum matched by the prior of St John of Jerusalem. Combined, these five loans constituted almost two-thirds of the entire sum raised.[14] Whittington had now been lending to England's kings for nearly thirty years. His willingness to do so was coming to an end; he had more peaceful and progressive purposes for his wealth, and in planning and implementing those he would work ever more closely with the man recently elevated as London's town clerk.[15] The two men were linked most by a common interest in education. Whittington's patronage of two libraries is frequently ascribed to Carpenter's influence and to that of John Colop, who managed the distribution of his estate in alms and in the dissemination of religious tracts known since as 'common profit books'. Following Carpenter's election, Whittington encouraged and may have provided financial support to his friend to enable him to write the *Liber Albus* or 'white book', generally regarded as the first book of English common law. Completed during Whittington's fourth and final term as mayor in 1419–20, this set out for the first time the historical and legal framework for statutes relating to the City of London.[16] The one evident divergence between the two men lay in their attitude to property. While Whittington acquired the 'burden' of property typically only when he had to, for example in the commuting of a debt or as repayment of an obligation, Carpenter was an acquisitive property owner and rentier, holding at the time of his death over 300 tenements in London alone.

35

FOUR TIMES MAYOR

October 1419

On 13 October 1419 London's outgoing mayor, the grocer William Sevenoke, made a striking contribution to the expanding ritualism of the mayoralty in his inauguration of a solemn Mass at the Guildhall Chapel, intended to mark the election of those who would follow him. This further solemnising of the mayor's office and his moral authority built directly on John Woodcock's initiative of 1406, establishing a tradition that, with a few refinements, has largely continued to the present day. In both instances the incoming beneficiary was Richard Whittington. He was 60 when he returned for his fourth and final term and, while a few of his peers had made it to 70, a far greater number had not passed 50. Increasingly aware of his own mortality, not least having seen his wife, his mentor and many of his friends die before him, he set out objectives for the short time he would have left and for the time beyond, pursuing them with vigour, urgency and, in an episode that startled some of those closest to him, a retribution that would alienate support and polarise opinion. If Whittington's health or stamina was failing him, it didn't show, and he appears to have been as energetic in his final term as he was during his earlier tenures. Yet his last tilt at social reform and a preoccupation with his will, more than three years before he would die, point to someone who knew that if illness or frailty didn't foreclose him, then age surely would. On returning to office in the autumn of 1419 he therefore determined to press on with his attempts to tear down and rebuild Newgate. Despite his own and Thomas Knolles's efforts to improve lives and alleviate conditions, Newgate had slipped further into ignominy. He had further reason to raze the place. His predecessor Sevenoke had recently called time on the practice, established nearly forty years earlier, of sending those adjudged to have committed minor crimes of corruption and financial malpractice to the relative leniency of Ludgate. He had closed the gaol and transferred many of its inmates to the overcrowded and filth-ridden Newgate. Six months later, it was Whittington who had to pick up the pieces, as 60 or more of these less hardy transferees were dead, probably the result of an outbreak of typhus.[1] He made no bones of his disgust and outrage, proclaiming: 'By reason of the foetid and corrupt atmosphere that is in the heinous gaol of Newgate many persons are now dead who would be alive' and reversed Sevenoke's decision, reopening Ludgate to accommodate 'all citizens and other reputable persons whom the Mayor, Aldermen, Sheriffs or Chamberlain of the City shall think proper to commit and send to the same.'

It was a sign of the crusading, uncompromising figure he would become during his last term. Myers describes this reversal as 'an act of charity for the public-spirited Richard Whittington'.[2] An even greater act would follow a few years later, in the generous provision for its rebuilding made in his will. Yet there is something of a conflict here: on the one hand he tackled overcrowding and reduced the unbearable strain on the lives of those committed to Newgate, but he also reinstated the separation, in law, of those whose wealth, reputation and connections placed them above those wretched unfortunates left behind. Whittington considered right was on his side: after all, he had relieved pressure on 'that heinous gaol' and he continued to push for Newgate to be demolished and rebuilt, with his own resources if need be. He may also have judged it politic to keep onside those in the City whose support would assist his ambitions to eradicate Newgate once and for all. Was he simply looking after the interests of his own class or manoeuvring to achieve a much greater and long-held good? Probably the latter. His plan would be fulfilled, but posthumously.

In the concluding months of his mayoralty, Whittington is reputed to have entertained Henry V and his queen consort, Catherine de Valois, at the Guildhall, an occasion when purportedly he was awarded a knighthood, though there is no record that he was ever offered one. Apparently, while Henry was examining the fire, scented with sweet woods and spices, Whittington is reported to have cast bonds of debt totalling £60,000 owed to him by the king into the flames. Lysons says that it provoked the salute from a surprised and grateful king—'never had Prince such a subject'—to which Whittington is said to have replied, 'Never had a subject such a Prince.' This demands a terminal suspension of belief. Even had the banquet taken place, and there is little evidence for it, such a melodramatic act of rescinding a debt owed by the Crown, and one so ludicrously exaggerated, equivalent to about half the Exchequer's annual revenue, is abject nonsense. Even its 'source', Samuel Lysons, writing misty-eyed 440 years later, accepts that the tale was improbable—in truth a confection—claiming that his own work would have been the poorer for not giving light to the 'tale', observing that 'History would lose ... half its charms if we were to deprive it of all its romance; it would present to us nothing but a lot of dry bones, without any marrow in them.'[3] Lysons's treatise on Whittington is admiring, romantic and written by someone who spent his early life in Rodmarton, an estate near Cirencester, long associated with the Whittingtons and their kin the Fitzwarins. It is also, in this instance, fanciful and inaccurate.[4]

Brewers

What is less in dispute is Henry's unshakeable confidence in Whittington's singular ability to resolve some of the most intractable obstacles to efficient revenue gathering, and in the mercer's deeply moral determination. In this case, the cause of the king's discontent was a resurgence in the corruption and malpractices of Whittington's old adversaries, the brewers. This had resulted in a breach of statute and a serious loss in revenue to the Exchequer. In Henry's estimation only one man had the stature, determination and integrity to bring them, once more, to book. 'A zealous, and perhaps unrealistic advocate of price control, he quarrelled repeatedly with the brewers over the rising price of ale ... during his third and last mayoralty, the wardens of the Brewers' Company were fined for overcharging by a reluctant court of aldermen "bot for to plese Richard Whityngton, for he was cause of alle the forsaid juggement".'[5] Whittington has been described in his last years as 'very active in prosecuting the forestallers of meat and sellers of dear ale'.[6] His long-standing dispute with the brewers reached back to his second term as mayor in 1397–8, and had simmered and then ignited during his third mayoralty in 1406. It would now flare into outright confrontation during his final period of office and continue to burn fiercely in the period that followed. The difference now was that it was Whittington himself who inflamed the confrontation. Unwin notes that in all matters concerning the regulation of trade, especially trade in victuals and drink, the mayor of London possessed extensive powers of control, while the 'natural desire' of the victuallers was to have these powers exercised in a manner that was conducive to their interests.

He describes this as 'one of the chief motive forces in London politics'. Whittington decided, quite unequivocally, that he would not just take on the brewers but would make an example of them. It is here that Whittington's uncompromising moral streak is most sharply drawn. Put simply, the brewers' commercial activities were essentially a matter of legal and fiscal abrogation, and they were not alone in this, but their disregard of community, mayoralty and state was in Whittington's eyes a far more serious matter, amounting to an overbearing contempt. It was also an affront to Whittington's own professional and moral codes. It was this personal and uncompromising pursuit of the brewers that many—in the City, the commonalty and even within his own circle—regarded as bordering on the vindictive. Indeed, other 'interests' within the City wondered where it would end, who would be next. Historically, the brewers had hardly helped their cause. It was the custom, for example, of this powerful company to mark out the susceptibility of London's mayors to ingratiation, incentive, bribery, and overtures of self-interest—marking them as friend or foe. In Whittington they faced the least amenable of all. 'One mayor was a good man, meek and soft to speak with, and the Brewers gave him an ox and a boar so he did them no harm. Another refused their gifts with thanks but promised to be just as kind as if he had taken them. The famous Richard Whittington they regarded as a sworn foe to the craft.'[7]

During his final term Whittington would prove to be a zealous, implacable and, at times, perhaps unrealistic advocate of price control, illustrated in his repeated and unyielding quarrels with the brewers over the rising cost and quality of their ale. Their malpractices—the shortening of measures, the watering of ale, the use in some instances of rank water to brew their products, their intimidation of landlords, their manipulation of elected officials, their disregard for statute, and a dismissive attitude which made it clear they regarded themselves as above the law and too powerful to bring to heel—were a red rag to an unbending moralist like Whittington, but there were other influences driving London's mayor in his rapidly deteriorating relations with the brewers. They already had a 'history'. The brewers had exercised a retail monopoly since 1364 and Whittington had confronted them in 1406–7 at the request of the king. Sixteen years later, in 1422 and 1423, violation of mayoral pricing and grading standards in nearly a third of London's wards all concerned breaches of the assizes of ale.[8] In 1420 the Brewers' Company brought forward a petition demanding that the City amend the ordinances made during the tenure of John Woodcock's mayoralty in 1405–6. Their aim was to deflect Whittington from any intended assault on their practices or privileges, firing a warning arrow across his path. They too were up for a fight, and they intended to take him on. For his part, Whittington adopted the position that with a history of malpractice, having breached the law in matters of pricing and weights and been proven guilty of diluting their products, some members of the company were, at the very least, corrupt. In the year that he laid the foundation stone and provided the greater part of the funding for the new library at Greyfriars, contributing £400 of the total cost of £456 16s 8d, he resolved to meet them head-on.[9] After all, he had the support of the king, the Corporation and many ordinary Londoners who had been cheated and made ill by dilution and adulteration. Yet there were signs early on that his efforts might falter as other interests voiced their concerns about interference, about where lines would be drawn, about rights of trade and, darkly, about the tone and personal acrimony that coloured Whittington's pursuit. These concerns were enunciated to him by one of his closest supporters, the Chancellor Henry Somer, who supported him throughout and commended him publicly in Parliament for his 'persistence' but also warned him of the physical threat to his person if he pushed too hard. It may have been Somer who insisted that he should have the protection of the Serjeant at Arms.

For their part, the brewers had not forgiven him for his assault on their practices or the high-handed way he had berated and reduced them in their previous encounters. Many felt they had been hung out to dry and their reputation, such as it was, had been irredeemably sullied. It didn't help either that many held a contempt for what they, and other guilds, saw as interference from a condescending mercer, although he was acting as London's mayor on each of the occasions they had clashed. They charged that he was using a 'civic' office, freely elected, to pursue them and inflict a commercial wound. Whittington knew in 1420 that his time was short. We have a picture of someone driven by a compulsion to deliver one final civic accomplishment, to lance a recurring boil, to root out and make an example of corruption. Friends warned that he had enraged a formidable, potentially vicious enemy, yet for Whittington they were a soft and necessary target. Make an example of the brewers and he would set an example for all. In this volatile mix there was also his pride, perhaps over-weening in this instance. Had not the king asked him personally to take on this task, and had he not made clear that Whittington was the only man in England sufficiently capable and honest to take it on and succeed? Then, there was the matter of his will. While he cast back over his life and worked through with Carpenter how he would sustain the moral compass that had guided him since he arrived in London, he was imposing it on this most amoral and unprincipled of adversaries. He was investing his pursuit with a religious zeal.

While the opening confrontations of Whittington's pursuit took place during his final term as mayor, these deepened after October 1420, unfolding and sharpening further over the course of 1421–2. Indeed, he continued to behave as if he still held the reins of office. His immediate successors—William Cambridge (1420–1), Robert Chichele (1421–2) and William Walderne (1422–3)—either distanced themselves by publicly standing apart from his activities or discreetly acquiesced, provided their mayoralty was not too implicated. In short, this was Whittington's hand, and he alone would play it. He did so by asserting his 'legacy' and borrowed authority as one of London's most renowned mayors; by virtue of the authority invested in him by the Crown; by drawing on his own resources and the support of close friends; and by sheer will, the force of his personal stature, and his unshakeable conviction that he was right, legally and morally. In this way, he was able to deploy a string of confrontational and disruptive measures, including harassing the officers of the Brewers' Company, visiting its meeting hall, and turning up unannounced at the premises of individuals under suspicion of malpractice. He had no intention of relenting or taking prisoners. In one notable instance he intervened directly in their trading by selling up, by proclamation, the entire stock of one brewer based at Long Entry, near the Stocks, and of others based at The Swan in Cornhill, The Swan by St Antony's and The Cock Tavern in Finch Lane. His persistence was so unrelenting that he prevailed in summoning a dozen of their number before the mayor, William Cambridge, and London's aldermen. The interrogation of their practices and behaviour clearly left a deep impression on the company because the account is recorded in the 'Brewers' First Book'. After they had been questioned and taken to task for their practices, we learn from the proceedings that

> the Mayor shewed hem diverse ensamples of malt yn the same court to which the malt the Brewers answered that thei cowd make no ale thereof … And the moste parte of the comones of the said cite seyden that it was a fals thing to sell here ale so dere while they myghten hae malt so good chepe, bote men syeden atte that tyme that Brewers were cause of the derthe of malt … Then seide the Mayor and alle the Aldermen that they

were condemned yn her bond of xxli, and the mayor ordained ... that the ... maistres of Brewers craft ... should be kept yn ward of the Chamberlayn ... And thus thei did abide.[10]

After the meeting, the brewers were instructed to attend the chamberlain and John Carpenter, by now London's town clerk, who then 'commanded' them to go home to their houses. In a striking insight into Whittington's extraordinary influence and relentlessness, Carpenter told them it was the decision of the mayor and aldermen that they should not be imprisoned nor suffer any loss of their goods but that, as they came to realise, they had been summoned by the mayor at the request of his predecessor, 'but for to plese Richard Whityngton'.[11] It is even more revealing to discover in the brewers' accounts for the following year an entry in the sum of £7 3s 4d 'for two pipes of wine for Richard Whetyngton's butler, also money given to divers serjeants of the mayor for to be good friends of our craft'. As there is no evidence that Whittington or his butler, presumably Henry London, accepted this gift of wine, we are bound to conclude that this was a weasel attempt to discredit him after the event. Whatever the truth or the reason, the Brewers' Company was neither cowed nor deflected from its traditional approach to public officers; the last line says it all—'for to be good friends of our craft'.[12]

Among Whittington's colleagues in the City, there were many who found his determination stifling. He was guilty of retribution, arrogance, intransigence. Where would he strike next, whose sharp trade would he swoop to blunt and regulate, whose errant behaviour would he punish in the courts? Even the Church weighed in, two bishops accusing him of insufferable rectitude and another of 'religious zeal'. For someone whose characteristics appear detached and balanced, Whittington was always likely to be seen as moralistic and judgemental, incapable of backing down, perhaps even from exoneration or leniency. In this very last episode of his career he comes across as fervid, crusading, unforgiving. Almost certainly he knew that he had reached a point where he could not retreat. His comfort that Henry V had urged him to follow this course and to see it through to the bitter end was ultimately a veil for his own unswerving bull-headedness. Carpenter and other close friends persisted in urging him to bow to the prevailing mood and to achieve a face-saving accommodation, to make his peace. With reasonable justification he might protest that it was he who was the injured party, the one who had been abused and threatened. Carpenter may have reminded him that it was London which would be the injured party if he did not bring this contest to an end. For others, Whittington's actions were discordant: he had become the issue, the questionable party—more so when it became known, through an approach to Carpenter, that the newly elected warden of the Brewers' Company had actively sought to put an end to the matter, to find common ground to work together. We can only conject what Carpenter said to him: 'You have won your argument, Richard. You have achieved what the king required of you, your task accomplished, your adversaries bowed and conciliatory. You have served London magnificently. There are no more battles to be fought.' He would have been given short shrift for even thinking it.

Perhaps there was an unexpected, unorthodox outcome to Whittington's dispute with the Brewers' Company, and one which he would have approved of: that it may have provided an impetus to the establishment of almshouses in London. Frank Rexroth notes:

> It is more likely that another incident ultimately led to the establishment of the almshouse in London: a dispute between the most famous late medieval Londoner, Richard Whittington, a mercer and alderman who served several terms as mayor, and the worshipful company of brewers. This dispute concerned the company's relationships to their poor, the conflict between *gula* and *caritas*, the disproportion between conspicuous consumption and discreet help for the needy. It showed Londoners the high legitimatory significance that an almshouse could attain for urban groups.[13]

36

CITIZEN OF LONDON

Of course, Whittington's continuing spats with the brewers, important and lively as they were, amounted to little more than a sideshow to the far more fundamental exigencies that beset the nation. In the spring of 1421 Henry V's need for money was once more urgent. He had travelled the country with his new consort, Queen Catherine, in part to observe at first hand and quell the disquiet and disaffection that his lords and many parliamentarians advised him were widespread and deepening by the day. Yet here was a useful opportunity to show off England's new queen, dazzle his subjects, and exploit this as a clever means to raise money for the next stage of the war. Effectively, this was Henry, England's leading celebrity, 'on tour', meeting, uplifting and softening his subjects for more taxation, further hardship and the fresh prospect of war. The country had not seen anything like it. In the north he turned up to pray at the shrines at Walsingham, Beverley and Bridlington. In the west and Midlands, he hauled up at England's second port of Bristol, at the cathedral town of Hereford, at Shrewsbury and at Kenilworth Castle, taking in industrious Coventry and Leicester along the way. Later, he arrived at the great religious centres of York and Norwich and dawdled at England's east coast port of Lynn.

On 6 May he was given the news he feared most, a treasury statement on the financial state of his kingdom. It was far more parlous than he could have imagined. In this latest balance sheet he was notified that the total expected income for the year ending Michaelmas 1421 would be of the order of £55,743, of which the greatest part, £40,676, would be raised from customs. A further raft of casual income would bring in £15,066. Set against this was a projected expenditure of £52,235. England had barely £3,500 worth of pennies to rub together. He was facing disenchantment at home and the likelihood of an underfunded campaign and, consequently, the prospect of defeat abroad. Nor was this the full financial picture. From this impoverished balance, if indeed it was accurate and had not already been overtaken by unaccounted and unforeseen expenditure, he would still have to find the wherewithal to meet the costs of his own household, the chamber, the privy wardrobe, the 'king's works', and the funding of a new defensive tower at Portsmouth, on England's vulnerable south coast. And there was more, much more: the remuneration of the king's naval clerk, fees due to the Constable of the Tower of London, the bill for artillery and ordnance for his army, the running of his various embassies, the feeding of the 'king's prisoners', the cost of his scriveners in producing reports, contracts and messages, and that of his messengers in delivering them. No provision had been made for his personal debts, those outstanding as king and those incurred before his accession, or for the expenditure of his wardrobe, an oversight which must have been of keen interest to Richard Whittington. Quite bizarrely there was an unaccounted bill for the custody of the king's lions. Yet all this was small beer when set against the most grave detail of the accounts: they did not provide for the debts of either Calais or Harfleur. His only course was to appeal for loans, from everyone and everywhere. Jacob refers to the liquidity that Henry had come to rely on.

> The remarkable thing was the amount of fluid capital that was about. The wealth of the speculator in lands and rents contrasts with the limited resources of the crown. In so far then as the lenders in question were either the great capitalists like Sir Robert Knolles, John Hende, Richard Whittington or Bishop Beaufort or favoured officials like Henry Somer, the Lancastrian chancellor of the exchequer, they secured their ample *quid pro quo* in a number of ways, among which lending at a heavy discount was perhaps the most common.[1]

They could and would help, but these regular sources would not be enough on their own. He would need to find new and more imaginative ways of raising finance. Had he not just reacquainted his people with the majesty of England and the promise of further triumph and prosperity; would the nation at large not respond to his call for the resources necessary to deliver both? He would soon have his answer. If his grand tour had been something of a gamble when he first set off, then it paid off shortly after his return. Just four days later, on 10 May, the first batch of loans arrived, assiduously pressed by a small army of commissioners who had followed in his wake. Day one produced 37 parties providing a total of £1,700. For a brief but nervous moment it looked as if no more would be forthcoming. Momentously, three days later, on 13 May, an unprecedented 535 loans arrived in a single day, producing the huge sum of £34,131. The 'political' gamble that many had warned would backfire had also paid off: he was 'loved' and revered after all. Regardless of whether we think him brave, politically astute, foolhardy or dangerously overconfident and out of touch with his subjects, his instincts proved to be right, and he won the day—as he now intended to do in France.

The principal lenders were the usual suspects—Beaufort led the way with loans totalling £17,666; the City of London did its duty, no doubt reminded of its trials during the time of Richard II, and raised £2,000; Henry's queen, Catherine, also set an unusual precedent in what we might today interpret as a public relations intervention, in expressing confidence in her husband and in England with a personal gift of £1,333; and Whittington was there as ever with £666, matching the Bishop of Bath and Wells. While the largest 24 loans generated over £25,000, the distinctive feature of the call was the balance of £9,000 derived from no less than 500 small lenders—many of them entire communities of villages and towns. It was a truly popular response that spoke volumes for the regard or the fear in which Henry V was held.

Loans and Payment of Interest, 1421

The means adopted by the king and his Exchequer for repaying loans varied. Some were repaid entirely in cash, others in the form of assignments, and others by grants or favours which might include certain rights in the export or taxation of goods. Other means of repayment took the form of an appointment to a particular office, the award of property, or tenure bearing attractive status such as keeper of a royal property. In other cases, a particular set of circumstances or the identity of the lender would not require the loan to be repaid in any material form. Some lenders were simply content to have contributed to the king's needs in the belief that they would become 'known' to the king and his court; they might receive invitations to events or even sit in on meetings—these were sufficient compensation. Alien merchants who traded regularly with London, some based or domiciled in the city, might simply take the view that it was politic from time to time to contribute a loan that would not be reimbursed. For them it simply strengthened their faint hold on 'citizenship' and might safeguard their livelihood and trade.

What is clear in the first quarter of the 15th century is that the needs of successive kings for money to finance their households or fund their military campaigns were for the most part met. London was prosperous and boasted a wealthy merchant class, Calais had strengthened English trade, the Church and the senior clergy understood the need and had the financial wherewithal to support the monarchy, and an alien merchant community provided additional rich pickings when encouraged or pressured. The primary fear of any king, chancellor or treasurer would always be not simply whether the financial support they required would be available, but whether it could be drawn on quickly, whether it was liquid. It was a particular attraction of Whittington that he had chosen from the outset of his career not to tie up his wealth in land and property and that he tended, so to speak, to have the 'readies' available. Notwithstanding his other merits, his position as one of London's wealthiest men, with cash in hand and as an influencer within London's merchant class, had from the early 1390s made him a favoured and frequently the first port of call when financial rescue was in the air. He was not the only source that could be relied upon. The likes of John Hende, Henry Beaufort and Thomas Knolles frequently appear in the lists. Nor was he alone in having cash to hand. Aside from its role as a European trading hub, domestically the City was a sizeable and expanding cash economy based on land and property speculation, on the development of the port and its infrastructure, and on the ceaseless fashion for mansions and fine housing. Wealth was abundantly available within London, and it frequently was held and changed hands as cash. Jacob has reported that one of the key functions of the King's Council at the start of Henry's reign was to include and bind to him men who could enable him to raise finance. That relationship was presumed to be ongoing. 'The addition on 1 November 1400 of three citizens of London—Richard Whittington, John Shadworth and William Brampton—indicated the king's need to get maximum help from the city.'[2]

As for Whittington, Caroline Barron has written that 'there is no case among Richard Whittington's 58 loans where the sum repaid is larger than that recorded as lent', adding that Whittington did not fit into that category of reluctant lenders who provided small sums when the king managed to represent it as their duty to do so. And, if he did not lend out of a sense of duty, then what were his motives? This connects with other events in 1421. While Whittington may have been preoccupied with the brewers throughout 1421 and 1422, his attentions were not exclusively devoted to their pursuit. Encouraged by the tenacity with which the mercer had taken on the task, Henry V laid a further challenge at his door: he was to preside over another matter of great contention, the London usury trials of 1421, a public sign that his own history as a lender was beyond reproach. Yet, away from the spotlight, his time was increasingly devoted to the mission that mattered to him most of all, the planning and writing of his will with the assistance of the man whose own reputation was now burgeoning and who would be his chief executor.[3]

Richard Whittington drew up his will on 5 September 1421, eighteen months before his death in March 1423.[4] He had considered it both in form and in content over a long period, almost certainly from the time of his wife's illness and the realisation that she would not live to see the fulfilment of their joint project at St Michael Paternoster. Provision for the endowment of a college and almshouses at St Michael's was at the heart of this vision and formed the centrepiece of the will. The endowment allowed for the establishment of a 'perpetual' college of priests charged with saying Masses for the couple. About half of the thirty or more bequests in Whittington's will required the recipient to offer prayers for himself and Alice. By the time he summoned John Carpenter to College Hill to work through the detail with him, he had already decided to leave his entire fortune to charity. His marriage to Alice had not produced children, he had no direct heir, he had little to do with his remaining family at Pauntley—though he made some minor bequests to his brother Robert— so his vision and his arrangements were cast much further afield, intended to support a much larger constituency in which he had numerous interests, or with which he had forged important relationships, or for whose part in his life he considered himself grateful or under obligation. This ensured that his will would be far-reaching, and his bequests demonstrate the sheer breadth of his social, moral, civic and spiritual interests and convictions. They embraced endowments to hospitals, the establishment of educational institutions, the funding and resourcing of a leading library, investment in public works and infrastructure, improvements to civic hygiene and sanitation, the alleviation of individual and group poverty, the rebuilding of London's most infamous prison, and improvements to the lives of prisoners.

Richard Whittington's will has been interpreted by some as impersonal because it did not centre on family, but this misses its essential purpose and true worth—it was at heart a programme for social reform and civic enlightenment and was largely dedicated to what Whittington saw as his enduring responsibility to create a better London. Sir Ivo Fitzwarin had captured this sense of responsibility perfectly in his own will nine years earlier when he described his son-in-law so precisely and lucidly as 'Richard Whittington, Citizen of London'. An unmistakable feature of the will was its emphasis on continuity. It was intended to both initiate and sustain, after his death, projects he had been unable to commence or conclude during his life. Whittington's death effectively freed his assets in their entirety, unlocking a huge cache of financial resources—a sum estimated in the region of £7,000—for this purpose of posthumous 'fulfilment'. His intention that his entire estate should be realised as far as possible in cash and deployed purposefully reflected his belief that liquidity rather than investments tended to make things happen, quickly and with more and lasting impact. He was not unusual in making bequests intended to promote social or civic improvement: this was a relative commonplace for members of London's wealthy merchant class and a touchstone for those who had held the office of mayor and wished to record the fact with some form of public gifting. But for the most part these were the peripherals of their after-death arrangements and were often tightly bound up with calculations for their salvation. Whittington was no less interested in redemption, and there are extensive provisions in the will for the saying of Masses, endowment of chantries, and support for individual churches, priests and religious orders, but it is radically distinctive for three reasons.

First, it places at its core social, educational and civic improvement. Second, there is the sheer scale of the will as a 'project' to be developed further after his death. Third, there was the exceptional freedom of action he awarded to his executors, and to Carpenter in particular, not only in their allocations to the specific causes he had identified but also in supporting initiatives which were not identified at this time, but which they were given encouragement to identify and 'interpret' as consistent with his general vision and purpose. In other words, he recognised that after his death other opportunities and needs would present themselves and, in order to anticipate these, he created space for them to make their own wise judgement. Whittington had briefed Carpenter on this very point as the will was evolving, and his appointment as chief executor, having the final say, underlines this pragmatism and forward thinking. There is no doubt that in the period from September 1421 until he was committed to his bed in March 1423 Whittington would have discussed with each of his executors how the projects he had identified would be completed and where else they could bring their common interests to bear. In modern terms Whittington's nominees were not simply his executors but a skilled and focused task and finish group.

The will instructed his executors to sell the house at St Michael Paternoster and his lands and tenements in the parishes of St Andrew by Baynard's Castle, St Michael Bassishaw and St Botolph without Bishopsgate and to distribute the proceeds. Of thirty or more bequests, at least half required the beneficiaries to offer up prayers for the mercer and his wife. The will was wide-ranging in its intent, and London would remember it: bestowing funds for the rebuilding of several churches, gifts to be made on the day of his death to paupers and those disabled by war and afflicted by wretched conditions, support for the poor in parishes he favoured, and gifts to the inmates of certain hospitals and the prisoners of London's gaols at Ludgate, Fleet and Marshalsea and those held by the King's Bench. He made provisions for the repair of London's highways, sums to be presented to the children of friends for their marriage dowries, emoluments to monastic houses, and a raft of residuary clauses that gave freedom to his executors to interpret his intent. After his death they were to establish a perpetual college of priests, ensure five or more secular chaplains were attached to the rebuilt church, and construct an almshouse so that he and Alice would know that their will should be done at St Michael's. Elsewhere, he had provided for the building of the south gate of St Bartholomew's Hospital and for the support of young women with children who had no man at their side or husband in their bed. This work was to be undertaken in part as repayment of a debt due for a quitrent of 20 shillings long overdue and payable out of the house of St Michael Paternoster. He left these works in the hands of his friend the cleric John White, until recently the master of that place. Funds were reserved for works intended to enhance the majesty of London's new Guildhall and to open the wonders of literature to scholars and to the people of London by enabling Carpenter to construct his library there.[5] In this regard he would match and exceed the bequest made by his fellow mercer William Bury, who at one point had been brought before him during the usury trials.[6]

Memorably, Whittington's executors were to commence and complete the project he had set in motion many years earlier at Newgate to ensure that it was rebuilt anew and its livid scar removed from the face of London. His provisions would make known his enduring pity and compassion for the daily crushing of life and breaking of spirit that he considered stained this quarter of his city. For him, there was no place more ravaging of body and ruinous of the soul. Though he would not live to see it, he would go to his grave knowing he had put in place measures to eradicate it. Prisoners were to be removed on the presentation of his petition to a temporary respite while the walls were torn down and a new place of detention rose in its place. There was room, he contended, at the compters to house them and no time should be wasted. He had arranged before his death that the mayor and commonalty, on behalf of his executors, would present his petition to the Privy Council on the day after he died. He had ensured in his discussions with Carpenter that, above all else, his will was to be his chief public act of remembrance, and had requested William Babington, the Attorney General, to supervise it. But it was Carpenter who would see it through and make the final judgements. In September 1421 he made clear to his chief executor that he would have every last penny, every tenement, every piece of land, every debt owing, and all other chattels for which he could raise funds to support a programme of works that would set an example for others to follow. He had estimated that the total cash raised would be in the region of £7,000, excluding any monies released by the sale of his tenements, assets still held in Gloucestershire and Berkshire, and all jewellery and personal effects. The bequest was on a scale never seen before: other wealthy figures such as de la Pole and Sir John Poultney may have had more to hand but had not invested their entire fortune in public and charitable works. Whittington had drawn the terms in such a way that Carpenter and his fellow executors would have considerable room to adapt some of his wishes and interpret them to suit the need and the day. London was changing so quickly that what he aspired to then could well be overtaken before he was cold in the ground. The two friends talked through how each of the executors should act and what authority Carpenter individually and the group collectively would have, confirming in writing what had already been proposed in principle. Much of the mercer's vision had been developed with his wife ten years earlier, and in one sense the will is a salute to her and almost elegiac in its range, purpose and form. Whittington's choice of executors was purposeful and tactical. All were close friends. John Coventre was well placed as a mercer and alderman to marshal the support of the Mercers' Company. John White, the former rector of St Michael's and now master of St Bartholomew's Hospital, was chosen to provide learned and wise counsel in all matters of church and public welfare. Well regarded by the middle clergy, White understood church politics and shared Whittington's view that the proceeds of his will should have a clear secular intent. Whittington would not tolerate any involvement in his closing affairs from what he regarded as an increasingly befuddled and uncaring Church. As the will moved through various stages of development and revision, it fell to another long-term

338

friend, William Grove, a highly regarded scrivener and notary, to act as clerk. Eventually it would read as follows: 'In the name of God and the Holy and Indivisible Trinity, Father, Son and Holy Ghost, amen. On 5 September 1421, in the ninth year of the reign of Henry V, I Richard Whittington, citizen and alderman of London, being sound in mind and memory, make this my testament in the following manner.'[7]

In the normal fashion Whittington entrusted his soul to almighty God, the Blessed Virgin Mary, and all the saints. He instructed that his body be buried in the church of St Michael Paternoster Royal on the north side of the high altar. Any debts he owed were to be paid in full. To cover the costs of his funeral and vespers, he set aside the sum of £100. The day following his death was to be marked by a Requiem Mass together with the first of a monthly remembrance for his soul, the souls of his father, his mother and his wife, 'my beloved Alice', and those of any others to whom he owed a debt of gratitude. To every poor man, woman and child, he instructed his executors to distribute one penny on the day of his funeral. A sum of 100 shillings was allocated to the high altar of St Michael's for tithes or offerings unpaid 'due to forgetfulness or negligence', and a sum of 6s 8d to each chaplain to pray for his soul and those of the others he had cited. In a notable personal gesture, he set aside 40 shillings for Thomas Kirton, lately rector of St Michael's, to fund prayers for his soul and those of others he had mentioned, and a further 100 shillings was to be distributed in alms, at the discretion of his executors, among that church's poor parishioners. The sum of 100 shillings was also given to his spiritual guide and executor John White, who had been at hand at the death of his wife and to whom he had first described their future burial arrangements. He credited White with the renewal of the St Michael Paternoster parish and owed him a great debt. White was also privy to Whittington's views on the alleviation of the distress experienced by young mothers who were either unmarried or had lost their men, and his concerns for children who were orphaned or fatherless. The two men shared an ambition to develop part of St Bartholomew's to address these needs, and the provisions of Whittington's will now made this possible.

There followed a list of churches to whose structural upkeep and repair of ornaments he wished to make contributions: these included 40 shillings to All Hallows in Honey Lane, 53s 4d to St Pancras, and the greater sum of 100 shillings to St Margaret Lothbury, part of which was intended to purchase prayers for the soul of a former rector. As someone who had played an influential part nearly twenty years earlier in pressing the case for a royal charter which would incorporate efforts to support the poor, it was no surprise that Whittington set aside £13 6s 8d 'for the alms of my craft the guild of the mercers of London'. His intention was to set an example that other mercers would follow, and here he looked to John Coventre to ensure that the seeds he sowed would germinate. We might imagine he hoped that within ten years every leading mercer in London would follow his example, making their own provisions for the poor and disadvantaged. An admiration for one of his mercer predecessors, William Elsing, a notable benefactor in the 1330s of churches, hospitals and the poor, was reflected in the 40 shillings he made available for maintaining the structural fabric of St Alphege Cripplegate, which Elsing had rebuilt at his own expense. His thoughts had also turned to where he had commenced his civic career as a common councillor. To St Stephen Coleman Street he gifted 40 shillings for distribution among the parish poor, and he left the same to those in the parish of St Michael Bassishaw. Similar provisions were put in place for St Mary Staining. In each case, their priests and parishioners were to acknowledge his bequest by praying for the souls he had listed in his will. This also extended to the donation of 100 shillings he made to each order of friars in London. A personal bequest of 100 shillings was made to the monastic house at Burnham in Berkshire, a small Augustinian settlement of nuns who had provided care to Alice during her long illness. Alice must have spent some time locally in their care or else nuns had been housed for a time at St Michael's to tend her there. Care for the sick was a recurring theme of the will, and Whittington was intent on either establishing or supporting hospitals to improve London's facilities and anticipate the needs of its population. Accordingly, money was to be distributed among poor people in three named hospitals, St Mary without Bishopsgate, St Mary of Bethlehem and St Thomas in Southwark, and among the lepers of Lock, Hackney, and St Giles without Holborn. Each would have £10. He also recognised the subsistence needs of the individuals who offered this care to the poor, and a sum of 20 shillings was therefore to be distributed among the poor brothers and sisters of Elsing Spital, the institution founded by the mercer whose work he admired. An insight into his excursions with Alice in both good and ill health was provided in some of the distributions. Funds were directed to a monastic house at Cheshunt and the same to the priories at Rowney near Ware and Bromhale near Windsor, which were noted as close to the hearts of the Fitzwarin family. To the house of the Carthusians, he bequeathed 100 shillings 'so they may pray for my soul and those of my family and associates'.

Readers of his will today might be struck by the £100 he provided for the 'marriage of virgins', to be distributed as his executors determined. Here we see an affirmation of Whittington's long-standing views on the sanctity of marriage and its vital role in social stability and in the fulfilment of duties to God. This promotion of marriage was intended to keep young women off the streets, to free them from sin and penury, and to prevent children being born into the City of London without knowledge of their father or deprived of financial support.

Amid the thicket of religious, social and hospital bequests, there were also down-to-earth distributions relating to transport, trade, hygiene and the needs of Londoners generally going about their business. As someone who had made his fortune from trading goods and services by road, bridge and water and who understood the importance of a well-maintained infrastructure to support London's economy, it was natural that Whittington should allocate the sum of £100 towards the improvement of roads deemed to be in bad condition, and his executors were free to distribute his generosity 'where the necessity is most felt'. The allocation of this sum was in part the personal fulfilment of a long-standing pledge made to Stephen Spilman, who had first encouraged him in this idea. How many times had he been in a rig when the horse had stalled because it refused a ramshackle bridge, or had a carter, carrying his goods, been inhibited in his deliveries by deep potholes, thick mud, unruly undergrowth and unsafe foundations?[8]

As a mercer and former mayor of London, he was also familiar with the holes in the city's finances. In fact, he was resuming exactly what London's first mayor, Henry Fitz-Ailwyn, had set out to do over 200 years earlier, to update and maintain a road system created by the Romans that had rarely been improved and never surpassed. Trading for many years with the Low Countries, Whittington and his executors must at times have been exasperated that the achievements of their engineers in reclaiming land from the sea and constructing safe and purposeful infrastructure could not be replicated in their own city, where so many of London's principal roads were little more than deeply perforated dirt tracks. In Carpenter, he had London's most knowledgeable and best-connected administrator, who knew not only every part of the city's infrastructure but also how to go about repairing or replacing it. Both men understood the importance of sound bridges and reliable roads not only to the city's economy and to overseas trade but also to the daily lives of ordinary Londoners. Similarly, sanitation, hygiene and cleanliness were each appreciated as essential to London's social and economic health. Carpenter himself had already captured some of these issues in his codification of London's governance in 1419.

> It is in the *Liber albus* (The White Book of the City of London) ... that we find the fullest record of the ordinances of the wards and it is also at the time of its compilation that the only surviving records of those courts in action were copied into the city's plea and memoranda rolls. This context of the Whittington/Carpenter reforms following a period of extreme civic discord provides us with both a motive and an opportunity for the increasing focus on cleanliness in London's neighbourhood records and on its streets.[9]

The centrepiece of the will, and the 'infrastructure project' for which Whittington is best known, was the rebuilding of Newgate, an ambition he had held for more than three decades and which he shared for a long time with close friends such as Thomas Knolles and, more recently, Carpenter himself. Here was the subject of his greatest passion, the state of London's foul prisons and the condition of those unfortunate enough to be held there. First there was the matter of 'alleviation': at the moment of his death the sum of £500 was set aside for the distribution of 40 shillings a week to be shared among those imprisoned at Ludgate, Fleet, Marshalsea, the King's Bench and, of course, hellish Newgate until this sum was exhausted. He had finally secured the king's licence to rebuild the most infamous of London's gaols and had recently taken the first steps that would lead to its reconstruction. He now invested Carpenter with the authority and funds to complete his vision and to initiate improvements in London's other prisons.

In addition to the liquid funds he made available, Whittington also left to his executors the entire tenement in which he lived in the parish of St Michael Paternoster, and all lands and tenements he held in the parish of St Andrew, near Castle Baynard, and in the parish of St Michael Bassishaw, as well as in the parish of St Botolph outside Bishopsgate, so that after his demise they might sell them and distribute the proceeds. The final provisions of the will relate to the executors themselves, naming them and setting out the remuneration with which he wished to reward them for their efforts both before and after his death.

> I appoint as the executors of this my testament John Coventre, John White as my clerk, John Carpenter as the senior executor and William Grove. I have asked William Babyngton to act as supervisor as required by law; and

I bequeath to the same John Coventre £20 for his labour, to John White £13.6s.8d for his labour, to John Carpenter £40 for his labour, to William Grove £10 for his labour, and to the supervisor £20 for his labour.[10]

Ultimately, the success of the will's implementation and the delivery of Whittington's reformist vision rested on the judgement, the diligence, and, to a significant extent, the anticipation and 'invention' of these friends and colleagues, each of them notable figures in their own right. The nature of their task was essentially collegiate and consensual: nothing Whittington instructed or bequeathed was to be decided or implemented without at least three of them being present at the decision and involved similarly in its outcome. The appointment of Babington as 'supervisor' was a legal requirement, and who better to provide expert counsel and balance than an old and dear friend who happened to be England's Attorney General? Yet collegiate as these appointments and arrangements were, Whittington ensured that there would be a *primus inter pares*, an 'executive chairman'. It was made abundantly clear that in every case Carpenter must be present, and no decision or course of action could be considered valid without his closest friend having participated. Into Carpenter's custody Whittington therefore placed the secure chest he kept in his library, bearing three locks and containing Whittington's jewels, an assortment of personal effects, and deeds and personal papers he would require in order to achieve at least some of the ends they had agreed. No single executor might remove anything from this chest without the consent or the presence of the entire group. Finally, Whittington turned to the arrangements he had in mind to address the welfare of his own house and staff. His executors were instructed to keep his household together, and to feed them, remunerate them and continue to accommodate them at College Hill for one full year following his death. That was the end of it.

* * *

Whittington's executors reported after his death:

The strongest desire and greatest preoccupation of a prudent, wise, and devout man should be to plan ahead and make provision for the state [of his soul] and the termination of his short life, through acts of compassion and benevolence. In particular, to provide for those poor people who have been crushed by severe hardship and cruel misfortune and who do not have the means to earn a living through a craft or manual labour. So that, at the day of the Last Judgement, he will find a place with those who are saved.[11]

On his deathbed he had given instructions to his executors to quickly establish an almshouse for the perpetual support of poor people, and his executors affirmed afterwards that they wished 'to do whatever we can to fulfill the commendable intent and beneficial wishes expressed in his will, as is our duty'. They moved quickly. As their first act, they founded in the church of St Michael Paternoster a college of priests and clerics to perform divine services daily for the souls of Richard and Alice. A residence for the master and priests of the college was constructed on a large empty plot of 'our' land to which they intended to add a churchyard. And fulfilling a singular aim of the Whittingtons, they established an almshouse for thirteen 'needy and devout poor people, well-behaved and of honest character' as a perpetual residence and place of sustenance for them and their successors. The building itself was erected on land they had purchased for this purpose, situated between the church and the wall enclosing a vacant plot to the rear of the high altar of the church, on the south side, and the great tenement that had until recently been Whittington's home, to the north. 'We wish and ordain that this house be forever known as God's House, or Almshouse, or the Hospital of Richard Whittington, and that Richard and his wife Alice be considered and credited by everyone forevermore as the true principal founders of that house and hospital.' It is in the establishment of the almshouse that we see at first hand the tangible connection with the mayoralty and with the Mercers' Company that Whittington had intended. His executors wished to

> ordain that the present mayor of the city of London and his successors who are mayors or wardens of the city are to be overseers of the [administration of] the almshouse; and that the present wardens of the community of the craft of mercery in London, and their successors as wardens of that craft, shall forever be and be known as conservators of that almshouse.

The mayor in question in 1423 was the draper William Cromer, succeeded in 1424 by a fishmonger, John Michell. But the name that captures attention is the incumbent in 1425, none other than one of Whittington's closest friends and one of his executors, John Coventre.

After the ensuing deaths of the executors—though John Carpenter did not die until 1442—the intention was that succeeding tutors would be appointed by the wardens of the Mercers' Company. If the company was neglectful of its duties or failed to appoint a tutor within the requisite period, then the appointment would fall in that instance to the mayor of London but without prejudicing the company's rights on subsequent selections. While this underscored the close ties that Whittington sought with his fraternity, he was determined to prohibit admission to the alms-house by poor men who had been mercers and those who had taken the livery of other companies. Whittington deemed that support for such men must be a matter for their own companies and must not under any circumstances dilute the resources he had invested at St Michael's. The implicit intention was that by setting an example and by excluding these groups, then their own companies and guilds would be obliged to make *their* resources available. In turn, this would extend the impact of Whittington's own objectives by other means. If his instructions were breached, then all such provisions and admissions would be deemed invalid. In such circumstances it would fall to the mayor or warden of the City of London to remove the offending individual and appoint another poor person in his place. However, poor and infirm men of the mercers' craft who had not been 'of the livery' of the mercers, and for whom the Mercers' Company was not obligated to provide support, were to receive preferential treatment in appointment to any vacancies among the fellows of the almshouse. Those admitted were obliged to attend Matins, Mass, Evensong and Compline and to offer prayers for the souls of Richard and Alice Whittington, for the souls of Whittington's parents, Sir William and Lady Joan, and for the souls of Sir Ivo Fitzwarin and Lady Maud, his wife. Next, prayers were to be said for the souls of those royal figures who had helped him on his way and with whom he had established close relation-ships. These included Richard II and Sir Thomas of Woodstock, Duke of Gloucester, who were described with affection as 'the particular lords and patrons of Richard Whittington', and Anne and Eleanor, the wives of that king and duke. They were also bound to pray for the good health and prosperity of the present king Henry VI, for the Archbishop of Canterbury, Henry Chichele, for the conservators and benefactors of the house, the Mercers' Company, and generally for those to whom Richard and Alice Whittington were indebted in any way during their lifetimes. The close details governing the day-to-day lives of those admitted to the almshouse are outside our scope here, but they included very precise instructions to live and remain 'continually' within the boundaries of the almshouse and to avoid 'idle and self-centred conversation'. Whittington's strong sense of social order is seen in the condition that those who ben-efitted must observe their station and the strictures he placed on what was often 'conditional welfare'. At St Michael's we are given an insight into a micro-regime of mutual self-help in which those of reasonable strength and health were expected to take care of fellow residents who were sick or feeble and assist them with their basic needs. Residents were required on their demise to cede all or a significant part of their personal possessions to the almshouse. In return for fulfilling a raft of moral obligations and social duties, the residents of Whittington's almshouse would receive in perpetuity weekly pensions or allowances for their food, drink and other essential needs. Finally, Whittington's executors earnestly entreated 'the tutor and poor people, present and future, to live together in harmony with each other, serving God, and praying devoutly for the souls mentioned.'

POSTSCRIPT

A LIFE BEYOND

The death of Henry V on 31 August 1422, a week short of his 35th birthday, marked the final chapter in Whittington's proximity to the monarchy. He had written his will, mapped out his benefactions, and completed his final term of office as mayor. He had concluded his work on Henry's commission investigating usury and had railed one last time at his old enemy, the brewers, attempting to enforce what he regarded as two of the essential imperatives of the mayoralty—the regulation of weights, measures and pricing of food and drink, and the bringing of law to bear against corruption. By the time the war with France resumed in 1423, Whittington too was gone. On 21 October 1422 Henry VI, a child of nine months, had succeeded his father. A regency was established until his coronation in 1429. Two years later he was crowned king of France. If Henry V's reign had marked the high point in the raising of loans by the monarchy during Whittington's lifetime, 'a peak period of borrowing by the crown ... and the increased efficiency of the government revenue collectors', it would soar again under his successor Henry VI. By then, Whittington could no longer be called upon.

Whittington was buried beside his wife Alice in the tomb he had constructed in the church of St Michael Paternoster. In accordance with his directions, he was interred on the north side of the high altar marked by an epitaph, according to Stow in Latin verse, describing him as *flos mercatorum* (flower of merchants) and *regia spes et pres* (hope and surety of the king). His tomb is said to have been rifled through for treasure in the reign of Edward VI by the parson of the church, intent on extracting the lead in which the body was rumoured to be lapped. It was replaced during the reign of Queen Mary, but his resting place was consumed with his church in the Great Fire of 1666.

After his death Whittington's executors acquired two sites which effectively completed the land assembly for the St Michael Paternoster project. The first was a large tenement called 'Le Tabbard on the Hoop', which had been excluded from Whittington's initial purchase of land from William Weston in 1409. The second was a group of four shops which adjoined the boundary of St Michael's, which would be acquired in February 1424 from Robert Chichele, to whom Whittington had originally conveyed them in 1411. The residue of the Weston land would later become the site for the college of priests, and the almshouses were built on the Tabbard site.

It is one of the great ironies of Whittington's story that in life he largely eschewed acquisition of property, preferring to preserve his wealth in cash or in the form of easily commutable jewellery and plate, yet after his death it was used by his executors to assemble a significant portfolio of land, buildings and rents intended to fund the works of charity and piety he had mapped in his will. A tranche of assets was purchased in the first two to three years after his death from fellow mercers in the parishes of St Mary Magdalen, St Lawrence Jewry and All Hallows Barking; tenements and shops in St Dunstan in the East were acquired from members of other companies. Development sites, tenements and rents were also acquired in St Stephen Coleman Street, where he had begun his civic career forty years earlier, and at St Leonard Eastcheap, St Margaret Bridge Street and St John Walbrook among other places. In December 1424 the Mercers' Company was appointed to supervise and sustain the college and almshouse after the death of two executors, John White and William Grove. A second wave of acquisitions led by John Carpenter would follow after 1430, including the purchase of a messuage and garden adjoining the college of priests from Whittington's old friend Thomas Knolles and his son of the same name. By 1431 Carpenter had accumulated sufficient property and rental income to secure the annual financial needs of both. Jean Imray tells us that it remained only to put in place the legal mechanisms that would bind the future entrustment of both institutions to the mercers. In May 1432 Carpenter conveyed both assets to the grocer and former mayor William Sevenoke, who, in turn, made a will transferring the property to the Mercers' Company 'provided that they carried out the trusts of the College and Almshouse'. Any revenue left over from the fulfilment of these 'trusts' was to be made available to assist mercers who had fallen on hard times, chiefly in the form of loans. Carpenter himself would die in 1442 and the properties were conveyed to form their endowment.

POSTSCRIPT

Whittington's Legacy

There are two principal parts to Richard Whittington's legacy, the first and substantive part comprising his endowments, his benefactions and an enormous sum of cash that his executors used imaginatively and skilfully to purchase the properties that would realise the completion of his and Alice's vision for St Michael's and to establish an income and investment foundation for the ongoing work of the Mercers' Company. The second is perhaps less widely understood: the 'legacy of the man'—the culture, wise judgement and social philosophy that drove his reforms both before and after his death and that created the template, set a challenge, and raised the bar for other wealthy like-minded reformers to follow. He was by no means the first leading Londoner or the first mercer to recognise the social, economic and regulatory inequities and deficits of London. The endeavours of London's first mayor, Henry Fitz-Ailwyn, and later of William Elsing just half a century before Whittington first took office, are two notable examples. Where Whittington does excel is in the sheer scale, range and ambition, and in the resources, energy and unfailing commitment he invested over a sustained period as mercer, investor, employer, property owner, office holder, mayor and testator. History focuses rightly on the scale and reach of his will and its impact in the twenty years *after* his death, but this is to underestimate or, worse, over-look the gifts, donations, charitable works, personal investment in social and economic infrastructure, relentless determination to improve London's prisons, sanitation, byways and watercourses and to fund works to hospitals, almshouses and libraries, and extraordinary long-term lend-ing and gifts to the Exchequer, some of which at least—unlike those to the Crown—served to benefit the commonalty. And in the matter of wider reform, intended to benefit ordinary Londoners, we must not overlook his endeavours to instigate reforms in food, drink, pricing, weights and measures, and usury, which placed him head-on in challeng-ing confrontations with the fishmongers, corn merchants, other victual-lers, backstreet loan sharks, and, of course, brewers. Indeed, if there is any foundation to the pantomime story of Dick Whittington, then per-haps it originates when as a young boy he first entered the household of Sir Ivo Fitzwarin. That millions of people since have been fascinated by his life for the best part of six centuries is proof enough that he was indeed unique, extraordinary in his endeavours, and memorable in his legacy. And all without the benefit of that mythical cat.

NOTES

INTRODUCTION

1. George Warner, ed., *The Libelle of Englyshe Polycye: A Poem on the Use of Sea-Power, 1436* (Oxford: Clarendon Press, 1926).
2. Samuel Lysons, *The Model Merchant of the Middle Ages Exemplified in the Story of Whittington and His Cat* (London: Hamilton Adams and Co., 1860), 71.
3. Richard Grafton, *Grafton's Chronicle, or, History of England* (London, 1659; republished 1809), vol. 1, 499.
4. John Stow, *Survey of London: Written in the Year 1598* (Stroud: Sutton, 1994).
5. E Arber, *A Transcript of the Registers of the Company of Stationers of London, 1554–1640 A.D.*, 5 vols. (London, 1875–94), vol. 3, 282.
6. George Chapman, John Marston and Ben Jonson, *Eastward Hoe* (London, 1636).
7. Francis Beaumont, *The Knight of the Burning Pestle* (London, 1635).
8. John Warrington, ed., *The Diary of Samuel Pepys* (London: Dent, 1964), vol. 3.
9. 'The Dick Whittington' historic pub located in Gloucester city centre, built as a 13th-century townhouse. The original owner claimed to have been Whittington's uncle. https://www.thedickwhittington.co.uk/history.
10. Andrew Duncan, *Secret London* (London: New Holland, 1995).
11. Christopher Turner, *London Churches Step by Step* (London: Faber and Faber, 1987).
12. Henry Chamberlain, *A New and Compleat History and Survey of the Cities of London and Westminster, the Borough of Southwark, and Parts Adjacent: From the Earliest Accounts, to the Beginning of the Year 1770* (London, 1770).
13. Thomas Pennant, *Pennant's Tour of London* (London, 1805).
14. Steve Roud, *London Lore: The Legends and Traditions of the World's Most Vibrant City* (London: RH Books, 2008).
15. http://www.kattenstoet.be/en/page/497–511/the-cat-throwing.html.
16. Henry B Wheatley, ed., *The History of Sir Richard Whittington, by T. H.* (London: Villon Society, 1885).
17. Walter Besant and James Rice, *Sir Richard Whittington: Lord Mayor of London* (New York: Merrill Baker, 1894).
18. James Tait, 'Richard Whittington', *Dictionary of National Biography* (Oxford, 1885–1900), vol. 61.
19. Osbert Sitwell, *The True Story of Dick Whittington* (London: Home and Van Thal, 1945);

see also Jean Harrowven, *Sir Richard Whittington's Secret* (Norwich: Borrowdale Press, 2000).

20. AGW Boggon et al., *Richard Whittington of Pauntley* (Gloucester: City and County of the City of Gloucester, 1959).

21. Michael Whittington, *The Whittington Story: From the Three Counties to the City* (Oxford: Parchment Press, 1988).

22. Jean Imray, *The Charity of Richard Whittington: A History of the Trust Administered by the Mercers' Company 1424–1966* (London: Athlone Press, 1968).

23. Caroline M Barron, 'Richard Whittington: The Man behind the Myth', in *Studies in London History Presented to Philip Edmund Jones*, eds. AEJ Hollaender and William Kellaway (London: Hodder and Stoughton, 1969); and Caroline M Barron, *London in the Later Middle Ages: Government and People, 1200–1500* (Oxford: OUP, 2004).

24. Anne Sutton, *The Mercery of London: Trade, Goods and People* (London: Routledge, 2000).

1. HOME

1. http://opendomesday.org/name/81250/ansfrid-of-cormeilles/.

2. AP Baggs, ARJ Jurica and WJ Sheils, 'Winstone: Manors and Other Estates', in *A History of the County of Gloucester*, vol. 11: *Bisley and Longtree Hundreds*, ed. NM Herbert and RB Pugh (London, 1976), 147–8, www.british-history.ac.uk/vch/glos/vol11/.

3. http://www.british-history.ac.uk/vch/glos/vol4/, 35–41; WG Hoskins, *Local History in England* (Oxford: Routledge, 1984), 238–9.

4. 'Medieval Gloucester: The Later Middle Ages', in *A History of the County of Gloucester*, vol. 4: *The City of Gloucester*, ed. NM Herbert (London, 1988), 35–41, http://www. british-history.ac.uk/vch/glos/vol4/.

5. 'Houses of Benedictine Monks: The Abbey of St Peter at Gloucester', in *A History of the County of Gloucester*, vol. 2, ed. William Page (London, 1907), 53–61, www.british-history.ac.uk/vch/glos/vol2/.

6. 'Houses of Benedictine Monks: The Abbey of St Peter at Gloucester'.

7. https://en.wikipedia.org/wiki/Gloucester_Abbey.

8. http://www.gatehouse-gazetteer.info/English%20sites/4761.html.

9. ARJ Jurica, ed., *A History of the County of Gloucestershire*, vol. 12: *Pauntley* (Woodbridge, 2010), 281–301, http://www.british-history.ac.uk/vch/glos/vol12/.

10. Walter Besant and James Rice, *Sir Richard Whittington: Lord Mayor of London* (New York: Merrill Baker, 1894), 32.

11. Besant and Rice, *Sir Richard Whittington*.

2. WHITTINGTON

1. James Tait, 'Richard Whittington', *Dictionary of National Biography* (Oxford, 1885–1900), vol. 61.

2. Michael Whittington, *The Whittington Story: From the Three Counties to the City* (Oxford: Parchment Press, 1988).

3. 'Parishes: Haselor', in *A History of the County of Warwick*, vol. 3: *Barlichway Hundred*, ed.

Philip Styles (London, 1945), 108–15, http://www.british-history.ac.uk/vch/warks/vol3/.

4. A somewhat perplexing version of the Pauntley descent was provided in 1837 by TC Banks though he does affirm that its acquisition was through the Solers. 'The family of Whitington was of great consideration at Pauntley in the county of Gloucester, which they obtained by marriage with the heiress of Solers, of Pauntley ... The Pauntley line terminated in the main branch in 1346 by the death of Thomas Whittington who left only female issue married into the families of St Aubyn, Berkeley, Bodenham, Throckmorton, Nanfant and Poole of Saperton.' TC Banks, *The Dormant and Extinct Baronage of England*, vol. 4 (London: Henry G Bohn, 1837).

5. Whittington, *The Whittington Story*, 10.

6. AGW Boggon et al., *Richard Whittington of Pauntley* (Gloucester: City and County of the City of Gloucester, 1959).

7. Jean Imray, *The Charity of Richard Whittington: A History of the Trust Administered by the Mercers' Company 1424–1966* (London: Athlone Press, 1968), 27 n. 3.

8. Caroline M Barron, 'Richard Whittington: The Man behind the Myth', in *Studies in London History Presented to Philip Edmund Jones*, eds. AEJ Hollaender and William Kellaway (London: Hodder and Stoughton, 1969), 198.

9. www.historyofparliamentonline.org/volume/1386–1421/member/whittington-robert-14234.

10. Walter Besant and James Rice, *Sir Richard Whittington: Lord Mayor of London* (New York: Merrill Baker, 1894); Henry B Wheatley, ed., *The History of Sir Richard Whittington*, *by T. H.* (London: Villon Society, 1885). See also https://catalog.hathitrust.org/Record/012203169.

11. Samuel Lysons, *The Model Merchant of the Middle Ages Exemplified in the Story of Whittington and His Cat* (London: Hamilton Adams and Co., 1860), 10.

12. Wheatley, *The History of Sir Richard Whittington*.

13. Acknowledging 1959 as the 600th anniversary of his birth, the City of Gloucester, County of Gloucestershire and Mercers' Company declared 'Richard's date of birth is by no means certain, but from his age at death it appears he was born in the 1350s. His eldest brother William was 23 at the time of their father's death in 1358 so that Richard may well have been the son of a second marriage.' Clearly, all three must have had some confidence in 1359 as the year of his birth given the publicity and expenditure spent on celebrating it.

14. Sir William Whittington was still deemed an outlaw in 1359. It has been suggested that his offence was marrying without licence Berkeley's widow, who went on to survive him and died in 1372. See 'Sir William Whittington', *Dictionary of National Biography*.

15. Corporation of London Records Office, Husting, Plea Roll 80.

16. The records show as grantor William de Southam, vicar of the church of St Lawrence Jewry. Grantee: William de Elsyngg, citizen and mercer of London. Place or subject: Grant of a rent from a tenement in the parish of St Lawrence Jewry. County: London. http://discovery.nationalarchives.gov.uk/details/r/C34296777.

17. British Records Society, *Inquisitions Post Mortem for Gloucestershire*, vol. XLVII (London, 1914).

18. Lysons, *The Model Merchant*, 15.

3. DEPARTURE

1. www.historyofparliamentonline.org/volume/1386–1421/member/whittington-robert-14234.

2. 'From 1382 onwards he evidently remained at home, being kept busy for the next 40 years in many tasks of local government. Indeed, in this respect he was perhaps the most active member of the community of Gloucestershire, for he served as a j.p. for about 31 years altogether, and discharged office as alnager, coroner, escheator (for four terms) and sheriff (for three); indeed, there was scarcely a year between 1390 and his death in 1423 when he was not placed in some position of responsibility.' See http://www.historyofparliamentonline.org/volume/1386–1421/member/whittington-robert-14234.

3. JFD Shrewsbury, *A History of Bubonic Plague in the British Isles* (Cambridge: CUP, 2008), 134–5.

4. 'Medieval Gloucester: Trade and Industry, 1327–1547' in *A History of the County of Gloucester*, vol. 4: *The City of Gloucester*, ed. NM Herbert (London, 1988), 41–54, http://www.british-history.ac.uk/vch/glos/vol4/.

5. See 'Medieval Gloucester: Topography', in *A History of the County of Gloucester*, vol. 4: *The City of Gloucester*, ed. NM Herbert, 63–72.

4. TO LONDON

1. Carol Davidson Cragoe, ARJ Jurica and Elizabeth Williamson, 'Bradley Hundred', in *A History of the County of Gloucester*, vol. 9: *Bradley Hundred: The Northleach Area of the Cotswolds*, ed. NM Herbert (London, 2001), 1–8, http://www.british-history.ac.uk/vch/glos/vol9.

2. Eileen Power, *The Wool Trade in English Medieval History* (Oxford: OUP, 1941), 50.

3. Eleanor Chance, Christina Colvin, Janet Cooper, CJ Day, TG Hassall, Mary Jessup and Nesta Selwyn, 'Communications', in *A History of the County of Oxford*, vol. 4: *The City of Oxford*, ed. Alan Crossley and CR Elrington (London, 1979), 284–95, http://www.british-history.ac.uk/vch/oxon/vol4/.

4. See William Woods, *England in the Age of Chaucer* (London: Hart-Davis, 1976).

5. Chance et al., 'Communications', http://www.british-history.ac.uk/vch/oxon/vol4/3–73.

6. https://historicengland.org.uk/listing/the-list/list-entry/1001978.

7. Catherine Arnold, *Bedlam London and Its Mad* (London: Pocket Books, 2008); https://historicengland.org.uk/research/inclusive-heritage/disability-history/1050–1485/from-bethlehem-to-bedlam/.

8. Holborn had begun to develop as a medieval suburb of the city, with houses that had

steadily increased in size and grandeur. The construction by the Bishop of Ely of a pala-
tial townhouse at present-day Ely Place served to underline its sense of self-worth. Its
13th-century chapel, dedicated to St Etheldreda, survives to the present day. The bishop's garden was noted for its strawberries and, in *Richard III*, Shakespeare has the Duke
of Gloucester say, 'My lord of Ely, when I was last in Holborn / I saw good strawberries in your garden there / I do beseech you send for some of them.' See http://hid-
den-london.com/gazetteer/holborn/; Walter Thornbury, 'Holborn: To Chancery
Lane', in *Old and New London* (London: Cassell, Petter and Galpin, 1878), vol. 2, 526–
42, http://www.british-history.ac.uk/old-new-london/vol2.

5. LEADENHALL

1. B Lambert, *The History and Survey of London and Its Environs, from the Earliest Period to the Present Time* (London, 1806), vol. 2.
2. George Edward Cokayne, Vicary Gibbs and H Arthur Doubleday, eds., *The Complete Peerage of England, Scotland, Ireland, Great Britain and the United Kingdom, Extant, Extinct or Dormant* (2nd edn, London: St Catherine Press, 1959); J Goronwy Edwards, *Calendar of Ancient Correspondence Concerning Wales* (Cardiff: Cardiff University Press, 1935); RW Eyton, *Antiquities of Shropshire* (London: JR Smith, 1854–60).
3. Janet Meisel, *Barons of the Welsh Frontier: The Corbet, Pantulf, and FitzWarin Families 1066–1272* (Lincoln: University of Nebraska Press, 1980), 35; P Brown, P King and P Remfry, 'Whittington Castle: The Marcher Fortress of the Fitz Warin Family', *Shropshire Archaeology and History* LXXIX (2004): 106–27; https://en.wikipedia.org/wiki/Fulk_FitzWarin; F Suppe, 'Fitzwarine Family (per. c.1145–1315)', *Oxford Dictionary of National Biography* online; 'Wantage Hundred: Introduction', and 'Parishes: Wantage', in *A History of the County of Berkshire*, vol. 4, eds. W Page and PH Ditchfield (London, 1924), 267–8, 319–32.
4. JS Roskell, L Clark and C Rawcliffe, 'Fitzwaryn, Sir Ivo (1347–1414) of Caundle Haddon, Dorset', *The House of Commons, 1386–1421*, eds. JS Roskell, L Clark and C Rawcliffe (Stroud: Sutton, 1993), http://www.historyofparliamentonline.org/volume/1386–1421/member/fitzwaryn-sir-ivo-1347–1414.
5. George Frederick Beltz, *Memorials of the Most Noble Order of the Garter* (London: William Pickering, 1841).
6. http://www.historyofparliamentonline.org/volume/1386–1421/member/fitzwaryn-sir-ivo-1347–1414.

6. CONNECTIONS

1. George Frederick Beltz, *Memorials of the Most Noble Order of the Garter* (London: William Pickering, 1841), 96–8; Sir William Dugdale, *Monasticon Anglicanum* (London, 1675–83), vol. 6, 746; John Hutchins, *History and Antiquities of the County of Dorset* (London: JB Nichols and Sons, 1863).
2. Liza Picard, *Chaucer's People: Everyday Lives in Medieval England* (London: Orion, 2017),

49; Ben Weinreb and Christopher Hibbert, *The London Encyclopaedia* (London: Papermac, 1993).

3. John Stow, *A Survey of London Written in the Year 1598* (Stroud: Sutton, 2009), 144–50.

4. AH Thomas, 'Notes on the History of the Leadenhall, 1195–1488', *London Topographical Record* 11 (1923): 1–22; HathiTrust Digital Library, University of Michigan, https://babel.hathitrust.org/cgi/pt?id=mdp. 39015049031902&view=1up&seq=8.

5. AH Thomas, ed., *Calendar of Select Pleas and Memoranda of the City of London, 1381–1412* (Cambridge: CUP, 1932), 122–3.

6. William Caferro, *John Hawkwood: An English Mercenary in Fourteenth-Century Italy*. (Baltimore: Johns Hopkins University Press, 2006).

7. Felix Barker and Peter Jackson, *London: 2000 Years of a City and Its People* (London: BCA, 1979), 71.

8. Thomas, 'Notes on the History of the Leadenhall, 1195–1488'.

9. Picard, *Chaucer's People*, 148; Stow, *A Survey of London*, 150–63; M Samuel and G Milne, 'The Ledene Hall and Medieval Market', in *From Roman Basilica to Medieval Market*, ed. G Milne (London: HMSO, 1992), 39–50; http://mapoflondon6.uvic.ca/.

7. FIRST DAY

1. Gordon Home, *Medieval London* (London: Bracken Books, 1994), 128; Jean Froissart, *Chronicles* (London: Penguin Classics, 1978).

2. As a religious fraternity drapers developed an early attachment to St Mary Bethlehem in Bishopsgate, 'founded in honour of the Virgin Mary by good people Drapers of Cornhill and other good men and women for the amendment of their lives'. The draper community was concentrated in the streets around Cornhill, Candlewick Street (Cannon Street) and Chepe (Cheapside) where they later adopted St Mary le Bow in Cheapside and later still St Michael, Cornhill—where the company continues to worship today—as their favoured churches. See https://en.wikipedia.org/wiki/Worshipful_Company_of_Drapers.

3. W Herbert, *The History of the Twelve Great Livery Companies of London*, 2 vols. (London, 1834); Robert B Ekelund Jr, Robert F Hébert and Robert D Tollison, 'The Political Economy of the Medieval Church', in *The Oxford Handbook of the Economics of Religion*, ed. Rachel M McCleary (Oxford: OUP, 2011); Sylvia Thrupp, *The Merchant Class of Medieval London, 1300–1500* (Ann Arbor: University of Michigan Press, 1962); Gary Richardson, 'Craft Guilds and Christianity in Late-Medieval England: A Rational-Choice Analysis', *Rationality and Society* 17 (2005). See also https://doi.org/10.1177/1043463105051631.

4. A useful insight into London life at this time is provided in 'Memorials: 1370', in *Memorials of London and London Life in the 13th, 14th and 15th Centuries*, ed. HT Riley (London: Longmans, Green and Co., 1868), 341–7, http://www.british-history.ac.uk/no-series/memorials-london-life/pp341–347.

5. After the inferno that swept London in 1212, the city's first mayor, Henry Fitz-Ailwyn,

introduced measures to replace timber-structured buildings with stone and those with thatched roofs with tile to prevent a recurrence. Where this was resisted or proved untenable, water barrels and fire rakes were required to be positioned adjoining those properties deemed likely to be engulfed by fire.

6. At the time of the Great Fire 1666 it was estimated that London had 109 medieval churches. A guide to what was lost can be found in Elizabeth and Wayland Young, *Old London Churches* (London: Faber and Faber, 1956); Gordon Huelin, *Vanished Churches of the City of London* (London: Guildhall Library Publications, 1966).

7. The City of London's 25 wards are: Aldersgate, Aldgate, Bassishaw, Billingsgate, Bishopsgate, Bread Street, Bridge and Bridge Without, Broad Street, Candlewick, Castle Baynard, Cheap, Coleman Street, Cordwainer, Cornhill, Cripplegate, Dowgate, Farringdon Within, Farringdon Without, Langbourn, Lime Street, Portsoken, Queenhithe, Tower, Vintry and Walbrook. They form a continuing thread in Whittington's civic and commercial careers. He represented Coleman Street and Lime Street. Farringdon was divided in 1394 into 'Within' and 'Without', defined by whether the ward was within or without the city (London) wall.

8. Paul Talling, *London's Lost Rivers* (London: Random House, 2011); Peter Ackroyd, *London Under* (London: Vintage Books, 2012).

9. DJ Keene and Vanessa Harding, *Historical Gazetteer of London before the Great Fire* (Cambridge: Chadwyck-Healey, 1987), http://www.british-history.ac.uk/no-series/london-gazetteer-pre-fire.

10. Writing in 1598, Stow reports that Goldsmiths Row, for example, was a section on the south side of Cheapside, by Cheapside Cross, which ran between Bread Street and Friday Street. Goldsmiths Row and the shops and homes of other wealthy merchants made the street an elite and attractive one. Stow claims that there were ten houses and fourteen shops on Goldsmiths Row and that they were easily the most beautiful in London. He adds that in 1491 the then sheriff of London, Thomas Wood, lived here and that he built the facades of some of the later beautiful houses on Goldsmiths Row and Wood Street which he 'garnished with the likeness of woodmen', suggesting that 'his predecessors might be the first owners, and namers of the street after their own name'. John Stow, *A Survey of London Written in the Year 1598* (Stroud: Sutton, 2009), 294–5, 257.

11. Ben Weinreb and Christopher Hibbert, *The London Encyclopaedia* (London: Papermac, 1993), 148.

12. Sir John Clapham, *The Concise Economic History of Britain from the Earliest Times to 1750* (Cambridge: CUP, 1957), 143.

13. For the present-day rankings, see https://en.wikipedia.org/wiki/Livery_company.

14. https://en.wikipedia.org/wiki/Livery_company.

15. Geoffrey Chaucer, *Troilus and Criseyde* (1374).

16. AR Myers, *Chaucer's London: Everyday Life in London, 1342–1400* (Stroud: Amberley, 2009), 59.

8. PLAGUE

1. Josiah Cox Russell, *British Medieval Population* (Albuquerque: University of New Mexico Press, 1948).

2. Daniel L Zimbler, Jay A Schroeder, Justin L Eddy and Wyndham Lathem, 'Early Emergence of *Yersinia pestis* as a Severe Respiratory Pathogen', *Nature Communications* 6 (2015).

3. Benedict Gummer, *The Scourging Angel: The Black Death in the British Isles* (London: Vintage Books, 2010), 62.

4. Philip Ziegler, *The Black Death* (Glasgow: Collins, 1969); J Hatcher, *Plague, Population and the English Economy, 1348–1530* (London: Macmillan, 1977); John Aberth, *The Black Death: The Great Mortality of 1348–1350: A Brief History with Documents* (London: Palgrave Macmillan, 2005); Ole J Benedictow, *The Black Death 1346–1353: The Complete History* (Suffolk: Boydell Press, 2004).

5. Michael Harrison, ed., *London Growing: The Development of a Metropolis* (London: Hutchison, 1965), 99.

6. Harrison, *London Growing*, 103.

7. Richard Holt and Gervase Rosser, *The English Medieval Town* (London: Longman, 1990).

8. Interview with Nils Stenseth, University of Oslo, http://www.bbc.co.uk/news/science-environment-42690577; http://www.iflscience.com/health-and-medicine/human-not-rat-parasites-were-responsible-for-the-black-death-new-research-finds/.

9. WG Hoskins, *Local History in England* (London: Longman, 1984).

10. Derek Keene, *The Walbrook Study: A Summary Report* (London: Centre for Metropolitan History, University of London, 1987).

11. Ziegler, *The Black Death*, 90–1.

12. T Amyat, 'Population of English Cities temp Edward III', *Acta Archaeologica* XX: 524–31.

13. Josiah C Russell, 'The Pre-plague Population of England', *Journal of British Studies* 5, no. 2 (1966): 1–21.

14. EA Wrigley and RS Schofield, *The Population History of England, 1541–1871: A Reconstruction* (London: Edward Arnold, 1981).

15. Tom James, *Black Death: The Lasting Impact* (BBC, Feb. 2011), http://www.bbc.co.uk/history/british/middle_ages/black_impact_01.shtml.

9. A NUMBERS GAME

1. MM Postan, 'Some Economic Evidence of Declining Population in the Later Middle Ages', in *Essays on Medieval Agriculture and General Problems of the Medieval Economy* (Cambridge: CUP, 1973).

2. Bruce Campbell, *Before the Black Death: Studies in the Crisis of the Early Fourteenth Century* (Manchester: Manchester University Press, 1991), 4.

3. Campbell, *Before the Black Death*, 5.

4. Postan, *Essays on Medieval Agriculture*.

5. Campbell, *Before the Black Death*, 22.

6. JMW Bean, 'Plague, Population and Economic Decline in England in the Later Middle Ages', *Economic History Review* 15, no. 3 (1963): 423–37, DOI: 10.2307/2592917, https://www.jstor.org/stable/2592917.

7. J Hatcher, *Plague, Population and the English Economy, 1348–1530* (Basingstoke: Macmillan, 1977), 15.

8. Hatcher, *Plague, Population and the English Economy*, 15; G Duby, *Rural Economy and Country Life in the Medieval West* (Columbia: University of South Carolina Press, 1968).

9. AR Bridbury, *Economic Growth: England in the Later Middle Ages* (London: George Allen and Unwin, 1961).

10. D Hawkins, 'The Black Death and the New London Cemeteries of 1348', *Antiquity* 64 (1990), https://doi.org/10.1017/S0003598X0007856X.

11. Goran Ohlin, 'No Safety in Numbers', quoted in Hatcher, *Plague, Population and the English Economy*, 14.

12. Philip Ziegler, *The Black Death* (Glasgow: Collins, 1969), 227.

13. Hatcher, *Plague, Population and the English Economy*, 25.

14. Hatcher, *Plague, Population and the English Economy*, 14.

15. J Bolton, 'The World Upside Down', in *Black Death in England*, ed. Mark Ormrod and Philip Lindley (Stamford: Paul Watkins Publishing, 1996).

16. Barbara F Harvey, 'Introduction: The "Crisis" of the Early Fourteenth Century', *Before the Black Death: Studies in the 'Crisis' of the Early Fourteenth Century*, eds. BMS Campbell (Manchester: Manchester University Press, 1991), 1–24.

17. Ole J Benedictow, *The Black Death 1346–1353: The Complete History* (Suffolk: Boydell Press, 2004).

18. Hatcher, *Plague, Population and the English Economy*, 31, notes that 'The immense loss in life in the plagues inevitably caused disruption and setbacks in production, but in greater part these appear to have been short-lived.'

10. RECOVERY

1. William Woods, *England in the Age of Chaucer* (London: Hart-Davis, 1976), 79.

2. Woods, *England in the Age of Chaucer*.

3. JL Bolton, *The Medieval English Economy 1150–1500* (London: Dent, 1980), 214.

4. Bolton writes that between 1377 and 1381 the government, in addition to normal taxes on movable property, introduced three new levies, the poll or head taxes raised on all those aged fourteen and above. The third poll tax of 1381 was the final straw and its collection was so ill presented and bungled 'it seemed as if another new tax was being taken without consent'. Bolton, *The Medieval English Economy*, 214.

5. Hatcher, *Plague, Population and the English Economy*.

6. Josiah Cox Russell, *British Medieval Population* (Albuquerque: University of New Mexico Press, 1948), 248; Bolton, *The Medieval English Economy*, 65.

7. NM Herbert, ed., *A History of the County of Gloucester*, vol. 4: *The City of Gloucester* (London, 1988), 35–41, http://www.british-history.ac.uk/vch/glos/vol4/pp35–41.

8. MC Prestwich, *Plantagenet England, 1225–1360* (Oxford: OUP, 2005).

9. Sir John Clapham, *The Concise Economic History of Britain from the Earliest Times to 1750* (Cambridge: CUP, 1957), 165.

10. Thomas James Beaumont, *The Palaces of Medieval England: Royalty, Nobility, the Episcopate, and Their Residences from Edward the Confessor to Henry VIII* (London: Seaby Press, 1990).

11. Eileen Power, *The Wool Trade in English Medieval History* (Oxford: OUP, 1941), 40.

12. Power, *The Wool Trade*, 64.

13. Power, *The Wool Trade*, 37.

14. See the extensive work of Anne Sutton, *The Mercery of London: Trade, Goods and People, 1130–1578* (London: Routledge, 2019).

15. Such as Alessandro de' Bardi, Bartolomeo de' Bardi, Pietro Bene, Dino Forzetti, Giovanni di Francesco, Francesco Grandoni, Jacopo Niccolini, and Pietro Rinieri. Edward racked up an extraordinary loan debt of 900,000 gold florins with the Bardis and a further 600,000 with their rivals, the Peruzzi. His refusal to repay either debt resulted in their bankruptcy. Applied History Research Group, 'Banking in the Middle Ages: The End of Europe's Middle Ages', University of Calgary, 1997; T Kunal, 'The Crash of the European Financial System in 1345', *Financial Engineer* (2013), https://thefinancialengineer.org/2013/03/31/14th-century-the-crash-of-peruzzi-and-the-bardi-family-in-1345/.

16. Ephraim Russell, 'The Societies of the Bardi and the Peruzzi and Their Dealings with Edward III', in *Finance and Trade under Edward III: The London Lay Subsidy of 1332*, ed. George Unwin (Manchester: Manchester University Press, 1918), 93–135, http://www.british-history.ac.uk/manchester-uni/london-lay-subsidy/1332/pp93–135.

11. LONDON'S MERCHANT CLASS

1. Caroline M Barron, *London in the Later Middle Ages: Government and People, 1200–1500* (Oxford: OUP, 2007), 45.

2. A useful study of London's population in the 14th century is offered in Robert E Hall, 'The Population of England in the 14th and 15th Century', paper, Stanford University, 12 January 1965, web.stanford.edu.

3. A recent and wide-ranging perspective on the impact of Sumptuary Laws is provided in Giorgio Riello and Ulinka Rublack, eds., *The Right to Dress: Sumptuary Laws in a Global Perspective, c.1200–1800* (Cambridge: CUP, 2020).

4. Gregory Clark, 'The Long March of History: Farm Wages, Population and Economic Growth, England, 1209–1869', *Economic History Review* 60, no. 1 (2007): 97–135; Colin Samuel, 'After the Black Death: Labour Legislation and Attitudes towards Labour in Late Medieval Western Europe', *Economic History Review* 60, no .3 (2007): 457–85.

5. See Peter Ackroyd, *Thames: Sacred River* (London: Chatto and Windus, 2007), 188; Ackroyd, *London: The Biography* (London: Vintage, 2001); Christopher Hibbert, *London: The Biography of a City* (London: Penguin, 1980); Simon Jenkins, *The City on the Thames* (London: Pegasus Books, 2020).

6. Norman Cantor, *In the Wake of the Plague: The Black Death and the World It Made* (New York: Free Press, 2001); Alexander Flick, *The Decline of the Medieval Church* (New York: Burt Franklin, 1967).

7. EL Veale, 'The Trade in Skins in the Thirteenth and Fourteenth Century', in *The English Fur Trade in the Later Middle Ages* (London: London Record Society, 2003), https://www.british-history.ac.uk/london-record-soc/vol38/pp57–77.

8. Chris Jones, 'Paris: Pinnacle of Gothic Architecture', in *The Great Cities in History*, ed. John Julius Norwich (London: Thames and Hudson, 2016), 128–32.

9. Ackroyd, *Thames: Sacred River*, 188.

10. Norwich, *The Great Cities in History*, 149–52.

11. Rainer Postel, 'The Hanseatic League and Its Decline', paper read at the Central Connecticut State University, 20 November 1996. First recorded in 1282 and described as a merchant community settled around a trading post on the Thames, the later named 'Steelyard' drew its legal status from a schedule of tax and custom concessions awarded by Edward I in a Carta Mercatoria proclaimed in 1303. Influential but also a focus of opposition in London throughout much of the 14th century, it was not until the early 15th century, when the London branch of the Hansa was driven by merchants from Cologne, that it increased its toehold on the English wool and cloth finishing industry, chiefly exporting through the port of Colchester. In exchange for their privileges the German merchants of the Steelyard undertook to maintain Bishopsgate, the gateway from London to their interests on the south-east coasts at Colchester, Boston and Lynn.

12. Ackroyd, *Thames: Sacred River*, 192.

13. http://www.portcities.org.uk/london/server/show/ConNarrative.37/chapterId/462/The-early-port.html.

14. Sir John Clapham, *The Concise Economic History of Britain from the Earliest Times to 1750* (Cambridge: CUP, 1957), 150.

15. Clapham, *The Concise Economic History of Britain*, 167.

16. Clapham, *The Concise Economic History of Britain*, 167.

17. Stephen Alford, *London's Triumph: Merchant Adventurers and the Tudor City* (London: Allen Lane, 2017), xi.

18. Alford, *London's Triumph*, xiii.

19. Alford, *London's Triumph*, xv.

12. MERCERS

1. Robert Seymour, *A Survey of the Cities of London and Westminster, Borough of Southwark and Parts Adjacent* (London, 1735), vol. 2, 337.

2. The Good Parliament sat from 28 April to 10 July, becoming the longest Parliament up to that time and taking place at a time when the English court was held by many

to be corrupt, wasteful and overbearing. It derived its name from the efforts of members to hold government to account and reform it.

3. AR Myers, *Chaucer's London: Everyday Life in London, 1342–1400* (Stroud: Amberley, 2009), 54.

4. John Stow, *A Survey of London Written in the Year 1598* (Stroud: Sutton, 2009), 413–7.

5. Stow reports that by 1531, in the reign of Henry VIII, there were at least 60 livery companies in the city. Stow, *A Survey of London*, 414–5.

6. For an early and recent list of London's livery companies, see https://en.wikipedia.org/wiki/Livery_company.

7. For a detailed account of a medieval London ward, see Christine M Fox and Timothy Hailes, *A History of Bassishaw Ward, 1200–1600* (ebook, 2014).

8. Nichols was one of the founders of the Camden Society and a product of the Merchant Taylors' School. See https://en.wikipedia.org/wiki/John_Gough_Nichols.

9. Roy Porter, *London: A Social History* (London: Penguin, 1994), 30.

10. Stow, *A Survey of London*, 236.

11. Stow, *A Survey of London*, 81.

12. John Watney, *Some Account of the Hospital of St Thomas of Acon, in the Cheap, London, and of the Plate of the Mercers' Company, London* (London: Blades, East and Blades, 1892).

13. Watney, *Some Account of the Hospital of St Thomas of Acon*.

14. Stow, *A Survey of London*, 86–7.

15. Sir John Clapham, *The Concise Economic History of Britain from the Earliest Times to 1750* (Cambridge: CUP, 1957), 124.

16. Stow, *A Survey of London*, 337–8.

17. See the timeline at https://www.mercers.co.uk/our-history/700-year-timeline#.

18. Anne F Sutton, *The Mercery of London: Trade, Goods, People, 1130–1578* (Abingdon: Routledge, 2005).

19. Anne F Sutton, 'The Merchant Adventurers of England: Their Origins and the Mercers', *Historical Research* 75, no. 1 (2002); EM Carus-Wilson, 'Early Development of the Merchant Adventurers Organisation in London as Shown in Their Own Medieval Records', *Economic History Review* (1933): 147–76; Laetitia Lyell, 'The Problem of the Records of the Merchant Adventurers', *Economic History Review* 5, no. 2 (1935): 96–8.

20. Stephen Alford, *London's Triumph: Merchant Adventurers and the Tudor City* (London: Allen Lane, 2017), 41.

21. Alford, *London's Triumph*, 47.

13. POLLUTION

1. Lynn I Perrigo, 'Plagues and Pollution in Medieval England', *Social Science* 46, no. 3 (1971): 133–8.

2. May McKisack, *The Fourteenth Century, 1307–1399* (Oxford: Clarendon Press, 1987), 379.

3. Peter Brimblecombe, 'Attitudes and Responses towards Air Pollution in Medieval England', *Journal of the Air Pollution Control Association* 26, no. 10 (1976), https://doi. org/10.1080/00022470.1976.10470341. Mark Jacobson writes that by 1200 London had been deforested and a switch began to 'sea-coal' that washed up on beaches. As early as the 1280s, there were complaints about smoke from burning coal. Attempts failed to ban burning then and again 250 years later during the reign of Queen Elizabeth I. Mark Z Jacobson, *Air Pollution and Global Warming: History, Science, and Solutions* (Cambridge: CUP, 2012).

4. William TE Brake, 'Air Pollution and Fuel Crises in Preindustrial London, 1250–1650', *Technology and Culture* 16, no. 3 (July 1975): 337–59, http://www.jstor.org/stable/3103030.

5. https://www.british-history.ac.uk/no-series/new-history-london/pp57–74.

6. McKisack, *The Fourteenth Century*, 372; Robert L Galloway, *Annals of Coalmining and the Coal Trade* (London: Colliery Guardian Company, 1898).

7. Ernest L Sabine, 'Butchering in Mediaeval London', *Speculum* 8, no. 3 (1933): 335–53.

8. For context, see Martha Carlin and Joel T Rosenthal, *Medieval London: Collected Papers of Caroline M Barron* (Kalamazoo: Western Michigan University Medieval Institute Publications, 2017).

9. 'This street is possessed for the most part by founders that cast candlesticks, chafing dishes, spice mortars, and such-like copper works, and do afterwards turn them with the foot and not with the wheel, to make them smooth and bright with turning and scratching (as some do term it), making a loathsome noise to the by-passers that have not been used to the like, and therefore by them disdainfully called Lothberie.' Walter Thornbury, *Old and New London* (London: Cassell, Petter and Galpin, 1878), vol. 1, 513–5, http://www.british-history.ac.uk/old-new-london/vol1/pp513–515.

14. OSMOSIS

1. J Bolton, *Money in the Medieval English Economy, 973–1489* (Manchester: Manchester University Press, 2012), 23–7; M Allen, *Mints and Money in Medieval England* (Cambridge: CUP, 2012); J Day, *The Medieval Market Economy* (Oxford: OUP, 1987); NJ Mayhew, ed., *Coinage in the Low Countries, 880–1500*, British Archaeological Reports, International Series (LIV, 1979), 95–161.

2. 'A Treatise on the Origin, Nature, Law and Alterations of Money', quoted in C Eagleton and J Williams, *Money: A History* (London: British Museum Press, 2007), 77.

3. 'A Treatise on the Origin, Nature, Law and Alterations of Money'.

4. Walter Besant and James Rice, *Sir Richard Whittington: Lord Mayor of London* (New York: Merrill Baker, 1894).

5. R Leach, *The Schools of Medieval England* (London: Methuen, 1916), https://warburg. sas.ac.uk/pdf/nlb220b2256346.pdf.

6. *Ars dictaminis* has been described as the art of prose composition, and more specifically of the writing of letters (*dictamines*), which was of relevance to apprentices charged

with acquiring skills in recording, correspondence, the writing of bills, etc. Frequently associated with the *ars dictandi*, which taught typically in Latin the composition of documents, it was therefore of interest to merchants and their scriveners. As a subject, composition fell within the wider study of rhetoric. See https://en.wikipedia. org/wiki/Ars_dictaminis. See also Janet Luehring and Richard Utz, 'Letter Writing in the Late Middle Ages: An Introductory Bibliography of Critical Studies', in *The Late Medieval Epistle*, eds. Carol Poster and Richard Utz (Evanston: Northwestern University Press, 1996), 191–221.

7. PW Hammond, *Food and Feast in Medieval England* (Stroud: Alan Sutton, 1993), 44–6.

8. Hammond, *Food and Feast*, 18–9, 46–7; Walter Thornbury, 'Fishmongers' Hall and Fish Street Hill', in *Old and New London* (London: Cassell, Petter and Galpin, 1878), vol. 2, 1–8, http://www.british-history.ac.uk/old-new-london/vol2/pp1–8.

9. John Stow, *A Survey of London Written in the Year 1598* (Stroud: Sutton, 2009), 187.

10. For a description of the dubious trade in fish, see Gustav Milne, *The Port of Medieval London* (Stroud: Tempus, 2003), 148–50.

11. John Noorthouck, 'Billingsgate Ward', in *A New History of London, Including Westminster and Southwark* (London, 1773), book 2, ch. 7, 551–3.

12. Gustav Milne and Chrissie Milne, *Medieval Waterfront Development at Trig Lane, London* (London: London and Middlesex Archaeological Society, 1982).

13. William Herbert, *The History of the Twelve Great Livery Companies of London* (London: self-published, 1834; republished by David and Charles, 1968), vol. 2. The two divisions of the trade are described as follows: 'The company of the fishmongers is one of the twelve great companies; it originally was divided into stockmongers and fishmongers; the first were incorporated in 1433; a period in which we had a very considerable trade with Iceland in that very article.'

14. 'The London Fishmongers were divided into two distinct classes, "Stock-fishmongers", and "Salt-fishmongers". Then Thames Street was known as "Stock Fishmongers-Row", and the old fish-market of London was "above bridge", what is now called "Old Fish-Street hill" in the ward of Queenhithe, not as now "below bridge" in Thames-street in the ward of Billingsgate.' Peter Cunningham, *Handbook of London: Past and Present; Its History, Associations and Traditions* (London: John Murray, 1849), vol. 1.

15. https://bendgong.wordpress.com/category/gong-farming/the-gong-farmer-of-the-middle-ages-and-tudor-england/.

16. Keene, Derek, *The Walbrook Study: A Summary Report* (London: Centre for Metropolitan History, University of London, 1987). Peter Ackroyd provides a more gruesome reference to the Walbrook's earlier history as a repository for skulls 'once believed to represent the victims of Boudicea's invasion of London in 60 AD … But the question then remains, why only the skulls?' Peter Ackroyd, *Thames: Sacred River* (London: Chatto and Windus, 2007), 372. See also Paul Talling, *London's Lost Rivers* (London: Penguin, 2011).

17. Ben Weinreb and Christopher Hibbert, *The London Encyclopaedia* (London: Papermac, 1993), 918.

18. Michael Harrison, *London Growing: The Development of a Metropolis* (London: Hutchinson, 1965), 99.

19. Weinreb and Hibbert, *The London Encyclopaedia*, 484.
20. Weinreb and Hibbert, *The London Encyclopaedia*, 752.
21. Weinreb and Hibbert, *The London Encyclopaedia*, 368.
22. Stow remarks that 'There be monuments in this church of Reginald Coleman, son to Robert Coleman, buried there 1383. This said Robert Coleman may be supposed the first builder or owner of Coleman Street; and that St Stephen's Church, there builded in Coleman Street, was but a chappel belonging to the parish church of St. Olave, in the Jewry.' Stow, *A Survey of London*, 246.

15. APPRENTICE

1. Scavage was a toll charged of non-resident merchants by mayors or towns on goods offered or sold in their districts. Tronage was a customary duty or toll for weighing wool; so called because it was weighed by a common trona, or beam.
2. John Stow, *A Survey of London Written in the Year 1598* (Stroud: Sutton, 2009), 102–4.
3. Stow, *A Survey of London*, 107.
4. The Stews were situated in Bankside and Maid Lane in Southwark and formed part of the estate owned by the Bishop of Winchester. 'Bankside', in Howard Roberts and Walter H Godfrey, eds., *Survey of London*, vol. 22: *Bankside (The Parishes of St Saviour and Christchurch Southwark)* (London, 1950), 57–65, https://www.british-history.ac.uk/survey-london/vol22; Martha Carlin, *Medieval Southwark* (London: Hambledon Press, 1996). In 1393 'the City decreed that all prostitution was to be banished to Cokkes Lane in Smithfield, and to the stews in Bankside. Stew Lane, a narrow street that still exists today on the City side of the River Thames, led down to the river and was where people would take a boat to cross over to the Bankside stews.' The women who offered their services there were mischievously known as 'Winchester Geese'. See 'Exploring Southwark', http://www.exploringsouthwark.co.uk/the-bankside-stews/4593475219.
5. The starlings were the timber pillars piled into the river which provided the bridge with its structural integrity but which also had the dangerous effect of causing the water in their immediate vicinity to churn and, during bad weather and changes of tides, to create small threatening whirlpools which could easily upset small boats. Their infamy produced the dangerous sport of 'shooting the bridge' during which the foolhardy (often drunk) would attempt to squeeze between them as the water rushed and roiled, leading to many deaths and injuries. It led to the saying that London Bridge was 'made for wise men to cross and for fools to go under'. Ben Weinreb and Christopher Hibbert, *The London Encyclopaedia* (London: Papermac, 1993), 468.

16. FROM GOOD TO BAD

1. D'Argentine was the son and heir of John d'Argentine by his second wife, Agnes de Bereford, and held extensive estates in Norfolk, Suffolk, Cambridgeshire and Herts. He fathered two daughters: Mathilda (Maud), who married Fitzwarin, and Elizabeth.

2. *Calendar of Inquisitions Post Mortem*, vol. 2, 217, 323; vol. 3, 454, cited in the *Dictionary of National Biography*.

3. Gerald Harriss, *Shaping the Nation: England, 1360–1461* (Oxford: OUP, 2006); AD Carr, *Owen of Wales: The End of the House of Gwynedd* (Cardiff: University of Wales Press, 1991).

4. David Nicolle, *The Great Chevauchée: John of Gaunt's Raid on France, 1373* (Oxford: Osprey Publishing, 2011).

5. Walter Thornbury, 'Upper Thames Street', in *Old and New London* (London: Cassell, Petter and Galpin, 1878), 17–28, http://www.british-history.ac.uk/old-new-london/vol2/; Paul Strohm, *The Poet's Tale: Chaucer and the Year That Made the Canterbury Tales* (London: Profile Books, 2014); Gerald Home, *Medieval London* (London: Bracken Books, 1994), 141.

6. Strohm, *The Poet's Tale*, 1–8, 16–21.

7. Robert Whittington continued to maintain contact with his widow, Lady Elizabeth, for whom he would stand surety at the Exchequer in July 1388.

8. Caroline Frances Eleanor Spurgeon, *Five Hundred Years of Chaucer Criticism and Allusion (1357–1900)*, 3 vols. (Cambridge: CUP, 1925).

9. Jean Froissart, *Chronicles* (London: Penguin Classics, 1978), 194.

10. May McKisack, *The Fourteenth Century, 1307–1399* (Oxford: Clarendon Press, 1987), 387–94.

17. INTEREST GROUP POLITICS

1. Anthony Kenny, 'Wycliffe, John (d. 1384)', *Dictionary of National Biography*, (Oxford University Press online, 2004); Gordon Leff, *John Wyclif: The Path to Dissent* (Oxford: OUP, 1966).

2. AK McHardy, 'Richard II: A Personal Portrait', in *The Reign of Richard II*, ed. Gwilym Dodd (Stroud: Tempus, 2000), 12.

3. A detailed commentary on the 'victuallers' party' is provided by Anne Sutton in *The Mercery of London: Trade, Goods and People, 1130–1578* (Abingdon: Routledge, 2005). See also Paul Strohm's account of the culmination of Nicholas Brembre's 'extreme partisanship' in the final days of his challenge to Richard II. Paul Strohm, *The Poet's Tale* (London: Profile Books, 2014), 173–80.

4. *The Court of the Common Council*, Information leaflet 13 (London Metropolitan Archives of the City of London).

5. Myers, *Chaucer's London*, 75.

6. William Woods, *England in the Age of Chaucer* (London: Hart-Davis, 1976), 30.

7. Caroline M Barron and Anne F Sutton, eds., *Medieval London Widows, 1300–1500* (London: Hambledon Press, 1994), 86–8. This 'guild reinforcement' can also be seen in Sylvia L Thrupp, *The Merchant Class of Medieval London, 1300–1500* (Ann Arbor: University of Michigan Press, 1962), 326; and in Frank Rexroth, *Deviance and Power in Late Medieval London* (Cambridge: CUP, 2007).

8. JS Roskell, L Clark and C Rawcliffe, eds., *The House of Commons, 1386–1421*, http://

www.historyofparliamentonline.org/volume/1386–1421/member/vanner-henry-1395.

9. The brewers' manipulation of weights, measures and quality of ale was an issue for London's mayors as early as the 1270s. See George Unwin, *The Gilds and the Companies of London* (London: Methuen, 1908), 65.

10. May McKisack, *The Fourteenth Century, 1307–1399* (Oxford: Clarendon Press, 1987), 377–8, 434–6.

11. Caroline M Barron and Laura Wright, eds., *The London Jubilee Book, 1376–1387: An Edition of Trinity College Cambridge MS 0.3.11, ff. 133–57* (Woodbridge: Boydell and Brewer, 2021).

12. Twyford was prominent in London's politics; an alderman of Coleman Street ward in 1376, he was sheriff in 1378 (*Calendar of the Patent Rolls: Edward III, 1377–81*, 146, 267). He belonged to John of Gaunt's party led by Northampton, opposed to the 'court party' led by Brembre. Brembre was mayor when Twyford clashed with him, having imprisoned a close goldsmith associate of Twyford. See HT Riley, ed., *Memorials of London and London Life in the 13th, 14th and 15th Centuries* (London: Longmans, Green and Co., 1868), 415–7; 'Nicholas Twyford', *Dictionary of National Biography*, https://en.wikisource.org/wiki/Twyford,_Nicholas_(DNB00).

13. https://www.historyofparliamentonline.org/volume/1386–1421/member/bamme-adam-1397.

14. Stephen Halliday, *Newgate: London's Prototype of Hell* (Stroud: Sutton Publishing, 2007).

15. John Stow, *A Survey of London Written in the Year 1598* (Stroud: Sutton, 1994), 15.

16. Halliday, *Newgate*, 14. 'These culprits had offended their fellow citizens rather than infringed the king's peace—broadly speaking they had committed civil rather than criminal offences. These were "respectable" criminals, many of them tradesmen and freemen of the city who had fallen on hard times. They had once associated with the mayor, sheriffs and members of the governing body, known as the Court of Common Council, which ran the Square Mile.'

17. 'In 1378 pestilence attacked once again, the fifth time it had come. On this occasion it seems to have bypassed the South of England, entering in at York directly from the continent and—in the words of Thomas Walsingham—"almost the entire region was rapidly stripped of its best men".' B Gummer, *The Scourging Angel: The Black Death in the British Isles* (London: Vintage, 2010), 404.

18. ARRIVAL

1. http://www.new.ox.ac.uk/college-history.

2. MH Keen, *England in the Later Middle Ages* (London: Routledge, 2004), 205–6.

3. May McKisack, *The Fourteenth Century, 1307–1399* (Oxford: Clarendon Press, 1987), 403.

4. John Noorthouck, 'Richard II to the Wars of the Roses', in *A New History of London, Including Westminster and Southwark* (London, 1773), book 1, ch. 5, 75–94, http://www.british-history.ac.uk/no-series/new-history-london/pp75–94.

5. HT Riley, ed., *Memorials of London and London Life in the 13th, 14th and 15th Centuries* (London: Longmans, Green and Co., 1868), 531–5, http://www.british-history. ac.uk/no-series/memorials-london-life/pp531–535; Caroline M Barron, 'Richard Whittington: The Man behind the Myth', in *Studies in London History Presented to Philip Edmund Jones*, eds. AEJ Hollaender and William Kellaway (London: Hodder and Stoughton, 1969), 197–248.

6. Samuel Lysons, *The Model Merchant of the Middle Ages Exemplified in the Story of Whittington and His Cat* (London: Hamilton Adams and Co., 1860), 96. Very little is known of Whittington's settlement and early life in London. The legend converts the Dorsetshire knight, his father-in-law, into a London merchant and his master, which Sir Walter Besant accepts as historical fact. But his first authentic appearance belongs to 1379, when he contributed 5 marks to a city loan. Riley, *Memorials of London and London Life*, 534, quoted in *Dictionary of National Biography*.

7. For a detailed note on Whittington's career in London, see JS Roskell, L Clark and C Rawcliffe, eds., *The House of Commons, 1386–1421* (Stroud: Sutton, 1993), http:// www.historyofparliamentonline.org/volume/1386-1421/member/whittington-richard-1423.

8. Thrupp, *The Merchant Class of Medieval London*, 91.

9. Eileen Power, *The Wool Trade in English Medieval History: Being the Ford Lectures* (Oxford: OUP, 1955), 4.

10. 'Houses of Benedictine Monks: The Abbey of St Peter at Gloucester', in *A History of the County of Gloucester*, vol. 2, ed. William Page (London, 1907), 53–61, www.british-history.ac.uk/vch/glos/vol2/.

11. Power, *The Wool Trade*, 19.

12. Power notes: 'large-scale cloth production and large-scale sheep farming were exceptional in their intrinsic character. They were also exceptional in the intimacy of their connection with each other. The economic, and a good deal of the political history of Europe has been profoundly influenced by the fact that the earliest homes of cloth manufacture were not identical with the most important centres of wool production. The wool producing areas found their chief market abroad and the cloth-producing areas were all working with imported raw materials.'

19. REVOLT

1. See George Unwin, *The Gilds and the Companies of London* (London: Methuen, 1908), 102–4, 159–60; W Herbert, *The History of the Twelve Great Livery Companies of London*, 2 vols. (London, 1836).

2. Whittington served Coleman Street ward from 31 July 1384 to 1386 before taking on the role of alderman of Broad Street ward from 12 March 1393 to after 24 June 1397, and Lime Street ward from 13 February 1398.

3. May McKisack, *The Fourteenth Century, 1307–1399* (Oxford: Clarendon Press, 1987), 377–8, 434–6.

4. Sylvia L Thrupp, *The Merchant Class of Medieval London, 1300–1500* (Ann Arbor: University of Michigan Press, 1962), 79–80.

5. Thrupp, *The Merchant Class of Medieval London*, 79–80.

6. JL Leland, 'Robert Tresilian', *Oxford Dictionary of National Biography* online.

7. Following the Merciless Parliament, which resulted in the execution of Brembre and Thomas Usk in 1388, Northampton was granted a full pardon in December 1390. His full citizenship was granted five years later in 1395. Usk had been Northampton's servant when he served as mayor from 1381 to 1383. In 1384, he was arrested but released in exchange for informing against his former master, stating that he had no desire to be 'a stinking martyr'. See EW Gosse, 'Thomas Usk', *Encyclopaedia Britannica*, 11th edn.

20. AT COURT

1. On St Mary Bethlehem see https://historicengland.org.uk/research/inclusive-heritage/disability-history/1050–1485/from-bethlehem-to-bedlam/. It was the Drapers' Company who in 1805 offered land at Islington for the rebuilding of a new hospital, only to find that the restrictions of trust ownership prevented it. C Arnold, *Bedlam, London and Its Mad* (London: Pocket Books, 2008).

2. Arthur Bryant, *Set in a Silver Sea* (London: William Collins, 1984), vol. 1, 339.

3. Bryant, *Set in a Silver Sea*.

4. https://en.wikipedia.org/wiki/Humphrey_Stafford,_1st_Duke_of_Buckingham.

5. Countess of Stafford (30 April 1383—16 October 1438). Anne had strong connections with Gloucestershire and was buried in 1438 at Llanthony Priory, a few miles from Whittington's family home in Pauntley. A seminal history of the Staffords is provided by C Rawcliffe, *The Staffords, Earls of Stafford and Dukes of Buckingham, 1394–1521* (Cambridge: CUP, 1978).

6. David Nash Ford, 'Sir William Fitzwarin', *Royal Berkshire History*, http://www.berkshirehistory.com/bios/wfitzwarin.html.

7. Eileen Power, *The Wool Trade in English Medieval History: Being the Ford Lectures* (Oxford: OUP, 1955), 121.

8. May McKisack, *The Fourteenth Century, 1307–1399* (Oxford: Clarendon Press, 1987), 468; FRH du Boulay and Caroline M Barron, *The Reign of Richard II: Essays in Honour of May McKisack* (London: Athlone Press, 1971), 178–9.

9. On 5 April 1376 Carlisle joined with Lyons, Twyford and two others in lending £1,000 to Edward III, who undertook to repay them out of the wool custom. In September 1377 a huge loan to the government of £10,000 was raised by a group of leading merchants. See https://www.historyofparliamentonline.org/volume/1386–1421/member/carlisle-adam-13991400. John Hadley was a notable lender and royal creditor throughout the 1370s, lending 40 marks to Edward III in February 1371, a co-contributor to royal loans of £3,000 in December 1374, and one of the contributors to the £10,000 loan of September 1377. Like Whittington, he was also a contributor to the 'gift' raised in January 1379 to entice the 'great lords of the realm' back to London. See https://www.historyofparliamentonline.org/volume/1386–1421/member/hadley-john-1410.

10. EB Fryde, *William de la Pole: Merchant and King's Banker, 1366* (London: Hambledon Press, 1988), 41–50, 51–2.

11. Anthony Bedford Steel, *The Receipt of the Exchequer, 1377–1485* (Cambridge: CUP, 1954); TF Tout, *Chapters in the Administrative History of Mediaeval England: The Wardrobe, the Chamber and the Small Seals*, 6 vols. (Manchester: Manchester University Press, 1920–33). The Great Wardrobe had moved in the early 1360s to a site north of Baynard's Castle and, during Whittington's time, it was not only a 'depository' for royal clothing, accessories and other finery but also the 'operational centre' for that part of the royal household and included storage, meeting rooms, lodgings for its staff, rooms for production and tailoring, and a private space for the king to meet, entertain and rest.

12. Caroline M Barron, 'Richard Whittington: The Man behind the Myth', in *Studies in London History Presented to Philip Edmund Jones*, eds. AEJ Hollaender and William Kellaway (London: Hodder and Stoughton, 1969).

13. Sylvia L Thrupp, *The Merchant Class of Medieval London, 1300–1500* (Ann Arbor: University of Michigan Press, 1962), 55.

14. Whittington's full list of offices include common councillor, Coleman Street ward, 31 July 1384–6; alderman of Broad Street ward, 12 March 1393—after 24 June 1397; Lime Street ward by 13 February 1398; mayor, London, 8 June 1397—13 October 1398, 13 October 1406 to 1407, 1419–20; sheriff, London and Middlesex, March 1393 to 1394. See https://www.historyofparliamentonline.org/volume/1386-1421/member/whittington-richard-1423.

15. John Stow, *A Survey of London Written in the Year 1598* (Stroud: Sutton, 1994), 241–8.

16. Walter Thornbury, 'Cripplegate' in *Old and New London* (London: Cassell, Petter and Galpin, 1878), 229–45, http://www.british-history.ac.uk/report.aspx?compid=45093.

17. *The Court of the Common Council*, Information leaflet 13 (London Metropolitan Archives of the City of London).

18. AR Myers, *Chaucer's London: Everyday Life in London, 1342–1400* (Stroud: Amberley, 2009), 75.

19. Jonathan Sumption, *The Hundred Years War: Cursed Kings* (London: Faber and Faber, 2015), 159, 162–3. Gaunt sailed on 9 July 1386 with a large Anglo-Portuguese fleet carrying an army of about 5,000 men plus an extensive 'royal' household including his wife and daughters. Pausing on the journey to use his army to drive off the French forces who were then besieging Brest, he landed at Corunna in northern Spain on 29 July.

20. http://www.historyofparliamentonline.org/volume/1386–1421/member/whittington-richard-1423#footnote11_87nf246.

21. http://www.historyofparliamentonline.org/volume/1386–1421/member/whittington-richard-1423#footnote11_87nf246.

22. Paul Strohm describes Chaucer's London job as controller of customs as 'always a precarious one'. He had been inserted as the 'fall guy in a major profiteering scheme',

his role being to certify the probity of powerful and influential customs collectors—including his associate the imperious Nicholas Brembre. Wool duties at this time contributed one-third of the total revenues of the realm. Towards the end of 1386 Chaucer was among the early casualties of Richard II's unpopularity and Brembre's impending fall. He was deprived of his much-coveted Aldgate apartment, denounced in Parliament and pressed to resign his controllership, leading to voluntary self-exile in Kent. Paul Strohm, 'Who Was Chaucer?', https://www.theguardian.com/books/2015/jan/24/who-was-chaucer-canterbury-tales.

23. *History or Narration Concerning the Manner and Form of the Miraculous Parliament at Westminster in the year 1386, in the tenth year of the reign of King Richard the Second after the Conquest, declared by Thomas Favent, Clerk*, http://www.arts.cornell.edu/prh3/310/texts/favent.html. See translation by Andrew Galloway in Emily Steiner and Candace Barrington, eds., *The Letter of the Law: Legal Practice and Literary Production in Medieval England* (Ithaca: Cornell University Press, 2002), 231–52.

24. Fryde provides a useful note on de la Pole's rise and demise. EB Fryde, *William de la Pole: Merchant and King's Banker, 1366* (London: Hambledon Press, 1988), 230–1.

25. De Vere was proclaimed by the Commons as undesirable and persona non grata through a bill of attainder, which enabled the state to acquire his estate on his demise. Michael Whittington, *The Whittington Story: From the Three Counties to the City* (Oxford: Parchment Press, 1988), 30.

26. See Anthony Goodman, *The Loyal Conspiracy: The Lords Appellant under Richard II*. (Miami: University of Miami Press, 1971). Thomas of Woodstock was imprisoned in Calais to await trial for treason. Infamously, he was assassinated during his internment on 8 September 1397 by a group of Richard II's close supporters believed to have been led by Thomas de Mowbray, Duke of Norfolk, and Sir Nicholas Colfox. The outcry at both his death and the circumstances of his murder provoked further unrest and served only to deepen Richard's unpopularity.

21. MERCER RISING

1. Arthur Bryant, *Set in a Silver Sea* (London: William Collins, 1984), vol. 1, 363.

2. Anthony Steel, *Richard II* (Cambridge: CUP, 1941), 7–8, quoted in AK McHardy, *The Reign of Richard II: From Minority to Tyranny, 1377–97* (Manchester: Manchester University Press, 2012).

3. Steel, *Richard II*, 174–5.

4. Nigel Saul, *Richard II* (New Haven: Yale University Press, 1997), 202.

5. McHardy, *The Reign of Richard II*, 16.

6. JG Edwards, 'The Parliamentary Committee of 1398', *English Historical Review* XL, no. CLIX (1925): 324–5.

7. FRH du Boulay and Caroline M Barron, *The Reign of Richard II: Essays in Honour of May McKisack* (London: Athlone Press, 1971), 173–4.

8. John Noorthouck, *A New History of London, Including Westminster and Southwark* (London, 1773), 75–94, http://www.british-history.ac.uk/no-series/new-history. For a

detailed study on sanitation in the medieval era, see Dolores Marie Jorgensen, 'Private Need, Public Order: Urban Sanitation in Late Medieval England and Scandinavia', PhD dissertation, University of Virginia, May 2008.

9. Noorthouck, *A New History of London*.

10. Buchanan Sharp, *Famine and Scarcity in Late Medieval and Early Modern England: The Regulation of Grain Marketing, 1256–1631* (Cambridge: CUP, 2016), 129.

11. Sharp, *Famine and Scarcity*.

12. *Knighton's Chronicon* was written during the 14th century by Henry Knighton, an Augustinian canon, comprising five chronicles, the last covering 1377–95. See Geoffrey Haward Martin, trans., *Knighton's Chronicle 1337–1396* (Oxford: Clarendon Press, 1995); and AR Myers, *English Historical Documents*, vol. 4: *1327–1485* (Oxford: Oxford University Press, 1969). Both cited at https://en.wikipedia.org/wiki/Knighton%27s_Chronicon.

13. Sharp, *Famine and Scarcity*, 129; Noorthouck, *A New History of London*; and Adam Anderson, *Historical and Chronological Deduction of the Origin of Commerce*, vol. 1 (London, 1764), 218.

14. Du Boulay and Barron, *The Reign of Richard II*, 178 n. 16.

15. Du Boulay and Barron, *The Reign of Richard II*, 169.

16. Du Boulay and Barron, *The Reign of Richard II*, 181.

17. Jean Imray, *The Charity of Richard Whittington: A History of the Trust Administered by the Mercers' Company, 1424–1966* (London: Athlone Press, 1968), 33.

18. George Unwin, *The Gilds and Companies of London* (London: Methuen, 1908).

19. The Bishop of Salisbury, the Chancellor (the Bishop of York) and the Duke of Gloucester 'weighed in' and the mayor and leading members of the council were made liable and imprisoned in several places and the governance of London was placed until Christmas in the hands of the king's appointees Dalyngrigge and Radyngton. Thomas Carte, *A General History of England*, vol. II (London, 1750).

20. LC Hector and Barbara F Harvey, eds., *The Westminster Chronicle, 1381–1394* (Oxford: OUP, 1982), 493–5.

21. Ian Mortimer, *The Fears of Henry IV: The Life of England's Self-made King* (London: Vintage, 2008), 104.

22. Mortimer, *The Fears of Henry IV*.

23. The northern boundary of Broad Street ward was formed by London Wall and what is today Blomfield Street and bordered Coleman Street ward. It had boundaries with Bishopsgate and Cornhill where it connected with the modern Throgmorton Street. Its western boundary snaked through the small courts and narrow alleys that ran alongside Moorgate. See https://en.wikipedia.org/wiki/Broad_Street_(ward).

24. Unwin, *The Gilds and Companies of London*, 106–7, describes the early congregation of drapers in and around Candlewick Street and later on at Cornhill, where he notes that 'the gild out of which the Drapers' Company grew was that founded in the Hospital of Our Lady of Bethlehem, in 1361, by the Drapers of Cornhill'.

25. https://web.archive.org/web/20110613033710/http:/www.cityoflondon.gov.uk/

Corporation/LGNL_Services/Leisure_and_culture/Local_history_and_heritage/sheriffs.htm.

26. 'Memorials: 1393', in *Memorials of London and London Life in the 13th, 14th and 15th Centuries*, ed. HT Riley (London: Longmans, Green and Co., 1868), 531–5, http://www.british-history.ac.uk/no-series/memorials-london-life/pp531–535.

27. https://www.historyofparliamentonline.org/volume/1386–1421/member/knolles-thomas-1435.

28. Alfred P Beaven, 'Chronological List of Aldermen: 1302–1400', in *The Aldermen of the City of London Temp. Henry III—1912* (London, 1908), 379–404, http://www.british-history.ac.uk/no-series/london-aldermen/hen3–1912/pp379–404.

22. THE COMPANY

1. TF Reddaway and Lorna EM Walker, *The Early History of the Goldsmiths Company, 1327–1509* (London: Edward Arnold, 1973), 262. The goldsmiths had received their first royal charter as early as 1327, giving them the right to enforce good authority and the standards within the trade, and emphasising the company's standing over provincial goldsmiths, marking its formal existence as a craft guild, with St Dunstan as its patron saint. See also https://www.thegoldsmiths.co.uk/company/history/history-of-the-company/.

2. 'As a former renter and warden of his livery company, Bamme played a prominent part in the acquisition by the Goldsmiths of land and rents in London after they had been granted their new charter by the Crown in February 1393. Although no record of the negotiations leading up to the award has survived, it seems likely that Henry and Adam Bamme, together with their associate Drew Barantyn, were chiefly instrumental in obtaining King Richard's favour.' http://www.historyofparliamentonline.org/volume/1386–1421/member/bamme-adam-1397.

3. John Noorthouck, 'Richard II to the Wars of the Roses', in *A New History of London Including Westminster and Southwark* (London, 1773), 75–94, http://www.british-history.ac.uk/no-series/new-history-london/pp75–94.

4. Sir John Watney, *An Account of the Mistery of Mercers of the City of London: Otherwise the Mercers' Company* (London: Blades, East and Blades, 1914). An exceptional history of the Mercers' Company is provided by Anne Sutton, *The Mercers' Company First Charter 1394* (London: Mercers' Company, 1994), 121–4, regarding their efforts to secure their charter in 1394.

5. https://www.thegoldsmiths.co.uk/company/history/history-of-the-company/.

6. Watney, *An Account of the Mistery of Mercers*.

7. In April 1397 the Mercers' Company acquired a licence in mortmain for three shops and three messuages in St Martin Outwich.

8. Whittington served as warden from 24 June 1395, and again in 1401–2 and 1408–9. Mercers' Company, Recs. Wardens acct. book, ff. 16v, 34, 47v.

9. St Thomas was from an early time the church of the mercer fraternity, located in Chepe. Watney describes as 'originally one of the houses of the military order of the

Knights of St Thomas of Acre, a small body of men who formed themselves into a semi-religious order on the model of the Templars; they wore a mantle with a red and white cross on it. The order was never numerous, and was probably poor.' Sir John Watney, *Some Account of the Hospital of St Thomas of Acon, in the Cheap, London and of the Plate of the Mercers' Company* (London: Blades, East and Blades, 1892), 36. Harrison reports that the order, though far smaller than the Templars, 'yet possessed considerable property in Poultry'. Michael Harrison, *London Growing: The Development of a Metropolis* (London: Hutchinson, 1965), 103.

10. Watney, *Some Account of the Hospital of St Thomas of Acon*, 36.
11. After the Dissolution of the Monasteries (1536–41), the hospital and chapel were purchased by the mercers only to be destroyed by the Great Fire of London 1666. A second hall was commissioned in 1676 but fell to the Blitz of 1941. Some of the original woodwork and stained glass were saved and incorporated in a replacement hall erected in 1958. A link with the original chapel remains in the form of the statue of Christ which lies at the entrance to the Mercers' Chapel, marking the Worshipful Company of Mercers as one of the few London livery companies to have its own private chapel. http://www.mercers.co.uk/700-years-history#. See Alan J Forey, 'The Military Order of St Thomas of Acre', *English Historical Review* 92 (1977): 481–503.
12. AR Myers, *Chaucer's London: Everyday Life in London, 1342–1400* (Stroud: Amberley, 2009), 90.
13. Myers, *Chaucer's London*, 90–2.
14. AP Baggs, ARJ Jurica and WJ Sheils, 'Stroud: Manors and Other Estates', in *A History of the County of Gloucester*, vol. 11: *Bisley and Longtree Hundreds*, ed. NM Herbert and RB Pugh (London, 1976), 111–19, http://www.british-history.ac.uk/vch/glos/vol11/pp111–119.
15. http://www.historyofparliamentonline.org/volume/1386–1421/member/fitz-waryn-sir-ivo-1347-1414. Whittington Castle was not of strategic importance and Fitzwarin gave it up before the spring of 1386, probably because of military commitments elsewhere. From September 1394 to April 1395, he served the king in Ireland with a small company of three esquires and four archers remunerated from the Royal Wardrobe. The award of Whittington almost certainly resulted from his family connections and was probably to safeguard the minority of his young kinsman, ending with Fulk's death in 1407.
16. Sylvia L Thrupp, *The Merchant Class of Medieval London, 1300–1500* (Ann Arbor: University of Michigan Press, 1962), 23.
17. Thrupp, *The Merchant Class of Medieval London*.
18. Thrupp, *The Merchant Class of Medieval London*.

23. THE MAYORALTY

1. Walter Besant and James Rice, *Sir Richard Whittington: Lord Mayor of London* (New York: Merrill Baker, 1894), 11.
2. Derek Keene, 'Henry fitz Ailwin (d. 1212)', *Oxford Dictionary of National Biography* online, https://en.wikipedia.org/wiki/Henry_fitz_Ailwin.

3. https://en.wikipedia.org/wiki/List_of_lord_mayors_of_London.

4. Helena M Chew and William Kellaway, eds., *London Assize of Nuisance 1301–1431: A Calendar* (London: London Record Society, 1973), ix–xxxiv, http://www.british-history.ac.uk/report.aspx?compid=35968.

5. 'Introduction', *London Assize of Nuisance 1301–1431*.

6. 'Chronicles of the Mayors and Sheriffs: 1188–1239', in *Chronicles of the Mayors and Sheriffs of London 1188–1274*, ed. HT Riley (London: Trübner, 1863), 1–8.

7. See https://www.cityoflondon.gov.uk/about-the-city/history/Pages/mayoralty.aspx; https://www.magnacartabarons.info/index.php/the-barons/hardel-william/.

8. Nigel Saul, *Richard II* (New Haven: Yale University Press, 1997); http://magnacarta800th.com/schools/biographies/the-25-barons-of-magna-carta/william-hardel/. Poole remarks that 'The inclusion of the mayor of London among the twenty-five barons elected to carry out the terms of Magna Carta is an expression of the important position which the boroughs had reached by the beginning of the thirteenth century.' AH Poole, *Domesday Book to Magna Carta, 1087–1216* (Oxford: Clarendon Press, 1986), 73–4.

9. Sir Maurice Powicke, *The Thirteenth Century, 1216–1307* (Oxford: Clarendon Press, 1987), 28–37.

10. The description is cited by Matthew Paris to a dialogue attributed to Pope Innocent IV. See MA Michael, 'Vere hortus noster deliciarum est Anglia', in *Medieval Art, Architecture and Archaeology at Canterbury*, ed. Alixe Bovey, British Architectural Association Conference Transaction XXXV (Abingdon: Routledge, 2013), 276.

11. Powicke, *The Thirteenth Century*, 78.

12. Gordon Home, *Medieval London* (London: Bracken Books, 1994), 96–7, considered Henry to be consumed by both envy and dislike of London. It provided for all his inexhaustible whims and needs but, because it could do so, it may have also been an object of suspicion. What if London denied him or turned against him?

13. Powicke, *The Thirteenth Century*, 136–7.

14. GM Trevelyan, *History of England* (London: Longman, 1973), 100.

15. See Home, *Medieval London*, 108–12, 260; Powicke, *The Thirteenth Century*, 188.

16. 'Waleys probably possessed private property or had significant commercial interests in France. This is evident from the fact that he was elected mayor of Bordeaux in 1275, the year following his London mayoralty.' Riley, *Chronicles of the Mayors and Sheriffs of London, 1188–1274*, http://www.british-history.ac.uk/no-series/london-mayors-sheriffs/1188–1274.

17. Charles Welch, 'Henry le Waleys', *Dictionary of National Biography*, https://en.wikisource.org/wiki/Waleys,_Henry_le_(DNB00).

18. Charles Welch, 'Gregory de Rokesley', *Dictionary of National Biography*.

19. Martin Allen, 'Italians in English Mints and Exchanges', in *Fourteenth Century England*, ed. Chris Given-Wilson (Woodbridge: Boydell Press, 2002), xxiv.

20. Michael Prestwich, *Edward I* (New Haven: Yale University Press, 1997); and *War, Politics and Finance under Edward I* (Lanham: Rowman and Littlefield, 1972), 178–9.

21. Robin R Mudhill, *England's Jewish Solution: Experiment and Expulsion, 1262–1290* (Cambridge: CUP, 2002).

24. SELF-PERPETUATION

1. Anne Sutton, *The Mercery of London: Trade, Goods and People, 1130–1578* (Abingdon: Routledge, 2005), 11.

2. Caroline M Barron, *London in the Later Middle Ages: Government and People, 1200–1500* (Oxford: Oxford University Press, 2007).

3. Sylvia L Thrupp, *The Merchant Class of Medieval London, 1300–1500* (Ann Arbor: University of Michigan Press, 1962), 65.

4. Ruth Bird, *The Turbulent London of Richard II* (London: Longmans, 1949).

5. Barron, *London in the Later Middle Ages*, 4.

6. Robert Dahl, *Polyarchy; Participation and Opposition* (New Haven: Yale University Press, 1971).

7. Barron, *London in the Later Middle Ages*, 5.

8. AR Myers, *Chaucer's London: Everyday Life in London, 1342–1400* (Stroud: Amberley, 2009), 73.

9. Myers, *Chaucer's London*.

10. Clapham writes that from the 13th to 15th centuries it was quite commonplace to find that 'the leading Londoners are immigrants, as their names show'. He cites among these figures le Waleys, the radical John of Northampton, and Richard Whittington, men whom he describes as 'fortune seekers'. Sir John Clapham, *The Concise Economic History of Britain from the Earliest Times to 1750* (Cambridge: CUP, 1957), 126.

11. http://www.historyofparliamentonline.org/volume/1386–1421/member/dallingridge-sir-edward-1346–1393.

12. http://www.historyofparliamentonline.org/volume/1386–1421/member/dallingridge-sir-edward-1346–1393.

25. EYES ON HEAVEN

1. https://en.wikipedia.org/wiki/Greyfriars,_London.

2. Further development of the church was led by le Waleys, a vintner not a mercer, who is thought to have constructed the nave or at the least provided the timbers. Jens Röhrkasten, *The Mendicant Houses of Medieval London, 1221–1539* (Munster: LitVerlag, 2004), 413–5.

3. It was Margaret who came to the rescue by purchasing the additional land required to build the choir, promoting and funding the construction of the new church and spending 2,000 marks on the enterprise before her death in 1318. In turn, her involvement paved the way for a second queen, Isabella, wife of Edward III, who provided the £700 necessary to complete the work. John Noorthouck, 'Addenda: The Mayors and Sheriffs of London', in *A New History of London Including Westminster and Southwark* (London, 1773), http://www.british-history.ac.uk/no-series/new-history-london/. See also 'Lord Mayors of the City of London from 1189', www.cityoflondon.gov.uk.

4. Citing just one example of the link between the charitable works of London's mercers and their eye on salvation, Cook notes that 'In the church of the hospital of St

Thomas of Acon, Cheapside, later to become the Mercers' chapel, were buried many eminent Londoners and several chantries were founded there.' GH Cook, *Medieval Chantries and Chantry Chapels* (London: Phoenix House, 1963).

5. Turner provides a useful guide to the 'flowering' of London's churches in the 14th and 15th centuries. See Christopher Turner, *London's Churches Step by Step* (London: Faber and Faber, 1987).

6. Sylvia L Thrupp, *The Merchant Class of Medieval London, 1300–1500* (Ann Arbor: University of Michigan Press, 1962), 99.

7. John Carpenter, *Liber Albus: The White Book of the City of London*, trans. HT Riley (London: White Press, 2017).

26. TWICE MAYOR

1. Thomas Walsingham, *Historia Anglicana*, quoted in AK McHardy, *The Reign of Richard II: From Minority to Tyranny, 1377–97* (Manchester: Manchester University Press, 2012), 29; see also HT Riley, ed., *Thomas Walsingham ... Historia Anglicana* (London, 1864. Another version of Walsingham's description may be found in G Stow, 'Chronicles versus Records: The Character of Richard II', in *Documenting the Past: Essays in Medieval History Presented to George Peddy Cutino*, eds. J Hamilton and P Bradley (Woodbridge: Boydell Press, 1989), 160.

2. Sylvia Federico, 'The Chivalry of Richard II, 1381–1399', in *The Reign of Richard II*, ed. Gwilym Dodd (London: Tempus, 2000), 51–6.

3. Federico, 'The Chivalry of Richard II, 1381–1399', 53; Chris Given-Wilson, ed., *Chronicles of the Revolution, 1397–1400* (Manchester: Manchester University Press, 1993), 241.

4. EW Stockton, ed., *The Major Latin Works of John Gower* (Seattle: University of Washington Press, 1962).

5. Federico, 'The Chivalry of Richard II, 1381–1399', 53.

6. Caroline M Barron, 'Richard Whittington: The Man behind the Myth', in *Studies in London History Presented to Philip Edmund Jones*, eds. AEJ Hollaender and William Kellaway (London: Hodder and Stoughton, 1969).

7. Christopher Phillpotts, 'Richard II and the Monasteries of London', in *Fourteenth Century England*, vol. 7, ed. W Mark Ormrod (Woodbridge: Boydell Press, 2012), 210.

8. Stephen Broadberry, Bruce MS Campbell and Bas van Leeuwen, 'English Medieval Population: Reconciling Times Series and Cross-Sectional Evidence', University of Warwick working paper, 27 July 2010, estimates that the total English population by 1400 was 2.08 million (Table 6, English population, 1086–1541 (millions)), https://warwick.ac.uk/fac/soc/economics/staff/sbroadberry/wp/medievalpopulation7.pdf.

9. 'In 1185 the estate was held of the Templars by Roger de Cauntelo, whose son Richard made an exchange of rights in Frampton with Richard de Clifford c.1230.' Cited in Kathleen Morgan and Brian S Smith, 'Stonehouse: Manors and Other Estates', in *A History of the County of Gloucester*, vol. 10: *Westbury and Whitstone Hundreds*, eds. CR

Elrington, NM Herbert and RB Pugh (London, 1972), 143–8, http://www.british-history.ac.uk/vch/glos/vol10. A further note about the Cauntelo and Clifford families can be found at https://epdf.tips/the-dependent-priories-of-medieval-english-monasteries.html.

10. 'Richard Whittington and Hugh of Bisley, who claimed that John's other lands were held as of their manors of Lypiatt and Bisley, established that his Frampton estate was held of John Clinton as of Temple Guiting manor. John's heirs were said to be his daughters Elizabeth and Anne. Elizabeth married John Staure, and in 1401 Richard Whittington and Hugh of Bisley complained that James Clifford and John Staure had ejected them from John Clifford's estate.' See Morgan and Smith, 'Stonehouse: Manors and Other Estates'.

11. Daneway passed with John Clifford's estate at Frampton on Severn to his daughter Alice, the wife of William Teste, and their heirs. AP Baggs, ARJ Jurica and WJ Sheils, 'Bisley: Manors and Other Estates' in *History of the County of Gloucester*, vol. 11: *Bisley and Longtree Hundred*, eds. NM Herbert and RBA Pugh (London, 1972), 11–20.

12. This refers to a situation in common law that transfers the property of a deceased individual without heirs to the Crown or state, thereby ensuring that property is not left in a legal limbo without a recognised ownership. Where a tenant-in-chief had died, the fee reverted to the king permanently, the property reverting once again to a mere tenantless plot of land.

13. 'Bamme, Adam (d. 1397) of London', in JS Roskell, L Clark and C Rawcliffe, eds., *The House of Commons, 1386–1421* (Stroud: Sutton, 1993), https://www.historyof-parliamentonline.org/volume/1386–1421/member/bamme-adam-1397.

14. First recorded in the 12th century and consumed in the Great Fire of 1666, St George Botolph Lane was located off Eastcheap, in Billingsgate ward, overlooking Pudding Lane to the rear. It was one of the 51 churches rebuilt by the office of Sir Christopher Wren but demolished in 1904. See http://lostbritain.uk/site/st-george-botolph-lane-2/.

15. 'And in June dysscessid the mayer, and for hym was schosyne Richard Wyttyngton and occupied un tyll sent Edwardes daye.' 'The Chronicle of the Grey Friars: Richard II', in *Chronicle of the Grey Friars of London*, Camden Society, OS, vol. 53, ed. JG Nichols (London, 1852), 6–9, http://www.british-history.ac.uk/camden-record-soc/vol53/pp6–9.

16. 'Woodcock, John (d. 1409) of London', http://www.histparl.ac.uk/volume/1386–1421/member/woodcock-john-1409; 'Shadworth, John (d. 1430) of London', http://www.histparl.ac.uk/volume/1386–1421/member/shadworth-john-1430. For Gilbert Maghfeld see Gustav Milne, *The Port of Medieval London* (Stroud: Tempus, 2003), 132–4.

17. Nigel Saul, *Richard II* (New Haven: Yale University Press, 1997), 231.

18. Anne Curry, 'Richard II and the War with France', in *The Reign of Richard II*, ed. Dodd, 37.

19. AK McHardy, 'Richard II: A Personal Portrait', in *The Reign of Richard II*, ed. Dodd, 18.

20. McHardy, 'Richard II', 18.

21. Ralph Pugh, *Imprisonment in Medieval England* (Cambridge: CUP, 1968), 181, 184–5, 191; FRH du Boulay and Caroline M Barron, eds., *The Reign of Richard II: Essays in Honour of May McKisack* (London: Athlone Press, 1971); *Calendar of the Patent Rolls Preserved in the Public Record Office, Richard II, A.D. 1377–1399*, vol. 4 (London, 1895).

22. De Vere, Duke of Ireland, had led Richard's forces to defeat at Radcot Bridge, Oxford, against the Lords Appellant in 1387. Worse still, he had fled the field, escaping to France. He was sentenced to death in his absence by the Merciless Parliament of 1388, forfeiting his lands and title. An early and influential introducer of business to Richard Whittington, he died abroad in a hunting accident in 1392. Richard II returned his body to England for an ill-judged reburial in November 1395, which ignited a lingering contempt for both men.

23. Du Boulay and Barron, *The Reign of Richard II*, 183–7; RR Sharpe, ed., *Calendar of Letter-Books of the City of London*, H, 391, http://www.british-history.ac.uk/london-letter-books/voli/; R. Higden, *Polychronicon* (London, 1865), IX, 273–4; *Calendar of the Patent Rolls Preserved in the Public Record Office, Richard II, A.D. 1391–6*, 100, 130, 171; HC Maxwell Lyte, ed., *Calendar of Close Rolls, Richard II*, vol. 5 (London, 1925), 2, 9, 12, 78, 88–9; AH Thomas, ed., *Calendar of the Plea and Memoranda Rolls of the City of London*, vol. 3 (London, 1932), 182–3.

24. He would also intervene in county elections where the candidates or results didn't suit his interest. Dodd, *The Reign of Richard II*, 80; Given-Wilson, *Chronicles of the Revolution*, 178.

25. Dodd, *The Reign of Richard II*, 80.

26. Cited in Emma Hatfield, *London's Lord Mayors: 800 Years of Shaping the City* (Stroud: Amberley, 2015).

27. J Bolton, *Money in the Medieval English Economy, 973–1489* (Manchester: Manchester University Press, 2012), 287.

28. See Richard Britnell, 'Blackwell Hall, London' in *Encyclopedia of Medieval Dress and Textiles*, eds. Gale Owen-Crocker, Elizabeth Coatsworth and Maria Hayward (Leiden: Brill, 2012), http://dx.doi.org/10.1163/2213–2139_emdt_SIM_000859. The later development of Blackwell Hall is described in Nick Bateman, 'From Rags to Riches: Blackwell Hall and the Wool Cloth Trade, c.1450–1790', https://www.tandfonline.com/doi/abs/10.1179/pma.2004.001.

29. Du Boulay notes that trade rivalry between English merchants and the Hanseatic towns of the Baltic, where they were intent on gaining a foothold, both intensified and deteriorated in the last quarter of the 14th century and that Richard II and the Hansa's nominal protector, the Teutonic Order, made concerted attempts to improve relations. It is interesting to note that it was Prussian merchants who complained of injuries done to them by their English counterparts rather than the contrary.

30. HT Riley, ed., *Memorials of London and London Life in the 13th, 14th and 15th Centuries* (London: Longmans, Green and Co., 1868), https://www.british-history.ac.uk/no-series/memorials-london-life.

31. *The Customs of London, Otherwise Called Arnold's Chronicle* (London, 1811).

32. Caroline M Barron, 'Richard Whittington: The Man behind the Myth', in *Studies in*

London History Presented to Philip Edmund Jones, eds. AEJ Hollaender and William Kellaway (London: Hodder and Stoughton, 1969).

33. May McKisack, *The Fourteenth Century, 1307–1399* (Oxford: Clarendon Press, 1987), 486–8.

27. CIRCLES

1. Clementine Oliver, *Parliament and Political Pamphleteering in Fourteenth-century England* (York: Medieval Press, 2010).

2. Oliver, *Parliament and Political Pamphleteering*, 76.

3. Oliver, *Parliament and Political Pamphleteering*, 76

4. https://www.historyofparliamentonline.org/volume/1386–1421/member/woodcock-john-1409.

5. https://www.historyofparliamentonline.org/volume/1386–1421/member/woodcock-john-1409.

6. https://www.historyofparliamentonline.org/volume/1386–1421/member/shadworth-john-1430.

7. https://www.historyofparliamentonline.org/volume/1386–1421/member/shadworth-john-1430.

8. Much of Shadworth's business was conducted from the Old Wool Quay, 'le Wollewharf', which had its origins in the 13th century or earlier. 'All Hallows, Barking-By-The-Tower, Pt II' (Survey of London, vol. 15: London County Council, 1934), 31–43.

9. https://www.historyofparliamentonline.org/volume/1386–1421/member/shadworth-john-1430.

10. www.historyofparliamentonline.org/volume/1386–1421/member/bosham-john-1393.

11. www.historyofparliamentonline.org/volume/1386–1421/member/bosham-john-1393.

12. https://www.historyofparliamentonline.org/volume/1386–1421/member/knolles-thomas-1435.

13. See Alfred P Beaven, *The Aldermen of the City of London Temp. Henry III—1912* (London, 1908), http://www.british-history.ac.uk/no-series/london-aldermen/hen3–191.

14. John Stow, *A Survey of London Written in the Year 1598* (Stroud: Sutton, 1994), 52–3, 108, 237–8.

15. http://users.trytel.com/tristan/towns/florilegium/lifecycle/lcdth12.html#p54.

16. Sylvia L Thrupp, *The Merchant Class of Medieval London, 1300–1500* (Ann Arbor: University of Michigan Press, 1962), 169.

17. TF Reddaway and Lorna EM Walker, *The Early History of the Goldsmiths' Company, 1327–1509* (London: Edward Arnold, 1975).

18. Reddaway and Walker, *The Early History of the Goldsmiths' Company*, 281; 'Memorials: 1400' in HT Riley, ed., *Memorials of London and London Life in the 13th, 14th and 15th Centuries* London: Longmans, Green and Co., 1868), 553–5, http://www.british-history.ac.uk/no-series/memorials-london-life/pp553–555.

19. https://www.historyofparliamentonline.org/volume/1386-1421/member/chichele-robert-1439; https://www.british-history.ac.uk/no-series/london-aldermen/hen3-1912/pp379-404.

20. Stow, *A Survey of London*, 228 JH Wylie, *History of England Under Henry the Fourth* (London: Longmans, Green, 1898), vol. 4; https://www.historyofparliamenton-line.org/volume/1386–1421/member/waldern-william-1424.

21. J Payling, 'Babington, Sir William (c.1370–1454)', *Oxford Dictionary of National Biography* online.

22. See Elspeth Veale, 'Gilbert Maghfeld', *Oxford Dictionary of National Biography* online.

23. He is described by one writer as 'Gilbert Maghfeld, ironmonger, credit broker and money lender'; the same writer notes that leading figures in London and 'their communities were connected to Maghfeld by his moneylending services, on which Maghfeld built his later career before his financial collapse and death in 1397.' Andrew Galloway, 'The Account Book and the Treasure: Gilbert Maghfeld's Textual Economy and the Poetics of Mercantile Accounting in Ricardian Literature', *Studies in the Age of Chaucer*, 33 (2011): 65–124.

24. JL Bolton, *The Medieval English Economy, 1150–1500* (London: Dent, 1980).

25. http://www.historyofparliamentonline.org/volume/1386–1421/member/standon-william-1410.

26. Fiona Somerset, '"No Man May Serue to Two Lordis": The Lollard Glossed Gospels as Spiritual Advice in John Colop's Common-Profit Book, CUL Ff.6.31', *Journal of the Early Book Society for the Study of Manuscripts and Printing History*, 22 (2019): 73–92.

27. For wider context on the role of Thomas Roos in Whittington's affairs see Caroline M Barron, 'Richard Whittington: The Man Behind the Myth', in *Medieval London: Collected Papers of Caroline M. Barron*, eds. Martha Carlin and Joel T Rosenthal (Kalamazoo: Western Michigan University Medieval Institute Publications, 2017), 267–334.

28. *Stow, A Survey of London, 49*. He also cites Thomas Faulconer's interest in improving hygiene and infrastructure as mayor in 1414, causing the town ditch to be cleansed and 'doing many other things for the same city' and in the same year providing a loan to Henry V 'towards maintenance of his wars in France.' He 'caused the wall of the city to be broken toward the moor which he also drained and dried, enabling citizens to walk from Moorgate upon the causeways to Iseldon and Hoxton. *Stow, A Survey of London, 49*, 108, 358.

29. John Coventre was admitted to the Mercers' Company in 1401 and was master of the Company in 1417 and 1423, the year in which Whittington died. He was mayor in 1425–26. His role as an executor is recorded in the National Archives: https://discovery.nationalarchives.gov.uk/details/r/C9061429. He and Whittington—and their wives—were closely connected to the town of Coventry: Dugdale Society, vol. xiii, 39–68. See also 'The City of Coventry: Crafts and Industries, Medieval Industry and Trade', in *A History of the County of Warwick, vol. 8: The City of Coventry and Borough of Warwick*, ed. WB Stephens (London: 1969), 151–7.

30. See Jean Imray *The Charity of Richard Whittington: A History of the Trust Administered by the Mercers' Company, 1424–1966* (London: Athlone Press, 1968), 13–4, 14 n 1;

Norman Moore, *St Bartholomew's Hospital in Peace and War: The Rede Lecture 1915* (Cambridge: Cambridge University Press, 1915), 26–7; Stephen Alsford, *Florilegium Urbanum* (ebook), http://users.trytel.com/tristan/towns/florilegium/community/cmreli17.html.

31. Imray, *The Charity of Richard Whittington*, 14 n 3 cites Grove Guildhall Library MS 5370, 'Common Paper' of the Scriveners' Company, 57. Imray also provides a detailed note on the work done by Whittington's executors on the Text of Ordinances: *The Charity of Richard Whittington*, 109–21. Of further interest here is Lisa Jefferson, ed., *The Medieval Account Books of the Mercers of London: An Edition and Translation* (Aldershot: Ashgate, 2008).

28. NEW KING, NEW CENTURY

1. Gwilym Dodd, ed., *The Reign of Richard II* (London: Tempus, 2000), 84.

2. Ian Mortimer, *The Fears of Henry IV: The Life of England's Self-made King* (London: Vintage, 2008), 199.

3. Chris Given-Wilson, ed., *Parliamentary Rolls of Medieval England* (Woodbridge: Boydell and Brewer, 2005).

4. FRH du Boulay, 'Henry of Derby's Expeditions to Prussia 1390–1 and 1392,' in *The Reign of Richard II: Essays in Honour of May McKisack*, eds. FRH du Boulay and Caroline M Barron (London: Athlone Press, 1971).

5. JH Harvey, 'Richard II and York', in *The Reign of Richard II*, eds. Du Boulay and Barron, 203.

6. Thomas Rymer, ed., *Rymer's Foedera* (London, 1739–45), vol. 8, 488, http://www.british-history.ac.uk/rymer-foedera/vol8. See Samuel Lysons, *The Model Merchant of the Middle Ages Exemplified in the Story of Whittington and His Cat* (London: Hamilton Adams and Co., 1860), appendix, for a list of loans.

7. 'Sir Ivo Fitzwarin (1347–1414), of Caundle Haddon, Dorset', in JS Roskell, L Clark and C Rawcliffe, eds., *The House of Commons, 1386–1421* (Stroud: Sutton, 1993), https://www.historyofparliamentonline.org/volume/1386–1421/member/fitzwaryn-sir-ivo-1347–1414.

8. 'Sir Ivo Fitzwarin (1347–1414), of Caundle Haddon, Dorset'.

9. Kathleen Morgan and Brian S Smith, 'Stonehouse: Manors and Other Estates', in *A History of the County of Gloucester*, vol. 10: *Westbury and Whitstone Hundreds*, eds. CR Elrington, NM Herbert and RB Pugh (London, 1972), 273–6.

10. Alfred P Beaven, 'Chronological List of Aldermen: 1302–1400', in *The Aldermen of the City of London Temp. Henry III—1912* (London, 1908), 379–404, http://www.british-history.ac.uk/no-series/london-aldermen/hen3–1912/pp379-404.

11. Caroline M Barron, *London in the Later Middle Ages: Government and People, 1200–1500* (Oxford: Oxford University Press, 2007), 14.

12. http://www.historyofparliamentonline.org/volume/1386–1421/constituencies/london.

13. AR Myers, *Chaucer's London: Everyday Life in London, 1342–1400* (Stroud: Amberley, 2009), 75.

14. John Noorthouck, 'Richard II to the Wars of the Roses', in *A New History of London, Including Westminster and Southwark* (London, 1773), book 1, ch. 5, 75–94, http://www.british-history.ac.uk/no-series/new-history-london/pp75–94.

15. Mortimer, *The Fears of Henry IV*, 220.

16. http://www.history of parliamentonline.org/volume/1386–1421/member/whittington-richard-1423.

17. The minutes of the Privy Council record his presence with William Brampton at a meeting on 15 June 1400, noting the prospect of summoning him to the Great Council in the following year. *Ord. Privy Council*, vol. 1, 122, 163.

29. PULSE OF THE NATION?

1. EF Jacob, *The Fifteenth Century, 1399–1485* (Oxford: Clarendon Press, 1961), 429.

2. Jacob, *The Fifteenth Century*, 19.

3. Ian Mortimer, *The Fears of Henry IV: The Life of England's Self-made King* (London: Vintage, 2008), 233.

4. FRH du Boulay and Caroline M Barron, eds., *The Reign of Richard II: Essays in Honour of May McKisack* (London: Athlone Press, 1971), 169.

5. Du Boulay and Barron, *The Reign of Richard II*, 169.

6. Du Boulay and Barron, *The Reign of Richard II*, 171–2.

7. TF Reddaway and Lorna EM Walker, *The Early History of the Goldsmiths' Company, 1327–1509* (London: Edward Arnold, 1975), 280.

8. An excellent account of one of England's earlier and most influential lenders is provided in EB Fryde, *William de la Pole: Merchant and King's Banker, 1366* (London: Hambledon Press, 1988).

9. Eileen Power, *The Wool Trade in English Medieval History: Being the Ford Lectures* (Oxford: OUP, 1955), 88–92.

10. Power comments on the earlier period that 'when the crown was no longer dependent on individual wool merchants, no wool merchant ever rose to a position of such overwhelming financial superiority as that enjoyed by de la Pole, Pulteney, Picard, Tideswell and their like'. Power, *The Wool Trade*, 121.

11. Derek Hurst, *Sheep in the Cotswolds* (Cheltenham: History Press, 2005).

12. CD Liddy, *War, Politics and Finance in Late Medieval English Towns: Bristol, York and the Crown, 1350–1400* (Woodbridge: Royal Historical Society, 2005).

13. William Stubbs, *The Constitutional History of England in Its Origin and Development* (Oxford: Clarendon Press, 1891), III.

14. Power, *The Wool Trade*, 17–18.

15. Mortimer, *The Fears of Henry IV*, 234.

16. Mortimer, *The Fears of Henry* IV, 244.

17. Mortimer, *The Fears of Henry IV*, 246, 253–4.

18. James Tait, 'Edward Plantagenet', *Dictionary of National Biography*.

30. MARRIAGE

1. Lisa Jefferson, ed., *The Medieval Account Books of the Mercers of London: An Edition and Translation* (London: Routledge, 2009).
2. RR Sharpe, ed., *Calendar of Letter-Books of the City of London*, vol. 1, 1400–1422, ff. xiv–xxix, October 1401, http://www.british-history.ac.uk/london-letter-books/voli/pp15–30.
3. Jefferson, *The Medieval Account Books*. Among the others he had enrolled was William Cavendish, noted earlier, cited elsewhere as someone given a 'second chance' by Whittington and known to him as the grandson of England's Chief Justice. Edmund Peyton and John Pyehard were taken on in 1391–2 and would have completed their service before 1400; and the others were John Weston, Nicholas Leming, Edmund Brigg and John Empingham.
4. Jean Imray, *The Charity of Richard Whittington: A History of the Trust Administered by the Mercers' Company, 1424–1966* (London: Athlone Press, 1968), 21.
5. Sir William Dugdale, *Monasticon Anglicanum* (London, 1675–83), vol. 6, 746. Alice is described as the daughter of Sir Ivo Fitzwaryn, a knight of considerable landed property in the south-western counties, who on several occasions represented Dorset and Devon in Parliament, by his wife Matilda or Maud Dargentein, one of the coheiresses of the well-known Hertfordshire family in which the office of royal cupbearer was hereditary. John Hutchins, *History and Antiquities of the County of Dorset* (London: JB Nichols and Sons, 1863), vol. 1, 327–8.
6. Imray, *The Charity of Richard Whittington*, 3–19.
7. Imray, *The Charity of Richard Whittington*, 16–17.
8. Imray, *The Charity of Richard Whittington*, 3–4; AE Stamp, ed., *Calendar of Close Rolls, Henry IV*, vol. 1 (London, 1927), 563; vol. 2 (London, 1929), 165; vol. 3 (London, 1931), 130.
9. EF Jacob, *The Fifteenth Century, 1399–1485* (Oxford: Clarendon Press, 1961), 76.
10. https://www.historyofparliamentonline.org/volume/1386–1421/member/chideock-john-1375–1415.
11. Jacob, *The Fifteenth Century*, 76; AB Steele, *The Receipt of the Exchequer, 1377–1485* (Cambridge: CUP, 1954), 86–7.
12. Jacob, *The Fifteenth Century*.
13. Michael Roberts, *The Early Vasas: A History of Sweden, 1523–1611* (Cambridge: CUP, 1968), ch. 1.

31. THREE TIMES MAYOR

1. JH Wylie, *History of England under Henry IV* (London: Longmans, Green, 1898), vol. 4, 2.
2. HT Riley, 'Election of Richard Whityngton to His Second Mayoralty', in *Memorials of London and London Life in the 13th, 14th and 15th Centuries* (London, 1868), https://www.british-history.ac.uk/no-series/memorials-london-life.

3. See Caroline Barron, 'Mass at the Election of the Mayor of London, 1406', in *Medieval Christianity in Practice*, ed. Miri Rubin (Princeton: Princeton University Press, 2009), 333–8.

4. http://www.historyofparliamentonline.org/volume/1386–1421/member/askham-william-141415.

5. http://www.historyofparliamentonline.org/volume/1386–1421/member/brampton-william-i-1406.

6. Riley, 'Election of Richard Whityngton to His Second Mayoralty'.

7. *The Court of the Common Council*, Information leaflet 13 (London Metropolitan Archives of the City of London).

8. Adam Anderson, *An Historical and Chronological Deduction of the Origin of Commerce, from the Earliest Accounts* (London, 1801), vol. 1, 233.

9. AH Thomas, ed., *Calendar of Select Pleas and Memoranda of the City of London, AD 1381–1412* (Cambridge: CUP, 1932), 283.

10. John H Munro, 'Bruges and the Abortive Staple in English Cloth: An Incident in the Shift of Commerce from Bruges to Antwerp in the Late Fifteenth Century', *Revue Belge de Philologie et d'Histoire* 44, no. 4 (1966): 1137–59.

11. http://www.merchantsofthestapleofengland.co.uk/.

12. This may have its roots in December 1406 when James Clifford had also quitclaimed to Robert Whittington land which had once belonged to his father in Frampton Mansell. See https://www.historyofparliamentonline.org/volume/1386–1421/member/clifford-james.

13. AP Baggs, ARJ Jurica and WJ Sheils, 'Stroud: Manors and Other Estates', in *A History of the County of Gloucester*, vol. 11: *Bisley and Longtree Hundreds*, eds. NM Herbert and RB Pugh (London, 1976), 111–9, http://www.british-history.ac.uk/vch/glos/vol11/pp111–119.

32. PESTILENCE AND ICE

1. Edward Seymour, *The Complete History of England*, vol. 1 (London, 1764).

2. John FD Shrewsbury, *A History of the Bubonic Plague in the British Isles* (Cambridge: CUP, 2008).

3. Charles Creighton, *A History of Epidemics in Great Britain from A.D. 664 to the Extinction of Plague* (Cambridge: Cambridge University Press, 1891).

4. Creighton, *A History of Epidemics*.

5. Shrewsbury, *A History of the Bubonic Plague*.

6. Creighton, *A History of Epidemics*, 221.

7. Sylvia L Thrupp, *The Merchant Class of Medieval London, 1300–1500* (Ann Arbor: University of Michigan Press, 1962), 94.

8. EF Jacob, *The Fifteenth Century, 1399–1485* (Oxford: Clarendon Press, 1961), 86.

9. Jacob, *The Fifteenth Century*, 89.

10. Anthony Steel, *Richard II* (Cambridge: CUP, 1941), 114–5.

11. JH Brazell, *London Weather: Frost Fairs on the Thames* (London: HMSO, 1968).

12. Brazell, *London Weather*; John Kington, *Climate and Weather* (London: Collins, 2010).

13. 'The Chronicle of the Grey Friars: Richard II', in *Chronicle of the Grey Friars of London*, Camden Society, OS, vol. 53, ed. JG Nichols (London, 1852), 9–12, http://www.british-history.ac.uk/camden-record-soc/vol53/pp9–12.

33. LOSS

1. AH Thomas, ed., *Calendar of the Plea and Memoranda Rolls of the City of London*, vol. 3 (London, 1932), 289–301, 'Roll A 40: 1408–09', http://www.british-history.ac.uk/plea-memoranda-rolls/vol3/pp289–301.

2. http://discovery.nationalarchives.gov.uk/details/r/C9537182.

3. Jean Imray, *The Charity of Richard Whittington: A History of the Trust Administered by the Mercers' Company, 1424–1966* (London: Athlone Press, 1968), 3, suggests that 1409 is the year that Whittington began rebuilding St Michael's and that this coincides with the death of his wife, but Alice died in the summer of 1411, two years later, and must therefore have played some part in developing the vision for what was intended at that time to be a shared project with her husband.

4. Jews had been expelled from England by Edward I on 18 July 1290. Except for a handful numbering six or seven dozen who had converted to Christianity and were confined within the precincts of the 'House of Conversion' in Chancery Lane, none had been allowed to remain on or return to English soil.

5. Ariel Hessayon, 'From Expulsion (1290) to Readmission (1656): Jews and England', http://www.gold.ac.uk/media/350th-anniversary.pdf.

6. A Weiner, 'Note on Jewish Doctors in England in the Reign of Henry IV', *Jewish Quarterly Review* 18, no. 1 (1905): 141–5; Matthew Dennison, 'In Search of the Real Dick Whittington', *New Statesman*, 11 December 2015, https://www.newstatesman.com/culture/2015/12/search-real-dick-whittington.

7. Ian Mortimer, *The Fears of Henry IV: The Life of England's Self-made King* (London: Vintage, 2008).

8. Thomas Gascoigne and James E Thorold Rogers, *Loci e Libro Veritatum: Passages Selected from Gascoigne's Theological Dictionary Illustrating the Condition of Church and State, 1403–1458* (Oxford, 1881).

9. Peter McNiven, 'The Problem of Henry IV's Health, 1405–1413', *English Historical Review* 100, no. 397 (1985): 747–72; https://wilson.fas.harvard.edu/stigma-in-shakespeare/henry-iv%E2%80%99s-apoplexy.

10. Weiner, 'Note on Jewish Doctors', 141–5.

11. Weiner, 'Note on Jewish Doctors', 141–5.

12. JH Wylie, *History of England under Henry IV* (London: Longmans, Green, 1896).

13. Thomas Brewer, *Memoir of the Life and Times of John Carpenter, Town Clerk of London in the Reigns of Henry V and VI* (London: Arthur Taylor, 1856), 118.

14. His family had originated in the French town of Cambrai though Carpenter himself was born in Hereford and baptised in its cathedral. His grandfather is reported as establishing the family at Dilwyn in Herefordshire, which must have been a notable

talking point with Whittington whose own grandfather William had intermarried with the de Solers family and in 1311 had inherited Pauntley from them; they were the owners of Herefordshire estates and manors which bore their name, including Dilwyn Solers.

15. Proved 5 February 1414. Cited in Agnes Gibbons and EC Davey, *Wantage Past and Present* (London, 1901).

16. Gibbons and Davey, *Wantage Past and Present*.

17. AL Brown and H Summerson, 'Henry IV (1367–1413)', *Oxford Dictionary of National Biography* online.

18. Beauchamp was summoned by Henry V to Westminster, accused of fomenting rebellion and of holding heretical views. Pleading not guilty, he was acquitted on 26 October of both charges by a jury. Almost certainly involved in stirring revolt, Beauchamp was able to secure his freedom and was not again accused of Lollardy. See http://www.historyofparliamentonline.org/volume/1386–1421/member/beauchamp-sir-thomas-1444.

19. Ian Mortimer, *1415: Henry V's Year of Glory* (London: Vintage, 2010).

20. Mortimer, *1415*.

34. NEW PURPOSE

1. The appointment may have bemused but also suited the impecunious and status-conscious poet. The work was well paid, far in excess of his salary as a comptroller, and he was also accorded the honorary appointment of 'keeper of the lodge' at the King's Park at Feckenham. 'For Geoffrey Chaucer. Richard by the grace of God king, etc., to the treasurer and barons of our exchequer, greetings. We command you that in the account which our dear Squire Geoffrey Chaucer, Clerk of our Works, is to present you in the execution of his office you will allow him on his oath the costs made for the scaffolds in Smithfield, which he had made for us and for our very dear companion the queen at Smithfield in the month of May now passed. *Given under our privy seal at Westminster, the first day of July in the fourteenth year of our reign.* Martin Crow and Clair C Olson, *Chaucer Life-Records* (Oxford: Clarendon Press, 1966), cited in https://chaucer.fas.harvard.edu/pages/chaucer-clerk-works.

2. In August 1415 Whittington was repaid the sum of 500 marks from the receiver-general of the Duchy of Lancaster.

3. http://www.historyofparliamentonline.org/volume/1386–1421/member/whittington-richard-1423#footnote21_nfxgog6.

4. Court of Common Pleas, 1425, CP 40/656, rot. 108d, http://www.british-history.ac.uk/no-series/common-pleas/1399–1500/hilary-term-1425#highlight-first.

5. For acclaimed accounts of Agincourt, see Juliet Barker, *Agincourt: The King, the Campaign, the Battle* (London: Abacus, 2006); Juliet Barker, *Agincourt: Henry V and the Battle That Made England* (London: Back Bay Books, 2007); Anne Curry, *The Battle of Agincourt: Sources and Interpretations* (Woodbridge: Boydell Press, 2009); Anne Curry and Malcolm Mercer, *The Battle of Agincourt* (New Haven: Yale University Press, 2015).

6. N Coldstream, '"Pavilion'd in Splendour": Henry V's Agincourt Pageants', *Journal of the British Archaeological Association* 165 (2012): 153–71; H Nicolas, ed., *A Chronicle of London from 1089 to 1483* (London: Longmans, 1827); F Taylor and JS Roskell, eds., *Gesta Henrici Quinti: The Deeds of Henry the Fifth* (Oxford: Clarendon, 1975); see also Anne Curry, *Agincourt: Myth and Reality* (online course, University of Southampton, 2015), https://www.futurelearn.com/courses/agincourt/0/steps/8865.

7. It is claimed that he represented London in one of the parliaments of 1416, but no returns seem to exist.

8. There was apparently little contact between Robert and his wealthy younger brother, although they shared some property interests. In 1388 they had together brought a legal action against Bishop Gilbert of Hereford over the next presentation to Westbury church, Gloucestershire, and both were involved in lawsuits against James Clifford over lands formerly held by their kinsmen the Maunsells. See http://www.historyofparliamentonline.org/volume/1386-1421/member/whittington-robert-14234.

9. JA Sharpe, 'The History of Crime in England c.1300–1914: An Overview of Recent Publications', *British Journal of Criminology* 28, no. 2 (1988): 124–37.

10. JS Roskell, L Clark and C Rawcliffe, eds., *The House of Commons, 1386–1421* (Stroud: Sutton, 1993), http://www.historyofparliamentonline.org/volume/1386-1421/member/whittington-robert-14234.

11. Samuel Lysons, *The Model Merchant of the Middle Ages Exemplified in the Story of Whittington and His Cat* (London: Hamilton Adams and Co., 1860), 23; 'Whittington, Richard (d. 1423) of London', in *The House of Commons, 1386–1421*, eds. JS Roskell, L Clark and C Rawcliffe.

12. In 1419 Guy was appointed escheator of Gloucestershire and he was elected to Parliament the following year. His father's influence was probably instrumental in securing both positions. Three months before his death in July 1423, and three after that of his brother Richard, Robert named Guy as principal beneficiary and executor of his will. He succeeded to the Whittington estates in Gloucestershire, Herefordshire and Worcestershire. See http://www.historyofparliamentonline.org/volume/1386-1421/member/whittington-guy-1440.

13. Thomas Brewer, *Memoir of the Life and Times of John Carpenter, Town Clerk of London in the Reigns of Henry V and VI* (London: Arthur Taylor, 1856), https://www.loc.gov/item/03007452/.

14. Henry was so short of funds to sustain his campaigns in France that he pawned his crown for a period of up to eighteen months to his uncle the Bishop of Winchester for 100,000 marks and used some of his jewels as collateral for a £10,000 loan from the City of London. Laurence Echard, *The History of England from the First Entrance of Julius Caesar and the Romans to the End of the Reign of King James Ist* (London, 1707), vol. 1.

15. RA Newhall, *The English Conquest of Normandy, 1416–1424* (New Haven: Yale University Press, 1924), 144.

16. John Carpenter, *Liber Albus: The White Book of the City of London*, trans. HT Riley (London: White Press, 2017).

35. FOUR TIMES MAYOR

1. Stephen Halliday, *Newgate: London's Prototype of Hell* (Stroud: Sutton Publishing, 2007).

2. AR Myers, *Chaucer's London: Everyday Life in London, 1342–1400* (Stroud: Amberley, 2009).

3. Samuel Lysons, *The Model Merchant of the Middle Ages Exemplified in the Story of Whittington and His Cat* (London: Hamilton Adams and Co., 1860), 60.

4. In fact, this association is noted at the very time that Whittington is purported to have made his grand gesture. The Whittington family had long-standing connections with Rodmarton, and the manor was held by a William Fitzwarin around 1420. William was the latest in a line in which all the heads had also taken the ancestral name Fulk. The barony with the castle and lordship of Whittington in Shropshire had descended from father to son until the death of Fulk XI in 1420. It then passed down the female line into the Bourchier family. The 11th Baron Fitzwarin, John Bourchier, was created Earl of Bath in 1536.

5. JS Roskell, L Clark and C Rawcliffe, eds., *The House of Commons, 1386–1421* (Stroud: Sutton, 1993).

6. George Unwin, *The Gilds and Companies of London* (London: Methuen, 1908), 195.

7. Unwin, *The Gilds and Companies of London*, 232–3.

8. Sylvia L Thrupp, *The Merchant Class of Medieval London, 1300–1500* (Ann Arbor: University of Michigan Press, 1962), 93–4.

9. A notable inmate was Friar Thomas Wynchelsey, and it is likely that through his influence the Greyfriars benefitted from Whittington's will. Wynchelsey himself and the then guardian, William Russell, were benefactors of their house. CL Kingsford, *The Greyfriars of London* (Aberdeen: Aberdeen University Press, 1915), 170; see also http://www.british-history.ac.uk/brit-franciscan-soc/vol6/, 15–27.

10. Unwin, *The Gilds and Companies of London*, 233.

11. Brewers' first book quoted in Unwin, *The Gilds and Companies of London*, 235.

12. Unwin, *The Gilds and Companies of London*, 235.

13. F Rexroth, *Deviance and Power in Late Medieval London* (Cambridge: CUP, 2007), 232; Mia Ball, *The Worshipful Company of Brewers: A Short History* (London: Hutchinson, 1977).

36. CITIZEN OF LONDON

1. Jacob sets out the details of Henry's financial woes. EF Jacob, *The Fifteenth Century, 1399–1485* (Oxford: Clarendon Press, 1961), 192, 202–7, 440–2, 439–40.

2. Jacob, *The Fifteenth Century*, 429.

3. Brewer notes that as one of Whittington's executors, John Carpenter 'conferred essential benefits on the city by promoting various public works, especially the erection of Conduits, the rebuilding of Newgate, the enlargement of the Hospital of Saint Bartholomew, the completion of the Guildhall, and the formation of a Library attached thereto, to which he subsequently bequeathed sundry rare books for the benefit of

students. In token of his eminent services, he was honoured both by his sovereign and fellow citizens with peculiar immunities and privileges.' Thomas Brewer, *Memoir of the Life and Times of John Carpenter, Town Clerk of London in the Reigns of Henry V and VI* (London: Arthur Taylor, 1856), 122.

4. The outstanding extrapolation of Whittington's will is provided in Jean Imray's seminal work. Jean Imray, *The Charity of Richard Whittington: A History of the Trust Administered by the Mercers' Company, 1424–1966* (London: Athlone Press, 1968).

5. Carpenter's literary interests were significant and his collection notable and growing. In his own will, dated March 1442, he left 'an extremely interesting and eclectic list of books, ranging from legal formularies and treatises on letter writing (a predictable interest in view of his career) to architecture, works of Aristotle, Seneca and Petrarch and (aptly) Richard de Bury's *Philobiblon*. Theological works loom large, and some of these items reflect the widening interests of the literate gentry in his day.' Margaret Aston, *Faith and Fire: Popular and Unpopular Religion, 1350–1600* (London: Hambledon Continuum, 1984).

6. Anne Sutton describes Bury as one of 'two exceptional London mercers of Suffolk origin whose careers cross the first decades of the fifteenth century: a benefactor of a library'. 'London Mercers from Suffolk c.1200 to 1570: Benefactors, Pirates and Merchant Adventurers (part 1)', http://suffolkinstitute.pdfsrv.co.uk/customers/Suffolk%20Institute/2014/01/10/Volume%20XLII%20Part%201%20(2009)_London%20mercers%20from%20Suffolk%20c.1200–1570%20A%20F%20Sutton_1%20to%2012.pdf.

7. Sources transcribed in EF Jacob, ed., *The Register of Henry Chichele, Archbishop of Canterbury, 1414–1423* (Oxford: Canterbury and York Society, 1937), vol. 2, 240–4; and Jean Imray, *The Charity of Richard Whittington: A History of the Trust Administered by the Mercers' Company, 1424–1966* (London: Athlone Press, 1968), appendix 1. See also Stephen Alsford, *Florilegium Urbanum* (ebook), http://users.trytel.com/tristan/towns/florilegium/community/cmreli17.html.

8. Valerie Allen and Ruth Evans, *Roadworks: Medieval Britain, Medieval Roads* (Manchester: Manchester University Press, 2016), 115–6.

9. John Carpenter, *Liber Albus: The White Book of the City of London*, trans. HT Riley (London: Griffin and Co., 1861).

10. Imray, *The Charity of Richard Whittington*.

11. Sources transcribed in Jacob, *The Register of Henry Chichele, Archbishop of Canterbury, 1414–1423*, vol. 2, 240–4; and Imray, *The Charity of Richard Whittington*, appendix 1.

BIBLIOGRAPHY

Aberth, John, *The Black Death: The Great Mortality of 1348–1350; A Brief History with Documents* (London: Palgrave Macmillan, 2005).

Ackroyd, Peter, *The Canterbury Tales: A Retelling by Peter Ackroyd* (Harmondsworth: Penguin, 2010).

———, *London: The Biography* (London: Vintage Books, 2001).

———, *Thames: Sacred River* (London: Chatto and Windus, 2007).

———, *London Under* (London: Vintage, 2012).

Akbari, Suzanne Conklin and Jill Ross, eds., *The Ends of the Body: Identity and Community in Medieval Culture* (Toronto: University of Toronto Press, 2013).

Alford, Stephen, *London's Triumph: Merchant Adventurers and the Tudor City* (London: Allen Lane, 2017).

Allen, M, *Mints and Money in Medieval England* (Cambridge: Cambridge University Press, 2012).

Allen, Valerie and Ruth Evans, *Roadworks: Medieval Britain, Medieval Roads* (Manchester: Manchester University Press, 2016).

Amyat, T, 'Population of English Cities temp Edward III', *Acta Archaeologica* XX: 524–31.

Anderson, Adam, *Historical and Chronological Deduction of the Origin of Commerce*, vol. 1 (London, 1764).

Applied History Research Group, 'Banking in the Middle Ages: The End of Europe's Middle Ages', University of Calgary, 1997.

Arber, E., *A Transcript of the Registers of the Company of Stationers of London, 1554–1640 A.D.*, 5 vols. (London, 1875–94).

Arnold, Catherine, *Bedlam London and Its Mad* (London: Pocket Books, 2008).

Ash, Bernard, *The Golden City: London between the Fires, 1666 and 1941* (London: Phoenix House, 1964).

Aston, Margaret, *Faith and Fire: Popular and Unpopular Religion, 1350–1600* (London: Continuum, 1984).

———, *The Fifteenth Century: The Prospect of Europe* (London: Thames and Hudson, 1968).

Bagley, J and P Rowley, *A Documentary History of England, vol. 1 (1066–1540)* (Harmondsworth: Pelican, 1966).

BIBLIOGRAPHY

Baker, TFT, JS Cockburn and RB Pugh, eds., *A History of the County of Middlesex*, vol. 4: *Harmondsworth, Hayes, Norwood with Southall, Hillingdon with Uxbridge, Ickenham, Northolt, Perivale, Ruislip, Edgware, Harrow with Pinner* (London: Victoria County History, 1976).

Baker, Timothy, *Medieval London* (London: Cassell, 1970).

Ball, Mia, *The Worshipful Company of Brewers: A Short History* (London: Hutchinson, 1977).

Banks, TC, *The Dormant and Extinct Baronage of England*, vol. 4 (London: Henry G Bohn, 1837).

Barker, Felix and Peter Jackson, *London: 2000 Years of a City and Its People* (London: BCA, 1979).

Barker, Juliet, *Agincourt: The King, the Campaign, the Battle* (London: Abacus, 2005).

———, *Conquest: The English Kingdom of France, 1417–1450* (London: Little, Brown, 2009).

———, *Conquest: The English Kingdom of France in the 100 Years War* (London: Abacus, 2010).

Barron, Caroline M, 'The Government of London and Its Relationship with the Crown 1400–1450', PhD thesis, University of London, 1970.

———, *London in the Later Middle Ages: Government and People, 1200–1500* (Oxford: Oxford University Press, 2007).

———, 'Richard Whittington: The Man behind the Myth', in *Studies in London History Presented to Philip Edmund Jones*, eds. AEJ Hollaender and William Kellaway (London: Hodder and Stoughton, 1969).

Barron, Caroline M and Nigel Saul, *England and the Low Countries in the Middle Ages* (Stroud: Sutton, 1998).

Barron, Caroline M and Anne F Sutton, eds., *Medieval London Widows, 1300–1500* (London: Hambledon Press, 1994).

Barron, Caroline M and Laura Wright, eds., *The London Jubilee Book, 1376–1387: An Edition of Trinity College Cambridge MS 0.3.11, ff. 133–57* (Woodbridge: Boydell and Brewer, 2021).

Bean, JMW, 'Plague, Population and Economic Decline in England in the Later Middle Ages', *Economic History Review* 15 (1963).

Beaumont, Francis, *The Knight of the Burning Pestle* (London, 1635).

Beaumont, Thomas James, *The Palaces of Medieval England: Royalty, Nobility, the Episcopate, and Their Residences from Edward the Confessor to Henry VIII* (London: Seaby Press, 1990).

Beltz, George Frederick, *Memorials of the Most Noble Order of the Garter* (London: William Pickering, 1841).

Benedictow, Ole J, *The Black Death, 1346–1353: The Complete History* (Woodbridge: Boydell and Brewer, 2004).

———, 'Plague in the Late Medieval Nordic Countries', *Epidemiological Studies* (1996).

BIBLIOGRAPHY

Bennett, HS, *Life on the English Manor: A Study of Peasant Conditions* (Cambridge: Cambridge University Press, 1962).

Besant, Walter and James Rice, *Sir Richard Whittington, Lord Mayor of London* (New York: Merrill Baker, 1881).

Billings, Malcolm, *London: A Companion to Its History and Archaeology* (London: Kyle Cathie Limited, 1994).

Bird, Ruth, *The Turbulent London of Richard II* (London: Longmans, Green, 1949).

Blackham, Robert James, *The Soul of the City: London's Livery Companies, Their Storied Past, Their Living Present* (London: S Low, Marston and Co., 1931).

Boggon, AGW et al., *Richard Whittington of Pauntley* (Gloucester: City and County of the City of Gloucester, 1959).

Bolton, JL, *The Medieval English Economy, 1150–1500* (London: Dent, 1980).

Bolton, J, *Money in the Medieval English Economy, 973–1489* (Manchester: Manchester University Press, 2012).

Bovey, Alixe, ed., *Medieval Art, Architecture and Archaeology at Canterbury*, British Architectural Association Conference Transaction XXXV (Abingdon: Routledge, 2013).

Brabrook, EW, *The Worshipful Company of Mercers of the City of London* (London: Mercers' Company, 1889).

Brake, William TE, 'Air Pollution and Fuel Crises in Preindustrial London, 1250–1650', *Technology and Culture* 16, no. 3 (July 1975).

Brazell, JH, *London Weather: Frost Fairs on the Thames* (London: HMSO, 1968).

Brewer, Thomas, *Memoir of the Life and Times of John Carpenter, Town Clerk of London in the Reigns of Henry V and VI* (London: Arthur Taylor, 1856).

Bridbury, AR, *Economic Growth: England in the Later Middle Ages* (London: George Allen and Unwin, 1961).

Brimblecombe, Peter, 'Attitudes and Responses towards Air Pollution in Medieval England', *Journal of the Air Pollution Control Association* 26, no. 10 (1976).

British Records Society, *Inquisitions Post Mortem for Gloucestershire*, vol. XLVII (London, 1914).

Britnell, RH, *The Commercialisation of English Society, 1000–1500* (Cambridge: Cambridge University Press, 1993).

Broadberry, Stephen, Bruce MS Campbell and Bas van Leeuwen, 'English Medieval Population: Reconciling Times Series and Cross-Sectional Evidence', University of Warwick working paper, 27 July 2010.

Brown, AL, *The Governance of Late Medieval England, 1272–1461* (London: Edward Arnold, 1989).

Brown, P, P King and P Remfry, 'Whittington Castle: The Marcher Fortress of the FitzWarin Family', *Shropshire Archaeology and History* LXXIX (2004).

Bryant, Arthur, *The Medieval Foundation* (London: Collins, 1966).

———, *Set in a Silver Sea* (London: William Collins, 1984).

BIBLIOGRAPHY

Caferro, William, *John Hawkwood: An English Mercenary in Fourteenth-Century Italy* (Baltimore: Johns Hopkins University Press, 2006).

Calendar of the Patent Rolls Preserved in the Public Record Office, Richard II, AD 1377–1399, vol. 4 (London, 1895).

Campbell, Bruce MS, *Before the Black Death: Studies in the Crisis of the Early Fourteenth Century* (Manchester: Manchester University Press, 1991).

Cantor, Norman F, *In the Wake of the Plague* (New York: The Free Press, 2001).

Carlin, Martha, *Medieval Southwark* (London: Hambledon Press, 1996).

Carlin, Martha and Joel T Rosenthal, *Medieval London: Collected Papers of Caroline M Barron* (Kalamazoo: Western Michigan University Medieval Institute Publications, 2017).

Carpenter, John, *Liber Albus: The White Book of the City of London*, trans. HT Riley (London: White Press, 2017).

Carr, AD, *Owen of Wales: The End of the House of Gwynedd* (Cardiff: University of Wales Press, 1991).

Carte, Thomas, *A General History of England*, vol. II (London, 1747).

Carus-Wilson, EM, 'Early Development of the Merchant Adventurers Organisation in London as Shown in Their Own Medieval Records', *Economic History Review* (1933).

———, 'Trends in the Export of English Woollens in the Fourteenth Century', *Economic History Review* 3 (1950): 162–79.

Chamberlain, Henry, *A New and Compleat History and Survey of the Cities of London and Westminster, the Borough of Southwark, and Parts Adjacent: From the Earliest Accounts, to the Beginning of the Year 1770* (London, 1770).

Chapman, George, John Marston and Ben Jonson, *Eastward Hoe* (London, 1636).

Chaucer, Geoffrey, *The Canterbury Tales* (Harmondsworth: Penguin Classics, 1982).

Chew, Helena M and William Kellaway, eds., *London Assize of Nuisance 1301–1431: A Calendar* (London: London Record Society, 1973).

Clapham, Sir John, *The Concise Economic History of Britain from the Earliest Times to 1750* (Cambridge: Cambridge University Press, 1957).

Clark, Sir George, *English History: A Survey* (Oxford: Oxford University Press, 1978).

Clark, Gregory, 'The Long March of History: Farm Wages, Population and Economic Growth, England, 1209–1869', *Economic History Review* 60, no. 1 (2007): 97–135.

Clouston, WA, *Popular Tales and Fictions* (Edinburgh: William Blackwood and Sons, 1887).

Cokayne, George Edward, Vicary Gibbs and H Arthur Doubleday, eds., *The Complete Peerage of England, Scotland, Ireland, Great Britain and the United Kingdom, Extant, Extinct or Dormant* (2nd edn, London: St Catherine Press, 1959).

Coldstream, N, '"Pavilion'd in Splendour": Henry V's Agincourt Pageants', *Journal of the British Archaeological Association* 165 (2012): 153–71.

Cole, Hubert, *The Black Prince* (London: Purnell Books, 1976).

Cook, GH, *Medieval Chantries and Chantry Chapels* (London: Phoenix House, 1967).

Corrigan, Gordon, *A Great and Glorious Adventure: A Military History of the Hundred Years War* (London: Atlantic Books, 2013).

Coulton, George, *Chaucer and His England* (London: Methuen, 1963).

Creighton, Charles, *A History of Epidemics in Great Britain from A.D. 664 to the Extinction of Plague* (Cambridge: Cambridge University Press, 1891).

Crossley, Alan and CR Elrington, eds., *A History of the County of Oxford*, vol. 4: *The City of Oxford* (London, 1979).

Crow, Martin and Clair C Olson, *Chaucer Life-Records* (Oxford: Clarendon Press, 1966).

Cunningham, Peter, *Handbook of London: Past and Present; Its History, Associations and Traditions*, vol. 1 (London: John Murray, 1849).

Curry, Anne, *Agincourt: Myth and Reality* (online course, University of Southampton, 2015).

———, *The Battle of Agincourt: Sources and Interpretations* (Woodbridge: Boydell Press, 2009).

Curry, Anne and Malcolm Mercer, *The Battle of Agincourt* (New Haven: Yale University Press, 2015).

The Customs of London, Otherwise Called Arnold's Chronicle (London, 1811).

Dahl, Robert A, *Polyarchy and Opposition* (New Haven: Yale University Press, 1971).

Dalzell, WR, *Shell Guide to the History of London* (London: Michael Joseph, 1982).

Daniell, Christopher, *Death and Burial in Medieval England, 1066–1550* (London: Routledge, 1997).

Davies, Norman, *The Isles: A History* (London: Papermac, 2000).

Day, J, *The Medieval Market Economy* (Oxford: Oxford University Press, 1987).

Deanesly, Margaret, *A History of the Medieval Church 590–1500* (London: Routledge, 1989).

Ditchfield, PH, *The City Companies of London and Their Good Works: A Record of Their History, Charity and Treasure* (London: JM Dent, 1904).

Dobson, RB, *The Peasants' Revolt of 1381* (London: Macmillan, 1983).

———, 'Urban Decline in Late Medieval England', *Transactions of the Royal Historical Society* 27 (1977).

Dodd, Gwilym, ed., *The Reign of Richard II* (Stroud: Tempus, 2000).

Dols, MW, *The Black Death in the Middle East* (Princeton: Princeton University Press, 1970).

Du Boulay, FRH and Caroline M Barron, *The Reign of Richard II: Essays in Honour of May McKisack* (London: Athlone Press, 1971).

Dugdale, Sir William, *Monasticon Anglicanum* (London, 1675–83).

Duncan, Andrew, *Secret London* (London: New Holland, 1995).

Eagleton, C and J Williams, 'A Treatise on the Origin, Nature, Law and Alterations of Money', in *Money: A History* (London: British Museum Press, 2007).

Echard, Laurence, *The History of England from the First Entrance of Julius Caesar and the Romans to the End of the Reign of King James Ist* (London, 1707).

BIBLIOGRAPHY

Edwards, JG, *Calendar of Ancient Correspondence Concerning Wales* (Cardiff: University Press Board, 1935).

————, 'The Parliamentary Committee of 1398', *English Historical Review* XL, no. CLIX (1925).

Ekelund, Robert B, Jr, Robert F Hébert and Robert D Tollison, 'The Political Economy of the Medieval Church', in *The Oxford Handbook of the Economics of Religion*, ed. Rachel M McCleary (Oxford: Oxford University Press, 2011).

Elrington, CR, NM Herbert and RB Pugh, *A History of the County of Gloucester*, vol. 10: *Westbury and Whitstone Hundreds* (London, 1972).

Eyton, RW, *Antiquities of Shropshire* (London: JR Smith, 1854–60).

Feiling, Keith, *A History of England from the Coming of the English to 1918* (London: Macmillan, 1950).

FitzStephen, William, *Norman London* (New York: Italica Press, 1990).

Flick, Alexander, *The Decline of the Medieval Church* (New York: Burt Franklin, 1967).

Forey, Alan J, 'The Military Order of St Thomas of Acre', *English Historical Review* 92 (1977): 481–503.

Fox, Christine M and Timothy Hailes, *A History of Bassishaw Ward, 1200–1600* (ebook, 2014).

Froissart, Jean, *Chronicles* (London: Penguin Classics, 1978).

Fryde, EB, *William de la Pole: Merchant and King's Banker, 1366* (London: Hambledon Press, 1988).

Fullbrook-Leggatt, L, *Anglo-Saxon and Medieval Gloucester* (Gloucester: John Jennings, 1952).

Gairdner, James, *Three Fifteenth-Century Chronicles with Historical Memoranda by John Stow* (London, 1880).

Galloway, Andrew, *Studies in the Age of Chaucer* (Notre Dame: University of Notre Dame Press, 2011).

Galloway, Robert L, *Annals of Coalmining and the Coal Trade* (London: Colliery Guardian Company, 1898).

Gardiner, John, *The Life and Times of Chaucer* (London: Jonathan Cape, 1977).

Gardiner, Juliet and Neil Wenborn, *The History Today Companion to British History* (London: Collins and Brown, 1985).

Gascoigne, Thomas and James E Thorold Rogers, *Loci e Libro Veritatum: Passages Selected from Gascoigne's Theological Dictionary Illustrating the Condition of Church and State, 1403–1458* (Oxford, 1881).

Gater, GH and Walter H Godfrey, eds., *Survey of London*, vol. 15 (London: London County Council, 1934).

Gibbons, Agnes and EC Davey, *Wantage Past and Present* (London, 1901).

Gillingham, John and Ralph A Griffiths, *Medieval Britain: A Very Short Introduction* (Oxford: Oxford University Press, 2000).

Given-Wilson, Chris, ed., *Chronicles of the Revolution 1397–1400* (Manchester: Manchester University Press, 1993).

BIBLIOGRAPHY

————, *Fourteenth Century England* (Woodbridge: Boydell Press, 2002).

————, ed., *Parliamentary Rolls of Medieval England* (Woodbridge: Boydell and Brewer, 2005).

Goodman, Anthony, *The Loyal Conspiracy: The Lords Appellant under Richard II* (Miami: University of Miami Press, 1971).

Grafton, Richard, *Grafton's Chronicle, or, History of England* (London, 1659).

Gray, HL, 'The Production and Exportation of English Woollens in the 14th Century', *English Historical Review* 39 (1924): 13–35.

Gross, Charles, *The Gild Merchant: A Contribution to British Municipal History* (London: Clarendon Press, 1890).

Guildhall Historical Association, *Richard Whittington* (1975), www.guildhallhistoricalassociation.com.

Gummer, Ben, *The Scourging Angel: The Black Death in the British Isles* (London: Vintage Books, 2010).

Hall, Robert E, 'The Population of England in the 14th and 15th Century', unpublished paper, Stanford University, 12 January 1965.

Halliday, Stephen, *Newgate: London's Prototype of Hell* (Stroud: Sutton Publishing, 2001).

Hamill, John, *The Craft: A History of English Freemasonry* (Wellingborough: Crucible, 1986).

Hamilton, J and P Bradley, eds., *Documenting the Past: Essays in Medieval History Presented to George Peddy Cutino* (Woodbridge: Boydell Press, 1989).

Hammond, PW, *Food and Feast in Medieval England* (Stroud: Alan Sutton, 1993).

Hanawalt, Barbara A, *Growing Up in Medieval London: The Experience of Childhood in History* (Oxford: Oxford University Press, 1993).

Harrison, Michael, ed., *London Growing: The Development of a Metropolis* (London: Hutchinson, 1965).

Harriss, Gerald, *Shaping the Nation: England, 1360–1461* (Oxford: Oxford University Press, 2006).

Harrowven, Jean, *Sir Richard Whittington's Secret* (Norwich: Borrowdale Press, 2000).

Hartley, Dorothy, *The Land of England* (London: Macdonald and Jane's, 1979).

Hartnell, Jack, *Medieval Bodies: Life, Death and Art in the Middle Ages* (London: Profile Books, 2019).

Hatcher, J, 'England in the Aftermath of the Black Death', *Past and Present* 144 (1994).

————, *Plague, Population and the English Economy, 1348–1530* (Basingstoke: Macmillan, 1977).

Hatfield, Emma, *London's Lord Mayors: 800 Years of Shaping the City* (Stroud: Amberley, 2015).

Hawkins, D, 'The Black Death and the New London Cemeteries of 1348', *Antiquity* 64 (1990).

Hays, Denys, *A General History of Europe* (London: Longmans, 1968).

BIBLIOGRAPHY

Hazlitt, William Carew, *The Livery Companies of the City of London, Their Origin, Character, Development and Social and Political Importance* (London: Swan Sonnenshein and Co, 1892).

Heath, Peter, *Church and Realm, 1272–1461* (London: Fontana, 1988).

Hector, LC and Barbara F Harvey, eds., *The Westminster Chronicle, 1381–1394* (Oxford: Oxford University Press, 1982).

Herbert, NM, ed., *A History of the County of Gloucester*, vol. 4: *The City of Gloucester* (Oxford: Oxford University Press, 1988).

————, *A History of the County of Gloucester*, vol. 9: *Bradley Hundred: The Northleach Area of the Cotswolds* (London, 2001).

Herbert, NM and RB Pugh, eds., *A History of the County of Gloucester*, vol. 11: *Bisley and Longtree Hundreds* (London, 1976).

Herbert, W, *The History of the Twelve Great Livery Companies of London*, 2 vols. (London: self-published 1834; republished 1968).

Hibbert, Christopher, *The English: A Social History (1066–1945)* (London: Grafton Books, 1981).

————, *London: The Biography of a City* (Harmondsworth: Penguin, 1980).

Hicks, Michael, *Who's Who in Medieval England 1272–1483* (London: Shepheard-Walwyn, 1991).

Hindle, Paul, *Medieval Roads and Tracks* (Princes Risborough: Shire Archaeology, 2010).

Hingeston-Randolph, FC, *The Register of Edmund Stafford A.D. 1395–1419* (London, 1886).

Hirst, LF, *The Conquest of Plague* (Oxford: Oxford University Press, 1953).

Hollaender, AEJ and William Kellaway, eds., *Studies in London History Presented to Philip Edmund Jones* (London: Hodder and Stoughton, 1969).

Holmes, George, *The Later Middle Ages 1272–1485* (New York: Norton, 1962).

————, *The Oxford Illustrated History of Medieval Europe* (Oxford: Oxford University Press, 1986).

Holt, Richard, 'Gloucester in the Century after the Black Death', *Transactions of the Bristol and Gloucestershire Archaeological Society* 103 (1985): 149–61.

Holt, Richard and Gervase Rosser, *The English Medieval Town* (London: Longman, 1990).

Home, Gordon, *Medieval London* (London: Bracken Books, 1994).

Hope, Valerie, *My Lord Mayor* (London: Weidenfeld and Nicolson, 1989).

Hoskins, WG, *Local History in England* (London: Routledge, 1984).

Huelin, Gordon, *Vanished Churches of the City of London* (London: Guildhall Library Publications, 1966).

Huizinga, Johan, *The Waning of the Middle Ages* (London: Penguin, 1985).

Hurst, Derek, *Sheep in the Cotswolds* (Cheltenham: History Press, 2005).

Hutchins, John, *History and Antiquities of the County of Dorset* (London: JB Nichols and Sons, 1863).

BIBLIOGRAPHY

Imray, Jean, *The Charity of Richard Whittington: A History of the Trust Administered by the Mercer's Company 1424–1966* (London: Athlone Press, 1968).

Inwood, Stephen, *A History of London* (London: Papermac, 2000).

Jacob, EF, *The Fifteenth Century*, Oxford History of England series (Oxford: Clarendon Press, 1961).

———, ed., *The Register of Henry Chichele, Archbishop of Canterbury, 1414–1423* (Oxford: Canterbury and York Society, 1937).

Jacobson, Mark Z, *Air Pollution and Global Warming: History, Science, and Solutions* (Cambridge: Cambridge University Press, 2012).

James, Tom, *Black Death: The Lasting Impact* (BBC, Feb. 2011).

Jefferson, Lisa, ed., *The Medieval Account Books of the Mercers of London: An Edition and Translation* (London: Routledge, 2009).

Jenkins, Simon, *The City on the Thames* (London: Pegasus Books, 2020).

Joseph, George, *Metropolitan Communities: Trade Guilds, Identity and Change in Early Modern London* (Stanford: Stanford University Press, 1997).

Jurica, ARJ, ed., *A History of the County of Gloucestershire*, vol. 12: *Pauntley* (Woodbridge, 2010).

Kahl, William, *The Development of London Livery Companies: An Historical Essay and Select Bibliography* (Boston: Harvard Graduate School of Business Administration, 1960).

Keen, MH, *England in the Later Middle Ages* (London: Routledge, 2004).

Keene, Derek, 'Medieval London and Its Supply Hinterlands', *Regional Environmental Change* 12, no. 2 (2002).

———, *The Walbrook Study: A Summary Report* (London: Centre for Metropolitan History, University of London, 1987).

Keene, DJ and Vanessa Harding, *Historical Gazetteer of London before the Great Fire* (Cambridge: Chadwyck-Healey, 1987).

King, Edmund, *Medieval London* (Stroud: Tempus Publishing, 2001).

———, *The Greyfriars of London* (Aberdeen: Aberdeen University Press, 1915).

Kington, John, *Climate and Weather* (London: Collins, 2010).

Kunal, T, 'The Crash of the European Financial System in 1345', *Financial Engineer* (March 2013).

Labarge, Margaret Wade, *Medieval Travellers: The Rich and Restless* (London: Hamish Hamilton, 1982).

Lambert, B, *The History and Survey of London and Its Environs, from the Earliest Period to the Present Time* (London, 1806).

Leach, R, *The Schools of Medieval England* (London: Methuen, 1916).

Leff, Gordon, *John Wyclif: The Path to Dissent* (Oxford: Oxford University Press, 1966).

Le Goff, Jacques, *Medieval Civilisation, 400–1500* (Oxford: Basil Blackwell, 1989).

Lewis, Jon E, *London: The Autobiography* (London: Constable, 2008).

Leyster, Henrietta, *Medieval Women: A Social History of Women in England, 450–1500* (London: Weidenfeld and Nicolson, 1996).

Liddy, CD, *War, Politics and Finance in Late Medieval English Towns: Bristol, York and the Crown, 1350–1400* (Woodbridge: Royal Historical Society, 2005).

Lipson, E, *The Exchange History of England*, vol. I: *The Middle Ages* (London: Adam and Charles Black, 1945).

———, *The Growth of English Society* (London: Adam and Charles Black, 1959).

Lobel, Mary, *A History of the County of Oxford*, vol. 7: *Dorchester and Thame Hundreds* (Oxford: Oxford University Press, 1962).

London Museum, *Medieval Catalogue* (London: HMSO, 1940).

Lyell, Laetitia, 'The Problem of the Records of the Merchant Adventurers', *Economic History Review* 15, no. 2 (1935).

Lysons, Samuel, *The Model Merchant of the Middle Ages* (London: Hamilton Adams and Co., 1860).

Lyte, HC Maxwell, ed., *Calendar of Close Rolls, Richard II*, vol. 5 (London, 1925).

———, ed., *Calendar of the Patent Rolls Preserved in the Public Record Office: Edward III, 1370–1374* (London, 1891).

Martin, Geoffrey Haward, trans., *Knighton's Chronicle 1337–1396* (Oxford: Clarendon Press, 1995).

Mayhew, NJ, ed., *Coinage in the Low Countries, 880–1500*, British Archaeological Reports, International Series, LIV, 1979.

McHardy, Alison K, *The Reign of Richard II: From Minority to Tyranny, 1377–97* (Manchester: Manchester University Press, 2012).

———, 'Richard II: A Personal Portrait', in *The Reign of Richard II*, ed. G Dodd (Stroud: Tempus, 2000).

McKisack, May, *The Fourteenth Century, 1307–1399*, Oxford History of England (Oxford: Clarendon Press, 1987).

McNiven, Peter, 'The Problem of Henry IV's Health, 1405–1413', *English Historical Review* 100, no. 397 (1985): 747–72.

Meisel, Janet, *Barons of the Welsh Frontier: The Corbet, Pantulf, and FitzWarin Families, 1066–1272* (Lincoln: University of Nebraska Press, 1980).

Miller, Edward and John Hatcher, *Medieval England: Rural Society and Economic Change, 1086–1348* (London: Longman, 1978).

Milne, Gustav, ed., *From Roman Basilica to Medieval Market: Archaeology in Action in the City of London* (London: HMSO, 1992).

———, *The Port of Medieval London* (Stroud: Tempus, 2003).

Milne, Gustav and Chrissie Milne, *Medieval Waterfront Development at Trig Lane, London* (London: London and Middlesex Archaeological Society, 1982).

Moore, Norman, *St Bartholomew's Hospital in Peace and War: The Rede Lecture 1915* (Cambridge: Cambridge University Press, 1915).

Morgan, Kenneth O, *The Oxford Illustrated History of Britain* (Oxford: Oxford University Press, 1984).

Moriarty, Catherine, *The Voice of the Middle Ages in Personal Letters, 1100–1500* (Luton: Lennard, 1989).

Morris, John, ed., *Domesday Book: Gloucestershire* (Chichester: Phillimore, 1982).

Mortimer, Ian, *The Fears of Henry IV: The Life of England's Self-made King* (London: Vintage Books, 2008).

————, *The Greatest Traitor: The Life of Sir Roger Mortimer, 1327–1330* (London: Vintage Books, 2010).

————, *The Time Traveller's Guide to Medieval England* (London: Bodley Head, 2009).

Mount, Tony, *Everyday Life in Medieval London* (Stroud: Amberley Books, 2015).

Mudhill, Robin R, *England's Jewish Solution: Experiment and Expulsion, 1262–1290* (Cambridge: Cambridge University Press, 2002).

Munro, John H, 'Bruges and the Abortive Staple in English Cloth: An Incident in the Shift of Commerce from Bruges to Antwerp in the Late Fifteenth Century', *Revue Belge de Philologie et d'Histoire* 44, no. 4 (1966): 1137–59.

Myers, AR, *Chaucer's London: Everyday Life in London, 1342–1400* (Stroud: Amberley, 2009).

————, *English Historical Documents*, vol. 4: *1327–1485* (Oxford: Oxford University Press, 1969).

————, *England in the Late Middle Ages, 1307–1530* (Harmondsworth: Pelican, 1963).

Newhall, RA, *The English Conquest of Normandy, 1416–1424* (New Haven: Yale University Press, 1924).

Nichols, JG, ed., *Chronicle of the Grey Friars of London*, Camden Society, OS, vol. 53 (London, 1852).

Nicolle, David, *The Great Chevauchée: John of Gaunt's Raid on France, 1373* (Oxford: Osprey, 2011).

Noorthouck, John, *A New History of London, Including Westminster and Southwark* (London, 1773).

Norwich, John Julius, *The Great Cities in History* (London: Thames and Hudson, 2016).

Ohlin, Goran, 'No Safety in Numbers: Some Pitfalls of Historical Statistics', in *Industrialization in Two Systems: Essays in Honor of Alexander Gerschenkron* (New York: Wiley, 1966).

Oliver, Clementine, *Parliament and Political Pamphleteering in Fourteenth-Century England* (York: York Medieval Press, 2010).

Ormrod, Mark and Philip Lindley, *The Black Death in England* (Stamford: Paul Watkins Publishing, 1996).

Owen-Crocker, Gale, Elizabeth Coatsworth and Maria Hayward, eds., *Encyclopedia of Medieval Dress and Textiles* (Leiden: Brill, 2012).

Page, William, ed., *A History of the County of Buckingham* (London: Archibald Constable, 1925).

Page, William and PH Ditchfield, eds., *A History of the County of Berkshire* (London: Archibald Constable, 1924).

401

BIBLIOGRAPHY

Parry, JH, *The Age of Reconnaissance: Discovery, Exploration and Settlement, 1450–1650* (Berkeley: University of California Press, 1981).

Pennant, Thomas, *Pennant's Tour of London* (London, 1805).

Perrigo, Lynn I, 'Plagues and Pollution in Medieval England', *Social Science* 46, no. 3 (1971): 133–8.

Picard, Liza, *Chaucer's People: Everyday Lives in Medieval England* (London: Orion, 2017).

Pierce, Patricia, *Old London Bridge* (London: Review Books, 2001).

Pirenne, Henri, *Economic and Social History of Medieval Europe* (London: Routledge Kegan Paul, 1961).

Platt, Colin, *Medieval England: A Social History and Archaeology from the Conquest to 1600 AD* (London: Routledge).

Poole, Austin Lane, *From Domesday Book to Magna Carta, 1087–1216* (Oxford: Clarendon Press, 1951).

———, *Medieval England* (Oxford: Clarendon Press, 1958).

Pooley, Ernest, *Guilds and the City of London* (London: Clark and Maxwell, 1947).

Porter, Roy, *London: A Social History* (London: Penguin, 1996).

Porter, Stephen, *The Great Plague* (Stroud: Amberley Publishing, 2009).

Postan, MM, *Essays on Medieval Agriculture and General Problems of the Medieval Economy* (Cambridge: Cambridge University Press, 1973).

———, *The Medieval Economy and Society: An Economic History of Britain in the Middle Ages* (Harmondsworth: Penguin, 1975).

Postel, Rainer, 'The Hanseatic League and Its Decline', *paper read at the Central Connecticut State University, 20 November 1996.*

Poster, Carol and Richard Utz, eds., *The Late Medieval Epistle* (Evanston: Northwestern University Press, 1996).

Power, Eileen, *The Wool Trade in English Medieval History* (Oxford: Oxford University Press, 1941).

———, *The Wool Trade in English Medieval History: Being the Ford Lectures* (Oxford: Oxford University Press, 1955).

Powicke, Sir Maurice, *The Thirteenth Century, 1216–1307* (Oxford: Clarendon Press, 1987).

Prestwich, Michael, *Edward I* (New Haven: Yale University Press, 1997).

———, *Plantagenet England: 1225–1360* (Oxford: Oxford University Press, 2005).

———, *The Three Edwards: War and State in England, 1272–1377* (London: Routledge, 2003).

Previté-Orton, CW, *The Shorter Cambridge Medieval History* (Cambridge: Cambridge University Press, 1955).

Pugh, Ralph, *Imprisonment in Medieval England* (Cambridge: Cambridge University Press, 1968).

Rawcliffe, C, *The Staffords, Earls of Stafford and Dukes of Buckingham, 1394–1521* (Cambridge: Cambridge University Press, 1978).

BIBLIOGRAPHY

Reddaway, TF and Lorna EM Walker, *The Early History of the Goldsmiths' Company, 1327–1509* (London: Edward Arnold, 1973).

Rexroth, Frank, *Deviance and Power in Late Medieval London* (Cambridge: Cambridge University Press, 2007).

Richardson, Gary, 'Craft Guilds and Christianity in Late-Medieval England: A Rational-Choice Analysis', *Rationality and Society* 17 (2005).

Richardson, John, *London and Its People: A Short History from Medieval Times to the Present Day* (London: Random House, 1995).

Riello, Giorgio and Ulinka Rublack, eds., *The Right to Dress: Sumptuary Laws in a Global Perspective, c.1200–1800* (Cambridge: Cambridge University Press, 2020).

Riley, HT, ed., *Chronicles of the Mayors and Sheriffs of London 1188–1274* (London: Trübner, 1863).

————, *Memorials of London and London Life in the 13th, 14th and 15th Centuries* (London: Longmans, Green and Co., 1868).

————, *Thomas Walsingham … Historia Anglicana* (London, 1864).

Roberts, Howard and Walter H Godfrey, eds., *Survey of London*, vol. 22: *Bankside (The Parishes of St Saviour and Christchurch Southwark)* (London, 1950).

Roberts, Michael, *The Early Vasas: A History of Sweden, 1523–1611* (Cambridge: Cambridge University Press, 1968).

Röhrkasten, Jens, *The Mendicant Houses of Medieval London, 1221–1539* (Munster: Lit Verlag, 2004).

Roskell, JS, with L Clark and C Rawcliffe, eds., *The House of Commons, 1386–1421* (Stroud: Sutton, 1993).

Roud, Steve, *London Lore: The Legends and Traditions of the World's Most Vibrant City* (London: RH Books, 2008).

Rowley, Trevor, *The High Middle Ages, 1200–1550* (London: Paladin, 1988).

Rubin, Miri, ed., *Medieval Christianity in Practice* (Princeton: Princeton University Press, 2009).

Rudder, Samuel, *A New History of Gloucestershire* (Cirencester, 1779; republished by Alan Sutton, Stroud in collaboration with Gloucestershire County Library: Nonsuch, 2006).

Russell, Josiah Cox, *British Medieval Population* (Albuquerque: University of New Mexico Press, 1949).

Sabine, Ernest L, 'Butchering in Mediaeval London', *Speculum* 8, no. 3 (1933): 335–53.

Saul, Nigel, *A Companion to Medieval England, 1066–1485* (Stroud: Tempus Publishing, 2000).

————, *Richard II* (New Haven: Yale University Press, 1999).

Selby, WD, *The Charters, Ordinances and Bye-laws of the Mercers' Company* (London, 1881).

Seward, Desmond, *A Brief History of the Hundred Years War: The English in France, 1337–1455* (London: Robinson, 2003).

BIBLIOGRAPHY

Seymour, Edward, *The Complete History of England* (London, 1764).

———, *A Survey of the Cities of London and Westminster, Borough of Southwark and Parts Adjacent* (London, 1735).

Sharp, Buchanan, *Famine and Scarcity in Late Medieval and Early Modern England: The Regulation of Grain Marketing, 1256–1631* (Cambridge: Cambridge University Press, 2016).

Sharpe, JA, 'The History of Crime in England c.1300–1914: An Overview of Recent Publications', *British Journal of Criminology* 28, no. 2 (1988): 124–37.

Sharpe, RR, ed., *Calendar of Letter-Books of the City of London*, vol. 1: *1400–1422* (London, 1909).

Sheppard, Francis, *London: A History* (Oxford: Oxford University Press, 1999).

Shrewsbury, JFD, *A History of Bubonic Plague in the British Isles* (Cambridge: Cambridge University Press, 2008).

Shumaker, WA, *The Cyclopedic Dictionary of Law* (Chicago: Callaghan, 1901).

Sitwell, Osbert, *The True Story of Richard Whittington* (London: Home and Van Thal, 1945).

Smith, Al, *Dictionary of City of London Street Names* (London: David and Charles, 1970).

Smith, Brian S and Elizabeth Ralph, *A History of Bristol and Gloucestershire* (Henley-on-Thames: Phillimore, 1996).

Smith, John Thomas, *Ancient Topography of London* (London, 1815).

Spurgeon, Caroline Frances Eleanor, *Five Hundred Years of Chaucer: Criticism and Allusion (1357–1900)* (Cambridge: Cambridge University Press, 1925).

Stamp, AE, ed., *Calendar of Close Rolls, Henry IV*, vol 1. (London, 1927), vol. 2 (London, 1929).

Steel, Anthony, *Richard II* (Cambridge: Cambridge University Press, 1941).

Steele, AB, *The Receipt of the Exchequer, 1377–1485* (Cambridge: Cambridge University Press, 1954).

Steiner, Emily and Candace Barrington, eds., *The Letter of the Law: Legal Practice and Literary Production in Medieval England* (Ithaca: Cornell University Press, 2002).

Stephens, WB, ed., *A History of the County of Warwick*, vol. 8: *The City of Coventry and Borough of Warwick* (London, 1969).

Stevenson, WH, ed., *Calendar of the Records of the Corporation of Gloucester* (Gloucester: J Bellows, 1893).

Stockton, EW, ed., *The Major Latin Works of John Gower* (Seattle: University of Washington Press, 1962).

Stow, John, *A Survey of London Written in the Year 1598* (Stroud: Sutton, 1994).

Strohm, Paul, *The Poet's Tale: Chaucer and the Year That Made the Canterbury Tales* (London: Profile Books, 2014).

Stubbs, William, *The Constitutional History of England in Its Origin and Development* (Oxford: Clarendon Press, 1891).

BIBLIOGRAPHY

Styles, Philip, ed., *A History of the County of Warwick*, vol. 3: *Barlichway Hundred* (London: Victoria County History, 1945).

Sumption, Jonathan, *The Hundred Years War: Cursed Kings* (London: Faber and Faber, 2015).

Sutton, Anne F, *The Mercers' Company First Charter 1394* (London: Mercers' Company, 1994).

———, *The Mercery of London: Trade, Goods and People, 1130–1578* (London: Routledge, 2000).

———, 'The Merchant Adventurers of England: Their Origins and the Mercers'', *Historical Research* 75, no. 1 (2002).

Swanson, Heather, *Medieval Artisans: An Urban Class in Late Medieval England* (Oxford: Oxford University Press, 1989).

Tait, James, 'The Common Council of the Borough', *English History Review* XLV1 (1931).

———, 'Whittington, Richard', *Dictionary of National Biography*.

Talling, Paul, *London's Lost Rivers* (London: Random House, 2011).

Tawney, RH, *Religion and the Rise of Capitalism* (London: Penguin, 1987).

Taylor, Christopher, *Roads and Tracks of Britain* (London: Orion, 1994).

Taylor, F and JS Roskell, eds., *Gesta Henrici Quinti: The Deeds of Henry the Fifth* (Oxford: Clarendon Press, 1975).

Thomas, AH, ed., *Calendar of the Plea and Memoranda Rolls of the City of London*, vol. 3 (London, 1932).

———, *Calendar of Select Pleas and Memoranda of the City of London, 1381–1412* (Cambridge: Cambridge University Press, 1932).

———, 'Notes on the History of the Leadenhall, 1195–1488', *London Topographical Record* 11 (1923).

Thomson, John AF, *The Transformation of Medieval England 1370–1529* (London: Longman, 1982).

Thornbury, Walter, *Old and New London* (London: Cassell, Petter and Galpin, 1878).

———, *Old London: Charterhouse to Holborn* (London: Alderman Press, 1987).

Thrupp, Sylvia, *Medieval Industry 1000–1500* (London: Fontana, 1971).

———, *The Merchant Class of Medieval London, 1300–1500* (Ann Arbor: University of Michigan Press, 1962).

Thurley, Simon, *The Buildings of England* (London: William Collins, 2013).

Tout, TF, *Chapters in the Administrative History of Mediaeval England: The Wardrobe, the Chamber and the Small Seals*, 6 vols. (Manchester: Manchester University Press, 1920–33).

Treharne, RF, *Essays on Thirteenth Century England* (London: Historical Association, 1971).

Trevelyan, GM, *England in the Age of Wycliffe* (London: Longmans, 1909).

———, *English Social History: A Survey of Six Centuries; Chaucer to Queen Victoria* (London: Longmans, Green, 1947).

————, *History of England* (London: Longman, 1973).

Turner, Christopher, *London Churches Step by Step* (London: Faber and Faber, 1987).

Unwin, George, ed., *Finance and Trade under Edward III: The London Lay Subsidy of 1332* (Manchester: Manchester University Press, 1918).

————, *The Gilds and Companies of London* (London: Methuen, 1908).

Veale, EL, *The English Fur Trade in the Later Middle Ages* (London: London Record Society, 2003).

Warner, George, ed., *The Libelle of Englyshe Polycye: A Poem on the Use of Sea-Power, 1436* (Oxford: Clarendon Press, 1926).

Warrington, John, ed., *The Diary of Samuel Pepys* (London: Dent, 1964).

Watney, Sir John, *An Account of the Mistery of Mercers of the City of London: Otherwise the Mercers' Company* (London: Blades, East and Blades, 1914).

————, *Some Account of the Hospital of St. Thomas of Acon, in the Cheap, London, and of the Plate of the Mercers' Company, London* (London: Blades, East and Blades, 1892).

Waugh, Scott L, *England in the Reign of Edward III* (Cambridge: Cambridge University Press, 1991).

Weiner, A, 'Note on Jewish Doctors in England in the Reign of Henry IV', *Jewish Quarterly Review* 18, no. 1 (1905).

Weinreb, Ben and Christopher Hibbert, *The London Encyclopaedia* (London: Papermac, 1993).

Weir, Alison, *Britain's Royal Families: The Complete Genealogy* (London: Vintage Books, 2008).

Wells-Furby, Bridget, *The Berkeley Estate 1281–1417: Its Economy and Development* (Bristol: Bristol and Gloucestershire Archaeological Society, 2012).

Wheatley, Henry B, ed., *The History of Sir Richard Whittington, by T. H.* (London: Villon Society, 1885).

Whittington, Michael, *The Whittington Story: From the Three Counties to the City* (Oxford: Parchment Press, 1988).

Willey, Russ, *Chambers London Gazetteer* (Edinburgh: Chambers Harrap, 2006).

Woods, William, *England in the Age of Chaucer* (London: Hart-Davis, 1976).

Wylie, JH, *History of England under Henry IV* (London: Longmans, Green, 1898).

Young, Elizabeth and Wayland Young, *Old London Churches* (London: Faber and Faber, 1956).

Ziegler, Philip, *The Black Death* (Glasgow: Collins, 1969).

Zimbler, Daniel L, Jay A Schroeder, Justin L Eddy and Wyndham Lathem, 'Early Emergence of *Yersinia pestis* as a Severe Respiratory Pathogen', *Nature Communications* 6 (2015).

INDEX

INDEX

INDEX